Culture, Economy, Power

SUNY series in Anthropological Studies of Contemporary Issues
Jack R. Rollwagen, editor

Culture, Economy, Power

Anthropology as Critique,
Anthropology as Praxis

EDITED BY

Winnie Lem and Belinda Leach

STATE UNIVERSITY OF NEW YORK PRESS

Published by
State University of New York Press, Albany

© 2002 State University of New York

All rights reserved

Printed in the United States of America

No part of this book may be used or reproduced in any manner whatsoever without written permission. No part of this book may be stored in a retrieval system or transmitted in any form or by any means including electronic, electrostatic, magnetic tape, mechanical, photocopying, recording, or otherwise without prior permission in writing of the publisher.

For information, address State University of New York Press,
90 State Street, Suite 700, Albany, NY 12207

Production by Diane Ganeles
Marketing by Anne M. Valentine

Library of Congress Cataloging-in-Publication Data

Culture, economy, power : anthropology as critique, anthropology as praxis / edited by Winnie Lem and Belinda Leach.
    p. cm.—(SUNY series in anthropological studies of contemporary issues)
    Includes bibliographical references and index.
    ISBN 0-7914-5289-1 (alk. paper)— ISBN 0-7914-5290-5 (pbk. : alk. paper)
    1. Marxist anthropology. 2. Political anthropology. I. Lem, Winnie.
II. Leach, Belinda, 1954– III. Series.
GN345.15.C85 2002
306—dc21
                                               2001032250

10 9 8 7 6 5 4 3 2 1

For Bill Roseberry

In Memory

Contents

Chapter 1. Introduction
    Winnie Lem and Belinda Leach   1

Part 1: Nations and Knowledge

Chapter 2. Bicentrism, Culture, and the Political Economy of Sociocultural Anthropology in English Canada
    Thomas Dunk   19

Chapter 3. The Political Economy of Political Economy in Spanish Anthropology
    Susana Narotzky   33

Chapter 4. Anthropological Debates and the Crisis of Mexican Nationalism
    Guillermo de la Peña   47

Chapter 5. Political Economy in the United States
    William Roseberry   59

Chapter 6. "A Small Discipline": The Embattled Place of Anthropology in a Massified British Higher Education Sector
    John Gledhill   73

Part 2: States and Subjects

Chapter 7. Sentiment and Structure: Nation and State
    Dipankar Gupta   91

Chapter 8. Communists Communists Everywhere!: Forgetting the Past and Living with History in Ecuador
    Steve Striffler   107

Chapter 9. "We Were the Strongest Ones Here": Transformed
  Livelihoods in Contemporary Spain
  Claudia Vicencio   121

Chapter 10. The Italian Post-Communist Left and Unemployment:
  Finding a New Position on Labor
  Michael Blim   136

Chapter 11. The Language of Contention in Liberal Ecuador
  A. Kim Clark   150

Part 3. Hegemonies and Histories

Chapter 12. The Decline of Patriarchy? The Political Economy of
  Patriarchy: Maquiladoras in Yucatan, Mexico
  Marie France Labrecque   165

Chapter 13. Remembering "The Ancient Ones": Memory, Hegemony,
  and the Shadows of State Terror in the Argentinean Chaco
  Gastón Gordillo   177

Chapter 14. Class, Discipline, and the Politics of Opposition in Ontario
  Belinda Leach   191

Chapter 15. Militant Particularism and Cultural Struggles as Cape
  Breton Burns Again
  Pauline Gardiner Barber   206

Chapter 16. Acquiescence and Quiescence: Gender and Politics in
  Rural Languedoc
  Winnie Lem   221

Chapter 17. Red Flags and Lace Coiffes: Identity, Livelihood, and
  the Politics of Survival in the Bigoudennie, France
  Charles R. Menzies   235

Chapter 18. Out of Site: The Horizons of Collective Identity
  Gavin Smith   250

References   267

Contributors   289

Index   293

CHAPTER 1

Introduction

Winnie Lem and Belinda Leach

> The philosophers have only *interpreted* the world . . . : the point is to *change* it.
>
> —Marx, *Theses on Feuerbach*

Provoked by Marx's well-known, oft-cited statement, countless scholars have committed their intellectual labor toward deciphering the inner workings of the modern world with the view that such endeavours might serve in some way to transform it. Among those incited by this declaration of purpose and challenged by Marxist analysis are numerous anthropologists whose efforts in ethnography and theory have been devoted toward generating a critical body of knowledge, directed ultimately at contributing toward political programs of change. In *Culture, Economy, Power* the work of some of those anthropologists is presented. This volume brings together a group of scholars who share the view that anthropological knowledge implies critique—a critique of the modern world and a critique of capitalism—and that to engage in and with anthropology represents an act of praxis. As such, our work in anthropology is committed to the emancipatory projects that find their origins in historical materialism, the critique of political economy, Marx's thoughts on class conflict and programs for social equality. Indeed, such ideas have laid the foundations for the massive social and economic transformations that have been inaugurated in many different national contexts in the twentieth century. Yet as we live in our contemporary world, in a period that extends well beyond the lifetime of Marx, such ideas and programs for change have become discredited. Indeed, the decline of socialism and the triumph of a neoliberal political and economic order in recent years have fanned the flames of criticism ignited by Marx's detractors and supporters alike. But criticisms of his framework and declarations that he was wrong are as old as Marxist thought itself. Turn of the twentieth century populist and liberal critiques, as well as more recent poststructuralist, feminist, and Foucauldian assaults on Marxist analysis (and also responses to them) have come to be so familiar, and to some extent mantric, that to review them here would be an exercise in redundancy. While the contributors in this volume agree that there is much to criticize in Marxist analysis, they nonetheless assert through their essays that there is much that has been of value and will continue to be of value as we confront the changes in the modern world in our intellectual and everyday lives and as we seek to understand the lives of the anthropological subjects with whom we are privileged to work.

The authors here are concerned therefore to explore the ways in which the precepts of Marxism continue to illuminate and enhance our understanding of culture, economy, and politics, both in the contemporary world as well as the past, despite and also because of the turns in recent history. But in their efforts to do this, they do not slavishly follow any doctrinal orthodoxy. Because, as their essays will show, much has been learned from challenges to Marxist analysis, the authors make significant attempts to modify and move beyond strict and strictured analytical frameworks. This is done, however, not by rejecting the fundamental precepts of Marxist analysis, but by extending and expanding upon its framework. As all Marxist inspired programs, visions, and activities have been initiated by individuals who act in concert, it is fitting to begin with a history of the way in which this collectivity of contributors to *Culture, Economy, Power* was formed.

Our Past

The essays in this collection emerge from a process of collaboration among a group of anthropologists whose work is informed by a materialist approach to understanding and analyzing culture. We share the view that culture, a pivotal concept in anthropology, is a phenomenon that is produced and reproduced in its relation to material forces. Our collaborations began in 1991 as a series of impromptu conversations that took place at the meetings of the Canadian Anthropology Society/Société Canadien pour Anthropologie (CASCA).[1] At that time, our efforts were galvanized by the way in which our discipline was responding to the postmodern "turn" in scholarship and the neoliberal "turn" in the larger political and economic order. The postmodern turn was inclining our discipline toward the textual approach, and a growing preoccupation with an ungrounded "culture" was coming to displace questions that were critical to address in the increasingly neoliberal world. To many of us, it was critical to confront the precise ways in which neoliberal economic policies and practices were engendering the restructuring of capitalism. It was a matter of urgency to understand precisely how the forces of globalization were altering processes of production, patterns of consumption, and relations in work. Furthermore it was important to understand how these forces related to social and political movements that were appearing and reappearing on the political and cultural landscape. Finally, to many of us, an analysis that was devoted to understanding how contemporary capitalisms were sustained and perpetuated reached a new immediacy. Despite the fact that overall, in anthropology, the space devoted to these questions became diminished, many of us individually pursued these concerns in our academic and everyday lives. From our individual research programs, it was clear that neoliberal forces were engendering new class configurations, new forms of domination and new contours of power, while older forms of subjection and exploitation were coming to be intensified. In the 1991 meetings, building on conversations that were taking place in the halls, over coffee, and at book exhibits while panel after panel focused on discourse, voice, self, identity, and narrative, a group of us gathered to talk about reinvigorating an agenda for anthropology that addressed domination, exploitation, class, structure, social process, political economy, and the production of culture.

Since those first conversations, a series of workshops, symposia, and sessions that focused on materialist approaches to the production of culture have been initiated both as part of the program of CASCA meetings and also apart from them. For those who participated[2] in these different fora, the point of departure was that to be engaged in anthropology is inherently a political act and that as individual anthropologists we continually make choices about how to express those politics through our intellectual orientations. Therefore, the consequences of these choices became reinforced at that 1991 meeting where reflexive and textual anthropology was coming to occupy more and more hegemonic space. Yet, as many of the contributors to this volume point out in their essays, hegemony is seldom total, and so we claimed a space for pursuing alternatives. Our efforts became focused on developing an understanding of culture as an inseparable part of daily and historical praxis. In general, we focused on three key areas of concern. First, we addressed the question of analysis. We pursued the problem of understanding the ways in which class allows us to grasp the dynamics of social relations under the different spatial and temporal configurations of capitalism. We also considered how an interpretively sensitive approach to culture in our analysis might affect our understanding of the relationship between culture and class. The second key area we explored focused on methodology. We addressed the implications for ethnographic method of considering culture as a phenomenon that is not sui generis, but produced and reproduced in relation to political and economic forces. Finally, we confronted the question of politics. We focused on the problem of the organizational and strategic questions that disempowered people face in their projects of collective action and we posed the question of what our relationship as anthropologists should be to such cultural/class projects. Our exchanges on politics were framed overall by certain fundamental epistemological concerns, particularly the question of the ways in which political context influences the formation of knowledge. We were concerned to examine the ways in which different intellectual projects are sustained or constrained within changing economies and structures of power. As the questions we broached in this area are foundational in nature, it is apposite to begin the volume by addressing the ways in which the culture of anthropology is produced and reproduced within different national settings.

In Part 1, *Nations and Knowledge,* the contributors explore the ways in which anthropologists both participate in contemporary political economies and are affected by historical changes in capitalism as intellectual workers who are engaged through their labor in the production, transformation, and reproduction of bodies of knowledge. Each author begins from the proposition that intellectual production is a process that is at once strongly institutionalized and politically charged. They explore the ways in which historical and contemporary conjunctures and conditions within nations privilege distinctive trajectories of inquiry within the field of anthropology, while deterring others. In recognizing that the influence of such conjunctures is not delimited by national borders, they also explore how conditions within one nation exert an influence over and define research agendas in other national contexts. Focusing on the Canadian context for social anthropology, Dunk (chapter 2) for example argues that agendas for research in anthropology in Canada can be determined by ideas, issues, and problems largely generated from outside its national borders. These emanate from countries that occupy a place of prominence in the intellectual field, usually Britain and the United States, where the majority of anthropologists are trained. Dunk argues that much of the work that is characteristic of Canadian anthropology reflects more the out of country training of the anthropologist concerned than the nature of Canadian society itself. Given the political and economic forces that have shaped the academy and intellectual pursuits in the United States and Britain, where Marxism and political economy have been relegated to the periphery (see Roseberry, chapter 5 and Gledhill, chapter 6), Canadian anthropology has reflected these trends. Thus, Canadian anthropology has suffered from the marginalization of Marxist anthropology and political economy, and the displacement from research agendas of the priorities and problems specific to Canada.

Narotzky's contribution (chapter 3) continues the discussion introduced by Dunk, on the nature of power relations in the development of anthropology in specific national contexts. She is concerned with the ways in which those relations have shaped anthropology in Spain and the anthropology of Spain. Her contribution is an examination of the ways in which both the changing political climate of Franco and post-Franco Spain as well as the intellectual influences emanating from non-Spanish nations have been critical to the shaping of Spanish anthropology. Narotzky emphasizes that the legacy of fascism not only involved the marginalization and the active persecution of Marxist intellectuals under Franco but it also meant the persistence of the intellectual dominance of culture and folklore studies, into the post-Franco era. This was a field of inquiry permitted in Fascist Spain and one that is still pursued by once and still powerful anthropologists who dominate Spanish anthropology. The consequences of these forms of intellectual domination for reinforcing certain webs of power, as well as its economic consequences for the privileging of particular research trajectories and defining the discipline within Spain, are drawn out by Narotzky.

Pursuing the theme of relationship between power, knowledge, and anthropology in Mexico, de la Peña (chapter 4) examines the relationship between Mexican anthropology and the state's quest for a unified national culture. He identifies three phases in the formation of Mexican anthropology that are linked to the official policies concerning the relationship of indigenous peoples and the peasantry to the state. While the state has tried to incorporate anthropology into its project, in practice materialist anthropology has provided a counterhegemonic discourse, opposing the homogenizing strategies of the state, making class a central concern, while downplaying the significance of "ethnic" difference. The question of "ethnic" difference is taken up also by Gupta (chapter 7). He focuses on the problem of how the state addresses the central political and economic tensions generated by ethnic divisions that exist within the nation-state that is inclined toward generating homogeneity in the creation of citizens.

At the other side of what some have called a "colonial relationship" are Britain and the United States, with their long histories of producing anthropologists, and in the process, reproducing colonial relationships with anthropological subjects (Asad 1973; Wolf and Jorgensen 1970). Within both these contexts, the space for a materialist anthropology has been squeezed with shifts in the political economy of contemporary Britain and the United States. Roseberry (chapter 5), like Narotzky, identifies processes in the United States that have marginalized political economy within the academy and within anthropology itself. He articulates the implications of this for left-oriented academic inquiry in terms of an academic enclosure, on the one hand, and anthropological enclosure, on the other. Like Dunk, Roseberry takes up the issue of the production of academics in anthropology and suggests that this has serious implications for generations of graduate students and marketplace decisions about who become members of the anthropological force of intellectual workers and who do not.

The British context for anthropological political economy has also been affected by the conservative retrenchment of the 1980s and 1990s. Examining the nature of university institutions, Gledhill (chapter 6) argues that the restructuring and globalization of education, and specifically the legacy of Thatcherite economic and cultural policies in Britain, has had radical implications for the contemporary politics of doing anthropology and the roles of anthropologists as public intellectuals. Under fiscal crises produced by the Fordist-Neo-Keynesian mode of capitalist regulation, education tends to be targeted for reduction in public expenditures. Gledhill argues that the restructuring of education is intended to produce people who might serve the ends of the capitalist accumulation process, thus higher education must fit that role, that is, train people in this way in order to qualify for the public purse. According to Gledhill, these dynamics are a reflection of the ideological dimensions to the neoliberal climate of regulation, which produces the university as a kind of battlefield where fights are fought over the nature of research, and where socially and politically critical research is declining. Within the academy a Foucauldian climate of self-regulation defines who is in and who is out as the internal politics intensify.

In Part 1, then, authors raise crucial questions, which are posed directly in Gledhill's contribution. They attend to the question of whom anthropologists produce knowledge for and they address the problem of whose interests are served by anthropological knowledge. From this set of essays also emerges the different political and economic circumstances in different historical contexts that enable or disable intellectuals to openly define themselves as Marxists, or invoke and teach Marxist literature and the implications that distinctive configurations of power have had for shaping the discipline. The contributions discussed above make clear the ways in which contemporary anthropology is contingent upon shifts and continuities in the political economies of the states in which it is practiced. Such shifts not only are critical in shaping the discipline, but they also shape our fields of inquiry and influence the subjectivities of the people we study.

In Part 2, *States and Subjects,* therefore, the contributors are engaged in an analysis of the ways in which hierarchies of power and forms of state domination figure in the formation of subjectivities in ethnographic settings that differ in time and place. Through case studies, the authors analyze the ways in which people experience and respond to nation-state practices over time. They also address the question of the processes that foster differentiation and the assumption of an identity based on difference that consigns particular categories of persons to the margins, while other classes are integrated into the centers of power. For example, Gupta (chapter 7) focuses his discussion of the question of ethnic difference and pluralism within the Indian nation-state. He argues that in the context of India, where universal franchise and minority rights came with independence, multiculturalism became integral in the formation of the postcolonial state. He suggests further how the interests of minority groups and minority group identities can be sustained so long as they do not come into conflict with the binding force of the "root" metaphors of the nation-state. Gupta's presentation is also an example of how anthropologists can study the nation-state. His perspective is derived from working within a context in which the political prerogatives involved in reconciling diversity with the homogenizing tendencies of the nation-state exists as a central political and economic tension. The contributions in Part 2, then, raise questions concerning the state, how the state governs its subjects and how subjects are incorporated into the state. Clark (chapter 11) pursues this question by examining the ways in which Ecuadorean Indians/peasants were drawn into the modernizing project of the state during the liberal period in Ecuador. She examines the ways in which the state intervened in the conflicts between the coastal elite and the highland elite by using a liberal discourse in which a common language and common categories actually marked differences in ideas and projects. By focusing on the keywords that emerged in liberal discourses, she argues that the state was able to support the interests of certain classes or class factions, and was in turn supported by certain classes and certain interests. The issue of how state strategies ensure support for the state is also addressed by Blim (chapter 10), and he directs attention to the struggles that occur within contending political parties to develop a form of a welfare state that would remedy Italy's employment problem while securing consensus for the new Italian state.

It is clear from these contributions, then, that the authors are concerned with specifying the "political" of political economy by examining structures of power and how power is exercised in different contexts. Questions are explored that concern the processes of class formation, class structure and interests, with the position of various groups to each other structurally, spatially, and historically, as well as with the structure and role of states as they reflect the concerns raised in Marx's political and historical surveys (Roseberry 1997). As the position of various groups to one another and vis à vis the state is often that of subordinate to superordinate or of the powerful to powerless, that relationship often involves domination. Often that domination occurs not as a simple display of strength or force, but as the authors above show, in the execution of certain projects and the implementation of specific visions of the nation and the national economy. This has involved projects of modernization in manifold contexts. Therefore, the forms that the state's (usually, but of course not always) modernizing project takes also require careful interrogation since it is the practices of state power, among other things, that give rise to certain forms of collective action and preclude others.

Striffler (chapter 8) and Vicencio (chapter 9) both provide cases in which state power is invoked and exercised to manipulate histories and shape subjectivities in their respective research settings. Striffler addresses the question of how and why dominant groups succeed in turning their history into the version of history that prevails over others. He examines how history was and is produced following the worker takeover of the hacienda in Ecuador. His analysis touches on the way in which the state constructed the takeover as communist-led and how this had the effect of simplifying and fixing the events, so that they would fail to serve the purpose of invigorating political projects in the present. As Striffler argues, where alternative histories are repressed, future oppositional projects are much more difficult to envisage.

The reinforcing role of state strategies and the effects that state power has in defining the past is also a central concern of Vicencio's chapter. Vicencio uses oral histories of a factory-owning couple in Franco's Spain to highlight the contradiction between the discursive construction of the past, characterized apparently by harmony and unity, and a material lived experience, characterized by divisiveness and suspicion. She argues that the reconstruction of the past, including a failed attempt at a producer cooperative among *capacho* (sisal basket) makers, impedes peoples' ability to imagine alternative forms of collective action in the present under changing global political economies. The effect of state strategies in both Vicencio's and Striffler's case studies is to constrain attempts at resistance. As these writers show, resistance and consent are not natural states and political quiescence an immemorial cultural attribute. They are produced and reproduced through material conditions.

The essays in Part 3, *Hegemonies and Histories,* are concerned precisely with an exploration of material conditions that are implicated particularly in the production of culture. They do this through their examinations of the ways in which class, gender, ethnicity, racialized forms of ethnicity, as well as regional and national identities are configured through the relationships involved in making a living under late capitalism. This is done in many contributions by problematizing the role of history and by elucidating upon the subtleties of the process of hegemony. Gordillo (chapter 13), for example, presents us with insights on the ways in which hegemonic visions and values are challenged in his analyses of the ways in which the social memory of the Tobas, an indigenous group in Argentina, is constructed. He illustrates the ways in which ideas about free and unfree labor are used in the Tobas' construction of the past. Gordillo argues that in these constructions there is a tension between past vision and present forms of consciousness. Tobas remember their ancestors as free, though innocent of their exploitation. In the present, however, they are dependent on, and clearly conscious of, their exploitation by the state. Gordillo discusses the ways in which the Tobas reconstruct old battles to represent themselves as victors, in ways that belie the facts of dominant histories. He argues that this process of reconstruction evokes and captures meanings of resistance to domination. But downplaying the terror and suffering of the past, while it permits people to draw on heroic qualities in their own more recent experiences of terror and suffering, undermines their capacity to turn these memories into a more critical political tool.

Indeed, many authors in this volume use the idea of hegemony to explore questions of conflict and struggle in which working people are engaged and they also explore the ways in which different forms of compliance are secured. Leach (chapter 14), for example, shows that for steelworkers in Ontario the outcome of industrial restructuring is a much less militant approach to politics. Turning to Gramsci and his ideas on the way in which the social subject becomes created under different forms of capitalism, she argues that the system of disciplining labor in unions operates to constrain political action. Barber (chapter 15) also examines the effects of industrial collapse, and she explores the ways in which hegemony is negotiated and tradition reworked in the contemporary struggles amongst mine workers in Cape Breton. She explores the conflicts engendered by the retreat of both the state and capital from its bargain with labor and its abdication of its role in the sustenance of Cape Breton communities. Her analysis focuses on the ways in which differential meanings in the language of community inform contemporary struggles to make a living under conditions of industrial restructuring. The effects of restructuring are also pursued by Lem's discussion (chapter 16) of the agrarian economy in Languedoc. Again, drawing on Gramsci's notion of hegemony, Lem focuses on the question of consent and discusses the ways in which rural women, the wives of small farmers, have become assimilated to key political and economic projects during particular periods in the capitalist transformation in France. Her discussion focuses on the ways in which the assimilation to one political project, particularly the project of modernization, has resulted in the alienation of women from another political project, the project of regional nationalism and the consolidation of regional culture and identity. The question of regional identity is also explored in Menzies's (chapter 17) discussion of fishers in Brittany. Menzies argues that the collapse of the industrial fish canning industry stripped away the class basis of identity (and, also, in this case a militant past), and opened the way for Bigouden regional identity. He thus explores the ways in which nationalist identity superseded class-based identity and asserts that in fact what underlies the shroud of identity politics was the class interest of a group of petty capitalists struggling to maintain their social and economic position.

From the essays in Part 3, and throughout the volume, it is clear that many of the contributors make an attempt to move beyond some of the conceptual and analytical boundaries of Marxism. They do this not by jettisoning the precepts and suppositions embedded in his analytical framework but, in fact, by reconfiguring them in ways that attempt to remedy some of the shortcomings or omissions that have been identified in his work and to pursue some of the questions that are raised. This is shown in the contributions that discuss gender and the attempts by many writers to modify and extend the analysis of capitalism in terms of gender analysis. For example, the question of how surpluses are extracted necessarily raises questions concerning gender, since capitalism tends to use men's and women's labor differently, in different times and places. In Part 3, for example, several contributors explore the question of the ways in which women's labor has been transformed by and inserted into the global economy. Labrecque (chapter 12) focuses on the women maquiladora workers in the Yucatan to trace the changes in gender relations that result from the economic crises and changing power relations that follow in the wake of the process of new forms of global capitalism that are emerging. She examines the ways in which the redefinition of gender relations results from economic crisis, and the troubling forms those take under specific conditions of gendered production. In her contribution, and also in the cases examined by Barber, Leach, Lem, and Menzies, gender is seen as embedded in social institutions and in ideologies, highlighting the gendered nature of capitalism and of local resistances to it.

While the framework for the analysis of capitalism has become extended through the contributions of many anthropologists whose work explores gender relations, identity, and women's labor, this has been accomplished within attempts to grasp the transformations of capitalism itself.[3] Indeed, contemporary capitalism has become altered in ways that were not altogether anticipated in Marx's writings. One of those changes, which some would argue reveal the limitations of Marx's framework, is often referred to as globalization. Yet globalization and also economic restructuring are probably the most cited and least understood contemporary processes. Globalization, taken to mean the process by which production, distribution, and exchange have become increasingly and intensively internationalized, is, as Roseberry (chapter 5) argues, a trend that is often taken for granted by anthropologists, and used either as a backdrop for ethnographic studies or as the theoretical underpinning for reflecting on population flows, cultural shifts, and the emergence of new social identities. Yet, some anthropologists have taken as central to their work the analysis of globalizing processes and its implications for men and women whose lives are directly touched by those forces. Labrecque's work particularly shows that anthropology is uniquely situated to address issues central to the changing organization of the global economy by drawing attention to the ways in which global processes are historically and regionally contextualized. In turn, this shifts our thinking about social movements that have arisen in late capitalism and the way that social subjectivity is constituted. Instead of seeing social movements as "new," we can see them as necessarily continuous, and in certain ways discontinuous, with older, often localized, forms of political mobilization, but always underpinned by material relations and situated practices.

Leach (chapter 14) and Barber (chapter 15) both discuss locations of industrial work in Canada and they trace the economic consequences of restructuring on the lives of people working in primary industries, where the global changes in systems of production have resulted in the deindustrialization of specific localities. Such discussions attend to local forms of change that are consequent upon such macro forces and they reinforce the analytical significance of the local and locality. In some work on globalization, especially that focused on diaspora, transnationalism, and mobility, the local has been effectively erased, considered as irrelevant to what is happening globally. Yet in many of the chapters here we pause to think about the nature and significance of locality in this highly mobile world. Smith (chapter 18), for example, suggests that the argument that presents contemporary economic reality as a radical break with the past, is one that actually derives from a failure to conduct locally and historically specific studies, and consequently to see the precise ways in which contemporary processes build upon older ones. Indeed, recent debates on the nature of globalization (Lash and Urry 1987; Smart 1993; Giddens 1990; Harvey 1989) point to the need for finely grained ethnographic studies that keep the global and the local in play simultaneously, so that the kinds of restructuring that globalization requires can be understood in a nuanced and locally specific way.

As a volume of essays that are written by anthropologists who approach their discipline through a commitment to the framework of political economy, *Culture, Economy, Power* is both an illustration of the relationship that prevails between anthropology and Marxism and a recent chapter in the history of that relationship. Indeed, anthropology and Marxism, as bodies of thought, modes of analysis as well as fields of investigation, have been shaped and reshaped through a long history of interaction and mutual influence. Any history of anthropological thought will no doubt outline the ways in which Marx's ideas have influenced the discipline of anthropology. But it is important to recall, as several writers have pointed out, that anthropology also influenced Marx in the development of key ideas in his work.[4] In recent years, many works have appeared that have given much attention to the critical relationship that has prevailed between Marxism and anthropology.[5] What these studies reveal is that while this relationship has been fraught with tension at times,[6] overall the relationship has been of a deep dialectical nature. Moreover, they expose the multiplicity of thematic areas and critical issues that have been the focus of anthropological attention in Marxist anthropology. While it is well beyond the scope of this introduction to review them, we will end this introduction by exploring some of the fundamental themes and the ways in which the essays attend to them.

Political Economy and Capitalism

The analysis of capitalism is clearly a key thematic area in Marxism and anthropology and those engaged in it would identify themselves as political economists. Yet it is often recalled that Marx actually engaged in a critique of political economy. This has led to questions of the compatibility of political economy and Marxism as modes of analysis. Marx critiques political economy in two senses. On the one hand he critiques the assumptions of the classical political economy of Smith, Ricardo, and Mill, and he also critiqued political economy as a body of knowledge and an intellectual tradition that claims to grasp the reality of the nature of material life (Levine 1979). As a critic of political economy, he rejected neoclassical explanations in economics for the workings of capitalism. On the other hand, his critique is also directed at material life itself, and through his critique of classical political economy as a body of knowledge, he intended to reveal the contradictions of the system of political economy itself, that is, capitalism (Levine 1979). In this respect, then, a Marxist approach and the approach of political economy are not incompatible. It is important to remember that while Marx begins with a critique of political economy, he also ends with it. As Roseberry (1997) reminds us, Marx is a political economist who worked within, while writing against, the basic ideas contained in the political economy of the day. So as a political economist Marx was nonetheless most concerned with the organization, mobilization, and appropriation of labor under capitalism, as well as how surplus labor is extracted from direct producers. In anthropology, continuing attention is being directed at these issues in studies of the question of the transition to capitalism (see, for example, Clark, chapter 11 and Striffler, chapter 8) and the dynamics within it. More recently, many writers concerned with the analysis of capitalism are also engaged in the effort to extend Marx's analysis to take into account the contemporary working of what has been called late capitalism, and to understand what capitalism means following its reorganization in the 1970s under what is often called post-Fordism. For example, what is often revealed is that the organization of contemporary capitalism is indeed different from the organizing principles that Marx so meticulously analyzed. Yet, as Labrecque (chapter 12), Leach (chapter 14), Barber (chapter 15), Menzies (chapter 17), and Lem (chapter 16) reveal, it is clear that the fundamental logic of surplus appropriation and the essential dynamics of capitalist economies remain unaltered.

Materialism and History

Perhaps the most important starting point of the approach in anthropology that has come to be known as political economy is its grounding in history and historical materialism. As anthropologists concerned with studying the political economy of past and present societies and cultures, each of the contributors uses, as a point of departure, notions contained in the historical materialism of Marx as well as in his analysis of capitalism and his analysis of political consciousness and collective action. The point of departure for Marx's materialism was the idea that through human actions, people enter into relations and act collectively in and on nature. In so doing, they commit their labor to the transformation of nature and the material conditions necessary for the reproduction of life. These ideas are summed up in one of the most famous passages that Marx ever wrote, in the *Preface* to *A Contribution to the Critique of Political Economy (1859)*. Hence, the concept of labor and the ways in which labor is organized are central precepts in Marx's notion of materialism. But the materialism of Marx is a historical one. It is historical in the sense that modes of organizing labor, the relations involved in mobilizing labor, are historically situated. As Striffler (chapter 8), Barber (chapter

15), and Clark (chapter 11) show, history itself is constituted by people acting collectively to reproduce and transform relations, institutions, and practices.

The thematic area of historical materialism is explored by most authors in the volume as they seek to problematize the special historical and material circumstances by which the labor of anthropological subjects and anthropologists themselves are organized. Pursuing the issue of how labor is organized for social reproduction, many of the contributors have focused on work contexts and the organization of livelihoods in distinctive periods under distinctive power configurations. Thus, for many of the contributors in this volume, the anthropological subject is constituted as people who labor, people who work. Many of the essays, therefore, use an analytical framework that views the social world as made of classes—members of the laboring class and members of classes who do not make a living employing the labor of others. Menzies (chapter 17), for example, focuses on small-scale fishers in Brittany and explores the relations and different interests of skippers and deckhands. He poses the question of why they persist despite the trend of the concentration of capital. Leach (chapter 14) argues for attention to class aspects of broad-based political mobilization in southern Ontario and describes how the specificities of the changes in the labor market militates against political action. The anthropological subjects in Labrecque's (chapter 12) contribution are again members of the laboring class. Workers and members of the laboring classes in Italy also represent the focus of Blim's (chapter 10) discussion. However, his intervention presents the other side of the question of work and employment that has come to configure the experience of increasing numbers of people in contexts of globalization and economic restructuring, that is, the experience of being out of work and unemployed. His contribution traces the different political initiatives taken on by the political Left and Right in contemporary Italy to address the question of regional differences in patterns of unemployment. These examples again illustrate the importance of locality and local processes in shaping class relations and politics, and together they reinforce Smith's view that questions the importance to which people's embeddedness in place remains significant in developing an understanding of the contemporary world. The field of inquiry, for anthropologists who are concerned with production and workers, is political and economic transformations in the conditions and circumstances within which people live and work.

In many of these contributions there is an attempt to move beyond what is often perceived as a strictly materialist focus. This is often interpreted as a form of materialist determination in Marx's work; for example, that the form of the state as well as ideas, beliefs, and consciousness, in other words the cultural realm and subjectivity, are all determined materially. Clark (chapter 11), Gordillo (chapter 13), Lem (chapter 16), Leach (chapter 14), and Barber (chapter 15) are concerned with the question of how subjects and subjectivities are created, and each addresses this issue, not by jettisoning materialism in favor of an epistemological idealism, but by employing Gramsci's concept of hegemony to shed light on the intricate connections between the material and the ideal.

As these essays illustrate, Marx's version of materialism involves change, history, and temporality. The temporality embedded in a Marxist framework has translated itself into a concern in anthropology with history, not simply as temporal change, but as change that specifically involves the forces of power and its relationship to economy. The critical importance of a historical approach is evident from all the chapters. Those dealing with the context within which anthropological knowledge is produced show clearly how those contexts change over time. In other chapters, historicizing present-day processes becomes a key methodology for developing a better understanding of those processes. Attention to history permits deeper knowledge of the shifts in forms of domination and exploitation, concepts that take a central place in all the work presented here. Historical analysis also reveals the vicissitudes of capitalist formation and reformation, and the forms of social differentiation that they engender. Correspondingly, class, as the way in which collectivities of people are inserted into relations of production and reproduction (Smith 1999, 92), and what class "means," both discursively and materially, emerges most forcefully through a historical approach. In the ways in which history is invoked, it becomes clearer to the analyst how processes of domination and exploitation come about, move in this and that direction over time. It also becomes clear how they are discursively reconstructed in the present, in many cases to enable and also to constrain political action in social movements.

Politics and Consciousness

Many of the authors are concerned with analyzing the structures of power and specifying how power is exercised in different contexts in an effort to also analyze how power can be seized, overturned, contested, and resisted. As the contributors in this collection self-consciously concern themselves with history, class, exploitation, and domination, problematics explored in Marx's historical and political surveys, the question of the distinctive character of social movements and also the absence of them, is broached in their papers. Leach (chapter 14) and Menzies (chapter 17), for example, undertake to examine forms of collective action by pursing the historical continuities and discontinuities that give them shape, rather than assuming radical breaks between "old" and "new" social movements. They examine movements engaged in class-based, regional, national, gender, and autochthonous struggles, and their relationship to overarching state projects in different phases of capitalist development. Taking up the theme of collectivity, they explore some of the questions that were raised in the Eighteenth Brumaire on how the "feeling of community" is generated, and how people acting in their relations with others transform the worlds in which they live. The concern with the political runs not only to understanding how the material relations and historical understandings of the past and present infuse identities, and how consciousness of the collective ignites forms of collective action, but there is also a concern with understanding what mitigates against the creation of communities of interests. For Striffler (chapter 8) and Vicencio (chapter 9), this is a historical question, while for Lem (chapter 16), this is a question that concerns the interplay between the state, modernization, culture, and hegemony.

In these various ways, then, each of the authors addresses the multidimensioned thematic areas that arise in part as Marx's intellectual legacy, but also in part from the real world of shifts and changes within capitalism in its early, modern, and late forms. We acknowledge a great debt to what has been called the "postmodern turn" in the social sciences and anthropology, for it gave us the impetus to think in concert about how some of the key concerns in anthropology might be rethought. We conclude, then, with two propositions. We propose that the realm of the cultural—in other words culture itself—should be explained and not taken as an untheorized catchall tool for explanation. To this we add that theorization necessarily involves a confrontation with the economic and political realm in history. We also propose that the agenda for anthropology should be reinvigorated by a commitment to exposing the "innermost secret" of the social structure of a system of economic and political organization based on the appropriation of labor, the appropriation of surplus (Marx 1967, 791). Inasmuch as some may take these propositions as provocations, we are eager to rise to the challenge of debate.

Notes

1. At the time, the society was called the Canadian Ethnology Society/Société d'ethnologie canadien.

2. The people involved have changed from year to year, with a fairly consistent core attending each year, others taking part as schedules permitted. Among some of those who have participated frequently over the years and whose ideas have shaped the collective agenda but whose contributions do not appear in the present collection, are: Claire Bélanger, Malcolm Blincow, John Calagione, Kirk Dombrowski, Lindsay Dubois, Glynis George, Leslie Jermyn, Tania Li, Micaela di Leonardo, David Nugent, the late, Daniel Nugent, Nicole Polier, Stuart Philpott, Albert Schrauwers, Veronica Schild, Gerald Sider, Krystyna Sieciechowicz.

3. There is a voluminous literature on these issues. For useful anthologies see di Leonardo (1991); Lancaster and di Leonardo (1997); Lamphere, Ragoné, and Zavella (1997).

4. See for example, Donham (1990) and Levine (1979).

5. See for example, Bloch (1985), Donham (1990), Kahn and Llobera (1981), Roseberry (1997), Sayer (1991), Vincent (1985), Wessman (1981).

6. Donham (1990, 3) has pointed out that anthropology and Marxism are in some ways opposed in their critical perspectives. Anthropology at its best, so he asserts, has stressed an unceasing respect for cultural differences. At its worst, it has descended into a wearied relativism that is devoid of any critical edge. On the other hand, Marxism at its best has been devoted to the deconstruction of ideologies that perpetuate human oppression. But at its worst, it has degenerated into a disregard for other ways of living and indeed contempt for people who do not share in the vision of an emancipatory project.

PART 1

Nations and Knowledge

CHAPTER 2

Bicentrism, Culture, and the Political Economy of Sociocultural Anthropology in English Canada

Thomas Dunk

Discussing the concept of a national culture and a national tradition of anthropological research is fraught with potential complications because both depend on the idea that there is a distinct nation that could generate a national tradition. While it is true that nationalism has been a powerful force in world history in the last two centuries, in many cases the existence of a national culture can be, and often is, contested. Canada is one of the modern states that lacks consensus about its national culture; indeed, in this sense it is more accurate to speak of the Canadian state rather than the Canadian nation precisely because there is not one hegemonic imagined community. Officially, there are at least two embedded in the Canadian constitution, those derived from the officially recognized founding nations, France and Britain. The First Nations have vigorously argued for and won a unique constitutional position by virtue of being the first peoples, thus giving at least three nations, and perhaps hundreds if we consider the cultural and political heterogeneity of the First Nations. Canada is officially a multicultural nation suggesting that competing ideas of Canadian culture and identity are welcome. Beyond these formally recognized expressions of different ideas about the national culture are the regional ones: the East, the West, and the Center, and even within each of these regions there are differences between the urban regional centers and the extensive hinterlands that they control politically and economically.

A second problem when discussing the national setting, culture, and anthropology in Canada is that there is not a distinctively English Canadian theoretical tradition in sociocultural anthropology, at least not in the way that one can relate specific paradigms with, say, French, British, or American anthropology (cf. Howes 1992, 155). Although First Nations studies form a prominent part of the subject matter of anthropology in English Canada (Darnell 1997), there is no unique theoretical perspective to call upon. It is perhaps a logical expectation that in a state that lacks a strong sense of a national culture one is hard pressed to find a national theoretical tradition of anthropological research.

Thus, if one is to try to explain what is distinctive about Canadian culture, and anthropology as one small element of that culture, one must set about trying to explain an evident lack, the presence of an absence so to speak. This problem is often seen to have its origins in the fact that, as the official state ideology would have it, Canada was founded by and has henceforth tried to protect its two founding cultures as well as various others. Thus, whereas other nation-states try in the official ideology to describe who they are—in other words to formulate a core identity—Canada has, officially at least, resisted this. What is said to make Canada distinctive is its diversity.

A Tradition That Is Not One

Recent analyses of this apparent bicentrism, or inability to imagine a whole that is not internally divided, have taken it to define a distinctive Canadian psyche, which is reflected in Canadian culture and in Canadian anthropology (Howes 1992; Harries-Jones 1997, 251–252). In other words, a negativity is, in fact, a positivity. What defines Canadian culture is its very lack of definition. Canadian identity is forever contingent and Canadian anthropology is, thus, a "'tradition that is not one,' like the identity of which it is, in part, an expression" (Howes 1992, 155). Although the notion of Canadian content as employed by state bureaucrats out to promote or protect Canada's cultural industries is dismissed as "preposterous" (Howes 1992, 156), a distinctively Canadian culture is identifiable on the basis of its formal structural properties, its bicentrism (Howes 1992, 163–164). The best in Canadian anthropology, as in high culture more generally, thus, are works that express this "tendency towards bicentrism" (Howes 1992, 166). This is juxtaposed to an American tendency toward "concentricity."

This analysis is interesting for at least two reasons. Firstly, it is an effort to go beyond the tendency to bemoan the absence of a distinctive Canadian culture and (English) Canadian anthropology by shifting our attention from content to formal, structural principles. Secondly, it explains the particular nature of this formal structural principle of Canadian thought by reference to a unique Canadian psyche, one that is reflected in Canadian political and legal history.

On the other hand, such reasoning runs aground on a number of issues. It is not clear that bicentrism as a formal structural principle is unique to Canadian culture, especially given the current configuration of global economics and culture. And while bicentrism may indeed be reflected in certain politico-legal documents such as the Canadian constitution, it is doubtful that this represents a national-popular will, as opposed to the particular thinking of a class or class fraction. Finally, there are some other straightforward political, economic, and cultural realities that Canada has always had to deal with and which a distinctive brand of Canadian political economy has tried to address. This tradition helps to explain the absence of a unique anthropological perspective in English Canada. The structures of importance are not in the Canadian psyche, but rather in global political economy.

Howes argues that the absence of a clearly centered culture and identity makes Canada different but this is now said to be true of all cultures. The common idea that Canadian identity consists solely or primarily of contingent relationships—that, for example, it primarily is defined as the binary opposite of American culture—is reflective of the principal of identity formation in much poststructuralist theorizing which emphasizes the relational, contextual, and contingent nature of all meaning (Laclau and Mouffe 1985). From such perspectives to say that Canadian national culture is characterized by an absence of essence, or that it is bicentric, no longer clearly separates it from any other national culture or identity. It may reflect a much more widespread "postmodern" condition, which only now is being recognized in numerous other locations; a condition that is a symptom of the compression of time and space brought on by recent technological and economic developments (Harvey 1989).

The juxtaposition of Canadian bicentrism and American concentrism reflects the familiar idea that the United States is a cultural "melting pot" whereas Canada is a nation that respects, indeed even protects, cultural diversity. This is why defining a Canadian culture is so difficult. Americans know or are told what they are to be or become, whereas Canadians have never settled on a uniform vision of who they are. While the political constitutions of the two states do reflect contrasting views on the appropriate relationship between the state and the individual, the differences between Canada and the United States, especially with regard to the respect for cultural variation within the two states, are often overdrawn. The history of the treatment of First Nations people by the Canadian state and the non-aboriginal population, and the efforts to assimilate non-Anglophone or non-Francophone immigrants into a dominant set of values and norms, indicates that there were and are powerful ideas about and desires to impose an "appropriate" uniform Canadian identity on the population (Stasiulus and Jhappan 1995; Valverde 1991). The ideas expressed by these actions may not be part of current official state doctrine but they are still present in Canadian culture. Anxieties about threats to a perceived homogeneous culture underlay the Canadian history of racist reactions to immigrants, especially Asian immigrants (cf. Ward 1978). Canadians have, periodically, expressed the same yearning for social, cultural, and biological homogeneity as have other national populations.

Indeed, while the "French fact" in Canada was recognized to some extent in law at the time of Confederation in 1867, the official declaration of Canada as a bilingual state dates from the 1960s. The federal act declaring Canada a multicultural society was not passed until the 1980s. Prior to the 1960s, most of the country paid little heed to the idea of bilingualism, and immigration regulations often explicitly discriminated against specific ethnic/racial groups. Unlike Mexico, where early twentieth-century nationalist projects celebrated an indigenous *mestizo* culture (see de la Peña this volume), nationalism in English Canada looked to its white, nordic biological and cultural heritage as the source of the nation's presumed future greatness.

There is a long tradition of sociological work comparing Canadian and American values. While much of this research supports the idea that Canadians and Americans vary with regard to issues such as the emphasis they place on individualism and competition, these differences are of a statistical rather than an absolute nature (Lipset 1990). Research on levels and kinds of prejudice and discrimination in the two countries suggests that the differences between Canadians and Americans are rather limited (Reitz and Breton 1994). The Canadian conceit that we are more tolerant of "otherness" than our American neighbors is both self-serving and inaccurate, even if as a small nation Canada is not guilty of the kind or extent of imperialist crimes historically committed by, say, the United Kingdom, France, or the United States.

There is also a tradition that interprets Canada's bilingualism and multiculturalism as a form of ideology rather than an expression of an essential Canadian identity. Bilingualism and multiculturalism are seen as attempts to undermine Quebecois nationalism by drowning the minority French language and culture in a sea of competing otherness and/or coopting unassimilated Quebecois and other ethnic leadership. In other words, Canada's bicentrism may reflect a technique for solidifying a uniform Anglo-dominated bourgeois hegemony, rather than a deep bicentric structure of the Canadian mind (Moodley 1983).

Such an analysis is supported by a growing literature on the ways in which contemporary multiculturalism meshes a little too easily with contemporary global capitalism. Katharyne Mitchell (1993), for example, has shown how multiculturalism is used by those speaking on behalf of international capital when they are opposed by local populations who perceive their lifestyles and economic interests jeopardized by developments brought on by foreign capital. Homeowners opposed to the secretive real estate dealings of Hong Kong investors are derided as racists and Canada's multicultural heritage is celebrated by those wishing to attract and benefit from this foreign investment.

Multiculturalism plays an important ideological role in the reproduction of the power and influence of capital in Canada and on a global scale. The notion of multiculturalism focuses attention on ethnicity as the core form of identity, as opposed to a multitude of other potential sources of identity. As state policies, bilingualism and multiculturalism foreground vertical divisions—different but equal cultures—and distract attention from horizontal divisions based on class and gender.

In a world in which large multinational corporations and huge investment firms look upon the entire globe as their field of action, local efforts to resist their designs are frequently treated as expressions of outdated localism, nationalism, or even racism. For the upper and upper-middle classes who have the means and ability to benefit from the free flow of capital, goods, and services, multiculturalism is a congenial idea. At its core, however, there is a certain "falsity": "the contemporary 'politically correct' liberal attitude which perceives of itself as surpassing the limitations of its ethnic identity ('citizen of the world' without anchors in any particular ethnic community), functions, *within its own society,* as a narrow elitist upper-middle-class circle opposing itself to the majority of common people, despised for being caught in their narrow ethnic or community confines" (Žižek 1997, 47).

In the current context, such facts and ideas should at the very least lead one to question the notion that bilingualism or multiculturalism reflect some primordial Canadian essence that one can see reflected in high culture and intellectual pursuits such as anthropology. If bicentrism is an element of Canadian culture, it may say more about the peculiar class/ethnic/regional structure of the dominant class or class fractions in Canada, or about the way in which the dominant social categories are integrated into global capitalism, than it does about a unique Canadian psyche. Underlying this apparent official respect for ethnic variation is a uniform set of capitalist social relationships, which stultify anything other than superficial difference.[1]

This brings me to a second observation. Howes argues that the merit of the criteria (evidence of bicentrism) he proposes for deciding whether or not a work should belong to the Canadian anthropological canon stems from the fact that they are general and "constitutional (that is, they are legal and cannot therefore be dismissed as 'purely political')" (Howes 1992, 156). This is a curious claim. Laws and constitutions are the product of very political processes; they are the object that political institutions and processes explicitly produce. They may not be "purely political" but they are highly political.

A Marxian-influenced perspective begins not by positing the autonomy of the legal system but by asking how the legal system reflects relationships of power and which segment of society, in terms of social classes or class fractions, it is that dominates the law-making process. In other words, which class's specific interests become embodied in laws that are then projected as an expression of national will and imposed upon everyone. The question that emerges from this perspective is, whose interest is represented in the Canadian constitution?

The processes by which a new state is created are always complex. However, it is well known that the "Fathers of Confederation" were largely merchant capitalists concerned, among other things, to secure a substantial hinterland for their control, a hinterland threatened by forces from within and without that sought to achieve political independence or absorption into the United States. The structure of the Canadian state reflects the accommodation reached by an ethnically divided class fraction so as to foster circumstances that allowed it to proceed in its goal of creating economic opportunities from which its members would benefit.

This is not to suggest that there were not or are not real divisions between the English-speaking and French-speaking populations that transcend a simplistic class analysis or that a reductionist Marxist argument suffices to explain the nature of the ongoing process of state formation in Canada. I simply want to draw attention to the fact that it is another form of simplistic reductionism to suggest that, for example, the constitutions of states can be read as expressions of some national essence or imaginary.

Indeed, it is arguable that the threats to national unity in Canada are at least partly a product of the fact that the Canadian constitution does not reflect the real Canadian imaginary, whatever it might be. Howes argues that the "bicentric propensity, this refusal to synthesize, is a manifestation of the strength of the Canadian constitution" (1992, 164). This is very much the official line, and one particularly meaningful among the central Canadian educated middle or upper class, especially Anglophones in Quebec and Francophones in Ontario. It is precisely the perspective that is under attack from many regions in the country, particularly the West, but also in the regions where Quebecois separatism is strongest, and among segments of the Anglophone white working class. In English Canada, the appeal of the populist right wing, such as it is, partly is based on its critique of bilingualism and multiculturalism (cf. Leach 1997, 1998; Patten 1996). The Canadian constitution may reflect an admirable principle of bicentrism, but it is a principle that many segments of the Canadian population find disagreeable.

All of this suggests that if we want to understand what is unique about Canadian culture we should look beyond the constitution and unresolvable questions about the particularity of a Canadian psyche or imaginary. What makes Canada unique is the particular way in which the human populations living within the country have been and have resisted being tied into a global economy over the last five hundred years. Indeed, a uniquely Canadian theoretical perspective has been developed precisely to try and understand this political and economic experience.

Canadian Political Economy and the Absence of a Strong National Culture

While there is no distinctively Canadian sociocultural anthropology, there is a widely recognized uniquely Canadian tradition of political economy. The "Canadian school," as it is referred to in communications studies (Martin 1997, 39–45), begins with Harold Innis and focuses on the relationship between the means of communication and political organization, a concern derived in part from analyzing the problems the Canadian state faced managing an economy spread over a vast and thinly populated territory.

The Canadian state has always had to contend with what is now seen to be a widespread phenomenon: the decentering of identities and cultures that deep embeddedness in global markets seems to entail and the inevitable reactions and backlashes that this experience generates. This may be explained in the Canadian case in part by reference to some of the principal concerns of Innis's political economy, particularly relationships between natural environmental conditions, technology, world markets, and the spatial organization of production, distribution, and settlement in Canada. In the words of Daniel Drache, one of Innis's main contemporary interpreters, a central focus of Innis's work was "the costly and uncontrollable effect of international markets on people and communities" (Drache 1995, xiv).

Indeed, at least some of the current concern in anthropology and other disciplines with the spatial dislocations and reorganizations that globalization is having are foreshadowed in Innis's theory of staple development and the effects this has had on Canada (Innis [1956]1995, 3–24). The staple theory argues that because of the unique and specific characteristics of reliance upon the export of staple products (themselves partly determined by environmental conditions) Canada's economic and cultural development took specific forms. Issues such as the environmental limits to certain kinds of economic activity, problems inherent in a reliance on export-led growth, import penetration of domestic markets, foreign ownership, and the arguable absence or relatively weak position of indigenous entrepreneurs meant that exogenous forces have played a role in Canadian economic and cultural history that they may not have elsewhere.

Another prominent theme in the staple theory is that the development of staple products and their export involves huge public investment in infrastructure, which leads, in turn, to high levels of public debt which then limit the state's options in terms of economic, social, and cultural policy, especially given a reliance on high levels of foreign investment and access to foreign markets. These themes are central to the current discourse on globalization, the nation-state, public finances, and the restructuring of production, distribution, and culture.

Following the general outlines of this approach, if Canadian identity is fractured, it is the product of each region's historical origins as staple-producing zones, rather than the hegemonic ideology of bicentrism. Newfoundland culture, tradition, and folklore is rooted in the fact that it was based upon the production of codfish for the mostly European market. Features of both the cod itself—for example, being a natural resource whose ecology meant it could not easily be incorporated into systems of private ownership—and the market—being of European peasants and workers and therefore with a limited price ceiling but a very elastic floor—had important consequences in terms of settlement patterns, returns on investments, and the social relations of production, such as, for example, the merchants' drive to externalize costs and risks of production. More recent changes in technology and the organization of production have had devastating effects on the environment and on the communities dependent on the fishery (see Kennedy 1997 for an overview of the anthropology of Newfoundland).

Quebecois culture is, of course, derived at one level from its French origins. But the Canadian side of French Canada is also inextricably bound up with the unique agro-forest economy developed in relationship to the early fur trade, the slow development of commercial agriculture, the nineteenth-century square timber trade, and the twentieth-century pulp and paper economy. Moreover, current issues such as Quebecois nationalism have their origins in part in the differential success of Quebec and Ontario (Lower and Upper Canada) in the early wheat economy. Because of environmental and economic conditions, petty commodity producers in Upper Canada/Ontario enjoyed a success that stimulated backward and forward linkages and thus contributed to the development of a more dynamic industrial capitalist culture in Ontario than in Quebec. Quebecers' sense of being "poorer cousins" in the confederation stems partly from this historic economic situation, which in certain respects they are still trying to overcome, but whose origins lie not in culture but in environment and markets (Panitch 1981, 15).

That the West has been historically reliant on grain, coal, oil, and gas production or the boreal forest region of central Canada on the production of fur, timber, and more recently pulp and paper has had a significant influence on the nature of migration, settlement, labor markets, and cultural identities in these regions.

The relationship between First Nations and the anthropological community in Canada has a long and important history. Some of the principal concerns of that research reflect the key role of First Nations people in the fur trade and the importance of the fur trade in Canadian economic development. This has left a continuing legacy in terms of relationships between the Canadian state and First Nations. As the importance of fur trade in the national economy waned, the Canadian state concerned itself with removing Native people so that other kinds of staple production could proceed—a process that is still ongoing and which has generated the endless struggles between the federal and provincial governments and First Nations over forestry, mining, oil, gas, and hydro-electric projects. This conflict has generated employment and research opportunities for many anthropologists (cf. Dyck and Waldram 1993).

Thus, Canada's unique cultural identity, or lack of cultural identity, is rooted in Canada's long and regionally variegated integration into global capitalism. Staple theory, as a unique Canadian contribution to political economy, attempts to both explain and express this historical experience. Like all theories, it has not gone unchallenged or unmodified.

By the 1970s, it was being reworked in what was referred to as the "new Canadian political economy" to avoid what some perceived as its environmental determinist overtones and to better fit with the "dependency" literature, the origins of which lay in efforts to understand the development of underdevelopment in Latin America. In this context Canada was seen as an anomaly—a rich but nonetheless underdeveloped nation. Emphasis was placed upon the role of imperialism and the problems of foreign control over key economic sectors in thwarting what was seen as a "normal" course of industrialization.

This literature was soon enough subjected to a neo-Marxian criticism; namely, that in its emphasis on exchange and trade patterns it ignored class, particularly the constitutive role of class struggle in determining the actual living conditions of subaltern populations and the range of power and options open to both indigenous and foreign capitalists. Class relations within Canada from the nineteenth century were very different from Latin America. Of particular importance was the fact that petty commodity producers and wage laborers were formally free, unlike much of Latin America where bonded forms of labor were far more common. This had important repercussions for the development of market relationships and a system of commodity production based upon the purchase of commodities in Canada and the lack of such an outcome in Latin America (Panitch 1981).

One element of this critique that is particularly pertinent to the current discussion is the way it focused on the cultural aspects of Canada's domination by imperial powers such as the United Kingdom and the United States. It is here that one finds a potential political economic explanation of Canadian anthropology being "a tradition that is not one." In the postwar era, the role of U.S. culture in Canadian life has been overwhelming. The high culture of Canadian intellectuals involved more resistance to American cultural imperialism than was true at the level of mass culture but it was not immune to it.

The Anthropological Labor Market in Canada

Anthropology developed as part and parcel of the postwar growth of the mass education system in Canada and this was made possible by, and Canadian anthropology has been indelibly shaped by, the nature of the continental intellectual labor market. What may most significantly distinguish anthropology in Canada from other national situations is the extent to which it relies on practitioners who were trained elsewhere, especially in the United States. This is especially important in those departments that are producing the new generation of faculty, which is supposedly going to fill the vacancies that are predicted in the near future. In the late 1990s, after two decades of hire-Canadians-first policies, the eleven departments that offer a doctorate in sociocultural anthropology overwhelmingly still were staffed by individuals who earned their degrees in the United States, United Kingdom, or elsewhere. Of the 142 full-time faculty in these departments, whose field of expertise is sociocultural anthropology, only forty-one (29 percent) have doctorates from Canadian universities.[2]

There are a number of reasons for this unique situation. Anthropology was established in universities in Canada only after World War II. Harries-Jones asserts that a brain drain from Canada to the United States, Great Britain, and elsewhere in the 1960s contributed to a shortage of Canadian-trained personnel for the expanding university system (1997, 250). This may or may not have been a causative factor in the shortage of Canadian anthropologists but there is more to the story than this, particularly given the hegemonic influence American culture has within Canada. Until the late 1960s, there were relatively few Ph.D.s granted by Canadian anthropology departments (Preston and Adelard-Tremblay 1988). As the universities launched their rapid expansion in the 1960s, they had to look elsewhere for the skilled labor required to staff them. In doing so they were following a common pattern in Canadian history, one whose explanation lies in part in Canada's historic staples-based economy. Shortages of skilled labor have often been overcome by importing this labor from elsewhere, rather than training and educating Canadian workers (Swift 1995, 70–93).

A large number of retirements and the fact that Canadian universities now produce a steady supply of individuals with doctorates in sociocultural anthropology may soon change this situation. There is, however, another factor at play, which is likely to mean that foreign-trained faculty will continue to be highly valued in Canadian anthropology programs.

The higher education system in Canada is influenced by the same trends that exist in popular and elite culture. Individuals always have and probably increasingly will look to a global culture for legitimation. Success within Canada often is dependent upon initial recognition and approval in the United States or, to a lesser extent, Europe. Unless the pattern changes, the transmission of the anthropological culture in Canada is always going to be through the filter of perspectives that originate elsewhere because degrees from certain foreign countries and universities possess more symbolic capital within Canada than degrees from Canadian institutions. This reflects the overwhelming role of foreign, especially American, culture in Canada.

Of course, Canada is not alone in being heavily influenced by the intellectual traditions that derive from the major present or past imperial nations. The grand paradigms that guide most social research can be historically connected to certain nations: German idealism, French rationalism, British empiricism, and American pragmatism. The intellectual cultures of all the smaller nations have been influenced by these traditions to some extent and even today the global domination of the United States and to a lesser extent the United Kingdom, France, and Germany is seen in such everyday realities as the fact that most so-called "world-class" journals and publishers are based in one of these countries. To become a "known" scholar requires being published in journals that, despite their particular national origin and setting, project and/or are perceived to reflect universal interests and concerns.

The forces working against the development of a distinctively English Canadian anthropological tradition may be understood in terms analogous to those that influence other academic disciplines. Efforts to establish a uniquely Canadian version of cultural studies have been hampered by the fact that the mix of traditions this new field brings together is imported from countries where intellectuals read their own culture as "exemplifying global developments, without needing to think about the specific relation of those developments to their national context" (Wernick 1993, 300). Because of Canada's subordinate position in the global system, its researchers in the social sciences and humanities are constantly reminded of the limitations of the "localness" of their work Academics who are based in the major powers tend to project (consciously or not) their empirical research and theoretical interests as having universal significance. Some academic research is deemed parochial while other research is seen by those in positions to define what is and is not significant as "world class" and globally important. As Narotzky (this volume) points out, sometimes local anthropologists in smaller states are treated as informants rather than professional colleagues by anthropologists from globally dominant nations. The culture of anthropologists is as deeply enmeshed in the powerful cultural, social, and economic forces that comprise the hierarchical global system as any other transnational academic (or non-academic) subculture and this is inevitably reflected in what comes to be seen as important theoretical, methodological, or even topical developments.

An example of this fact is the relative lack of impact that the applied anthropological analysis of First Nations communities that has been dominant in Canadian anthropology has had on the discipline as a whole. Despite the abundance and sophistication of this work, it has had very little if any influence on broader theoretical developments in the discipline. To understand the reasons for this would require a full-scale analysis in and of itself. But one short, although admittedly incomplete, answer to this puzzle is simply that the terms of debate(s) within the discipline as a whole are set by researchers based in the major Western imperial powers, that is, primarily by researchers based in the United States and to a lesser extent (reflecting their faded imperialist status) the United Kingdom and France.[3] In these states, relationships with First Nations never was, or in the United States no longer is, a central political problem, at least not compared to relationships with external former colonies or contemporary neocolonies. Moreover, Canada's relatively late industrial expansion into its hinterlands involved more explicit state planning and direction than in, for example, the United States. The negotiations that these more corporatist arrangements have involved have been a major source of employment for anthropologists in Canada.

As in Mexico (see de la Peña this volume), much anthropological research in Canada has been and continues to be focused upon issues relating to relations between the state and indigenous peoples. It is practical, applied, and "local" as opposed to academic, theoretical, and "foreign."[4] This creates a division of labor of sorts within the profession. In terms of conducting their research, anthropologists working in foreign locales have to deal with the day-to-day realities of living and working with their "subjects." But in terms of their academic careers, the day-to-day survival strategies are focused on negotiating their way through the middle-class intellectual culture of the universities at home where they live and work. The disjunction between theory and practice is thus matched by a disjunction between home and away. In the rarefied atmosphere of the university world, the sometimes ploddingly practical concerns of local applied anthropology simply lack the feel of heightened erudition that academic culture celebrates. What Roseberry (this volume) refers to as academic enclosure elides in Canada with the cultural forces that render Canadian training and, often, anthropological research on specifically Canadian issues a barrier—not an impenetrable barrier, but a barrier nonetheless—to career success within Canadian academic institutions.

The overdetermination of Canadian anthropology by paradigms derived from elsewhere is perhaps more important in explaining an apparent absence of a distinctive tradition and lack of concentric theorizing than some psychic deep structure derived from the historic French/English divide within the Canadian state. As a relatively small, albeit wealthy, power in the global system Canada has been heavily influenced by external developments since its inception. To the extent the Canadian psyche is bicentric—a problematic generalization as I have tried to show—it may be that what Dorothy Smith argues is true for women working in disciplines and living in an everyday world based on masculine language and concepts may be true of all subaltern social groups. Canadians may have developed a "bifurcated consciousness" (Smith 1990, 11–28) trying to negotiate their way through a world dominated by more powerful states and national cultures while at the same time having to develop cultural modes appropriate to immediate local environmental, economic, and cultural settings.

Conclusions

Anthropology's relationship to imperialism is by now, of course, an old subject. It is still relevant, however, if one wishes to understand the nature of the anthropological tradition, or lack of tradition, in Canada. The common subjects of anthropological research within Canada are peoples who have been colonial or neocolonial subjects of the dominant central Canadian Anglophone society—First Nations, Quebecois, and Newfoundlanders, groups that have a historically unique connection to Canada's staple-based economic history. Beyond this, Canadian anthropology reflects the influence of Canada's historic relationships to imperial powers, particularly with the United Kingdom and the United States on the Anglophone side while the historic cultural connection to France is visible on the Francophone side.[5] In other words, anthropology practiced within Canadian borders has reflected the parameters of internal colonial and neocolonial relationships, relationships that are to a significant extent the product of Canada's history of deep entanglement in global economic processes of the kind that Canadian political economy has attempted to understand. Canadian-based anthropologists practising in foreign lands have pursued global issues and theories as defined by anthropologists based in the leading imperialist nations. Thus, the "tradition that is not one" that is Canadian anthropology reflects the global political and economic forces that have forever determined the Canadian experience.

Notes

1. This is not to suggest that toleration and respect for racial and ethnic variability is not a desirable goal. It is a matter of comparing actually existing multiculturalism with the idea of an egalitarian, culturally diverse society. An analogous situation is the comparison of the idea of socialism with the reality of what were "actually existing socialisms." To critique actual practice is not necessarily to refuse the more utopian idea.

2. The numbers come from *The American Anthropological Association Guide 1997–98* (Arlington, Va.: AAA, 1997). The eleven departments are: Alberta, British Columbia, Calgary, Laval, Manitoba, McGill, McMaster, Montreal, Simon Fraser, Toronto, and York. Simon Fraser also has a separate Department of Archaeology which offers a Ph.D. My calculation of 142 sociocultural anthropologists is based upon the areas of interest listed beside each individual's name. In terms of national origins of the degrees held the breakdown is as follows: United States = 66; Canada = 41; United Kingdom = 19; Other = 16.

3. And even for the British and French global intellectual prominence now may be dependent upon acceptance and reinterpretion in the United States. See, for example, Lamont's (1987) discussion of Jacques Derrida.

4. There may be two contrasting developments currently influencing the division between applied and academic anthropological research. Gledhill (this volume) notes the pressure within the United Kingdom for anthropological research to become increasingly focused on internal social issues related to managing the crises generated by neoliberalism, a development that might help lessen the distinction between academic anthropology conducted in foreign locales and applied local anthropology. Roseberry (this

volume) notes how the employment crisis in anthropology in the United States may also create favorable conditions for a rapprochement between the academy and popular progressive organizations and movements as increasing numbers of anthropologists look to these organizations for jobs. I would argue that in Canada there is still a long way to go before applied research on Canadian issues receives the same recognition in academia as more academic research conducted in more exotic places.

5. This is how I would interpret the differences Maranda (1983) notes between Francophone and Anglophone anthropology in Canada. The influence of Marxism and semiotics among Canadian Francophone anthropologists reflected the dominant intellectual currents in France at the time, while the dominance of American anthropology among Anglophone anthropologists reflected the influence of the United States culture in English Canada.

CHAPTER 3

The Political Economy of Political Economy in Spanish Anthropology

Susana Narotzky

In this chapter, I explore the relations between the development of political economy in Spanish anthropology and the political context in Spain during the last forty years. I will also explore the connections of such development within the context of Spain to political economic trends in anthropology itself more generally, and the implications they have for a political economy of knowledge. First, I will describe the introduction of different Marxist theories in Spain and how this was related to antifascist and nationalist political dissent within the university during the Franco years. Second, I will present the work of some Spanish anthropologists who have worked within what can be termed a political economy framework. The collection of work to which I refer is not exhaustive. My point in drawing attention to it is to illustrate the different ways in which anthropologists have used the political economy perspective in their studies. Third, I will address the question of why some anthropologically innovative work advanced by Spanish anthropologists, who, again, work within the framework of political economy, has been ignored by Anglophone Europeanist anthropologists who claim a similar theoretical orientation. Moreover, the consequences of this situation will be explored. I will look therefore at the relation between American anthropologists doing political economy analyses of Spain and their local Spanish colleagues. My point in examining these questions is to stress that the combination of bypassing and treating as irrelevant local colleagues and of choosing particular anthropologists as "representing" Spanish anthropology as a whole has important political and economic consequences both in and out of Spain.

The overall objective of this chapter is to illustrate the connections between the ways in which anthropology is pursued and the local knowledge context where relations are political and economic. In speaking of Spanish anthropologists I am not referring to nationality. However, residence in a country, Spain, obviously means a shared experience of a particular political environment and this has informed the practice of anthropology. It is also true that anthropologists from elsewhere doing fieldwork in Spain also experience the Spanish political environment and react to it in different ways. Then, the experience of a particular political context and the anthropological practice that emerges within it forms a meaningful ground of contact between local anthropologists and anthropologists doing fieldwork in Spain. Another point of contact is the wider arena of anthropological knowledge where the presence or absence of communication between Anglophone and non-Anglophone anthropologists has scientific and political implications for the discipline as a whole.

I would first like to present the relations between the development of political economy in anthropology and the political context in Spain during the last forty years. After the Spanish Civil War (1936–1939), academics and intellectuals on the Left were either dead or in exile.

Under Franco

During the early 1970s the generation born after the war was beginning to enter the university as junior faculty and at the same time political opposition to Franco's dictatorship was becoming more organized and vocal. Links with the socialist and communist parties in exile in France were important in mobilizing protest in Spain, and the university was one of the main centers of political dissent. Political nationalism was also becoming relevant in the fight against Franco in certain regions: the Basque Country, Catalonia, and Andalusia.

In this context, two main currents of Marxist anthropology were introduced in Spain during the early seventies. First, the son of Angel Palerm, a Spanish anthropologist living in exile in Mexico, Juan Vicente Palerm, who was at the Universidad Complutense in Madrid, introduced a Marxist neo-evolutionist trend of anthropological thought.[1] Moreover, Palerm organized periodic informal meetings of anthropologists interested in Peasant Studies, where a comparative research project of different regions in Spain began to take form. J. V. Palerm was key in disseminating his father's vision of anthropology, which included a mix of ecological and historical constructions of social relations (see also de la Peña, this volume).[2]

The second current was French Marxism. The French Marxists Claude Meillassoux, Maurice Godelier, Pierre Philippe Rey, and Emmanuel Terray were the first to introduce a certain version of Marxism into Spanish anthropology (see also de la Peña, this volume). Moreover, anthropology at that time tended to be included in philosophy or history curricula and these were being strongly influenced by Althusser and the *Annales* school respectively. Godelier's brand of Marxist anthropology was dominant in Spain until the late seventies. For many anthropologists beginning their career in the 1970s, Godelier's introduction to

Marx's *Formen* in its French edition (1978), and his *Rationalité et irrationalité en économie* (1974) and *Horizon, trajets marxistes en anthropologie* (1977) were probably the most influential books, and these proposed the articulation of different modes of production in concrete historical social formations as the basic theoretical model.

Political Experience and Political Economy in Spanish Anthropology

In Spain, however, political experience was one of the main factors that geared anthropologists toward a Marxist perspective in the study of society and history (see Roseberry, this volume). The struggle against the Francoist regime in the 1960s and early 1970s had a stronghold in the university and was centered around class issues and around nationalist issues. Joan Frigolé (at the Universitat de Barcelona) is a good example of this. When I interviewed him on how he got his political economic approach to anthropology, he answered:

> I graduated in Philosophy but my real "training" was organizing political and union activities at the university. . . . I had to think in terms of the local context, the faculty, the university district, even and uneven rhythms of the organization of union activity in the other university districts, their coordination, the politics of the ministry, repressive activities of all sorts from the state apparatus and our response to them. . . . I learnt a way of action and analysis that I did not know before, that was not a part of my view of life. The local and the global, as we would now say, were connected, had constant feedback effects and we could see it, we were experiencing it every day. (Frigolé, personal written communication, 1998)

This political involvement was very strong in the case of Frigolé during the 1965–1967 period. He was student representative for the Barcelona university district and a member of the Catalan communist party (PSUC). He was forcibly removed from the university for a year in 1967–1968. When he returned he felt estranged from active politics, but he was attracted to anthropology: "I think, in part anthropology became for me—with nuances—the continuation of the spirit of political activism under a different guise, using different means." He began fieldwork in Murcia in 1971, in an area with a very unequal pattern of access to land, with extreme social differentiation and still suffering from the deep confrontations that exploded during the Civil War years (1936–39). In 1972 he was imprisoned for several months. In 1973, at the "First Meeting of Spanish Anthropologists," Frigolé wrote a paper with the title "*Algunas consideraciones sobre las unidades de análisis cultural*" (1975a) that can be considered the first explicit political economic program in Spanish anthropology. In this paper he insisted on the need to view research problems in their connection to different material and cultural processes. He also stressed the need to take into account the global social system, the state, and "a certain conception of history that will explain all these connections, the direction of the process and the emphasis placed on a specific element in the circuit of reciprocal connections" (Frigolé 1975a, 180). On the other hand, Ignasi Terradas's, another anthropologist's (Universitat de Barcelona), political experience was located in a Catalan nationalist project. It was through political nationalism that he made his way into political economy. He needed history in order to explore the roots of national Catalan identity, and national history led him to the *Annales* historians, particularly the work of Pierre Vilar and Fernand Braudel. He was also led to the work of the Anglophone neo-Marxists E. P. Thompson, Maurice Dobb, and Perry Anderson, as well as to Marx and Engels.

Likewise, Isidoro Moreno, another anthropologist at the Universidad de Sevilla, had both a radical political experience in the anti-Franco resistance movement and a strong nationalist feeling that led him to think of Andalusía as an economically and politically colonized region. His anthropological perspective developed into a dependency theory approach focusing on the political and economic position of Andalusía within the national and international context. This led him to search for material and cultural processes that could explain the dependent status of Andalusía, and also its fight for an autonomous identity (Moreno 1971, 1975, 1984).

For the group of young anthropologists[3] who were turning to a Marxist perspective in those years, the presence of Juan Vicente Palerm in Madrid was crucial. He launched the project of making a global, comparative study of rural regions in Spain, that followed a well-structured methodology based on a theoretical framework that combined multilineal evolution, an emphasis on irrigation, and historical materialism. Angel Palerm was a clear intellectual influence in this project. His influence, however, seems to have been opposed by Esteva Fabregat who was the chair of the anthropology department at the Universitat de Barcelona (Romaní 1996, 67). Fabregat aimed to exert control of the recently formed discipline by preventing the introduction of alternatives that would challenge the theoretical hegemony of the Culture and Personality school, which he favored. Palerm's theoretical perspective offered this challenge, and the result of this was a closing of the ranks of anthropology and academia similar to the processes of enclosure discussed by Roseberry (this volume). First, Angel Palerm was discouraged from applying for a position at the Universitat de Barcelona, when in the 1970s he wished to return from exile. Second, the Catalan members of this study group were opposed by Fabregat when seeking positions in the Universitat de Barcelona, and many ended up in jobs elsewhere.

Jesús Contreras, a student of Esteva Fabregat, however, managed to remain at the department in Barcelona and was able to introduce the political economy perspective despite strong resistance from Fabregat and in opposition to his Culture and Personality views (Contreras 1991a, 1991b). This dispersal of other anthropologists engaged in Marxist anthropology foreclosed the possibility of effectively completing the project begun with Juan Vicente Palerm to institutionalize the development of a political economy anthropology in the university.[4]

At the end of 1975 Franco died. The monarchy was reestablished. All the political parties agreed to a democratic constitution, which was established in 1978. Slowly, power relations began to change in the academy. In philosophy, Marxism began to reappear and Gramsci's work in particular began to be influential. In anthropology, the door began to be opened to Marxism. In 1977, the founding of the *Institut Catalá d'Antropologia,* the first association of anthropologists to exist in Spain (associations were banned during the dictatorship), was also a statement in favor of a materialist framework in anthropology. During the first five years seminars were organized with the aim of getting members to know what had been happening in the field of anthropology abroad. Invitations were sent to foreign anthropologists, such as Palerm, Henry Bernstein, Jonathan Friedmann, Maurice Bloch, and Josep Llobera, many of whom worked within the framework of political economy, although some quite loosely.[5] This gave rise to a very heterogeneous set of theoretical influences including dependency theory, world-system theory, and modes of production theory. A loosely defined "Marxist approach" that was mainly based on the French version of the modes of production theory became to be popular. The result was a somewhat syncretic Spanish Marxist approach that was preoccupied with "articulation" issues, and with "transition" to capitalism issues. It was also a very anticulturalist form of anthropology. In fact, in this version of Marxist anthropology, "culture," as opposed to "society," was conceived as merely superstructural, and its study was seen to be misdirected, misguided, and highly reactionary.[6]

The Work of Marxisant Spanish Anthropologists: 1970–1997

It is clear that Marxist approaches were exerting an influence in Spanish anthropology and many anthropologists were attempting to use the different approaches in their studies. In the 1970s and early 1980s, anthropologists were attempting to apply such frameworks in their community studies of peasant villages throughout Spain. For example, the work by Alberto Galván in Taganana in the Canary Islands (1980) and the work of Isidoro Moreno (1971) in an Andalusian community are clearly located within a modes of production framework. They tried to analyze the penetration of capitalist relations of production in a peasant community. Their work was also concerned with power relations and conflict between different groups within the community. However, generally, their analyses were limited by their methodological adherence to the idea of a closed bounded community. Moreover, the absence of any sense of history as both a global and local process that shapes present-day relations contributing to the processes of social differentiation also weakens these studies.

The work by Juan Martínez-Alier and Joan Frigolé stands in contrast to the above cited works. Martínez-Alier's (1968) study of the persistence of *latifundia* in the Campiña de Córdoba and Frigolé's (1983, 1991, 1998) studies of the process of differentiation and the cultural construction of unequal and exploitative relations among peasants in the Alto Segura in Murcia both break loose from the conceptual limitations posed by the concept of the bounded community. They are particularly sensitive to the wider historical and political context. Their studies take into account the consequences of the Civil War for working people and their capacities of gaining a livelihood and of expressing dissent in an enormously repressive political context. They also take into account the agrarian policies of the different Francoist governments and the general economic trends in the organization of production relations. Their work, thus, links local processes to national politics and historical developments. Also, both Martínez-Alier's and Frigolé's works pay particular attention to the production of culture and how it becomes a material force, an aspect of power in respect to local and national issues. In a similar vein, Ignasi Terradas's work on the industrial villages *(Colonies industrials)* in Catalonia (1995 [1979]) paid attention to the confluence of the construction of a nationalist politics, a paternalist socioeconomic ideology, and the rise of labor/capital conflicts in a particular economic conjuncture. During the 1980s he continued working in the study of historical processes linking material and ideological questions with their political expression in the Catalan region (*El món històric de les masies,* 1984b; *El cavaller de Vidrà,* 1987).

Last, I want to talk about some of the work being done in the 1990s. In Andalusía a number of people are doing important work using a political economy framework.[7] I would like particularly to highlight Cristina Cruces's (1994) analysis of the transformations in the structure of petty producers in an area of intensive family agriculture (Sanlucar de Barrameda, Cádiz). Her work shows how changes in people's lives are tied to the different policies of governments (during and after Franco), to the pressure of transnational agribusiness, to the strategies of local middlemen, as well as to the construction of gender, class, and regional identities. Cruces discusses the transformation of subsistence family agriculture into intensive commercial agriculture, showing how changes in work loads with the "new intensive agriculture," and therefore increasing female and child labor, are tied to cultural constructions of gender. By comparing this process with the production and reproduction relations of day laborers working directly in the wine-producing estates for international firms and their construction of "local proletarian" identities, she is able to show the local consequences of two different relations between capital and labor occurring simultaneously.[8]

Some work done from a political economic perspective does not concern problems localized within the boundaries of the Spanish state. Verena Stolcke's work on European cultural fundamentalism and Paz Moreno's work on survival within extreme forms of social exclusion (1994, 1998) are examples of this. Stolcke compares several European polities such as France and Britain (1993b, 1995) and Catalonia (1993a) and argues that the emergence of a new rationale for exclusionary practices of immigrants is not based on "race" criteria but on "cultural" criteria. This, she stresses, marks a significant move from using "innate" natural differences as the motive for sociopolitical discrimination, that is, racism, toward the use of an assumption of a national homogeneous "cultural" identity that supports the political integration of the nation-state. Cultural fundamentalism enables exclusionary practices in respect to "cultural others" conceived as alien to the spatio-cultural congruence of the nation. This move is historically located in a post–World War II context where Western political culture could not accept racism as an exclusionary rationale.[9]

Foreign Anthropologists in Spain

At this point I would like to discuss the work of some foreign anthropologists who have done work on Spain using the perspective of political economy. I begin with a brief discussion of José María Arguedas's (1987) work on an area of common pasture land. Arguedas was a notable Peruvian novelist and anthropologist. While his work was undertaken in the 1950s and published in Peru in 1968, it was not published in Spain until 1987. Appearing in Spain so much later than elsewhere, it had no influence on anthropology students at the time when it was first published. Moreover, it has been consistently ignored by Anglophone anthropologists. Arguedas did his fieldwork at the same time as Pitt-Rivers. If we compare the framework used in Arguedas's work with that of Pitt-Rivers (1954, published in Spanish in 1971, still during Franco's lifetime), it is worth taking note that Arguedas used a political economic framework (albeit in a somewhat disorganized manner). He speaks of the experience of repression after the Civil War and how this affected social relations, in particular political forms of expression, in the communities he studied. He tries to link the changes on the communal forms of work and the organization of access to resources to the wider national and international processes. It is significant therefore that his work was not published until more than ten years after Franco died, during the period of socialist government.

After Arguedas, in the 1980s, another study based on fieldwork done in the mid-seventies was published. Raul Iturra, a Chilean refugee trained in France and Great Britain and established in Lisbon's ICSTE (Instituto de Ciencas Sociais del Trabalho e Economia), presented a study of a Galician rural community, based on fieldwork done in 1975–1978 (Iturra 1988). He examined how the development of a multinational dairy company in the area transformed the social relations of production. He focused on reciprocal exchange of labor between households and analyzed how the meaning attributed to these interhousehold transferences of work obscured economic motives and relations that could be exploitative. In this work there was an explicit interest in social reproduction and transition issues. But, paradoxically, it was very much a "community" study, with a certain functionalist bias and not much of a historical background. Iturra has had a lasting influence on some Galician anthropologists such as José María Cardesín, who has fostered an interest in the idea of social reproduction by offering a nuanced historical approach in his study of Terra Cha in Galicia (1992).

However, it was mostly North American anthropologists that explicitly framed themselves as doing political economy (Roseberry, this volume). Among them let me mention Hansen (1977), Harding (1984), Behar (1986), Collier (1987), G. Smith (1990), and more recently Kasmir (1996). Collier's and Kasmir's studies are particularly exemplary. Collier attempts to understand the construction of a group of people, "the socialists," in a mining area of Andalusía, from economic, political, and cultural perspectives. He does this by linking the formation of this group to the historical, local, and national processes that affected important transformations in everyday life experience during the republican, Civil War, Franco, and post-Franco years. His perspective also breaks radically with community studies. It follows the life histories of the "socialists" that survived the Civil War, and links postwar repression and emigration flows to the industrial urban and peri-urban areas of Barcelona and Madrid, to the construction of a working-class politics. Kasmir's recent work on the Basque town of Mondragón and its well-known (and much studied) worker cooperatives reveals the connections between different strands of Basque nationalist politics, the economic policies of Francoist governments, and the construction of a "cooperative," nonconflictual ideology, as opposed to other local, confrontational, working-class strategies.

In contrast to the rigorous work of Collier and Kasimir, many of these studies have been the subject of intense criticism, particularly of the way in which history is used.[10] This applies to the case of Behar's (1986) study of the "web of use rights" in village agriculture and herding. William Roseberry (1988) in his influential paper on political economy comments that her work "is an ethnography of the commons, one that enriches our understanding of historical instances of open field agriculture elsewhere in Europe" (1988, 175). However, Roseberry also comments that

> continuity is stressed, but the differentiating effects of, for example, the move towards hiring herders in the late 19th century are not emphasized. Had some of the processes of change within a continuous system of open field agriculture

been more fully integrated into her account, the extraordinarily rapid changes that came with enclosure might have seemed less abrupt. (1988, 175–76)

In the following, I want to explore more fully some of the issues raised by such comments.

Behar takes the "common herd" (1986, 202–12) as a self-evident expression of mutuality. Following historical accounts, however, it could more likely be a result of the twelfth- and thirteenth-century expansion of the production of wool in the area. This process of expansion of sheep husbandry was encouraged by the kings of Castile through various privileges given to the church, secular lords, and *concejos comunales*. The process also produced regulation of transhumance that forced the union of small herd owners in order to claim pasture and surveillance rights during seasonal migration. In the course of several centuries (up to the liberal policies of the eighteenth century), claims over pasture land all over Castile opposed small and large herd owners, marginal users of pasture, transhumant herds, and local herds, and these conflicts constantly reshaped the "commons" and the "web of use rights." Historians of this area have pointed to the complex struggles that confronted ecclesiastical and secular lords, the king and the *concejos* around sheep herding and around the possession, usurpation and open access to "common" pastures. Moreover, the *concejos* appear to have hardly been a solidarity group, but instead were highly differentiated internally, with an oligarchy who benefited especially from the common pastures, while others were very marginal users of those use rights (Pastor 1973a; Ruiz Martín and García Sanz 1998). In practice, one can speak of differential use rights in continuous transformation for this area.

My critique is that Behar uses history ahistorically. History can be used to explain structure and continuity but it has to be history. Her use of history is tenuous, as she seems to jump back and forth into centuries, pick here and there what better suits a need to justify a particular idea of the past and a particular idea of its persistence in the present. What seems relevant to this discussion is how Behar's lack of awareness of the work of Spanish historians using a political economy perspective severely limits her historical knowledge about the uses and transformations of the commons in the area of Castile that she studied. Therefore, her perspective about the "web of use rights" and the continuity of the commons is mostly fictional, in the way that structural-functionalist accounts could be.

In sum, Behar's study is a classic "community study" with all its virtues and problems. One of its problems is that it lacks a real historical vision. That is to say, the commons were not used in the same way through the centuries, and differentiation and homogenization within a community must be studied as processes dialectically linked with wider institutional forces. Thinking in historical terms means never thinking in terms of "survival" or "persistence" of forms of life, of "the old rural culture that had endured" (Behar 1986, 13, even with her disclaimer on page 14 "recasting the forms of the past in the idiom of the historical moment," and 193). History means precisely the continuous transformation of the form and the substance in practice.

I would like at this point to raise another issue that has political economic consequences for anthropology in Spain. With the exceptions of Jane and George Collier, Gavin Smith, and Oriol Pi Sunyer, few foreign anthropologists seem to have exhibited an interest in discussing their ongoing work with the local anthropologists who were working in a political economy framework.[11] When they have contacted local anthropologists they have tended to treat them as informants instead of colleagues. Paradoxically, this has revealed to Spanish anthropologists the differential status of these two categories of "locals" in their own eyes.

What is also surprising about foreign anthropologists doing work in Spain, particularly those who define themselves as using a political economic framework, is the degree to which they seem to lack a consciousness of their position in the political debates within anthropology in Spain. An anthropologist such as Behar (1986), when referring to previous anthropological work done in Spain, refers only, with one exception (see below), to Anglophone anthropologists at a time when there was a sizable amount of published work by local scholars (cf. note 8 to her Introduction, page 341). Moreover, the only Spanish anthropologist she mentions is Carmelo Lisón (Universidad Complutense de Madrid). This helps to construct a certain image of Spanish anthropology internationally: that represented by the eclectic, structural-functionalist *cum* culturalist version of Lisón's method. This recognition from abroad has helped to reinforce and enhance his powerful position in the Spanish university system, building his authority to produce generations of uncritical young anthropologists who have espoused his eclectic and also conservative perspectives.

Foreign anthropologists should, I think, be aware of the effects that selecting a "privileged" local anthropologist has both in Spain and in the international academic arena. Locally, it serves to build up the reputation of the anthropologist (not only informally, but also formally, i.e., citations in Anglophone books or journals get more points in the evaluation of research productivity). It generally increases his/her power in gaining access to scarce funding resources. Internationally the image is that those who get cited and references are the "best" anthropologists around and that they fully represent the work that Spanish anthropologists are doing. This is often an inaccurate image, which fails to take into account the very signficant factors of the political history of Spain.

The Political Economy of Negligence

I would like to return to the work of Ignasi Terradas and use it as an example of a deeper problem affecting political economic anthropology more generally.

American Europeanists read mostly what gets published in English because the Anglophone publishing circuits are hegemonic in setting "reputations" and in pointing at debate issues. This occurs in a context where non-Anglophone European Europeanists have to write in a foreign language (English) in order to get published in Anglophone journals[12] if they want to be read even by the most politically sensitive of Anglophone anthropologists. In turn, this situation has a paradoxical unawareness effect on the dominant Anglophone academia, because non-Anglophone anthropologists tend to read widely in English and other languages, while the reverse is less frequent. The present situation, then, is both a hindrance to the production of knowledge in political economic anthropology and a reproduction of unequal relations of knowledge production between scholars of English educational and speaking background and the rest.

This problem is illustrated by a recent discussion on European ethnography published in the *American Anthropologist*. In that discussion, J. Schneider (1997) asks the following question: "Could there be a historical anthropology of England that would render cultural specific (i.e. exotic) this former epicenter of industrial, capitalist and imperialist power, distinguishing it within Europe and inverting its normally acultural role as emblem of universalism and social thought?" (1997, 723). Schneider then attempts to understand England's "long-term processes of marginalization." She writes of English clothiers whose "reasoning hinged on imagining displaced persons as only temporarily put out and easily mollified. Their ties to families, their suffering from the loss of livelihood, and their bitterness at being pushed to the edge of society were not considered a cost factor to weight against the benefits" (1997, 723). Schneider's project is, it seems to me, an extremely crucial one for anthropology.

However, it is worth noting that Terradas does precisely that kind of work in a piece published five years earlier, in Spanish: *Eliza Kendall. Reflexiones sobre una antibiografía* (1992). I have been surprised at how close Terradas's and Schneider's perceptions are. The thought of "inverting" England's "normally acultural role as emblem of universalism and social thought," as Schneider points out (1997, 723), and the thought of rendering significant—for the understanding of the social and cultural productions of English and European history—the unknowable life of a poor young working woman, whose suicide appears as a footnote in Engels's *The Condition of the Working Class in England* (1958), partake, I think, of the same feeling of inverted relevance. This procedure he calls an anti-biography, that is, "the part of void, of biographic negation, which nevertheless can reveal to us aspects of the treatment that a civilization gives to concrete persons" (1992, 13). Around this idea of "inverting" the value of an insignificant biography, the author presents his analysis of the social and cultural construction of life expendability at the margins, as the clue to (English) capitalist and imperialist civilization. He shows how the value-maximizing axiom (cf. Schneider's "improvement" concept) hinges on "the paradox of the necessity of the expendable" (1992, 30), whereby the life of certain persons is absorbed by the tension inherent to "being consumed maximally as a productive necessity and being given minimally as an expense and as a nuisance" (1992, 30).

Eliza Kendall's anti-biography serves to illuminate among other processes the construction of a hegemonic cultural formula—that of classical political economy and later marginalist economy—which sets at the margins the central tenets of value, including human value. In sum, Terradas's contribution is to show us that "[s]ome marginalised and marginally utilized persons posses the clue to the extreme foundations of a civilization: that is, how far it can go in order to benefit or injure those persons that form it. The manner in which one person can get treated (. . .) is the way reserved for all the rest" (1992, 43). What I wanted to point at in this particular case is both the convergence of interest and intent of two political economic anthropologists working on Europe, Jane Schneider, an Amercian scholar, and Ignasi Terradas, a Spanish scholar, and the lack of awareness, albeit unintended, that the American scholar has of her colleague's production, which was published a few years before her paper. This is in no way a personal critique; it is meant as an example of what I think is an issue that anthropology should confront, that the syndrome of lack of awareness has political economic consequences for the academic community.

Conclusion

I conclude with reflections on some of the main problems that are impairing the political economy approach in Spain. It seems to me that the fashionable obsession with identities is potentially a problem for a political economic perspective in anthropology. Although studies of identity formation are crucial within political economy and, in fact, are frequently included in many studies, there is a danger that the indiscriminate proliferation of identity studies being sponsored by the regional autonomous governments in Spain and other local institutions will mean a re-folklorization of anthropology as it becomes ever more involved in the instrumental production of an ideology of "local culture" emphasizing political homogeneity. The danger is also a paradoxical one that both homogenizes and individualizes the anthropological subjects through the overemphasis on collective and personal identities as the motor of agency. Structure gets completely lost in the process. The use of identity as the meaningful concept for structuring action instead of practical consciousness (in Raymond Williams's terms, 1977) or experience is something that should be debated. Identity should not simply be used as a substitute for practical consciousness.

In my view, every person, in her life, gets to interact with other people, and this experience will in many ways structure future action and experience. This everyday practice builds a consciousness of self and of the connection of self to others which we might call "identity" (both the feeling of uniqueness and the feeling of non-uniqueness and their reciprocal and changing relationship). But even the consciousness of our experience of a single event is continuously recast in our memory as other practices and experiences build and transform our consciousness of self (Portelli 1989). We enter into relationships with other people (alive and dead) in a terrain doubly mapped by history: the aggregate processes of social interaction in time that make "History," that create a structure of different groups of people doing different things; and our personal history, our ongoing "life history" (including its partial social structuration by biographic fiction in Bourdieu's sense, 1989) that creates a sense of being different. There is a dialectical tension between doing and being that relates to the tension between structure and agency, in history. But the studies on identity are often trying to understand social processes in terms of the interactive (or instrumental) constructions of being, instead of looking into the production of experience, consciousness, and collective agency through the negotiating practices of doing and being (a good example of how this can be done is Joan Frigolé's last book *Un hombre* 1998).

Finally, the main threat to anthropological political economy in Spain is linked to the political economy of funding institutions, both nationally and within the European Union (see Gledhill, this volume). This issue is related to power struggles within the academy in Spain, the outcomes of which determine the priorities of research agendas. It is also related to the very varied degrees of power of national groups of researchers within the European Union. This again is related to the fact that our work is silenced and ignored by anthropology journals in the English-speaking realm, and consequently, by the English-speaking anthropological community, even by those working on Spain. In this context, many are working in what gets funded locally or in Europe: that is, regional identity, local culture, museums, immigration, housing problems, anthropology of food, kinship and family studies, etc. Few, however, are able to transcend the narrow functionalistic frame of renewed topic fragmentation and insert their work into a truly critical political economy framework.

Notes

I would like thank Jesús Contreras, Joan Frigolé, and Ignasi Terradas for their information. Ana Rodríguez (CSIC, Madrid) has been my guide in historical matters. Gavin Smith has given helpful comments, Winnie Lem did a wonderful editing job. However, I only am responsible for the text that follows.

1. J. V. Palerm published a journal *Cuadernos de antropología social y etnología* where the work of Angel Palerm, Karl Wittfogel, Julian Steward, Eric Wolf, and others got published.

2. This owes much to Ignasi Terradas (Universitat de Barcelona) who told me about these meetings in a personal communication.

3. Other anthropologists loosely associated with the group that took form around Juan Vicente Palerm were Pau Comas, Joan Prat, Jesús Contreras, Alberto Galván, Carlos Giménez, Montserrat Camps, Carme Viader, Alberto Gordillo, Juan José Pujadas, Dolors Comas, Gloria Romaní, Isidoro Moreno.

4. I am indebted to Ignasi Terradas's comments on Palerm for this paragraph.

5. Josep Ramón Llobera was a key figure in helping contact Anglophone anthropologists. Through his direction of an anthropology series for a Barcelona publisher (Anagrama) he was also instrumental in introducing key texts in critical anthropology to the Spanish reading public.

6. This is a sketchy overview of the ways in which political economy entered the Spanish anthropological arena. Other views can be found in Prat (1991) and Romaní (1996).

7. Pablo Palenzuela, Emma Martín, Félix Talego, Carmen Mozo, and Cristina Cruces are some of them.

8. Other anthropologists presently doing work in a political economic framework may include: Paz Moreno, Lourdes Méndez, Oriol Beltrán, Carmen Mozo, Félix Talego, Marie José Devillard, Verena Stolcke, Emma Martín, José Pascual, Agustín Santana, Fernando Estévez, Victor Bretón, Carles Salazar, Gonzalo Sanz.

9. Ubaldo Martínez (1997), an anthropologist at the Universidad Autónoma de Madrid, has recently studied immigration processes, trying to analyze the relationship between the different national and local political economic as well as cultural processes in the migrant's country of origin and the local situation (labor market, housing policies, repression) in the different parts of Spain where they relocate. Another strand of work emerges as the study of unregulated production relations (Narotzky 1990; Smith 1999), addressing the commodification of affective relations as they are used to organize relations of production that are articulated with local, national, and international flows of capital and accumulation strategies, and to theorize on how this process transforms the cultural construction of those affective relations.

10. For example, Hansen's work has been criticized by Oriol Pi-Sunyer (1985) for his poor knowledge of the historical political situation.

11. Some anthropologists not working in a political economic framework, such as Susan Tax Freeman, Stanley Brandes, or James Fernandez, have had much friendlier and continuous relationships with their Spanish colleagues.

12. Moreover, peer reviewers—all pertaining to the Anglophone hegemonic academia—will also suffer from the syndrome of the unaware.

CHAPTER 4

Anthropological Debates and the Crisis of Mexican Nationalism

Guillermo de la Peña

From 1920 to 1968, the practice of anthropology in Mexico was strongly linked to a state discourse that extolled the virtues of nationalism and proclaimed the need for a unified national culture. In this official discourse, which received the name of *Indigenismo,* anthropology was defined both as the study of the indigenous population and their "problems," and as the scientific method by which Indians would become Mexicans. In turn, the creation and consolidation of a national culture was grounded on a vast social, economic and political program, which included government actions in the realms of education, communications, health, agricultural and industrial development, and agrarian reform. Since 1968, however, Mexican anthropologists have questioned this "official" definition of their discipline. During the 1970s and 1980s, social anthropological research became oriented toward the understanding of the conditions of exploitation and political subordination of the peasantry and the urban poor. Indigenismo was rejected as paternalistic and inefficient; moreover, it was denounced as the mask that disguised the true repressive nature of the Mexican state (Warman et al. 1970). The very category "Indian" was deconstructed and exposed as a sign of colonialist continuity (Bonfil 1970). But, at the same time, the crisis of Indigenismo and official nationalism has led to a quest for the importance of both ethnic differences and new cultural inventions in the construction of a democratic society. In the last decade of the century, after the collapse of European communism, this quest has been related to the discussion of the role of anthropology in the age of globalization and open-ended political transition.

At the risk of oversimplification, one might talk of three theoretical stages for Mexican anthropology throughout the twentieth century, the first related to modernization and developmentalist theories, the second to political economy approaches, and the third to a variety of post-Marxist and postmodern orientations (de la Peña 1997). Yet this characterization, to be adequate, would have to take into account the ongoing debate on the meaning of Mexican nationalism, which has modified and redirected theoretical analyses. In this chapter, I shall attempt to examine both the changing role of anthropologists in Mexico, and the nature of anthropological conceptual constructions, such as *"indios"* (Indians), *"campesinos"* (peasants), "acculturation," "ethnicity," etc., in the historical context of competing and often contradictory nationalistic discourses.

Indigenism, Mestizaje, and Revolutionary Nationalism

After a decade of violent strife (1910–1920)—what is known as "the Mexican Revolution"—the emerging revolutionary regime envisioned the task of national unification as a necessary condition for the rebirth of Mexico as a just, civilized, and peaceful country. This task was in many ways a sequel to nineteenth-century policies, which fought "centrifugal" ideologies and sentiments through public patriotic rituals and educational campaigns. Since the years of the consolidated Liberal Republic (1858–76), children at government schools were expected to pay particular attention to the study of Spanish, "the national language," and of "the history of the fatherland" *(historia patria)*, defined as a succession of glorious feats performed by Mexican heroes. But Liberal governments, and then Porfirio Díaz's dictatorship (1876–1910), had neglected to undertake any direct action to convert the often rebellious indigenous population into active participants in the construction of the nation. Even though Porfirio Díaz used the images of pre-Hispanic monuments (such as the Pyramid of the Sun in Teotihuacán, or the round stone Calendar of Tenochtitlan) and Aztec emperors as emblems of "Mexico's glorious history," in practice the descendants of the pre-Hispanic peoples were regarded as a hindrance to progress; they would have to be either removed or totally assimilated. In contrast, the governments of the Revolution were trying to define a positive strategy to understand the Indians as contemporary Mexicans. Such strategy was embodied in the discourse of Indigenismo.

Indigenismo, however, had two different streaks, which often contradicted each other. There was on the one hand the tendency to find "positive characteristics" in the living Indians: their generosity, family cohesion, frugality, physical resistance, and artistic sense (Dawson 1998). It was even said that certain key goals of the Revolution, such as the creation of agricultural cooperatives, were in fact germane to the indigenous tradition of communal organization. The cultural and educational movement led by José Vasconcelos when he was minister of education (1921–1924) and then continued by other politicians and educators sought to revive Indian art in a variety of ways: in the murals that covered the walls of public buildings, in the recovery of visual motives for the teaching of drawing, and in the incorporation of native instruments and tunes in the concerts of the National Symphonic Orchestra. In turn, the institution of the

Cultural Missions—brigades of teachers, artists, artisans, and agronomists—was designed to instill a new, revolutionary spirit to preexisting community values and practices.

On the other hand, Indigenismo was also a defense of cultural homogenization, symbolized in the figure—and the myth—of the *mestizo*. The *mestizo* was the result of a mixture that was both biological and cultural. The praise of such mixture was first sung by Andrés Molina Enríquez, a prominent lawyer, agrarian ideologist—he helped to devise and shape the constitutional article that legitimated land distribution in 1917—and amateur anthropologist. In his book *Los grandes problemas nacionales* ([1909] 1981), inspired by Herbert Spencer, Molina Enríquez declared the *mestizo* "race" to be the fittest for survival in the Mexican milieu, whereas the Indians and the whites were destined to disappear. Later, José Vasconcelos ([1925] 1960) coined the term *cosmic race (raza cósmica)* to refer to the people of the future, which would be an amalgam of all the "races" of the world, and which had its first important manifestation in Mexico and Latin America. Thus, the exaltation of the Indian virtues did not imply the negation of the Spanish-European heritage but the search for a synthesis of "the best" of the two cultures.

Professional anthropologists swam between those two tides. Manuel Gamio, who had been a student of Franz Boas's both in Mexico and the United Sstates but did not share his mentor's extreme cultural relativism, devised in 1921–1922 a vast regional research project in the Valley of Teotihuacán which purported to be a blueprint for future studies (Gamio 1922). The cornerstone of this study was a concept of "regional culture" that recognized and appreciated its historical peculiarities and values, but without idealizing them; that is, cultural change could and should be induced in order to bring indigenous peoples to civilized life. Another important concept in Gamio's thought was "incorporation," meaning that the process of culture change should not destroy "positive native values and practices"; on the contrary, it should allow people to incorporate Western knowledge and technology as well as a sense of national solidarity into their own way of life. Although Gamio himself was unable to carry on more studies in the fashion of the Teotihuacán project, his basic formula would be adopted by many Mexican anthropologists after him. The formula included field investigation on all aspects of indigenous life within a relatively homogeneous region, preferably with the help of a multidisciplinary team, followed by a systematic account of all the findings and a diagnosis of the main regional problems and their possible solutions. This would provide the foundation for an educational program for adults and children, specifically attuned to their needs. It would also orient government developmentalist actions.

Such an approach was adopted for instance by Moisés Sáenz—also an alumnus of Columbia University, like Gamio, but more influenced by John Dewey than by Boas—in his 1931 "experimental station" in the area known as

Cañada de los Once Pueblos (Canyon of Eleven Villages) in the state of Michoacán (Sáenz 1936). However, Sáenz's experiment ended in failure, since he encountered an angry reaction on the part of most villagers, already bitterly divided by issues of land, politics, and religion. This failure led Sáenz to criticize the notion of incorporation, because it implied a vision of the Indians as passive recipients of external influences and put the emphasis of change in the good will of anthropologists, teachers, and government agents. Instead, Sáenz preferred the term *integration,* in order to highlight the importance of local initiatives and grassroots participation. In addition, he strongly denounced the phenomenon that he called "revolutionary *caciquismo.*" The traditional *caciques* were authoritarian rural bosses of indigenous origins who derived their power from their function as mediators between local people and the landlords. The new bosses were no less authoritarian and functioned as brokers between the villages and the postrevolutionary bureaucracy. In order to avoid the corruption and abuse of power frequently linked to *caciquismo,* it was necessary to foster democratic organizations at the local level (see Sáenz [1939] 1976).

Following Sáenz's advice, President Cárdenas created in 1934 the Autonomous Department for Indigenous Affairs, in charge of promoting research and channeling grassroots mobilizations. The Department convoked several Regional Indigenous Congresses, where demands from different ethnic groups were voiced, including territorial autonomy. Alfonso Fabila, a social anthropologist working for the department, documented the demands from the Yaqui, an indigenous group in the state of Sonora with a long rebellious history, and helped to draft an agreement by which, for the first time, the Mexican state recognized the validity of indigenous forms of government (Fabila [1940] 1978). In Michoacán, the Department initiated an ethnolinguistic project to teach literacy in the Purhepecha (or Tarascan) language and encouraged the production of texts by Indian writers. But all this innovative activity was cut short in 1940, when President Ávila Camacho, Cárdenas's successor, dismantled the Department of Indigenous Affairs as being dangerous for the new policy of national unity, deemed to be necessary in the context of World War II.

In the period from 1940 to 1968, anthropological research became increasingly academic and was mainly confined to the National Institute of Anthropology and History (INAH, created in 1938) and its teaching branch, the National School of Anthropology and History (ENAH).[1] There, archeology became prominent among all anthropological disciplines, since pre-Hispanic monuments were again rhetorically constructed as national symbols and remodeled as tourist attractions. Nevertheless, a new government office, the National Indigenist Institute (INI), founded in 1948, recovered the idea of applied social anthropological research in indigenous regions, but now with an explicit and unequivocal assimilationist purpose.[2] In the 1950s, the work of the INI became theoretically oriented by the model of the "regions of refuge." This sophisticated model, created and developed by Gonzalo Aguirre Beltrán (1967), who had in turn found inspiration in the works of Gamio, Melville Herskovits, Robert Redfield, and Bronislaw Malinowski, reconstructed the historical notions of "Indianness" and "Indian culture" in a multidimensional context.[3]

Aguirre Beltrán contended that Indians did not live in isolation; on the contrary, since the colonial period, their communities have been integral parts of complex territorial systems, each of them articulated by the dominion of an urban center. This urban center, or primate city, is the residence of the non-Indian population *(blancos,* and *mestizos* or *ladinos)*. They have control over the most valuable resources, and they exercise power by monopolizing the institutions of local authority and all relationships with the central government. Thus, to be an Indian means to be excluded from access to strategic resources as well as from the benefits of urban life. It also means to be used and exploited as a reserve of cheap labor. Consequently, goes on Aguirre Beltrán, public action has to be directed at modifying the regional power system, by enforcing republican institutions such as the democratic *municipio*,[4] distributing land, opening rural markets, multiplying schools, and undertaking community development programs. Since Indian culture is a culture of subordination, the emancipation of the Indians and their conversion into citizens equal before the law would entail a process of "genuine acculturation" (not incorporation nor integration) leading to the flourishing of a rich *mestizo* culture, which would be both national and modern.

These ideas influenced the routes taken by social and cultural anthropology, not only in Mexico but also in other parts of Latin America. It allowed for a type of field inquiry that clearly superseded the ahistorical, localistic approach of "community studies" favored by U.S. scholars during the 1950s and 1960s. In Mexico, works such as the study of the Tepalcatepec basin by Aguirre Beltrán himself (1952) or the prospect of the consequences of the displacement of Mazatec villages for the construction of a dam in the Papaloapan River, written by Villa Rojas (1955), contributed to a much better understanding of the complexity of the forces affecting the life chances of indigenous peoples. The same has to be said of Plancarte's comprehensive regional study of Sierra Tarahumara (1954) and Marroquín's monograph of Tlaxiaco, a market town in the Sierra Mixteca (1957). However, Indigenist applied-oriented inquiries found it difficult openly to include government corruption, bureaucratic inefficiency, and political repression in their analysis of the hindrances to national integration and "obstacles to development" suffered by the Indians. And the voices and demands of the Indians themselves were taken into account only when they complied with the official tenets of government policy.

Anthropology and the Critique of Capitalist Modernization

After World War II, the Mexican government had launched an ambitious program of import-substitution industrialization, market protectionism, and overall economic modernization. Official nationalism was no longer phrased in revolutionary terms nor linked to mass mobilization in favor of popular demands, but to discipline and work for the future. The construction of "the Indian" as an economic, political, and cultural anachronism was therefore consistent with the need to create a new type of labor force, literate, culturally standardized, and willing to accept the ideal of upward mobility through individual effort. Concomitantly, the critique of anthropology articulated after the brutally repressed 1968 student movement also implied a critique of the state discourse on modernization.

The challenge to established wisdom had as a starting point the denunciation of the style of Mexican development: the country's staggering economic growth in the 1950s and 1960s had not eliminated poverty nor gross social and economic inequalities. Upward mobility was drastically limited to a minority. In the countryside, the *municipio* did not appear to be so much a democratic institution as a space for political manipulation on the part of the ruling Institutional Revolutionary Party (PRI), which in the case of the Indian regions actually reinforced a situation of "internal colonialism." Out of this critique, a vast although rather shapeless movement of the Left—made up of emerging political parties, students, intellectuals, independent unions, middle-class professionals, and radical urban and rural grassroots organizations—created a new nationalistic discourse emphasizing the opposition between "the [true] nation of the people" on the one hand and on the other the antinational interests of capitalism and imperialism. Curiously enough, the government itself tried to appropriate a part of this discourse for its own purposes, for instance in President Echeverría's rhetoric and public postures in defense of the Third World. In this context, anthropological debates were no longer exclusively centered on the indigenous question. On the contrary, anthropologists began to develop research categories in order to analyze problems such as the relationships between social inequality and capitalist modernization, class formation in the countryside and the city, and the nature of political domination.[5]

In the 1970s, the debate on the nature of the *campesinado* (peasantry) came to occupy the center of the Mexican anthropological scene. Predictably, it did not begin within the INAH, the ENAH, or the INI, but in institutions such as the National University (UNAM), the Iberoamericana University (a private institution run by Jesuits), the CIESAS (a new State research center created with the support of Aguirre Beltrán himself), and El Colegio de Mexico (a research institute founded by Spanish republican exiles in the Cárdenas period). An aspect of the debate was carried out by ethnohistorians who, under the leadership of Angel Palerm (see also Narotzky this volume) and Pedro Carrasco (1976), used Marx's concept of Asiatic Mode of Production to analyze the political economy of the pre-Hispanic Mesoamerican societies.[6] This implied that, after the Spanish conquest, the new colonial bureaucracy refunctionalized a tributary system in which the rural population—the peasantries—were not dependent on feudal lords but directly on a centralized state.

Palerm and his students went on to analyze the colonial social formation as a complex dynamic whole playing an active role in the creation of a world economic system (Palerm 1980). There was even a certain continuity between the Aztec polity and the colonial regime, insofar as state control over rural labor conditioned the development of a peasantry that produced food for the cities and mining towns and provided surplus labor for commercial haciendas and plantations. In turn, social anthropologists studying contemporary peasants in Morelos, Jalisco, the Bajío, Michoacán, etc., led by Palerm but also inspired by the writings of Eric Wolf and Alexander Chayanov, framed their studies in a *longue durée* process of regional formation, where the interaction between commercial haciendas and peasant communities conditioned patterns of production and dense spatial organization (Warman 1976). They argued that in the twentieth century, after the revolution and the agrarian reform, such spatial patterns were radically transformed, but peasants nevertheless continued to be crucial for the production of foodstuffs and labor surpluses, now in a context of subordination to national and international market structures and an increasingly centralized state apparatus. An important issue was that agrarian reform under the aegis of the new revolutionary state had contradictory effects, since it made the peasantry more vulnerable to vast market forces and more subordinated to the vertical power of the central bureaucracy. A particularly controversial question was whether capitalist hegemony would inevitably destroy peasant organization and totally "proletarianize" rural labor, or, on the contrary, dependent capitalism would refunctionalize and reshape peasant production to its own advantage. This controversy was never conceptually resolved, but it gave wide circulation to concepts borrowed from French Marxists, such as "articulation of modes of production" and "permanent primitive accumulation."

In any case, it was recognized that many peasants were increasingly unable to survive on their land and that—consequently—the selling out of labor through temporary or permanent migration to cities and the United States was an important feature of "the peasant way of life." Lourdes Arizpe (1980) coined the concept of "relay migration" to show that rural households were organized in such a way that their members would take turns to go in circular labor-migration trips, even long-distance trips, without losing their household connections. Several studies (for instance in Jalisco) also demonstrated the active participation of peasants in heterogeneous markets, thus highlighting the artificiality of established dichotomies such as rural versus urban, or traditional versus modern (Escobar, González de la Rocha, and Roberts 1987). Network analysis was introduced to examine the different types of ties that mediated the various social domains in which people participated. Vertical ties of patronage/clientelism, associated with the refunctionalized phenomenon of *caciquismo,* helped to explain the ways in which the PRI apparatus operated. Conversely, horizontal ties with kin, neighbors, and fellow villagers constituted a space of trust where strategies of survival in many different milieus were possible (Lomnitz 1994). The coexistence of both types of ties also related to the paradoxical nature of peasant culture, where strong horizontal solidarity was not necessarily an obstacle to political compliance (nor to authoritarianism), although the outbreak of frequent movements in the past and the present indicated "the revolutionary potential of the peasantry" when grievances could not be neutralized by available social resources; furthermore, awareness of the nature of such grievances could even result in the development of a class consciousness (Warman 1972, 1976).

In sum, the emerging literature postulated a nation differentiated not in terms of "degrees of civilization" but in terms of class; where cultural discourses were a function of the dialectics between domination and revolution; where the State's cultural policies had the purpose of justifying the expansion of capitalism and disguising its exploitative and oppressive condition; and where Indigenismo was, of course, basically "bourgeois anthropology."

In the late 1970s and 1980s many anthropologists focused their attention on urban groups, partly as a result of the discovery of the astounding importance of rural-urban migration. Again, a central preoccupation was the critique of the ideology of modernization: a large proportion of the expanding urban population was not gaining access to stable jobs in the industries or the services, nor to proper housing or urban services. The term *marginalization,* imported from the writings of South American sociologists (Anibal Quijano and José Nun) and anthropologists (José Matos Mar) was firstly used to conceptualize the situation of poor urban dwellers, but it was soon replaced by the term *informality,* coined by British economic anthropologist Keith Hart. As in the analysis of the peasantry, the emphasis was on household survival strategies, job diversification within the same family unit, and reliance on both horizontal (kin and neighborhood) and vertical (clientelistic) ties (González de la Rocha 1986). At the same time, the urban poor were conceptualized as an exploited class, since their informal activities had to be understood as subordinated to the interests of capital, as in the cases of the subcontracting of domestic manufacturing *(maquila doméstica)* and of the use of street vendors as cheap labor by big commercial distributors (Alonso 1980). In these cases, surplus value was extracted from workers by indirect means. Thus, the culture of the urban poor was not "the culture of poverty" categorized by Oscar Lewis in the 1950s, but the culture of a class struggling to find its own awareness.

Studies such as the collective one led by Jorge Alonso (op. cit.) in Mexico City attempted to discover the class component in urban social movements of squatters and tenants, but the authors of such studies had to reckon with the tremendous heterogeneity of beliefs, motivations, justifications and symbols articulated by the participants. Was it possible, in terms of class formation, to make sense of the coexistence and multifarious combinations of cultural forms and practices variously related to—for instance—folk Catholicism, northern border music, Mexican soap operas, government propaganda, extended family organization, Hollywood role models, and *cholo* styles? What would be, in the mid-eighties, the articulating force of working-class culture, in both urban and rural context, if most unions were constituted as corporatist extensions of the PRI, which still had the strength to epitomize Mexican culture in the discourse of "revolutionary nationalism"? To answer these questions, anthropologists had again to revise their concepts of culture as well as their own political positions on the question of nationalism.

Anthropology and the Critique of Nationalism After 1980

The decade of the 1980s brought the worst economic crisis in Mexico's recent history, which resulted in the opening of markets and the end of protectionist policies. It also brought bankruptcy to the PRI government. The politics of clientelism were in terminal crisis. The dispensation of subsidies had been suspended, and in 1992 the Program of Agrarian Reform was officially declared dead. The lives of the peasantry and the urban poor were more than ever defined by a frantic search for survival resources drawn from multiple sources and places. Hoping to build a new legitimacy, both within the country and in the international scene, the Mexican regime opened the way to civic and political liberties, and to reasonably clean elections. In this context, anthropological discussions in the last fifteen years have turned around three key issues: the constitution of new social identities vis à vis the globalization process; the relationship between popular culture and the emergence of civil society; and the meaning of citizenship. However, these discussions have more often than not been framed in a new debate on the meaning of nationality and the rediscovery of Indian culture.

On the concept of nationality, we find two opposing theses, one that engages anthropologists in the rewriting of Mexican history from the point of view of grassroots indigenous movements, and another one that reacts against the nostalgic reification of the past and demands a full commitment to modernity. Two books that represent these contradictory positions are respectively Guillermo Bonfil's *México profundo* (1989) and Roger Bartra's *La jaula de la melancolía* (1987). Bonfil argues that the real Mexico is the indigenous one, which was never fully destroyed by conquest and colonization. Buried under a veneer of pseudo-Westernized culture, it is reemerging in the new ethnic movements that contest the myth of the *mestizo*. In contrast, Bartra accuses intellectuals, and particularly anthropologists, of being imprisoned within an idyllic but false view of the rural and indigenous world. This "cage of melancholy," which rejects modernity, has in fact been very useful for the maintenance of the PRI authoritarian regime, insofar as paternalistic and clientelistic practices can be justified as protecting national essences. Therefore, in order to break the cage, anthropologists should deconstruct nationalistic mythologies and defend a concept of nation that goes beyond culture and history by emphasizing civil and political liberties.

Without falling into these extreme positions other anthropologists are addressing the issue of national culture in a variety of ways that recover the interest in class analysis but also attempt to incorporate the importance of localist and regional identities, political and cultural intermediation, migration experiences in different cultural settings, and the goals and discourses of heterogeneous social movements. For instance, Larissa Lomnitz's (1994) comparative study of hegemony in two regions shows the complex interplay among dominant elites, local intellectuals, and the interests of the subaltern classes, where the construction of unifying nationalistic myths becomes an arena for both contention and consent; thus, peasant and indigenous cultures can be examined without reducing them either to pure subordination or pure resistance. In a very different vein, Néstor García Canclini (1990) has introduced the concept of "hybrid cultures," which draws attention to, and tries to make sense of, the necessary juxtaposition of heterogeneous elements in the age of mass media and mass migration. In turn, the studies of migration are throwing new light on the existence of communities that are no longer bounded by a single territory; such communities constitute veritable laboratories for cultural innovation but at the same time they do not lose a strong sense of community. Striking examples of this are the Mixtec and Zapotec migrants who recognize localities in three or four different places as their own, to wit, their original villages in Oaxaca and Guerrero, other areas of central and western Mexico which they visit as agricultural laborers, Mexican cities on the northern border, and towns in the California valleys. In all these places, along with the adoption and adaptation of multiple Western elements, they have experienced a revival of their language as well as the strengthening of a discourse of ethnic solidarity, which is also used to justify demands for social justice, human rights, and political participation.

The cases of the Mixtec and Zapotec are not isolated. Guillermo Bonfil was right in saying that there is a proliferation of ethnic movements all over the Mexican territory. Most of these movements are not claiming for the return of an idealized past but they rather redefine ethnic identities and cultures in the context of a multicultural nation or even a multinational state. Significantly, among their leaders we find university graduates in anthropology and history, who successfully resisted one-dimensional acculturation. These new intellectuals are constructing new concepts of indigenous cultures and nationalism, historically rooted on their quest for ethnic citizenship.

Conclusion

If the constitution of anthropology as an intellectual discipline is unavoidably linked to the emergence and development of a discourse on culture, the case of Mexico demonstrates the peculiarities of this discourse in a context marked by the experience of postcolonialism and peripheral capitalism. The rejection of the colonial legacy implied the building of a nation endowed with its own autonomous identity, for which the indigenous past provided a rich repository of legitimizing symbols. At the same time, the search for a place in the "civilized world" demanded the new identity to look at the future, not at the pre-Hispanic past. Hence the idea of a national, homogeneous culture, assuming the indigenous but aspiring to Western modernity, which would put the myth of the *mestizo* at its center.

From such premises it followed that, if Mexican anthropologists were to study indigenous cultures, they would do so in the perspective of their relation to a purported future of *mestizaje*. The unlikely marriage of Boas's cultural relativism and Molina Enríquez's social Darwinism provided an initial analytical frame (in Gamio's work), although it was soon questioned by a critique of the politics of incorporation (in the work of Sáenz) and by the emergence of indigenous cultural movements and demands for autonomy (which were supported by anthropologists employed by the Department for Indigenous Affairs during the 1930s). With the founding of the National Indigenist Institute in 1948, there was a reaffirmation of a concept of national culture as homogeneous, democratic, and "modern," in contrast to heterogeneous indigenous cultures, now defined not only as obsolete and transitional but also as symbols of subordination and symptoms of the traditional oppression that modernity, through government action, would abolish.

This discourse on the dynamics of Mexican culture lost its clout when the concept of modernity was attacked as an ideological justification of peripheral capitalism. The argument was that, because of the nature of peripheral capitalism, "traditional" economic forms (such as the organization of the indigenous peasantry) would suffer a distorted incorporation into the market, which would allow for their refunctionalization and reproduction. Class emancipation was then postulated as a necessary precondition for the emergence of a national culture. At the same time, the reappearance of indigenous movements (particularly after 1980) and the irruption of Indian scholars in the anthropological profession led to the construction of a new discourse, which denied that national culture should be defined as homogeneous and questioned the relevance of a concept of modernity impervious to the persistence of ethnic identities in the context of a multicultural society. At the turn of the century, in a context of economic dislocation, mass migration, blurred national frontiers, multidimensional mass communications, and shifting political power, ethnic solidarity has become not a mechanism of isolation but a strategy for participation in uncertain—but inevitable—national and international ventures.

Have anthropological discourses on culture in Mexico lost their raison d'etre? It is undeniable that anthropologists face a major dilemma. They must either to renounce the concept of national culture altogether and accept a "postmodern," unpredictable fragmentation as their sole object of interest, or to construct concepts of national diversity where the meaning of cultural relativism would be recreated in terms of positive convergence: from respect to the distant other to conviviality with the different (and equal) neighbor.

Notes

A first version was presented at the Symposium on Political Economy and the Production of Culture, CASCA/American Ethnological Society joint meetings, Toronto, May 1998. My gratitude to Belinda Leach, Winnie Lem and Gavin A. Smith for their invitation and comments, and to all the participants for many stimulating debates.

1. Organizing the Indians and voicing their social, cultural, and political demands became dangerous; anthropologists who tried to carry on their labor of grassroots agitation (as in the 1930s) were even threatened by government repression.

2. The founding director of both INAH and INI was Alfonso Caso, a prominent lawyer, archeologist, and ethnohistorian, who was also a powerful politician. He wrote the legal charters for these (and other) institutions, became a cabinet minister, and was a close adviser to presidents of the Republic in the 1940s and 1950s.

3. A disciple of Melville Herskovits at Northwestern University in the early 1940s, Aguirre Beltrán worked close to Gamio and was well acquainted with the work of Robert Redfield in Tepoztlán and Yucatán and with the research project undertaken by Bronislaw Malinowski in the Oaxaca valley (see Drucker-Brown 1980). Aguirre Beltrán's model is at the same time a radical critique of these authors and an original synthesis of their ideas.

4. The *municipio* is a territorial, political, and administrative unit, under the rule of a council that, since the Revolution, has to be democratically elected.

5. Two journals were influential in redefining the direction of anthropological research: *Historia y Sociedad* (linked to the Communist Party) and *Nueva Antropología* (predominantly Marxist but with a plural orientation).

6. Palerm and Carrasco were part of a congeries of scholars transplanted to Mexico from Spain after the civil war. Both studied anthropology in Mexico during the 1940s, moved to the United States in the 1950s (since their ideas were not agreeable to Alfonso Caso, whose figure dominated official anthropology from 1940 to 1960), and came back to teach in Mexico after 1965.

CHAPTER 5

Political Economy in the United States

William Roseberry

In order to understand the development of anthropological political economy in the United States, it is helpful to think of the history of anthropological work in terms of particular generations of graduate students, the intellectual and political milieus in which they were formed, and their interests and activities. Although an explicit "political economy" is most clearly identified with one of these generations, the concerns of a broadly understood political economic perspective have figured in each of them. An account of the intellectual and political development of anthropological political economy requires, then, placement within a history of cohorts of graduate students that situates particular generations in relation to each other.

Consider three such generations, at twenty-year intervals, since World War II. A first, from the late 1940s and early 1950s, made a number of related moves: (1) it rejected Boasian particularism and embraced a range of evolutionary narratives; (2) it moved beyond a concentration on "primitive isolates" toward studies of "complex societies," including new types of social groups (e.g., peasantries, rural workers, urban populations) within them; and (3) it began to make more differentiated, sociological analyses of culture, distinguishing between "core" and "secondary" features and exploring the ways in which secondary features might be shaped by social groups and forces within the core.

A second, from the late 1960s and early 1970s, developed around the language of "critique": (1) of past anthropological collusion with colonial powers and administration; (2) of the failure of anthropologists to examine certain groups of people (women, for example, in the then typical conception of anthropology as the "study of man"), or certain characteristic social relationships marked by inequality (gender, class, race, ethnicity), or certain broad sociohistorical forces (capitalism, colonialism); and (3) of prevailing intellectual styles (empiricism, positivism).

A third, from the mid-1980s through the early 1990s, also developed around the language of critique, but it turned its skeptical eye in different directions. If we take the three areas of criticism mentioned for the second generation, the third generation developed each in markedly different ways. (1) It offered a criticism of colonialism, but it conceived colonialism less as a system of political and economic relationships and more as a culture of social relationships that both emerges from and shapes the very categories with which people conduct their daily life, interact with others, and construct the classificatory practices of administration or social science. The use of the neologism, "coloniality," marks this shift in emphasis. (2) It extended the criticism of anthropological failures to study particular groups, relations, and forces, but it both took for granted the critical moves of the second generation and explored their inadequacy. Thus, it moved from an anthropology of women to an anthropology of gender, stressing differences among women marked by class, ethnicity, national origin, and (especially) race. It faulted the second generation for overemphasizing class in its conceptions of inequality, ignoring the salience of other forms of inequality (gender, ethnicity, race) and identity. Indeed, the work of this generation increasingly took class-based relations of inequality for granted and concentrated on the construction of particular forms of identity within them. (3) Its criticism of intellectual styles and formations within anthropology included the work of the two immediately preceding generations among its critical objects. It shared the second generation's rejection of empiricism and positivism, but it saw a good portion of the second generation as unacknowledged positivists. Three preoccupations mark this generation's intellectual project: (a) a rejection of "grand narratives," or attempts to fit local and particular histories within wider sociological or historical frameworks (something each of the preceding two generations had done); (b) a rejection of "realism" as an ethnographic genre; and (c) a concern with "representation," as both intellectual and political practice. Here, the third generation is especially anxious to reject the classic anthropological practice through which white, Western anthropologists represent non-Western peoples for a white, Western reading public. The concerns addressed here are at least double: one having to do with the development of new forms and genres of communication, in which the representational authority of the outside ethnographer can be undercut, and the other having to do with the cultivation and promotion of a range of nonwhite or non-Western voices.

This sketch is schematic and partial, concentrating on a few innovative trends in intellectual work rather than attempting to capture the whole range of anthropological practices. Its concentration on generations of graduate students is not intended to ignore the contributions of senior scholars. Indeed, no full appreciation of the innovations of the first generation can ignore the influence of Julian Steward or Leslie White as writers, teachers, or inspiration. Similarly, scholars such as Eric Wolf, Sidney Mintz, Marvin Harris, Marshall Sahlins, Eleanor Leacock, or June Nash, graduates of the first generation, were important and formative influences—in very different ways, of course—on the second. Moreover, within the period of a generation's formation, important works were published by these senior scholars that serve, in retrospect, to stand for a whole line of work. Steward's (1955) *Theory of Culture Change* or the collaborative project produced by Steward and his students (1956), *The People of Puerto Rico*, appear as paradigmatic examples of the new work of the 1950s. And Wolf's (1969) *Peasant Wars of the Twentieth Century* or Harris's (1964) *Patterns of Race in the Americas*, at the beginning of the second generation, and Wolf's (1982) *Europe and the People Without History*, toward its end, serve as examples of the work produced during the second period. Similarly, Marcus and Fischer's (1986) *Anthropology as Cultural Critique* and Clifford and Marcus's (1986) *Writing Culture*, texts written by scholars who came of age during the second generation, profoundly affected the formation of the third. My concentration on cohorts of graduate students is not meant to indicate the most important producers of intellectual innovation at a particular moment but to draw attention to the process of intellectual production itself—the complex interaction between teacher and student, the formation of students within particular intellectual, institutional, and political milieus, the subsequent development and fate of their careers, and the later history of writing and publication.

The details of that complex history would have to be pursued elsewhere, though the generational scheme serves to organize the analysis of the present essay.[1] Here, my aims are more modest. Where, in this sketchy history of generations of anthropologists, does "political economy" fit? There are two answers, depending on the definition we give political economy itself. In a narrow sense, political economy has had two different but related meanings. On one hand, it refers to the study of capitalism, its formation as a structured and hierarchical system, and its economic, social, and political effects on particular regions and localities and the people who live in them. On another hand, it refers to the explicit use of Marxian perspectives within anthropology. The second hand offers a particular theoretical approach to the substantive questions juggled by the first hand; the first hand may reach out for various theoretical approaches as it manipulates these questions. For either of these understandings of political economy, which, though different, are often conflated, the second generation stands as the political economy generation *par excellence*. It was this generation that more fully embraced an explicit Marxism than any other, and a concern for the study of capitalism and its effects also clearly marked this generation's work.

But if by political economy we mean something a bit more broad, as, say, the study of the formation of anthropological subjects within complex fields of social, economic, political, and cultural power, then each of the generations has been involved in the history of anthropological political economy. The concern here is with the emergence of power relations more broadly, not solely under capitalism. For this, earlier moves toward the study of complex society, toward the study of civilizational processes in general, and toward a more differentiated understanding of culture, were critical, as are more recent questions regarding the kinds of narratives that can be constructed concerning the history of capitalism, the complex character of power and its effects through and beyond institutional loci, and the many forms and effects of inequality. Furthermore, the history of an engagement with Marx's work is somewhat more complex than a simple identification of a period of *explicit* Marxism would suggest.

Let us explore this problem more fully in terms of the two more narrow understandings of political economy mentioned above. If we take a study of capitalism and its effects as a central substantive question for political economy, the work of the "culture historians" of the 1950s, both in their ethnographic studies and in their comparative, typological exercises, was critically important (Manners 1960; Mintz 1959, 1974; Mintz and Wolf 1950; Wolf 1955, 1956, 1957, 1959; Wolf and Mintz 1957). Indeed, the move toward the study of "complex societies" placed on the intellectual agenda both the study of capitalism and the study of states—without necessarily labeling their subjects with these terms—that remain central to the concerns of anthropological political economy. Similarly, many members of this cohort came to their anthropological studies with prior exposure to and, in some cases, formation within Marxian theory. Because of the repressive atmosphere of the time—due to the combined effects of the relatively brief active period of McCarthyism and the long-term effects of the onset of the Cold War—their Marxism remained implicit and was even purged from texts in the journey from dissertation to book (Vincent 1990).

Much of the work of the third generation, in turn, has developed in constant and critical relation to the work and concepts of political economy. Taking the substantive questions surrounding the development of capitalism and its effects, we see an interesting trend. Although many authors reject both a historical and a systemic analysis of capitalism as irredeemably tied to the construction of "grand narratives," they situate their ethnographic studies within, and make theoretical reference to, some of the most recent developments of a capitalist world economy. This takes two forms. On one hand, it may be suggested that the capitalist world economy constitutes a kind of backdrop, a known system, that frames the actions and interactions of anthropological subjects. Anthropologists may take this system for granted as they pursue their more fine-grained ethnographic analyses (Marcus 1986). On the other hand, recent work on "flexible accumulation," "fast capitalism," and the purportedly new phenomena associated with "globalization" figure large in much recent work (Harvey 1989; Pred and Watts 1992; Soja 1989). Here, again, anthropologists contribute less as theorists of these phenomena. Instead, recent trends are taken for granted and serve either as backdrop for ethnographic work or as the starting point for theoretical reflection on the formation of new kinds of social and cultural movement and flows and the emergence of new identities within them (Appadurai 1996; Hannerz 1996; Kearney 1996; Marcus 1995). If we then turn to the question of Marxism, perhaps there has been no more consistent foil for recent critique, as

Marxian perspectives have come to stand for "grand narratives" *tout court*, representing all that was bad about earlier generations of anthropological work.

Academic Enclosure

I have thus far identified three generations and discussed, in broad strokes, some of their intellectual preoccupations and perspectives. It might be helpful to sketch certain aspects of a more social and material history. I have in mind four questions to address here. First, what, in the sense of political experience outside the academy, did particular generations of students bring with them to the academy? Second, how, and in what ways, did these outside experiences shape their intellectual formation? Third, how did their intellectual formation, specifically as anthropologists, shape their politics? Fourth, were their subsequent careers confined to the academy and did their writing reach beyond it?

Detailed answers to any of these questions would require a much longer work than the present one and would need to deal with various levels of analysis, including individual biography. Nothing in what I say is meant to characterize all of the members of a cohort. What follows may be taken as a set of hypotheses.

I wish to suggest that a reading of the work of each generation of anthropologists from their years as graduate students to their years as established or senior scholars requires us to consider two processes of "enclosure," one academic and the other anthropological. These are distinct but related, and we need to consider them separately and then examine their combined effects. In much of what follows, I concentrate on the second generation, which serves as a vantage point from which to look both backward and forward in time.

Let us consider, first, the process of academic enclosure. I suggest the following rough set of distinctions, based, again, on a structure of politics rather than individual political biographies—which were, for each generation, various. There are three issues that require consideration here, the first having to do with the line between academic and nonacademic political sites and movements (see also Gledhill, this volume), the second having to do with the organizational and intellectual centers of gravity for oppositional movements, and the third having to do with the issues around which movements were organized. At the beginning of the first generation, oppositional politics were associated with the issues and language of the traditional left (Wolf and Jorgensen 1970; Nader 1997, 121–129). The relation between wider political involvements and the academy was more likely to be balanced in that significant members of that generation brought to their academic lives and careers prior experience of Left politics. A more vibrant union movement, and the presence of communist and socialist organizations that, while never mainstream, were an expected part of the political landscape and had not yet been officially defined as treasonous, made for a situation in which the intellectual and organizational centers of Left politics were outside the academy. Two great political struggles animated the second generation—the Civil Rights movement and the opposition to the war in Vietnam. The first originated outside the academy, and its intellectual and organizational center of gravity remained outside of it, even as issues and demands became central to university-based struggles concerning curriculum, admissions, and hiring. The antiwar movement developed both on and off campuses, and the line between academic and nonacademic organizations and sites was less porous. That is, it was possible for students involved in antiwar activity to limit or concentrate their energies in the university in ways that were less likely for activists involved in Civil Rights struggles or class-based politics. A variety of new, identity-based, social movements, some of which began to emerge in the second generation and all of which operate in a more generalized atmosphere of conservative retrenchment, have marked the political scene during the third generation's formation. Although these new movements are active in both university and non-university settings, the line separating the settings seems to be sharper than at any other point, continuing a trend begun during the antiwar movement. Thus, it is entirely possible for a student to join a coalition or organization and for the issues and sites that animate that movement's politics to be entirely campus-based.

A large part of the story here is contextual—the long-term decline of the union movement and the purging of both socialist and communist perspectives from the realm of "legitimate" politics in the United States (see also Narotzky, this volume). The purge directly affected some members of the first generation and had profoundly altered the political landscape on campuses, and between campuses and a wider social field, by the 1960s. As campus activists engaged with wider political movements, they did not do so—at least explicitly—as Marxists. Indeed, the adoption of Marxian language was a sure route to marginalization or encapsulation within a campus milieu. Thus, as some campus radicals discovered Marx, their discovery did not necessarily lead them to join organizations or parties. Again, individual biographies are various, but the move to parties was a marginalizing one in any case, given the wider political history alluded to above. The structural effect was the development of a Marxism that remained academic in focus and audience. The process of academic enclosure was to become even more pronounced by the time the third generation began its studies.

I make this point neither to make false, nostalgic claims about earlier movements and organizations (which, in any case, had their own problems and repressions), nor to condemn individuals for the choices we have made. I simply want to point to certain political and social effects of academic enclosure. In his criticism of Salman Rushdie, Aijaz Ahmad makes a telling point about politics. Claiming that Rushdie offers critique without connection, he suggests that:

[P]olitics appears to me to be a matter not so much of opposition as of solidarity; it is always much less problematic to denounce dictators and to affirm, instead, a generality of values—"liberty, equality, fraternity," say, . . . but always much harder to affiliate oneself with specific kinds of praxis, conceived not in terms of values which serve as a *judgement* on history but as solidarity with communities of individuals, simultaneously flawed and heroic, who act within that history, from determinate social and political positions. (Ahmad 1992, 152)

Whatever one may say about the flaws in earlier organizations and movements, and these have, of course, been much noted, the severing of an active connection between them and Left academic thought and politics has meant that the academic Left most often develops, in Ahmad's terms, opposition without solidarities. As the line between university and non-university based movements becomes more sharply drawn, and as separate intellectual centers and audiences develop on each side of that line, oppositional politics within the academy more easily take the form of critique and less easily or successfully move toward community formation.

But the story of academic enclosure is not simply contextual. One needs to consider the role of the actors within the three generations as well. Here, the main point that needs to be made is that, whatever the range of extra-academic political activities engaged by individuals within particular generations of Left anthropologists, at least a portion of their activities was devoted to politics in and of the academy itself. Despite its magnificent name, the well-known Mundial Upheaval Society formed by a cohort of graduate students at Columbia University during the post–World War II years, was, and was intended to be, primarily a reading and discussion group. Anthropologists for Radical Political Action, formed during the anti–Vietnam War years, formed departmentally based collectives, each of which was responsible for a particular issue of a newsletter. While particular collectives might get involved with other groups in local, especially university-based, political issues and actions, the organization as a whole was focused on the production and distribution of the newsletter and preparation for the annual meeting of the American Anthropological Association (AAA). At the annual meeting, the group sponsored a section of the program, organizing "anti–imperialism" panels, and they organized for the business meeting, at which they presented resolutions calling on the association to take particular positions on political questions (opposition to the war, for example) or ethical issues (the participation of anthropologists in counterinsurgency research, for example).

These efforts reached their highest point at the 1971 annual meeting, which was the culmination of years of movement toward the adoption of a statement of ethics that looked askance at work by anthropologists for government agencies and sharply condemned secret research for governments or corporations. The move toward such a statement was made more urgent by the unveiling of Project Camelot in the mid-1960s and the later exposure of anthropologists' involvement in counterinsurgency research in Thailand. This problem came to light when students occupying administrative offices at the University of California at Los Angeles found incriminating documents naming individual anthropologists and sent copies to Eric Wolf, then of the ethics committee at the AAA. He and fellow member Joseph Jorgensen published details of the secret research in a 1970 issue of *The New York Review of Books*. The resulting controversy split anthropologists among those who condemned the secret research and those who condemned Wolf and Jorgensen for their public disclosure. Margaret Mead headed an ad hoc committee to examine the incident, and its report exonerating the researchers was rejected at the same annual meeting at which a statement of ethics was approved.

Over the whole course of the post–World War II period, these few years probably constitute the moment at which the linkage between an academic politics and a wider set of issues and struggles was most direct and consequent. Yet it is perhaps telling—not regarding the actions and concerns of the participants themselves but regarding the subsequent actions and careers of these and other anthropologists—that these incidents rarely figure in the wider history of the era. They do figure, importantly, in histories of late-twentieth-century anthropology and in the memoirs of the participants. This is, I think, indicative of the process of academic enclosure itself. In terms of the shaping of anthropology as a discipline and the moulding of individual careers, wider political events had a great effect. It would be hard to claim that anthropologists or anthropology shaped wider politics.

Perhaps the most important "internal" force pushing toward academic enclosure is the fact that the major employment and career track for professional anthropologists has been in the academy. Neither government nor business have actively sought anthropologists; nor have there been career tracks that pointed in either direction. Though increasing numbers of anthropologists have ended up with non-academic positions, this has been a result of a long-term crisis in academic employment. Moreover, even with the long crisis, and with recent moves by individuals into nonacademic careers, and with the inclusion of "practicing" anthropologists within the organizational structure of the American Anthropological Association, the principal route to and basis for professional status is through academic employment in the well-established hierarchy of university departments. The jobs most aspiring anthropologists aim for are in universities, the imagined audience they write for is in universities, and their careers and the most active part of their politics are often based in the academic departments where they teach.

This sharp dividing line between university-based and non-university-based employment and activity is both a condition for and a consequence of academic enclosure. Consider one consequence of this line—and the process of enclosure—for the second generation of students. Regarding the experience of that generation as a whole, Aijaz Ahmad writes:

> Those who were politically the most involved rarely found a coherent organizing center for their activity once the intensity of the mobilization had peaked; those who found such a center, for good or ill, disappeared into the anonymity of direct political work; few enough finished their Ph.D.s, and those who did rarely gained the academic sophistication to become theorists. Those who became theorists had been, as a rule, only marginally involved in the *political* movement. Most of them had known the "movement" mostly in its other kinds of social emphases: certainly the music, the alternative readings of Laing and Marcuse, surely the occasional demonstration—but there had been, through it all, the pressure to write brilliant term papers and equally brilliant dissertations. It was, in other words, the *survivors* of the "movement" who later became so successful in the profession. Radicalism had been, for most of them, a state of mind, brought about by an intellectual identification with the revolutionary wave that had gripped so much of the world when they were truly young; of the day-to-day drudgeries of, say, a political party or a trade union they had been (and were to remain) largely innocent. (Ahmad 1992, 66)

The only amendment I would want to make to this criticism of my generation is that it is important to see this process of academic enclosure structurally and not simply biographically. As we think of particular individuals, some were better, and some worse, than others at maintaining political connections, networks, and activities. As a group, however, anthropological political economy was developed within and communicated primarily to the academy. Its fate depended largely on the individual careers, and career choices, of those who worked in universities and wrote within the tradition. Organizational links beyond the academy were not developed. Think of the Union of Radical Political Economists and what it did and does as an organizational, public, and publishing unit, and then think of what Anthropologists for Radical Political Action could not do. Or, at another level, where is the anthropological equivalent (or anthropological section) of the Institute for Policy Studies?

Anthropological Enclosure

Let us turn now to a process of anthropological enclosure. Here, what I have in mind is simple but consequent. Whatever wider political perspectives and experiences students bring with them to anthropology, their formation as professionals requires training in and submission to a discipline: particular literatures, styles of work, forms of writing, and a community of fellow professionals. Consider, for example, the second generation of Left anthropologists, people who may have come to their studies reading *Monthly Review, New Left Review,* and the books published by these houses, as well as Marx and the Marxian canon of the day. What else were they reading, and what else were they doing? Not many graduate departments would let a student get past exams with this reading list alone, and despite the many criticisms of the politics and ethics of fieldwork floating around at the time (not, in most ways, unlike those published in the past decade), most departments expected students to do fieldwork. So students had to supplement their "political economy" reading with some anthropology, and they had to engage a literature on, and eventually get to know some people in, an area. The kinds of working bibliographies people constructed, then, were idiosyncratic. There was an immediately available literature in economic anthropology, especially with the French Marxian reformulation that placed Marxian perspectives within the intellectual genealogy of the subdiscipline (LeClair and Schneider 1968; Godelier 1972, 1977; Terray 1971; Meillassoux 1981). Depending on the department where one studied, students might also engage with one or more "materialist" (ecological, evolutionary) strains in anthropology. Some of the work itself seemed to speak to the students' concerns (and political economists could see themselves as resolutely materialist); moreover, the older generation of materialists themselves, as writers and teachers, often nurtured, protected, and promoted the students doing political economy.

Once past the exams, they went to the field. This involved an engagement with area-specific literatures, anthropological and non-anthropological, locally specific variants of political economic debates and Left politics, and people—local intellectuals, scholars, activists, officials, and the subjects of their research. These twin engagements—with literatures and with people—shaped the kind of political economic work done. This is, of course, a common story for almost all generations of anthropologists, regardless of theoretical inclination. I only draw attention to it here to explore a consequence for the political economic literature that is too often left out of retrospective surveys. Students were being formed in academic milieus for academic careers. They were learning to read and contribute to the literature of a discipline, and their subsequent success in the academy required that they show themselves to be "good" anthropologists.

The processes of academic and anthropological enclosure represented forms of capture and domestication, for good and ill. If political economic anthropology in the United States began at a certain distance from anthropological practice with overly schematic formula—of articulating modes of production in one line of work or the functioning of the world economy in another—it was precisely the "anthropologizing" of political economy over the seventies and eighties that produced work that rejected original questions or categories, or opened up on relationships that had been absent from the earlier schema, and that paid serious attention to locally and regionally specific relations of class or forms of capitalism. The original editors of *Critique of Anthropology* had noticed a similar process occurring among French Marxist anthropologists, in which French Marxists had set out to undermine or appropriate the terrain of social anthropology and had instead been captured by it. By this they meant that the French Marxists made the central questions and objects of inquiry of social anthropology their own, subsuming rather different Marxist questions to them, rather than transforming social anthropological practice via Marxist critique (Editorial Board, *Critique of Anthropology* 1979). The anthropological enclosure of political economy in the United States came in part with a changing political milieu, in part with the reading and fieldwork practice of the generation of sixties and seventies students, and in part with the employment and tenuring of some number of that generation. By, say, the early 1980s, they were less likely to assign (though they might still recommend) the Marxist classics, or even the debates of the 1960s and 1970s. Just as there had been a general burnout in economic anthropology on the formalist/substantivist debate, and few wanted to subject their students to its deadening detours, now few wanted to assign the original contributions to the dependency or mode of production literature. A review article or criticism would do. Indeed, no small number of the critiques and review articles were written by members of the sixties and seventies student generation themselves, along with monographs that were straightforwardly (or in other cases more vaguely) political economic. The original research for some of these might have been motivated by the debates on capitalism and modes of production, but by the time the books appeared the authors had abandoned the language and perspectives of the debates to ask new questions and challenge received categories of class, capital, capitalism, and so on.

As academically employed authors developed new perspectives, they reached out in various theoretical directions for inspiration—to French authors as different as Bourdieu (who offered a genuine critique of structuralism and made possible more empirical work on social fields) and Foucault (who offered Althusserianism without Althusser, that is, a continued structuralist theoreticism); or to previously neglected Marxian traditions as disparate as the English Marxist historians (Thompson most especially), British cultural studies as represented by Williams and Hall, or the revaluation of at least one "classic" Marxist (Gramsci). Some of these moves (Thompson and Williams especially) fit well with the more empirical practices engaged by some members of this generation and spoke to the kinds of cultural questions they now raised in their anthropological writing.[2]

Discourse and Political Economy

By the mid to late 1980s, then, when retrospective anthropological critiques began to appear with some frequency, the group of people actually doing what was being criticized was much reduced. Certainly world-systems theory, the favorite catchall label among the critics, had been a dead dog for a long time, and mode of production theory had suffered a similar demise. What, then, were the political economists in the academy, both the "old" ones from the first and second generations and their students, doing? Among the many intellectual and career moves, I discern two broad shifts. One has been a theoretical embrace of Foucault, and as Foucauldian perspectives have come to dominate U.S. anthropology in this period, this group fits within the mainstream of professional anthropologists. Some among this group seem to carry no visible marks of their political economic past. Others have used Foucault to distance themselves from their previous selves, the "preface to the new edition" of an earlier book being the most convenient vehicle for this sort of positioning. Others among the political economists have also moved beyond the perspectives and questions of the sixties and seventies, but partly because their dissatisfaction with that earlier literature was a disquiet concerning its theoreticism, they have embraced the more empirical and realist traditions of Marxian social history and cultural studies.

Here is where I see the critical academic divide at present. Both groups are asking remarkably similar questions concerning the formation and cultural construction of identities—gendered, ethnic, national, racial, class-based, and so on. But one group addresses these questions discursively, with a relatively thin sociology; the other addresses them more empirically, concentrating on the formation of institutional complexes and hierarchies. Both place great importance on power, but for one power is diffuse and capillary; for the other, in Fred Cooper's (1994) useful phrase, power is more arterial.

So we might see one branch of political economy remaking itself as a kind of Foucauldian anti-political economy and becoming part of what is now clearly the dominant discourse in U.S. anthropology. In their representations of the other group, it is less the Marxism of a relatively small number of writers that attracts critical attention and more their commitment to empirical practice and ethnographic realism. Here an interesting trick is performed, as the empirical practice is represented not as a critical response to the theoreticism labyrinth of Althusserian structuralism (and therefore, not so implicitly, a criticism of Foucauldian practice) but as an "old fashioned" commitment to, let us say, "monumentalist" anthropology. Thus, political economists of this sort can be conflated with, even made to stand for, several decades worth of the Tweedle Dum and Tweedle Dee of realist anthropology.

So far, this maneuver seems to be working, discursively and materially. Discursively, I have in mind the way in which issues are being constructed in review essays, M.A. curricula, and course syllabi. Thus far, political economists and others committed to empirical and sociological work have been less successful in presenting their work as a creative and critical response to structuralist theoreticism. Their responses have largely been defensive. Materially, I have in mind an issue associated with the reproduction of the field as a whole—the employment of anthropologists in the academy. Before exploring this, I should express more directly an evaluative judgment implicit in what I have already said. I regard the Foucauldian influence in anthropology as initially positive in its radical questioning of taken-for-granted categories and assumptions but actively unhelpful in its disdain for what I will broadly call sociological analysis. Foucauldian anthropologists have, of course, done ethnography, much of it insightful and provocative. But along lines followed by Sherry Ortner (1995, 1998) in a useful critique of resistance studies, I would argue that much Foucauldian ethnography is thin, *by design*. For example, one who hesitates to find power in particular institutional locations may also avoid detailed sociological analysis of economic and political institutions at work. Or an interpretation that stresses the commonalities and continuities in a "discursive formation" may produce insightful analyses of discourse but tell us relatively little about individual discourses and the relationships, incidents, and disputes that generate them.

It is here that a changing intellectual and academic milieu, in conjunction with the collapse of what was already a very tight academic job market in the early 1990s, has produced a real crisis for the reproduction of anthropological political economy—not for the generation of the sixties and seventies but for their students, and students of their students. In a related article, I have argued that the job crisis is radically narrowing the intellectual diversity of anthropology (Roseberry 1996). As the sociological/materialist strand of political economy loses the discursive battle with the Foucauldians, this situation will continue: their work stands for all of that which the "posts" claim to have superseded. And since one of the main functions of such discursive constructions is to classify literature so that individual works do not have to be read, it is exceedingly difficult for the actual contributions of individual authors to break through or undercut the constructions themselves.

Perhaps the main comparative advantage the present generation of anthropological political economists have in the long run will be the body of ethnographic work they will have produced during a period when much of anthropology had abandoned ethnography. Indeed, some extraordinarily good work is being done at the dissertation level by this generation. But for them to realize that comparative advantage, they will have to find someplace to publish their work, in a transformed publishing environment that now looks askance at the monograph, they will have to hope hiring committees actually read it instead of fitting it into convenient cubbyholes, and they will have to hang on for an indefinite period to diminishing hopes for academic employment.

This is clearly too much to ask. It is here that I would return to the academic enclosure of anthropological political economy, and the striking split between anthropologists in and out of the university, one with which many contributors to anthropological political economy have been complicit. This has been my generation's greatest failure, and the place where we see direct material consequences of the sort of personal trajectory Ahmad discerned. Thus, "practicing anthropology," which might have been a domain for Left and community-based work, has been cut off, both in imagination and practice, from political economy, and "practicing anthropologists" have been left to make their own way, in Non-governmental Organizations (NGOs) and nonprofits but also in investment banks and corporations. To the extent they made the latter move, "we" could look at them with the appropriate disdain. And, of course, by limiting itself to the academy, the generation had sharply curtailed the possibilities for genuine intellectual and political gains, the personal career successes of a few individuals notwithstanding.

The immediate tasks at hand are organizational, first within the academy in supporting autonomous efforts at unionization and pressure among adjuncts and non-tenure-track teachers and in resisting moves in our institutions toward flexible labor schemes and downsizing. But such moves, however necessary and important, are insufficient as long as they fail to address the larger structural problem—the enormous long-term gap between available positions and the number of Ph.D.s. This does not solely affect political economists, of course, but as political economists lose the discursive battle in the academy a disproportionate number of our students may lose the material battle on the job front. The only responsible move would be one that redresses the academic enclosure of political economy, that makes new kinds of organizational linkages, locally and regionally, that breaks out of university settings and creates new kinds of institutes, NGOs, and the like. That is, it is urgently necessary to do what earlier generations, including my own, did not do: to make real linkages between academic and nonacademic centers, institutes, and organizations. Simply to say this, of course, is not to provide solutions but to pose the problems in a slightly different way. The creation of such forms poses difficult problems of will, organizational capacity, and money. This conclusion is, then, less a call for action than a call for discussion, with the recognition that responsible action that takes the center of political economic activity beyond the university is necessary.

Notes

1. I have pursued this analysis in more detail in Roseberry 1995; 1996.

2. For representative examples, see Foucault 1980; Bourdieu and Wacquant 1992; Gramsci 1971; Thompson 1966, 1993; Williams 1977; Hall 1994.

CHAPTER 6

"A Small Discipline"

The Embattled Place of Anthropology in a Massified British Higher Education Sector

John Gledhill

In the wake of what have now become classical critiques of the relationship between anthropology and colonialism from inside and outside the discipline (notably Asad 1973; Said 1978), anthropologists were forced to reflect more on the relationship between their discipline and global political economy and macropolitics. Much of the academic critique of the classical anthropological project was mounted by diasporic intellectuals with apparent claims to speak for the former colonial world.

The problematic nature of such claims has not, of course, gone unrecognized; in, for example, the debates surrounding Gayatri Spivak's paper "Can the Subaltern Speak" (Spivak 1988), turning the nascent fields of cultural studies and postcolonial criticism into not merely a reproach but a potential challenge to the continued existence of social and cultural anthropology, anthropologists were also forced to reflect on the micropolitics of representation in their field of inquiry and the power relations established between ethnographers and their subjects. From Clifford's classic essay "On Ethnographic Authority" (Clifford 1983) onward, anthropology was drawn into a field of debate dominated by poststructuralist and postmodernist high intellectuals, although many of those involved sought to shun such labels or argued that anthropology's dilemmas were simply an aspect of a more generalized crisis of representation that corresponded to a "condition of postmodernity" that could be assigned a certain objectivity as a historical epoch (Harvey 1989; Jameson 1991; Knauft 1994).

Critical reflection on the nature of the critiques has also been voiced by some contributors to Clifford and Marcus's seminal *Writing Culture* volume itself (Clifford and Marcus 1986). Paul Rabinow, for example, argues that "the stakes in recent debates about writing are not directly political in the conventional sense of the term," because "the politics involved is academic politics" (Rabinow 1996, 49). Rabinow invokes Bourdieu's sociology, and in particular the

73

Bourdieu of *Distinction* and *Homo Academicus* (Bourdieu 1984a, 1984b), as his starting point for exploring this theme. For Bourdieu, authors need to be located in specific positions in specific fields of power (which, as I stress below, are not simply constituted by institutional frameworks, but also by broader social constituents of their habitus). So Rabinow argues, the political field in which "contemporary anthropological proclamations of anti-colonialism" emerged is clearly not that of the actual colonial world of the late 1950s, but the academy of the 1980s, within which such proclamations "must be seen as political moves within the academic community" (ibid.). Thus, Rabinow concludes:

> My wager is that looking at the conditions under which people are hired, given tenure, published, awarded grants, and feted would repay the effort. How has the "deconstruction" wave differed from the other major trend in the academy in the past decade—feminism? How are careers made and destroyed now? What are the boundaries of taste? Who established and who enforces these civilities? Whatever else we know, we certainly know that the material conditions under which the textual movement has flourished must include the university, its micropolitics, its trends. We know that this level of power relations effects us, influences our themes, forms, contents and audiences. (Rabinow 1996, 50–51)

Others have already begun to take up the questions Rabinow raises, notably Roseberry (1996 and this volume). As I noted above, it would also repay us to consider the broader social processes that guide the formation of individual scholars and their habitus—this would involve asking questions about personal social biography, as well as examining the effects of peer pressure, rewards, and disincentives within academic communities.

The shaping of institutions by broader power relations and the shaping of individuals within the microcontexts of academic communities are intimately related in influencing what academics say and the social and political significance of academic work. Although this has always been true, it is now urgent that we think more carefully about these issues. In what follows I argue that a global transformation of the nature of university institutions is underway that has radical implications for the contemporary politics of doing anthropology and the possible roles of anthropologists as public intellectuals. I focus my own discussion on the British case, pointing to some of its specific features as I proceed. There are, however, also ways in which the British case is simply an example of more general processes, which I explore in the next section.

The Political Economy of University Transformation

In the European tradition, the dependence of scholarly "autonomy" on the grace and favor of the politically powerful as a condition of existence of the university institution has a long history. It extends back into the thirteenth century to the founding of many British and European universities as they rapidly became instruments of royal authority in battles against the autonomy of the town and its burghers.[1] We also already know enough about the way our own discipline was pressed into the service of the state during and after World War II in the United States to resist the idea that the "autonomy" of the university institution in itself prevents those who run or work in such institutions from offering their services to the powerful (Gough 1968, Price 1998).

Nevertheless, the relative autonomy of university institutions as centers of knowledge production in the past does not seem a complete illusion. Most democratic states underwrote the rights of academics to express themselves freely, at least in principle, and some spaces for dissidence and debate were maintained in both private and public institutions despite Cold War witch hunts and the way recruitment and tenure decisions inevitably filtered out academics whose work was politically or intellectually offensive either to university cliques or to their establishment patrons outside. The question in Britain is whether the kind of state intervention that is taking place today is threatening these spaces of relative freedom with greater erosion even in a supposedly open and democratic society. Control of research funding has always been a powerful instrument for canalizing academic work, but one of the merits of a largely publicly funded higher education system is the scope that it has traditionally provided for the defense of minority subjects, while the importance of university autonomy lies in the power it has given academics to fight for a heterogeneous social knowledge base and the rights of critical and dissident views to find expression. As public funding is reduced and dependence on private sector finance increases, the defense of scholarly knowledge for its own (human) sake becomes increasingly dependent on the whim of elites and available tax breaks, while the likelihood of certain types of socially and politically critical research and teaching being funded inevitably diminishes. If, however, the shift in funding is also accompanied by interventions that interfere with the curriculum and diminish the relative autonomy of academic communities as sites where the politics of knowledge production can be fought out, then the implications are yet more radical and disturbing. Contests over knowledge production in universities have seldom been fought on equal terms, but the danger is that it will become impossible to fight meaningful battles in this arena at all.

Historically, in Britain both Conservative and also Labor governments have been eager to encourage new and more direct relationships between universities and the private sector, as universities have been under increasing pressure to demonstrate their "relevance" to the needs of a country seeking rejuvenation from a pattern of long-term economic decline particularly since the 1960s (Thompson 1970). It was, however, the government of Margaret Thatcher that embarked on the beginnings of a more radical process of intervention and restructuring in the universities, largely as a contribution to its overall strategy for managing that decline.

Although much of the reshaping of university institutions has to date been achieved indirectly by the extensive use of audit and "performance measurement" in a manner that will be described in more detail below, change has been enforced by two basic strategies of sustained pressure. One is a consistent and cumulative reduction in direct state finance, achieved through imposed "efficiency savings" and the progressive abolition of undergraduate grants. The other is an unfunded doubling of student numbers. The latter has placed academics in something of a dilemma, since access to higher education in Britain remained lower than in other European countries even after the increase in numbers of institutions in the 1960s, and broadening access to disadvantaged social groups is an aim that is difficult to oppose. Furthermore, the dilemma is compounded by the fact that the old "binary divide" between universities and polytechnics was abolished with the transformation of the latter into recognized university institutions: academics at "old" universities are often equally reluctant to appear "elitist."

Despite a continuing political rhetoric of "broadening access," this gap may be perpetuated. In Britain, the transition is essentially one from a higher education system in which undergraduate education was largely state funded and financial barriers to entry to elite institutions were supposedly removed by a universal system of means-tested grants, to a system in which students (or their parents or partners) are forced to foot an increasing proportion of the bill for their higher education.

Although it would be easy enough to magnify a sense of diversity in university organization by drawing out contrasts between the modern systems of the United States, Germany, or Holland, for example, and Britain, there is nonetheless, a pattern of global transformation behind this apparent diversity. The fiscal crisis of the Northern state produced by the Fordist-Keynesian mode of capitalist regulation in the old industrial centers is the most obvious factor, and has now been generalized by economic crises in East Asia and Latin America into a universal pattern of efforts to reduce public expenditure on higher education. A number of factors make higher education a relatively "soft" sector for such action. Students find it hard to counter the argument that they benefit personally from the training they receive in the form of higher than average earnings after graduation, and this diminishes the possibilities of making higher education finance a political issue. Academics find it extremely difficult to counter arguments that the research work they do should pass muster in terms of public accountability, and members of the public experiencing the increasing insecurity and austerity of late capitalist life are not particularly susceptible to persuasion about the merits of academics being paid from the public purse for research that offers no tangible benefit to the rest of society. The reasonableness of much of the current concern with establishing systems of accountability in Britain seems self-evident without any further questioning of what detailed criteria are being applied to the evaluations in question: this offers a powerful lever to those charged with implementing these systems and their political masters.

It is true that private capital is highly selective in its approach to substituting state funding provision, and in Britain is proving downright reluctant to increase corporate costs. This is of some concern to government, given that short-term commercial returns inevitably take precedence in decision making over longer term strategic planning: company managers are accountable to shareholders, and public finance has been important in the history of capitalism in both the West and East Asia as a means of ensuring that long-term strategic economic objectives are considered in the field of research and development (Wade 1990). Declining public investment in the science base in Britain is now seen as a problem, and in a world in which tourism and the sale of educational services in the global marketplace are significant elements of national economies, there is little scope for withholding state support entirely from areas of activity not directly related to the industrial manufacturing and financial services sectors of the economy. Nevertheless, there is a growing insistence that investments in any form of academic activity should show an economic return and that any kind of academic training students receive fit them for a world of "flexible labor" in which specific skills rapidly become obsolete and on the job training and retraining is becoming increasingly important.

Universities can no longer be left to determine what members of the professions know: their role is increasingly tied to serving the needs of the capitalist accumulation process and they must be seen to fulfill that role effectively as a condition for public funding. Expanding access to public education began as an issue of "civilizing the working classes" and making them fit to enjoy liberal citizenship rights, but the argument on access to higher education in the twentieth century increasingly mixed grounds of social equity with arguments addressing the need for a skilled labor force. The problem facing a utilitarian approach was simply that the relative autonomy of university institutions left students with personal choices that included a variety of intellectual and political options. Even in the absence of any ideological concern with the content of university curricula, this would become problematic as the principle of publicly funded higher education as a social right came under pressure. In Britain there is now an increasing emphasis on the way in which past failure to adopt policies to match students' choice of programs to available labor market opportunities ensured a persistent oversupply of graduates in some areas (including anthropology). This is seen as increasingly problematic for a world in which a broad liberal education is no longer seen as offering good "value for money" from the social (i.e., capitalist) standpoint.

The fact that graduates still seek jobs as university teachers has also played a role in facilitating the transformation of the university institution. Casualization of teaching labor through the use of fixed-term contracts, denial of tenure, and deployment of postgraduate teaching assistants in the undergraduate classroom, has proved a successful strategy in a period in which the higher education sector has been expanding (maintaining the idea that professional careers still exist even if many are disappointed by the final outcome of their career choice). As a transitional phenomenon, casualization has also been facilitated by the willingness of more privileged members of the academic community to be complicit in its extension and hostile (for reasons of perceived self-interest) to efforts by the victims of this development to defend themselves (DiGiacomo 1997). One of the most powerful effects of neoliberalism has been its capacity to make moral cowards of us all. The contradiction lies, of course, in the simple fact that people work in universities to make a living, and make a better living by competing with each other for the best possible share of the increasingly meager rewards that exist. Until the lives of (successful) university academics cease to have any attractions relative to alternative types of career and employment, recruitment will continue. The fact of continuing recruitment has already been identified as a likely basis for a refusal to concede any across the board improvements in levels of pay in the British system as a government inquiry deliberates on the issue. In the longer term, it may well be the case that the highest academic achievers will seek other kinds of careers, but there is currently no perception of difficulties that cannot be addressed by using "quality audits" to ensure that academic performance remains adequate.

A rhetoric that the national future lies in fostering a "flexible knowledge and skills-based society" has now become the common currency of governments that find the idea of the uncontrollable pressures of economic globalization a convenient pretext for a wide variety of measures that are beneficial to national (and transnational) capitalist interests and decidedly disadvantageous to their citizens. There clearly is still scope for pursuing different national policies toward education, and for debate about the balance between social and individual benefits in relation to levels of public expenditure. Nevertheless, the idea that higher education is a social good itself contains a potential sting.

In the discourse of New Labor in Britain it is coupled with the idea that universities have been elitist institutions and that turning them into providers of "relevant" training for personal advancement and general social benefit is a reform (which obscures the potential role of universities as centers for producing autonomous and anti-systemic knowledge). The late capitalist state is even less inclined than its predecessors to pay people for opposing it, and the mass university still depends on the late capitalist state in a fundamental way. Furthermore, one way in which capitalist corporations have removed the burden of supporting knowledge production from the taxpayer is through their increasing interest in doing research in house rather than contracting academics employed by universities. This further weakens the role of universities as communities where ethical and political debate can directly influence the production of knowledge.

Such trends can only be reinforced further by moves to streamline university governance now underway in Britain, which involve the reduction of elected and nonprofessorial members of governing bodies and their replacement with managerial appointees and users of university services such as industrialists and the managers of national health service trusts and other semiprivatized public sector agencies. The irony of these trends is that the scope for academics to continue to act as "negative workers" (Scheper-Hughes 1995), opposing both the restructuring of the academy itself and the kinds of services it is called upon to provide for capital and national programs of state social regulation, may be greatest in those elite institutions that enjoy the luxury of a secure private endowment income and fee-paying students from relatively affluent backgrounds.

The impact of neoliberal states on universities is clearly not simply a matter of economies in public finance or ensuring that public finance is directed toward economically useful purposes in the field of higher educational training. There is also a more directly ideological dimension to official efforts to direct university research in the social sciences toward regulatory projects that address the social consequences of capitalist restructuring, discussed in more detail below. It is nevertheless important to recognize the extent to which ideological shifts are the consequence of the mediation of scholarly production by the structures of professionalization and disciplinarity, which means that battles over the nature of research and learning are to a great extent fought out within the internal politics of academic institutions. Indeed, the kind of intervention that has been practiced by the state in Britain has largely succeeded, as I show in the next section, in producing a Foucauldian climate of self-regulation by academics themselves, reinforcing the longstanding role of informal mechanisms of inclusion and exclusion in disguising the ways academic work relates to broader configurations of power.

To pursue these issues further, it is necessary to focus on the specific roles that anthropology can perform within university institutions that are under increasing pressure to produce specific forms of knowledge in a specific late capitalist setting. This entails situating the possible politics of anthropology within the social sciences in general. For those who believe that anthropology is a relic of a colonial past, the disappearance of the subject from the curriculum would clearly be a positive development, but that is not the only factor working against us in the British context.

Britain: The Politics of University Restructuring and the Future of Anthropology

Thanks to the legacy of Malinowski, anthropology in Britain has predominantly meant social and cultural anthropology.

With fifteen institutions in the United Kingdom currently teaching the subject as a specialized undergraduate degree, and three more offering it as a major in a degree with another subject (ASA 1998), the discipline as a whole is tiny in comparison with sociology for example, which is taught within seventy-six institutions within England and Northern Ireland alone (HEFCE 1996). Yet anthropology is currently the second fastest growing field in the social sciences in terms of student demand.[2] Although HEFCE's assessors noted that "Anthropology is not widely distributed throughout universities and colleges, but is found typically in long-established institutions," new programs in anthropology are beginning to appear in the new universities created by the abolition of the distinction between universities and polytechnics under Margaret Thatcher. Given that anthropology is not taught in secondary schools, the fact that students arriving at university are opting in increasing numbers to study it is interesting. Furthermore, a significant proportion of the growing demand for anthropology courses comes from mature people with work experience of diverse kinds, much of it overseas (HEFCE 1995).

Growth of demand is not, however, matched by funding opportunities. Postgraduate research grants in England are provided by the government-funded Economic and Social Research Council (ESRC). Each year it cuts the number of available awards, so that anthropology candidates have to obtain significantly higher scores to get a grant than candidates from most other disciplines. In the 1998 competition for awards, social anthropology was initially allocated sixteen grants, making its ratio of grants to applications, 17 percent, the lowest of any of the seventeen subject areas funded by ESRC, though it was the subject with the fifth highest number of applicants (after politics and international relations, psychology, sociology, and human geography) (ESRC 1998a).[3]

Yet despite the fact that it funds only a small minority of anthropology postgraduate students, the ESRC has managed to dictate the terms under which all will be educated. Ph.D.s must now be completed in four years and all students must spend a year being trained in "skills" that the state deems relevant not simply to research, but to modern managerial culture. Ironically, however, the ESRC very seldom funds students in their first year of obligatory training. Anthropology's share of ESRC research money for faculty projects has remained relatively stable in terms of proportion of awards to applications. Yet the discipline's fortunes have declined dramatically in terms of absolute amounts of money allocated. In terms of the total amount of grants awarded, 242,091 pounds from a total of more than thirteen million pounds in 1996–1997, anthropology ranked thirteenth out of fifteen. The discrepancy is explained by the fact that grants to anthropologists are smaller than those secured by applicants from other disciplines, in a context in which between two-thirds and three-quarters of the applications the ESRC judges "fundable" are not actually funded.

Those who sit on the ESRC Research Grants Board generally accept the basic agenda of British social science set out by the ESRC through a series of published "thematic priorities" (ESRC 1998b). The thematic priorities define the mission of social science research as one of strengthening the U.K.'s economic competitiveness. Despite a small amount of recent rephrasing in the light of widespread protests about the apparent antagonism of the thematic priorities as originally defined to overseas or comparative research, and the introduction of a new "Transnational Communities Research Program" awarded 3.8 million pounds in funding, the ESRC continues to prioritize research on the U.K. while paying lip service to the value of cross-cultural research. With topics such as "technology and people," "innovation," "knowledge, communication and learning," "lifespan, lifestyles and health," and "social exclusion and inclusion" making up five of the nine principle themes (which also include "globalization, regions and emerging markets" as well as "economic performance and development") the ESRC is also clearly committing itself actively to projects of social regulation. Most funded social research seeks to provide "policy-orientated" quantitative indicators, and all research applicants must demonstrate the relevance of their results to "users." While users could include, for example, antiracist community groups or charities such as Oxfam (which now runs poverty alleviation programs in Britain itself), there is clear presumption that the bulk of British social science research should be more directly related to the management, if not containment, of the social consequences of neoliberalism and capitalist restructuring—the general decline in economic security and the growth of a relative surplus population condemned to a life on the margins of formal employment in a Britain whose once comprehensive welfare state is shifting to the workfare model and whose equally comprehensive public health service seems in terminal crisis. I will discuss some of the pitfalls of anthropologists articulating their research to this agenda later, but let me first say a little more about the implications of the transformation of undergraduate education and the new model of "lifelong learning" espoused by Tony Blair's New Labor government.

Blair's government is attempting to repeat its predecessor's effort to expand access to higher education while continuing to cut funding per capita. Part of this project is concerned with encouraging mature students to return to higher education periodically. This is the "lifelong learning paradigm" that is presented by Labor ministers as both a rational response to the world of flexible labor markets and a widening of opportunity within society. Lifelong learning is to be facilitated through a system of transferable credits and learning accounts. In other words, people can dip in and out of different institutions while continuing to work, and end up with higher qualifications. Yet, as of September 1998, undergraduate students in the U.K. ceased to be eligible for grants to meet the costs of their maintenance. Even the poorest students have to finance their maintenance from loans, and better-off students also have to pay one thousand pounds annually toward the costs of their tuition, though this charge is means-tested. There is currently a lively debate about whether universities will be allowed to charge additional fees on top of this, in the face of continuing chronic underfunding by government. An obvious problem is that the imposition of tuition fees and abolition of grants has acted as a major disincentive to recruitment of mature students, at least in the short term. The other side of the new system is an extension of sub-degree qualifications and vocational courses. More than half of Britain's Further and Continuing Education institutions are now technically insolvent, so pushing this scheme forward might mean transferring part of the money recouped from university sector tuition fees to those institutions, though this is being strongly resisted by the universities themselves at the present time through their representative body, the Committee of Vice-Chancellors and Principals (CVCP).

The quality of the education that students receive for the increasing amount of their own money that they must spend has, to date, been monitored by the Higher Education Funding Councils (HEFCE), which have dispatched review teams made up of fellow academics under the leadership of a HEFCE official (often a former secondary school inspector) to sit in on lectures and examine departments' procedures for delivering students pastoral care, tackling complaints and many other issues. The results of these Teaching Quality Assessments have been published (see, for example, HEFCE 1995). This system is to be replaced by a new regime, run by a separate Quality Assurance Agency (QAA). The QAA will be more concerned with the outcomes of the higher education process and the establishment of uniform degree standards between institutions than direct assessment of the quality of the student learning experience based on site visits and classroom observation, although QAA inspection teams will continue to descend on universities to sample their provision (as distinct from systematic review of all departments, subject by subject).

Although welcomed by some academics as representing a "lighter touch" in terms of bureaucratic intervention, the QAA presents new dangers in terms of possible intervention in the curriculum (though it has denied any intention to seek to create the same kind of national curriculum framework that exists for secondary education, and must, for the time being, be taken at its word). It is also possible that the QAA type of quality assessment will act to disguise a real deterioration in the kind of education students receive, by not considering the impacts of labor casualization, increasingly overcrowded classrooms, and understocked libraries as central issues in its refocusing quality issues on the standard of output and paper procedures.

These changes in systems of state intervention are clearly motivated by a desire to cut costs, though the fact that the previously separate departments of Education and Employment have been merged into a single ministry tells us something about the thinking underlying the audit regime. They are not, however, conducive to the interests of smaller subjects, since they raise the same issues of unequal competition for resources between disciplines that exist in the case of the ESRC's approach to research funding, and the pressure to merge anthropology with sociology ignores the extent to which anthropology cross-cuts divisions between the natural sciences, social sciences, and humanities. At the end of the day, these bureaucratic structures are part of the decision-making apparatus that determines the funding allocated to different disciplines.

Faced with a gamut of interventions of which the QAA is but one, it may seem odd that there has been no widespread and vigorous campaign of opposition on the part of academics. The situation is, however, less puzzling when one reconsiders the practical politics of all this. As I noted earlier, the abolition of the distinction between universities and polytechnics laid the basis for an improvement in Britain's figures for access to higher education without any additional public expenditure. It was politically astute because the new universities must compete with a number of small Ivy League institutions for funds and they must also set about competing with old universities as teaching institutions. This made them natural allies of a focus on innovative teaching technique as something to be valued, and it also predisposed their managers and academic staff to accept the agenda of refocusing undergraduate education on training for employment using techniques that facilitate mass education rather than a labor-intensive tutorial approach. Moreover, the persistence of successive forms of state intervention into higher education in the name of establishing national standards has resulted in a situation in which the mere threat of further intervention encourages academics to accept appropriate forms of self-regulation. This is very much the attitude to the new QAA, which was actually proposed by the university vice-chancellors themselves as a means of establishing a buffer between the institutions and funding councils. The new system of regulation and practice is legitimated as the only realistic approach to a massified higher education system, mirroring the broader tenor of neoliberal discourses on globalization and the end of the welfare state ("there are no practical alternatives"). The collaboration of academics is encouraged by maintaining the principle of subject-specific peer review in defining standards, but this regime actually places far more power in the hands of university managers, who insist that protecting the institution from more direct intervention depends on colleagues playing strictly by the rules of the game set by the audit process. It is also clear that considerable contradictions have developed within the new regulatory regime. It is almost certain that the way in which these will be addressed will recreate not simply the old binary divide that existed between the old universities and polytechnics, but a much stronger concentration of research activity on a reduced core of elite institutions, and perhaps also on favored disciplines or specific kinds of interdisciplinary programs dominated by researchers in favored fields and their paradigms. At this juncture, we can return to the specific implications for anthropology of these transformations.

The growth in demand for anthropology courses raises a number of interesting questions. Many students do not start their courses with a terribly clear idea of what the field offers them, but there seem, on the basis of my own experience in two institutions and that of other colleagues and students who have shared their impressions with me in National Network for Teaching and Learning Anthropology workshops, to be two principal attractions. First, the subject is seen as broader in scope than most disciplines, and in the case of some programs, as bridging the gulf between arts/humanities and sciences. Second, for many it is the global, comparative dimension of anthropology that is its attraction, in clear opposition to the narrow view of the world that is embedded in the official ESRC agenda for social science in the United Kingdom. Applicants want to understand other cultures and address questions such as global poverty and environmental crisis. Once in an anthropology program, students also seem attracted to critical perspectives on global political economy and social welfare issues, if they are offered such courses. Courses on sexuality and personhood taught from a cross-cultural perspective that run against the grain of neoliberal normalizing individualist rhetoric are also heavily oversubscribed. In my own university, where we have a general multidisciplinary social science degree as well as a social anthropology specialist degree, course numbers are growing to almost unmanageable proportions in the courses that pack the most punch as critical analysis. Students may well go on to pursue mundane careers after graduation, but this evidence suggests that they can be attracted by an anthropology that pursues big issues in a critical spirit, that seeks to make the West itself seem strange and forces new habits of thought. In other words, it is not difficult to sell anthropology to students on the basis that it offers the most comprehensive and challenging approach to the study of humankind, and in a way that makes a substantial critique of other disciplines. Anthropology courses in Britain are quite varied, and some do remain relatively traditional in orientation, teaching principally classical British ethnography and debates arising from that corpus of work. There are, however, encouraging signs of innovation in most parts, in part because we are so marginalized within academic power structures.

Many outside anthropology (and some, alas, inside) do, however, still see the discipline as a study of the "exotic." This can only strengthen the hand of those critics who regard our subject as an outmoded colonial project, and propagating the idea that the discipline focuses on the quaint and the trivial is also extremely convenient for the power holders in British social science. Competition for resources is increasing within universities. The relatively small number and small size of anthropology departments in comparison with sociology, political science, economics, and in the case of biological anthropology, the biosciences, creates a constant pressure for liquidation and merger. In this environment, it does not really matter what anthropologists actually do, since we have limited powers to represent ourselves.

Given that the bulk of research funding comes from the ESRC, many

"A Small Discipline" 85

anthropologists have striven to adapt their work to the ESRC agenda outlined above. This means, in particular, developing anthropological work in the U.K. ESRC research projects are also generating research assistant jobs for anthropologists contributing to the work of constructing social indicators, especially in the area of ethnic difference. The idea that anthropologists are specialists on ethnic minorities can easily suck us into uncomfortable positions (see also de la Peña, this volume). The official recognition of a multiplicity of ethnic groups and the creation of institutional channels for their representation has become a major strategy to divide and contain potential forces of resistance to the way economy and society are being restructured. Anthropologists have to think very carefully about how their work might fit into that agenda given the increasingly market-driven nature of higher education provision (also see Roseberry; Dunk, this volume). The state and business are principally calling the tune, and the ideological project that is at stake is the creation of a higher education system that can support policies of social normalization and reduce the study of the rest of the world to the issue of how Britain copes with economic globalization. New Labor has produced a certain amount of progressive rhetoric on questions such as overseas development and ethical foreign policy but the reality behind this rhetoric is deeply disturbing. For example, asylum seekers are still vilified as a combination of economic migrants and criminals, while Britain continues to stand four square behind the U.S. agenda in Iraq.

There is considerable scope here for anthropologists to act as vigorous public intellectuals running against the grain of official rhetoric and practice, and some are struggling to produce knowledge in precisely these areas of public controversy. The scope for doing this is, however, continually reduced by the transformation of academic life. Today's academics have poor salaries and growing work burdens, with few resources available for research. The pressures to go with the flow and seek what career rewards are still available are very great. This can mean accepting what the powerful define as appropriate subjects for anthropologists to study. It can also mean accepting fundamental changes to the curriculum that make anthropology a more "useful" applied subject orientated to achieving the employment outcomes that the state will judge acceptable. Many of our students are, of course, clamoring to be taught skills that will help them get a job, and I do not personally think that all the changes that are taking place are for the worse. It is, however, vital to defend the intellectual core of the discipline and seek to strengthen rather than blunt its critical edge.

Conclusion: Facing the Future, Facing Power

Adapting to change requires a different kind of reflexivity, one that is more self-conscious about two issues. One is, for whom do we produce knowledge— the holders of power or marginalized and subaltern social groups, Northern nation-states or those that their economic strategies and war machines victimize? The second concerns whose interests are served by particular forms of anthropological knowledge and particular analytical and interpretative positions.

Any scholar must remain entitled to a personal political and moral position, and there are no grounds for disallowing an individual the right to produce knowledge for the benefit of elites, the state, or national interest as defined for the state (though by the same token, other scholars should enjoy the right to criticize such endeavors on political and moral grounds, whatever the consequences for normal academic civility). What is not acceptable is refusal of self-consciousness or the persecution and marginalization of scholars who strive, however imperfectly, to produce knowledge that, for example, is inimical to nationalist positions that militate against the universal entitlement to "life, liberty, and the pursuit of happiness" of those who do not belong to a given national unit, or specifically seek to change the existing social and political balance of forces in the interests of greater equality and fairness. As I argued at the start of this chapter, an apparently radical discourse, such as that embodied in the literature of postcoloniality, may not make a profound contribution to the latter objective and could be seen simply as a move within the politics of academia itself, the effects of which are largely restricted to the academic field.

Answering these questions involves more than just contemplation. It requires us to spend time analyzing the social and political fields within which knowledge is produced. That means, inter alia, renewing the centrality of political economy in anthropology, since change in the academic field is clearly a facet of change and contradiction within capitalism. It also means pushing forward the kind of research on social and political realities that the funding structure seeks to inhibit in a more aggressive way. We have to think deeply about the likely consequences of everything we do, not merely in the classroom, but as professionals organizing our lives as workers in education and facing interventions to redefine and restructure our roles.

Academic (relative) autonomy and freedom are still worth fighting for, but to some extent they are eroded by powers that we can only feebly contest. When we consider the attractions of consultancy work for both in-post professionals and our postgraduates, we need to be prepared to debate the ethics and the politics of these kinds of engagements. There are an increasing number of opportunities offered by mining companies and other transnational agencies operating in the South, looking for ways to tackle global indigenous rights movements and anti- or alternative development protest movements. There are also many more opportunities to work for public regulatory agencies. None of these questions can now be decided in the abstract, from the security of a salaried academic job. In Britain, cash-strapped university managers are increasingly having to contemplate compulsory redundancies and departmental closures. The next millennium is going to be a difficult period, but I draw some comfort from the fact that anthropology as a profession is slowly showing signs of understanding the changes that are afoot and trying to confront them collectively in an organized way.

I would argue that we should no longer contribute to the production of culture as the masters of the exotic, and that we absolutely must not contribute to the production of culture as the gatekeepers of ethnic identities and a multicultural politics that disempowers and fragments disadvantaged groups. We can and should work on creating an increasingly politically engaged discipline, which argues against the narrow focus of organizations such as the British ESRC in defense of a truly global perspective. We may as well be aggressive in response to others, because pragmatic interest will ensure that they do us no favors and we need to shout to make ourselves heard. What we have going for us is that we do at least have one receptive audience to our message, the students whose experience of the world as it is or simple intellectual curiosity and a critical spirit draws them toward us.

Notes

1. For a discussion of the history of European universities, see Compton's Concise Encyclopaedia on CD-ROM, 1998 edition, and the World Wide Web pages of Oxford University, University College London, and Manchester University.

2. This finding is based on a review of the applications submitted through the Universities and Colleges Admissions Service (UCAS) by Dr. Sue Wright of Birmingham University, the coordinator of the National Network for Teaching and Learning Anthropology.

3. Social anthropology received 4 percent of awards made by the ESRC in 1994–1996, falling to 3 percent in 1996–1997, with a success rate of 29 percent, making the subject sixth out of fifteen disciplines according to this measure. These data are published in the Annual Reports of the ESRC Research Grants Board.

PART 2

States and Subjects

CHAPTER 7

Sentiment and Structure: Nation and State

Dipankar Gupta

Nation-State, Unity, and Difference

With the inauguration of the nation-state as a community, the numerous cultural spaces within a geographical unity begin to relate with one another supralocally. Cultural membership of a different kind now becomes available for the first time in history. The nation-state enlarges the scope for communication between hitherto closed cultural spaces, thus extending social boundaries (see Luhmann 1990, 175–183). The nation-state thus has a liberating effect that is often unrecognized. This is primarily because the original conditions behind the formation of nation-states have gradually been effaced from public memory, thus lowering the appreciation of the historical contributions of nation-states. Consequently, only the negative aspects of nation-states, such as the unbridled passions and violence they can and do generate, get a lot of attention and attract a lot of opprobrium.

This is where anthropology can be of help for it can quickly point out that human beings throughout history seek a sense of community bonding. Whether it is the Kachin, the Pueblo, or the Chinese, the sense of being superior to others is a common feature in all known societies, past and present. So it is not as if nation-states were the first to unleash wars based on primordial passions, nor is it that if nation-states were somehow removed from the face of the earth violence and prejudice would disappear. The nation-state is then a species of cultural membership, albeit with a wider area of resonance. This does not make its members more intense or passionate, but only signifies that its membership is much larger than existing cultural groupings and that its effects can be felt over a much larger space. There are some important differences too between nation-states and other forms of cultural memberships. We shall turn to these later. It is the similarities that need to be appreciated first.

Like other primordial memberships, such as those based on caste, language, or religion, the nation-state too invigorates certain root metaphors (see Turner 1974), and it is the adherence to these root metaphors that determines membership. The membership in this case is denoted by the term *citizenship*, but its base line passion is best captured by the term *patriotism*. The root metaphors of a nation-state vary from instance to instance, but everywhere they sacralize territory on the basis of popular acquiescence. So it is important to cognize what a nation-state does when it comes into being rather than charting a yellow brick road to nation-state-hood. The new space that the nation-state activates is necessarily more comprehensive than the earlier localized spaces of traditional communities. Therefore, while on the one hand the nation-state invokes membership according to its own set of root metaphors, it must also be able to accommodate other cultural spaces without compromising itself. This is the test most modern nation-states face; only some have come out of it with a reasonable degree of credibility.

The intensity of tensions between different sets of memberships depends on how certain spaces extend themselves. Religious spaces, on their own, rarely recall nation-state metaphors. This allows most marriages, or initiation ceremonies, to take place without incident. When it comes to a question of expressing religious identity contrapuntally against other religious identities, then the nation-state metaphors cannot but be recalled. In these moments it is impossible to observe religion as a private affair for it now takes on the Luhmannian "performative" dimension. Any nation in the course of its history, no matter how short that might yet be, has had to resolve issues of identity conflict, involving either religion, language, or caste. On occasions such as these, nation-state metaphors become salient, as religious spaces no longer either connect or collide dyadically. In most such confrontations in contemporary times the nation-state figures as an essential triadic node. This gives such antagonisms a certain valency that was not present in the medieval years.

For instance, Hindu-Muslim antagonisms, or Hindu-Sikh contradictions, in India, readily activate root metaphors of the nation-state. Linguistic quarrels too do the same. What needs to be emphasized again is that over time these experiences become part of the natural history of a nation's memory. To be a Hindu or a Sikh cannot be configured without these public extensions of religious memory playing a role. It is for this reason that what it is to be a Hindu demands a rooting in the territorial space of the nation-state of India. To be a Hindu in India, or a Muslim in India, or a Christian in India will be a vastly different experience from belonging to any of these denominations anywhere else in the world.

Part of the reason for the differences will lie obviously in the variations that exist in the very existential settings in which these religious denominations find themselves. Where else in the world will Hindus in such large numbers be found next to Muslims but in India. Particularities abound in different geographical locations, which is why contingencies exist everywhere. These particularities leave their impress on what it is to be a Hindu, or a Sikh, or a Christian, as indeed they did even in pre-nation-state epochs. When, however, we come to the question of examining how contradictions between religions are worked out and resolved in modern times, then the nation-state metaphors become significant in the making of cultural identities.

In the past, that is, before there were nation-states, the contradictions between religions were resolved largely on a dyadic basis. Sheer power played a critical role. The side that won took it all and the rest behaved until another opportunity arose (see Gupta 1996, 158–161, 67). Further, in the context of a closed economy with limited mobility, the supra-local factor could only be activated by little else than full-scale war. There were also centuries of peace, but this was a medieval peace. This peace was established on a hierarchical principle depending on who were the victors and who were the vanquished. Cultural diversities survived but in quietude and dared not clamor for attention.

Today, the situation is quite different. If the nation-state bonding is to be a viable one it must actively seek to integrate the marginal peoples within the territory. This is no easy task given the diversity of class positions in society (see Blim this volume). There is, of course, the option of going theocratic or fascist. In such cases, the majority (howsoever arrived at) denies equal rights to minorities. While such options do not take away from the legal fact of being a nation-state, they undermine the aspect of collective membership.

In the United States there was no consideration for blacks when the Constitution was first framed. The white settler colonizers saw themselves as the single force behind the American independence movement. It was as late as 1868, with the Fourteenth Amendment, that "equal protection under the law" was granted to blacks. With the Fifteenth Amendment of 1870, blacks got the right to vote. That America could be so dismissive of black presence till then was because the white population there did not consider blacks to be part of their quest for national sovereignty.

In the Indian case, the initial conditions of the national movement were such that lower castes and religious minorities were involved in the mass mobilizations of the anticolonial uprisings nationwide. Their inclusion was not just a matter of their physical presence, but was an outcome of conscious ideological articulations by the national movement on a variety of levels. In the Indian case, therefore, universal adult franchise and minority rights came together with the arrival of Independence.

The manner in which different nation-states come into being also determines how sensitive they are to the question of creating and maintaining harmony between different cultural groups and communities. Fascist and theocratic states suffer from no such constraints, but they are hardly models for emulation if seen from the perspective of the minority and disprivileged communities. If accidents of birth should be allowed to diminish one's status in a nation-state then the nation-state is still wanting in many respects. The contributions of liberal democracy, inadequate though they have been on a variety of occasions, provide a format for reconciling differences within the nation-state without sublating them by executive fiat.

The nation-state believes that it speaks in the name of all. This explains why modern nation-states are particularly embarrassed when faced with recalcitrant communities with their divergent cultural practices. As Claudia Vicencio (this volume) notes, unity is often imagined, and most often retrospectively. But such a compulsion never quite existed in pre-nation-state days. The vanquished were always well behaved and spoke only when spoken to. A nation-state, however, presumes a cultural community and a sacralized cultural space (or territory). There are several ways of solving this problem, some democratic and others not. One solution, under these circumstances, is to call the marginals aliens and enemies of the territory, as the Jews were characterized by the Third Reich. Jews were portrayed as people with loyalties outside Germany, perhaps even to the yet unformed state of Israel. To do this the Jews were first made into a homogeneous unity, and then, as they were the marginals everywhere, that factor was used to emphasize that they owed no allegiance to the nation-state of Germany, or to any other extant nation-state for that matter. "Statelessness," as Michael Walzer observed, "is a condition of infinite danger" (Walzer 1983, 32).

The other alternative is to devise a variety of laws and regulations that bring the marginals into the mainstream of the nation-state. It is not enough to just espouse such sentiments of integration without putting in place structures that will make them realizable. Such efforts may lead to the emergence of diverse metaphors. This could range from one of cultural assimilation, as with the melting pot metaphor, to the French metaphor of *laicite,* to cultural pluralist, or cultural laissez-faire metaphors as well (Parekh 1995). It must also be added that each of these metaphors are capable of conflicting interpretations (see also Clark this volume). But because these meanings must necessarily draw from the most literal meaning first, communication is possible even if it ends in disagreement. At this point I merely would suggest that nation-states try to take into account the diversity of cultures by relying on their root metaphors. Though this is never satisfactorily accomplished, cultural identities, nevertheless, cannot be innocent today of traces of belonging to a nation-state. Often anthropologists do not take this factor into consideration, which gives their accounts a certain ahistorical and idealized character. Contemporary cultural identities are not before the nation-state or after the nation-state but imbued with the nation-state.

When a quick survey is done into the prehistory of contemporary nation-states one finds that in their early and formative stages nation-states in Europe were indeed very intolerant of marginal cultures. At that point the bonding of the majority community, howsoever defined, was all that mattered. England, which prides itself in being the mother of democracy, too had a fairly murky past in the early years of its nationhood. It did not revoke the Test and Corporations

Act, which disprivileged the Jews and Catholics, until as late as the 1830s. All through the eighteenth century the Toleration Act of 1689 was in effect, which permitted everybody but the Catholics, Jews, and Unitarians to worship freely. It even outlawed Catholic religion for the English people. In terms of modern sensibilities, the Toleration Act could not have been more inappropriately termed. But this appears inappropriate to us only in hindsight. Toleration in the Toleration Act primarily referred to allowing free elections and free speech (for male Anglicans), control of Parliament over the Army, and so on.

Capitalism, Nation-State, Root Metaphors

In most cases, the actual fact of living in a capitalist economy has helped to congeal nation-state sentiments on an expanding basis in response to the question: Can capitalism survive without the nation-state? The answer has to be "yes, but. . . ." To the question: Can the nation-state survive without the instrumentalities that capitalism makes possible? The answer is "no, but. . . ." To the first question then. Capitalism can survive without the nation-state only if capitalism belongs only to the capitalists. Capitalists, as Lenin clarified, are out looking for markets regardless of nation-state boundaries. But capitalism is a practice that involves those who are not capitalists as well. If the roving instincts of capitalists disregard the interests of these others at the ground level on the shop floor, then the capitalist operation will face difficulties. The opposition to the capitalists will be of the kind that will accuse them of not taking the interests of the non-capitalists into account. This will invariably be portrayed in terms of national interests. One way or another, nation-state sentiments will surface.

Nation-state metaphors, too, cannot quite survive without capitalism in the sense that without capitalism and its undermining of local economies, economic practice would continue to be embedded by cultural metaphors that invigorate only confined spaces. This would impede capitalist operations, as a variety of local cultural metaphors and spaces would constantly come in the way. As the nation-state allows for a community that is supra-local, it provides capitalist economic practice a morality it would otherwise have lacked. Further, it can rely on this morality to evade the pressures of the strictly local. The relationship is therefore mutually advantageous and supportive. It is now even possible to talk of capitalist development in terms of national advancement.

Diversity, Alternatives, and Integration

The coupling of nation-state sentiments with capitalism also makes for a new understanding of diversity. In tradition there was no conception of diversity, for one could not quite rise above one's location in cultural space to view what happened elsewhere. Even when one was familiar with root metaphors in neighboring locales, interaction outside the strictly local space was limited and sporadic. In place of diversity, traditional societies talked of strangeness, of wildness, of the lack of godliness, but never really of diversity (see also Kluckhohn 1962, 69). Distances between cultural spaces were first ontologically marked. This gave "otherness" inhuman and consequently immoral qualities. Edward Said's *Orientalism* is all about how the Eastern cultures are seen as weak, effeminate, and given to wild swings in passion (Said 1978). It was only after nation-states triumphed the world over that the differences between cultures were signaled primarily in epistemological terms.

Diversity is a positive value today because the nation-state sentiment allows an elevation above the limitations of earlier encysted cultural spaces. The bonding that is brought about by nation-state's root metaphors makes it imperative not to dismiss those with whom one did not share overlapping cultural spaces. Though the call to respect diversity is often couched as if it were a call to respect tradition and traditionally oriented differences, it is really a very recent sentiment. To respect other cultural attributes within the overarching framework that the root metaphors of the nation-state creates is an outcome of modern times.

Though there is a moral judgment to respect diversity, it is also a fact that the greater the diversity in cultural spaces, and the weaker the insertion of nation-state's root metaphors in those spaces, the more traditional and backward a society tends to be. Diversities therefore are not good in themselves. They are good only so far as they do not conflict with the root metaphors of the nation-state. In that sense some of the isolation of earlier cultural spaces is overcome, though it cannot yet be said that they do not exist. Their existence, however, is not such that they do not allow a commonality of membership at a different plane. This naturally means that there should be a readjustment of the root metaphors of these prior cultural spaces to be able to make allowances for a supra-local community. To the extent that such adjustments are made, diversities can coexist within the nation-state.

Diversities that do not make room for this larger supra-local community are gradually eased out by the twin forces of capitalism and the nation-state. The nation-state's root metaphors make no concessions now, and can indeed be quite intolerant when faced with such situations. On occasions this can force a break within a nation-state, as with the emergence of Bangladesh. The eventual denouement in fractures such as this is not a nation-state-less conglomerate of cultural spaces, but another nation-state.

Diversities in tradition blocked movement, and encouraged suspicion across cultural spaces. Diversities can be a positive value today only if they do not carry the same features. In the past, diversities did not mean alternative lifestyles, but simply insurmountable differences. In fact, one can get a glimpse of this even as late as France between 1940 and 1944. After the German invasion of France, the Vichy regime under Marshal Pétain set about to emphasize French cultural purity where there would be no mixing of modern with antique; authenticity ruled. Groups in one region were discouraged from singing songs or performing dances that originated elsewhere. The performers had to be from the region they represented and costumed in what was deemed to be the traditional fashion (Lebovics 1992, 172). But in a modern liberal democratic nation-state diversities are acceptable and accepted only when they promote *alternative* life styles and choices, as well as actively sponsor a diversity of artifacts and products of diverse traditions. Kymlicka seems to accept this position but does not quite emphasize the difference between closed cultural practices and open alternative lifestyles (see Kymlicka 1995, 121–123). As Tamir points out: "Members of national communities unlike communists and vegetarians have no desire to persuade others to follow their way" (Tamir 1993, 149). In essence, then, diversities are compatible with nation-state sentiments as long as they free themselves from the past and present themselves as spaceless artifacts, or as alternative lifestyles that are open for adoption.

In the Indian case it should now be possible for Bengalis to live in Andhra and speak Telegu and take great pride in Telegu arts. Likewise, it should be possible for an ex-Untouchable to enter the Minakshi temple in South India, to wear a silk saree, and to conduct mortuary rites in the fashion that only Brahmins were allowed to do in the past. Only under these conditions can diversity be respected by, and made compatible with, the nation-state. Diversity by itself is not a virtue, but diversity tamed and opened is certainly not to be despised.

The above should act as a corrective to the simpleminded view that diversity is an unalloyed good in itself. To value diversity in this fashion is to ignore its premodern provenance (see Bhabha 1990, 208). Such an unqualified support to diversity is really quite anathemic to the spirit of, and to the root metaphors inaugurated by, the nation-state. As a matter of fact, the entrenchment of the nation-state metaphors gradually grows with the development of capitalism, which over time either effaces diversities or presents them as alternatives that exist within the territorial borders. The earlier cultural confines in America of Irish ghettos, or Polish ghettos, or Jewish neighborhoods no longer exist with the same kind of vibrancy as they did even forty years ago. The divisions between these communities were deep enough in those days so that even the socialist movement in America until the 1930s was divided into the Jerusalem Socialist Party, the Italian Socialist Party, and so on. Today, more than half a century later, but still within a lifetime, things have changed considerably. Even the Jews have now become "white folks" (Sacks 1994, 83–84).

This should not be taken to mean that Irish enclaves and the like are nowhere to be seen in America, but that their exclusiveness is fast disappearing. The only ghettos that still persist are the black neighborhoods. This is an outcome of the combination between class and race. Had it been just one or the other the matter would have been quite different. The gradual acceptance of East and South Asian migrants in white neighborhoods is quite remarkable. This is largely because class no longer differentiates them from the rest, though race still does. In the case of the Irish migrants, as race does not play such a distinctive role, class mobility has led to their absorption into an American way of life. In the case of blacks, both race and class are significant. This is why there are fairly distinct cultural spaces governed by black root metaphors. This diversity is not a positive feature of American society. It occludes movement across spaces and consequently threatens nation-state sentiments as well.

This should be a pointer to uncritical endorsements of diversity for diversity's sake. What is infinitely more preferable, given the direction of modernity and the gradual ascendance of allowing for alternatives and choices, is the sublation of diversities as distinct cultural spaces. In this quest the nation-state's metaphors act as potent solvents of past diversities. Poets such as Neruda, Tagore, and Yeats, who wrote movingly about grand nation-state sentiments (see Said 1994, 226, 232) did not qualify them by placing diversities at the same level as the "motherland." The attempt to accommodate diversities within the ambit of the nation-state is tellingly present in India's national anthem, itself a composition of Rabindranath Tagore.

The movement toward a cultural homogenization of space proceeds apace with the protection of diversities as artifacts. Museums, and the museum frame of mind, are widely promoted. Cultural historians, too, go about trying to rescue arts and crafts that are becoming defunct. There is nothing morally virtuous in such salvage operations, for as Mary Douglas said, we cannot learn something new unless we forget something old (Douglas 1995, 16). When universities give large grants for projects such as these it is yet another example of what Edward Said might call "Orientalism." This is an orientalization of one's own past, but only after it has been rejected and rendered inapplicable for enactment in contemporary practices.

Intersubjectivity, Public Sphere, and Res publica

The dissolution of distinct cultural spaces that the nation-state encourages brings about cultural homogeneity. This tendency cannot be doubted and may even lead to a lot of anguish among people as varied as de Tocqueville and Hegel. The positive side of homogeneity is that it brings about a greater degree of intersubjectivity (for example Schutz 1978, 134, 137) and the creation of a public sphere. This leads us from an examination of the *sentiment* of the nation-state to a study of its *structure*.

Jürgen Habermas once commented that higher levels of integration, such as those of the kind that the nation-state necessitates, require legal institutions based on moral consensus (Habermas 1984 vol. 2, 174–175). What he should have added is that this moral consensus can come from no other source than the root metaphors of the nation-state. As these metaphors are not always internally consistent they lead to diverse legal interpretations and disputes over points of law. What nevertheless comes to the fore is the emergence of a "public sphere." In this process cultural spaces of the past, including religion, lose their unchallenged authority and exclusivity (Habermas 1984 vol. 1, 340–343).

This public sphere, however, needs to be understood differently from the way in which Habermas has characterized it. This public sphere is not inhabited by a world that is rational to the extent that it keeps out "normatively ascribed arguments" (Habermas 1984 vol. 1, 340). Normatively ascribed arguments are not kept out, for then the requirement that legal statutes have a moral basis will have to be dropped. The public sphere emerges because the rules of arriving at an "achieved understanding" are agreed upon, leaving the door open for politics to determine which understanding is to gain primacy. In this sense the public sphere comes about not because there is an unanimity to keep out normative elements, but because there is a general agreement on how disagreements should be framed.

The moral content of the public sphere must also come from nation-state sentiments and can come from nowhere else. Between nation-states there is no ground for morality but only amoral bodies of regulations. There is no firm basis in international morality as there are no root metaphors at that level that are enacted by everyday, routine, popular participation. Universal brotherhood, or the dignity of human life, are features that figure in unworkable charters of human rights. Civil rights, on the contrary, have a firm moral base, as they are linked to nation-state metaphors and then to the public sphere.

What the public sphere does is allow for a greater degree of intersubjectivity of positions. The barriers that local cultural spaces traditionally erect become porous and frangible. This has already been hinted at when it was mentioned that diversities in nation-states must allow for choices in alternative lifestyles, where these alternatives still exist. It is this structured possibility of interchangeability of positions and intersubjectivity that makes the public sphere so public and the space so enlarged. As the rules of enactment are not to be found in prior cultural spaces, the public sphere derives its moral basis from the root metaphors of the nation-state. This moral basis need not be constantly invoked, nor need the participants always bear it uppermost in their minds. In fact, when it silently informs, without being aggressively dominant, its powers are the most persuasive (this is what Gramsci's "hegemony" is all about). It is only then that it becomes truly moral.

Diasporics, Minority Rights, and the Nation-State

The vibrance of root metaphors of the nation-state and the cultured territorial space they enliven can be felt even by diasporics when they settle in alien lands. Their conduct there, and particularly their struggle for minority rights in countries of their adoption, is charged by the vicarious spaces of the nation-state rather than by any subscription to universal laws of brotherhood. In this connection it is necessary to notice the timing when diasporics, as minorities, first began to raise their voices against discrimination. When ethnic pluralists began advocating greater tolerance between communities in Western democracies such as America, was also the time when ethnic distinctions were getting increasingly blurred, and there was indeed greater tolerance. The worst was already behind them (Steinberg 1989, 48–49). "In behalf of our sons," Irving Howe wrote in *The World of Our Fathers,* "the East Side [erstwhile working class migrant New York] was prepared to commit suicide; perhaps it did" (quoted in Steinberg 1989, 53).

In the days when immigrants from China, India, Africa, and South East Africa had few rights in North America there was hardly any demand from among them for equality of status. In America the Chinese were locked in filthy rooms by the dozens and denied the basic rights of citizenship. In Canada, for decades Indians of South Asian origin did not have the right to vote. Still there was hardly any energetic protest from these migrant quarters. If anything, the fight on this ground was carried out for them by benevolent Americans and Canadians. The Jews, too, hardly raised a voice regarding cultural discrimination against them. Hard though it may be to believe now, until the closing years of World War II Jews and blacks were on the same side.

It was among Jews, particularly in the United States, and in the rest of the Western European world more generally, that consciousness about their identity and rights was first articulated. This agitation coincides almost perfectly with the growing demand for, and the eventual realization of, a Jewish homeland in Israel. The establishment of such a homeland gave an enormous impetus to Jewish rights all over the world. To a very significant extent the persecution of Jews by Hitler's Germany focalized Jewish identity, but it was only with the realization of a Jewish nation-state that Jewish activism in countries all over the world became pronounced. In France the Jews had always lived as French, but now the Jewish identity was being stridently proclaimed even there. For centuries, the rabbinical model was the preferred template for the Jewish male. In their confined ghettos in most of Europe Jews adjusted to persecution by idealizing learning, particularly of the Torah (Prof. N. J. Demerath, personal communication). The aggressive warrior-like Jewish masculine ideal developed much later along with the gradual formation of the state of Israel. This explains to some extent why Jews were not prepared to resist the Nazis, and also explains why Jews need not be Zionists and yet remain extremely protective of the state of Israel. It is Israel as a sovereign nation-state, and not as a mythical promised land, that gave Jews the world over courage and dignity. Vicarious spaces have a powerful emotional charge and the manner in which they have been invoked to forward minority rights by diasporics proves the point.

The Jewish case might seem like an unusual one, co-mingled by the excesses of Nazi Germany, and by the extraordinary talents of the Jewish community wherever they may be located. A scientific experiment can nevertheless be conducted on a comparative basis by investigating when other communities, the Asians for example, first began to demand rights in diasporic locales.

Here too we find the extraordinary coincidence of the demand for minority rights by Asians and the emergence of the nation-state in Asian countries. After India became independent and Nehru came to Ottawa, the Indians in Canada began to assert themselves as a minority group and demanded parity with the rest of the Canadians. The same is true for the Chinese after China emerged from its revolution. This holds true for practically every country in Asia and Africa. The fact that there was now an independent and sovereign nation-state allowed for the recall of vicarious spaces to strengthen the demand for rights as minorities in diasporic conditions. The same Indians, the same Chinese, the same Arabs, lived incognito lives in America, and wherever else they went (see Burnet and Palmer 1988, 160). First with the stirrings of national liberation movements in the countries of their origin, and later with the actual establishment of nation-states in the formerly colonized parts of the world, the diasporic population from these countries found their voice in the lands of their adoption. From being immigrants they became members of a diaspora. Diaspora, as the historic genesis of the term suggests, connotes membership. It is only by being able to recall a vicarious space of an independent, sovereign homeland, that immigrants can make the transition from seriality to membership, and become a diaspora population.

This also accounts for why there is such a strong demand for ethnic pluralism at a time when communities have actually a much better position than what they ever had before. In the period when the conditions of the migrants were much harsher than today, it was the melting pot theory that was doing the rounds. Now that the immigrants are much better off it is the demand for ethnic pluralism that is being voiced from minority quarters. The capacity to recall a vicarious space, the nation-state, is what provides the minorities with their emotional and moral power.

The experiment can be carried even further. The two important communities that cannot recall a vicarious space of this sort, that is, a nation-state that is independent and sovereign, suffer the most, and their efforts are easily undermined. The first are the Native Indians. They cannot claim a sovereign nation-state, or even a series of nation-states to energize their demands. The fact that these Native communities are called nations and not nation-states is itself indicative of this fact. Nations can exist in the head, as so many artifacts can, but nation-states enliven a space, the sovereign territory, which can then be invoked as vicarious space for minority agitations, as the diasporic people do in America and in the rest of the Western world.

Blacks in America cannot recall a vicarious space either, for they do not identify with Africa or even with pan-Africanism. Some of the more articulate members of the black commuity may contrive to espouse such an identity but it is not a feeling that all blacks share. Black politics, too, is extremely vulnerable on this account and tends to turn viciously inward in moments of stress. Louis Farrakhan's emergence as a major black leader today is probably symptomatic of this condition. Further, blacks from the Caribbean are not akin to native-born blacks in America. This is why there are tensions between them (see Cox 1970, 380). In fact, it is widely believed that the Haitian migrants in America tend to distance themselves from other blacks because they were the first people of African descent to free themselves in the colonies.

Territory as the encultured space of the nation-state is far from being an exhausted empirical and conceptual phenomenon. It would be premature to say that for the diasporic peoples the lines between the homeland and the host land are blurred (Gupta and Ferguson 1997, 10). If what we have said above regarding the emergence of the demand for minority rights among the migrant minorities is even the least bit convincing it should demonstrate that the ability to recall a vicarious space plays a very strong role in diasporic lives. To suggest, as Appadurai does in a set of forceful essays on modernization, that in the new global order the nation-state has become obsolete is to overgeneralize from a highly privileged and mobile diasporic optic (Appadurai 1996, 169; see also Lash and Urry 1987, 300). Appadurai is probably convinced of his post-nation scenario for he believes that: "Everyone has relatives living abroad" (Appadurai 1986, 171). This is of course true, but only for a very small set who come from highly mobile and successful backgrounds.

Sentiment, Structure, and Citizenship

Anthropology can legitimately lay claim to the study of the nation-state as questions of root metaphors, cultural space, and community are involved in such an examination. There has been a reluctance among anthropologists to enter this domain for it was generally felt that the nation-state has to do with structures of legality and impersonal alienating practices that are not amenable to fieldwork or to concepts that are familiar to the anthropologists. This, we have tried to show, is far from true. Moreover, a nation-state cannot claim a durable or moral status if a body of rules and operational procedures is all that we are talking about. The nation-state is not based foundationally on what Weber would call *zweikrational*. A completely neutral nation-state can hardly arouse patriotism. Without uncalculating patriotism no nation-state can hope to survive for long.

It is important for anthropologists to realize how a study of nation-states with their root metaphors, regnant sets of meaning, and territorial spaces can give their discipline a contemporary relevance. By leaving behind the small group and its localized cultural spaces, anthropologists can contribute significantly toward the comprehension of modern, complex societies, all of which are today organized on nation-state principles. It may be argued that in some cases there is the structure of the nation-state without the sentiment, but it is structure and sentiment together that govern nation-states in most parts of the world.

It is true that no nation-state can survive without root metaphors whose regnant sets of meanings are enlivened through practice within a cultural space. But this is really the first step. In order that nation-states survive and reproduce themselves in time it is necessary that certain policy decisions be taken so that the sentiment that binds people together can be realized in as many instances as possible. The greater the instances of such commonality the stronger the nation-state tie will be within a particular territory. The more vivid, too, will be the recall of vicarious spaces by diasporics in far-flung lands.

Nation-states are built on popular endorsements of root metaphors, with their regnant set of meanings, which in practice enliven a cultural space that is the sovereign territory. This popular aspect of a nation-state can be undermined and lost sight of, for social relations are inherently unequal and hierarchical in most societies. Inequalities, when they are too sharp, offend the egalitarian principle on which the nation-state is founded (see Marshall 1963, 76, 81, 87). It is for this reason that appropriate policy measures are often contemplated that would realistically lessen the feelings of alienation that are bound to arise in a society where not everyone is actually equal in all respects, except perhaps in their patriotic fervor.

The nation-state belongs to all, rich and poor, privileged and the underprivileged. If classes and strata were left undisturbed by modern nation-states then the ties of commonality would soon wear thin and snap. This is where considerations of citizenship come up. The challenges of realizing citizenship in a substantive, and not just in a formal, way has been the concern of nation-states ever since the early years of the twentieth century. This is also the high noon of nation-state awareness, so it is only natural that the concerns of citizenship should accompany the development of nation-state sentiments. All established nation-states are concerned about realizing substantive citizenship, though the methods adopted may be different. The important point is that such public policy measures were hardly ever entertained in premodern times. The warp of such policy measures relies on the woof of nation-state sentiments. Historically, with nation-states, it has always been the sentiment first and policy next. Having dealt with sentiments, let us now go on to a study of the structures of the nation-state.

Nation-states are created in moments of what Sartre would probably call high "fusion." This euphoria, however, does not last for very long and the routine of seriality is bound to set in sooner or later. Once nation-states come into being the question of keeping foundational sentiments alive becomes an urgent task. There is no blueprint for it in tradition, or in spontaneous community organizations. To sustain the fraternity that was unleashed at the time of the formation of nationhood has to be accomplished by deliberate measures of statehood. The commonality that spurred the community of patriots and gave them the badge of membership, does not reflect itself in other aspects of social life.

There are vast differences in economic and cultural spheres within a nation-state. In addition, cultural and economic stratification can also reinforce each other. Unless statehood comes up with policies that inform the structures of governance that can keep fraternity going, the sentiments of a nation-state will be hard to sustain. The state must think now in terms of structures that can overcome the extant differences between members of a nation-state and give them a commonality that is not an evanescent one.

This is where citizenship figures as an active consideration. It is through citizenship that the fusion of sentiments is sought to be sustained. Subscription to nation-state metaphors is a necessary but not sufficient condition of substantive citizenship. Through the principles of citizenship the commonality that is threatened in the inequalities of social and economic life is addressed so that fraternity can still be preserved. This fraternity is not one that must compulsively make everyone equal in every respect. It should, however, give the individual a chance at realizing equality. The various theories of liberalism, beginning from Locke and culminating in John Rawls, are important in this context. An important theme in this connection is the reconciliation of liberal individualism with the protection and enhancement of fraternity. This implies that minority protection, the cultivation of freedom, the advocacy of positive discrimination must be attentive both to the individual and to the promotion of fraternity. It is not an easy task, but it is to this that we shall now turn.

While discussing issues relating to fraternity, it should also be clear that the nation-state necessitates a new kind of fraternity from the ones established by custom or tradition. The sense of fusion that the project "nation" brings about can only be consolidated by the framework of the "state" and its structures. The fraternity that is now relevant is a fraternity that is to be constructed. Fraternity, in other words, becomes a project, and is not a given solidarity. In fact all earlier solidarities are extremely suspect and must give precedence to the establishment of fraternity along lines of citizenship within the conditions of a civil society. These are still words, perhaps, but it is now up to the nation-state to give them meaning.

It needs also to be clarified that the root metaphors of the nation-state mimic the root metaphors of traditional cultural spaces, but are not identical with them. Tradition, when most tolerant, allowed for cultural spaces to coexist in a noninvasive sense. The root metaphors of the nation-state are not quite as quiescent and seek to actively intervene in the preexisting cultural spaces and in their memberships. With the nation-state's arrival there is a certain self-consciousness regarding how cultural spaces should conduct themselves for the larger glory of the whole. There are various ways of seeing the whole—the totalitarian and the liberal democratic are the two extremes in this regard. The totalitarian/fascist solution is a simple assertion of majoritarianism. It is the liberal democratic path that not only poses the greatest intellectual challenge, but also possesses greater liberating potential.

The metaphors of a nation-state are not only more invasive than traditional cultural metaphors, they are also more parlous in terms of the regnant sets of meanings that accompany each metaphor. This may seem surprising at first glance. When a set of metaphors commands such a large cultural space with so many members the unreflexive assumption generally is that the galaxy be richer and the regnant sets of meanings more varied. In actual fact the reverse is true, and with good reason. As the nation-state metaphors seek to supercede earlier cultural spaces and include them within the territorial space, the principles and sentiments for unification cannot allow for too many variations or exceptions. It is in this self-conscious drive to transcend and envelop parochial spaces that the root metaphors of the nation-state are quite different from the usual run of cultural metaphors. This again shows that logically the nation-state is not very supportive of closed spaces, nor of the kind of encysted cultural diversities that these spaces entail.

Perhaps the greatest difference between cultural metaphors and membership on the one hand and those of the nation-state on the other is in the range and depth of commitment. While cultural membership is intense and equally subscribed to, the situation is not quite as homogeneous with nation-state membership. In the making of the nation-state, while large numbers may have been involved, there are also significant chunks that were not participatory in the same sense. These are usually the less organized, less visible, less fortunate sections of the population. These categories of people become legal citizens, but are not substantively so. In other words, the root metaphors of the nation-state do not mean that all legal citizens are in a state of fraternity. All nation-states realize that the membership in this fraternity has to be enlarged, so that citizenship does not remain just a legal status. This is why there is a need for policies and structures of government. At different levels, and in different ways, regardless of whether a nation-state is liberal democratic or not, the question of substantive citizenship/membership is one that no nation-state can completely ignore. It is with liberal democracy, however, that the realization of enlarging and deepening fraternity is comprehensively recognized.

In spite of these and other differences between nation-state metaphors and cultural metaphors, there are also great similarities between them. This is what enables us to consider territory as the cultural space of the nation-state, and citizenship as a form of social membership. Like other cultural metaphors, the root metaphors of the nation-state need to be realized in practice. It is this that calls attention to the study of structures through which the nation-state metaphors can be realized. The most important consideration of social membership of a nation-state is the realization of citizenship. This, as we said earlier, is a task of great significance especially within the framework of liberal democracy. While liberal democracy is not alone in emphasizing that citizens have diverse origins and starting points, it is probably alone in protecting the right to political differences. The range of political differences allowed by liberal democracy is quite impressive, but everywhere its limits are set by the root metaphors of respective nation-states. A political opinion that attacks the basis of the cultural membership to the nation-state, or threatens to compromise on its cultural space—the territory—is first marginalized and then systematically pulverized. Yet when these limits are not transgressed liberal democracy allows for several visions of the good. In this sense liberal democracy does not advocate a perfectionist view. It canvasses instead for a state of affairs where a variety of conceptions of the good can compete in the public sphere for favor among citizens.

CHAPTER 8

Communists Communists Everywhere!: Forgetting the Past and Living with History in Ecuador

Steve Striffler

In March 1962, hundreds of workers took over Hacienda Tenguel, a banana plantation located in Ecuador's southern coast. The land invasion was important for a number of reasons. First, it occurred just after the Cuban Revolution, during a period when calls for agrarian reform and fears of communism were at their height in Ecuador and much of Latin America. The invasion not only put Tenguel on the front pages of Ecuadorian newspapers, but intensified national discussions regarding the influence of communism and the need for serious land reform. Second, the invasion took place in the country's most important industry and was carried out on an immense plantation owned and operated by the United Fruit Company, the largest producer and exporter of bananas in the world. By jeopardizing Ecuador's relationship with United Fruit, the invasion threatened the entire economy. Finally, the invasion forced United Fruit out of Ecuador and helped initiate a nationwide agrarian reform; Hacienda Tenguel was appropriated by the state, "delivered" to the workers, and transformed into the country's first and most important agrarian reform project. In short, the invasion mattered.

The primary concern of this chapter lies not in determining what the history of the invasion *was* (in any precise sense), but in understanding how that history *works*—how it was and is produced (Trouillot 1997). I seek to understand how and by whom the history of the invasion has been constructed, debated, and even fabricated, and what those constructions reveal both in terms of (1) the differential power relations involved in the production of history and (2) the contradictory and antagonistic relationships that people form in relation to their own history.

More simply, I attempt to explain, if only partially, an interesting contradiction surrounding the history of the history of the invasion. Why have Tengueleños, including those who actively participated in the takeover of the hacienda, continued (to the present day) to sustain the fiction that the invasion was communist-inspired—that communists led the workers into invading the hacienda? For the small minority of workers who were allied with United Fruit and aided elites in their efforts to define the invasion as "communist," this question is not particularly difficult to answer. The invasion was a direct threat to their own interests. For the majority, however, most of whom actively participated in the slaying of Goliath, the question poses something more of a challenge. Were elites so effective in writing a communist-paranoid history of the invasion that participants eventually came to believe that they had been pawns in a communist plot? If not, why would workers support this myth, thereby silencing their own quite substantial role in history (as the initiators of agrarian reform, as the invaders of the country's largest hacienda, etc.)? Indeed, given the invasion's David and Goliath quality, one would expect to hear a different set of tales about how a unified community, led by a few wise leaders, invaded a hacienda, overthrew a tyrant, and challenged the state—a narrative that is riddled with its own inaccuracies and historical problems but which is nonetheless understandable. Instead, although workers eagerly recount the history of the invasion, they are reluctant to elaborate or even admit their own involvement. This chapter attempts to explain why.

In so doing, the chapter contributes to a body of literature that has examined the role of social memory in the constitution of particular groups (Alonso 1988; Gordillo, this volume; Lamphere 1997; Passerini 1992; Portelli 1991; Sider and Smith 1997; Swedenburg 1991; Vicencio, this volume). The focus of much of this work has often been on the ideological struggles between state institutions, dominant classes, and popular groups, as more powerful sectors within society attempt to invent and impose a tradition, official history, or particular interpretation of the past (Hobsbawm and Ranger 1983). Part of this process necessarily includes attempts by dominant groups to suppress, and subordinate groups to reclaim, alternative histories (Alonso 1988). This type of ideological struggle, among the state, dominant classes, media, and workers, clearly took place in and around Tenguel during the months immediately following the invasion. The invasion, if only for a moment, was an important site of ideological struggle in which the workers were active participants, challenging official versions and promoting a counter-history. That they were not able to win this struggle is no more surprising than the fact that they lost control of the hacienda. They were simply outmatched.

At the same time, although this chapter is concerned with how and why dominant groups succeeded in turning *their* history of the invasion into *the* (public) history, it also tries to understand how and through what processes the workers themselves came to accept the official version. In other words, it may not be surprising that "the workers' history" was successfully suppressed from the public arena (i.e., relegated to the off-stage); but this does not explain why the workers in Tenguel came to accept and believe "the official history." Not only had they begun to articulate what could be called a counter-history, but their lived experience directly contradicted much of what constituted the dominant narrative. How, then, do we explain the emergence and acceptance of the official version by Tengueleños—by people who knew, better than anyone, that the invasion was not a communist conspiracy? The answer, it is suggested, lies not so much in the sophistication or force of dominant ideologies, or even in what subordinate groups have remembered. It is not enough to ask how certain traditions and histories are invented and then "internalized" (Hobsbawm and Ranger 1983); an important part of inventing and selecting certain histories and traditions is forgetting alternative ones. Why, and through what processes, have people forgotten, or rather, divorced themselves from, past experiences—experiences that could, should, and perhaps *must* be central to alternative histories that not only validate the past, but serve as a resource upon which future struggles can be grounded?

Remembering a Past

I conducted fieldwork in Tenguel in the mid-1990s, or just over thirty years after the workers invaded Hacienda Tenguel and forced United Fruit from the zone. Most Tengueleños proudly recounted how they helped United Fruit develop the most productive banana hacienda in Ecuador during the late 1940s and 1950s. They also remembered how their high wages, company-owned housing, subsidized food, and access to services were all threatened by an agricultural disease that destroyed the plantation's banana groves and forced United Fruit to lay off the bulk of the labor force by 1960. With surprisingly little pride, they described how they (or at least the bulk of "they") invaded the property and forced United Fruit from the zone.

The lack of nostalgia regarding the invasion is explained in part by Tengueleños' understandings of the subsequent three decades of state intervention, agrarian reform, popular struggle, and growing impoverishment (1962–1997). Virtually everyone agrees on two things. First, the invasion was a mistake brought about by communist outsiders. Second, the invasion was a defining moment that led to a failed agrarian reform and the emergence of contract farming, two interrelated processes that contributed to the further marginalization of peasant-worker families. In this sense, the takeover of Hacienda Tenguel is very much a "founding event"; people date occurrences in their lives in relation to the 1962 invasion. At the same time, it is not a founding event that is in any way celebrated. To the contrary, by pushing United Fruit out of the zone, the invasion is held responsible for a series of disastrous events and processes, including (1) agrarian reform (1962–1975), a particularly humiliating process that saw workers briefly acquire small plots of land through state-organized cooperatives; (2) the subsequent loss of that land to local capitalists; (3) and the emergence of contract farming, a system of production where, among other things, workers receive poor wages and no benefits. The invasion, in short, is responsible for a particularly difficult present.

There is, then, a general consensus that the invasion was communist (and that communism was an evil brought from the outside), even if there is significant disagreement over the particulars. In fact, debate about the specifics serves to solidify the broader consensus. The last three decades, generally seen through the lens of failure *(fracaso)*, can be blamed on a single event whose origins are explained by the intervention of communist agitators. The idea that communists were involved also serves to heal old wounds between Tengueleños, many of whom found themselves on opposite sides of the conflict. By agreeing that the invasion was an unfortunate, if defining, event brought about by communist outsiders, Tengueleños have in effect decided that the invasion should no longer be a source of ideological struggle. Those sites where the invasion's history is simplified and fixed through repetition—including family gatherings and Sunday afternoon chats around the soccer field—become places where a past is produced that is of little use for popular political struggles in the present.

How did this happen? Although the past three decades of "failure" (punctuated by a particularly difficult present) have served to sustain the belief that communist outsiders led the invasion of Hacienda Tenguel, it is still not clear how this interpretation emerged in the first place; or how a consensus initially formed; or how the counter-history was not only removed from public spaces, but disappeared from the "off-stage" as well. To address these questions, we must return to the last days of United Fruit's Hacienda Tenguel.

The War of Words

It was on March 24, 1962, several days prior to the invasion, that the Ecuadorian public first became aware that all was not well on United Fruit's Hacienda Tenguel. "Five Communist Agitators were in Tenguel to Foment Violence," declared a journalist on the back pages of *El Universo,* one of the country's major dailies (*El Universo* 3/24/62, 23). According to the article, anonymous "Bolshevik agitators" were "causing trouble" and had "begun to organize" the workers. The implicit message, from both the state and the mainstream media, was that the average worker had been content prior to the arrival of outside agitators. These disconnected disruptions were seen as local blemishes on the national road to progress. In the case of Tenguel, not only did outsiders put confusing ideas into the minds of the common folk, they provided organization. The more than two decades of union organizing was conveniently ignored: "The communists have begun to organize the workers" (*El Universo* 2/24/62, 23).

Due to a devastating plague that destroyed most of the property's banana trees, Hacienda Tenguel had been in decline. Contrary to newspaper reports, only a privileged minority were renting plots of land from United Fruit. Not only did forms of employment begin and end with United Fruit, but so too did access to housing, electricity, food, and even transportation. As the hacienda declined and United Fruit pulled out, services were withdrawn. By 1960, more than two thousand workers, or virtually the entire labor force, had lost their jobs and the workers' union was transformed into an increasingly militant organization that confronted United Fruit at every turn.

When the invasion took place several days later, the first newspaper report continued in the same (fictitious) vein, noting that "well informed sources" confirmed that there was a plan to convert the zone of Tenguel into a "communist outpost" (*El Universo* 3/28/62, 1). Well-trained communist militants from Guayaquil, Quito, Cuba, and Russia had trained the ex-workers in the use of arms, dynamite, and gas bombs. Techniques of guerrilla warfare had also been taught. Red flags could be seen on many houses and adorned the few bridges that had not been dynamited. Immediately prior to the invasion, the police, sensing that something abnormal was going to happen, captured five individuals who had revolvers, gas, and Molotov cocktails. Arrested as revolutionaries, this captured group had been accompanied by two Cubans (*El Universo* 2/28/62, 1).

Upon taking control of the hacienda, the ex-workers reportedly shouted slogans—"Viva Cuba" and "Viva la Reforma Agraria"—as they shot their pistols wildly into the air. Despite the best efforts of the police, the invasion succeeded. The list of casualties was extensive: five police were injured in their heroic defense of the hacienda; the house of Don Julio Arguello, United Fruit's superintendent, was dynamited; three employees of the company were taken hostage (whereabouts "unknown"); and a woman was killed (*El Universo* 2/28/62, 1). As the newspaper report explains:

> The workers . . . began to listen to the agitators of the extreme left and some of the leaders were converted who then began to agitate their *compañeros* into believing that they could get the hacienda parceled out to themselves. The atmosphere was ripe for communist propaganda and talk of agrarian reform. (*El Universo* 2/28/62, 1)

The communists were coming and Tenguel was just the beginning.

The populist government of Arosemena reacted quickly to the crisis. Guillermo Jaramillo Larrea, the Subsecretary of the Ministry of Social Welfare and Labor, led a commission comprised of high-level state officials that was ready to negotiate a solution (*El Universo* 3/28/62, 3). The state, however, was hardly unified with respect to the invasion or the broader issues of agrarian reform, popular uprising, and communism. A police invasion had not been ruled out, and the Ministry of Defense called for the violent eviction of the revolutionaries.

The struggle within the state over the invasion of Hacienda Tenguel emerged during the early stages of a nationwide transition in which populist sectors were slowly repressed by a tentative alliance between the military and landed classes. This shift was seen most conspicuously within the organizational terrain of the state, but was nonetheless visible throughout the political landscape between 1959 and 1963. In the middle of 1960, Velasco Ibarra, Ecuador's ultimate populist, was elected president for the fourth time on a wave of popular support. By the end of 1961, a little more than a year after his election, Velasco had managed to alienate virtually everyone and the country was in chaos. Demonstrations by students and workers were met by increasingly brutal repression from police and military forces as the streets of Guayaquil and Quito became a battleground. In an effort to avoid a full-scale military takeover, Velasco Ibarra fled the country in November 1961, leaving his vice-president, Carlos Julio Arosemena Monroy, to pick up the pieces (Cueva 1982; de la Torre 1993). President Arosemena managed to remain in power for well over a year, but the latter half of his presidency was essentially a transition to military rule. The military became increasingly brash in its attacks on peasant and labor organizations, laying the groundwork for a full-scale coup in July 1963, or a little more than a year after the workers had invaded Tenguel.

At the time of the invasion (March 1962), however, Arosemena still had relatively firm control over the government and—despite grumbling from the Ministry of Defense—was able to send the commission (and not the military) to Tenguel. Upon arrival, Subsecretary Jaramillo, himself a member of the socialist party, announced that the Ecuadorian government was going to buy the hacienda and that United Fruit had forty-eight hours to leave town. The assistant manager of United Fruit's operations in Ecuador was put under house arrest, and the police who had arrested the five workers were themselves placed in jail for mistreating the prisoners. The arrested workers, in contrast, were set free and honored as heroes (*El Universo* 3/30/62, 13).

Subsecretary Jaramillo announced that he had come to Tenguel on behalf of President Arosemena and was looking to restore peace. The government, he assured, wanted to resolve the problem quickly and deliver the hacienda to the workers. The other members of the delegation gave similarly positive speeches, emphasizing that with the government in Tenguel the workers' problems would be solved quickly (*El Universo* 3/30/62, 19). The National Director of Cooperatives, Dr. Rene Moreno, reaffirmed that the land would pass to the workers and that the system of cooperatives developed in Tenguel would be the model for all of Ecuador. According to newspaper accounts, he shouted that "agrarian reform was born in Tenguel." In return for worker discipline and obedience, the government would solve the problem, "prosperity would return in a year," and "Tenguel will be turned into a paradise" (*El Universo* 3/30/62, 19).

The day after the government commission came to Tenguel, met with workers, and made all sorts of fantastic promises, an ideological assault began against both Cooperative Juan Quirumbay, the organization that represented nearly all of the workers, and the state officials who supported its cause. Newspaper reports detailing the spread of communism in Ecuador increased after the invasion, and Tenguel was a central part of this discourse. One editorial noted that "the expansion of disorder towards neighboring zones . . . will quickly spread to the rest of the country" (*El Universo* 4/5/62, 4). This threat was due to "the lack of good sense and the failure to apply legal norms on the part of the Ministry of Social Welfare [Jaramillo] after the workers had clearly committed outrages against the hacienda" and United Fruit (*El Universo* 4/5/62, 4). The author suggested that this oversight should be corrected with "the severity that is required" and that a military contingent should be sent to take arms from the workers and root out "the clandestine agents of communism." This "repression" should be done quickly so that the "anarchist outbreak" does not spread to the country as a whole (*El Universo* 4/5/62, 4). Nor was such propaganda without its intended affects. On April 7, two days after the editorial, a military contingent was sent to Tenguel to make sure that people "were dedicated to agriculture" and nothing else (*El Universo* 4/7/62, 3). More significantly, Subsecretary Jaramillo became the ex-subsecretary, thereby ridding Cooperative Juan Quirumbay of its most important government ally (*El Universo* 4/7/62, 3). The removal from power of Jaramillo and other sympathetic state officials served to isolate the workers from the dominant producers of the invasion's history. Without the vocal support of at least some sectors within the state, the invasion was quickly defined as communist by the media.

This public relations assault lasted for more than a year after the invasion, continuing unabated until Cooperative Juan Quirumbay was destroyed by the military. One of the most visible forms of the ideological attack came in the form of an editorial written one month before the military took power on the national level (*El Universo* 6/12/63, 4). Ironically titled, "An example of how we will make Ecuador into another Cuba: Tenguel," the article began by asking "how much ink and paper, how much Russian and Ecuadorian money, had been spent to organize and mobilize the workers against United Fruit and to attack the police and military that guarantee the security of property and people?" Saenz, the rather creative editorialist, noted that outsiders used "psychological methods" to gain control of the minds of the peasants. The government had wasted endless amounts of money on the zone and the taxpayers had contracted an enormous debt—all in an effort to ensure that another Cuba was not built in Ecuador. Despite these efforts, Saenz insisted that "Tenguel represents the most eloquent contradiction of the speech, already suffocating, of the wisemen of agrarian reform." "No one, not the political leaders, not the technical experts . . . not the peasants, have wanted to transform the 17,000 hectares into minifundias or, according to the reformist lingo, 'family plots.'" But this was in fact what was happening, another Cuba existed in Tenguel where two cooperatives have formed, reflecting the divergent ideas of the leaders: "[O]ne is managed by the Communist Party and the other, which pretends not to be communist, is run by agents of Castro." "The ideological controversy that separates Peking from Moscow is being reproduced on a small scale in Tenguel" (*El* Universo 6/12/63, 4).

As sustained as the anticommunist propaganda against the workers was, several questions remain. First, to what extent, and in what form, did this discourse travel from national centers to the somewhat isolated area of Tenguel? Second, to what extent, and to what ends, did factions of workers adopt, reject, or modify the discourse? Finally, what was the relationship between the war of words, daily life in Tenguel, and the workers' own understandings of the invasion?

Power and Propaganda in Tenguel

The workers never held a uniform understanding of the invasion, United Fruit's relative virtues, the potential role the state, or the range of futures that they suddenly faced in 1962. Nevertheless, the decline of the hacienda, the massive layoffs, and the rapid impoverishment of a relatively privileged workforce served to unify the workers in the months just prior to the invasion. By March 1962, more than 80 percent of the workers had joined Cooperative Juan Quirumbay, the organization that led the invasion. At the same time, there was also a group of ex-workers, the majority of whom had been favored by the company and were renting small plots of land from United Fruit at the time of the invasion, who supported the status quo. Numbering fewer than one hundred at the time of invasion, this group came to form Cooperative Gala, a loose federation of ex-workers united by their opposition to Cooperative Juan Quirumbay.

After the invasion and Subsecretary Jaramillo's dismissal, Cooperative Gala quickly gained the upper hand in the ideological struggle. They formed alliances with local landowners and gained a privileged access to the media. By the end of 1962, Cooperative Juan Quirumbay had lost its allies within the state and the ideological war over the invasion's public/official history had ended. For the outside world, the invasion and Cooperative Juan Quirumbay were communist. The propaganda attack against the cooperative was accompanied by an on-the-ground assault carried out by local military and police forces. Members of Juan Quirumbay were harassed, jailed, and threatened as they slowly lost control of the hacienda.

It was these factors that led the majority of workers to abandon Juan Quirumbay and join Cooperative Gala between the end of 1962, when both the invasion and the workers had been defined as communist, and July 1963, when the military invaded the hacienda and destroyed both organizations. It should be stressed that although the workers left Cooperative Juan Quirumbay at different moments and for different reasons, most did so with considerable reluctance. They had put much of themselves into the organization and only joined Cooperative Gala after realizing that a continued alliance with Quirumbay could be dangerous. By mid-1963, it was clear that the final solution in Tenguel would be a military one and that any connection with the "communists" could be dangerous. As a result, more and more workers joined Cooperative Gala, denounced Juan Quirumbay as communist, and positioned themselves for a future whose broad contours they could no longer shape.

Within a week of taking over the national government in July 1963, the military government of Castro Jijón invaded Hacienda Tenguel. Thirty of Juan Quirumbay's most prominent members were immediately rounded up, paraded through town, and placed in a swimming pool filled with water up to their necks. They remained there for more than a day and were then permanently removed from the zone. As one ex-worker remembers:

> I asked the military commander what happened to the workers. He said the leaders of Juan Quirumbay had been taken prisoner. I said most were not leaders, but just workers like the rest. He then took me to the pool and showed me the workers. There were about thirty, all in the water with guns pointed at their heads. He asked if I had a question. I said nothing and turned away. I did not want to be put in the pool.

The imprisonment of the so-called leaders/communists was only the beginning of a long wave of military intimidation and repression that came to resemble something of a communist witch hunt. The people of Tenguel would be forced to turn their backs and remain silent many more times. Strict limitations were placed on people's movements and meetings of more than two people were forbidden. More importantly, workers were forced to turn on one another as the military searched for, and then expelled, the communists. As one worker recalls:

> I arrived one afternoon. I didn't know what was happening. My family was crying and the military was going through our stuff. They said they were looking for communist literature. We could barely read. They told me we had to leave the next day so we better get ready. Someone, perhaps a friend, had pointed me out [as a communist]. Why they picked some out and not others I don't know. I had worked for Juan Quirumbay but only on the land as a worker. That night when we were packing was awful. It was desperate. Our neighbors just watched. They were afraid. We were all crying. We were from here, all of our family. I had only been to Guayaquil a couple of times and we had no family outside the zone. The next day they dropped us at the edge of the hacienda. The people looked down on us and were told not to hire us. The people were afraid. What could they do? I don't know how we survived.

Narratives such as these were only recounted with great reluctance and, it should be stressed, were fairly rare. Most people who were removed from the zone did not return and are thus difficult to locate. Nevertheless, the evidence suggests that the military persecuted a significant portion of Tengueleños in a particularly arbitrary and random manner.

There is, of course, another side to this history of persecution. There are the experiences of those who remained in Tenguel and, either by temporarily leaving the zone, remaining silent, turning the other way, forming relationships with the military, or turning on their friends were able to remain in their homes, keep their families intact, and survive the wave of military repression. These were the people who hoped a strong and vocal stance against both "communism" and the invasion would be sufficient to avoid the attention of the military. In many cases, it was not. Interviews became confessions:

> The military came to my house. We were terrified. They said we had been involved in Juan Quirumbay and were known communists. They said we had to leave. This was crazy. Sure, I said I had belonged but had later quit when I saw the leaders were communists. I wasn't a leader, just a worker. The military said they had found communist propaganda in my house. They showed me a newspaper and asked where I got it. They kept pressing. I couldn't remember. It was just a newspaper. Finally, I told them I got it from someone who I thought had been more involved. He wasn't a communist, just a worker. But what could I do?

Although few workers and their families were confronted with such dramatic moments, many were left in circumstances where they had no choice—where they had to remain silent as friends were interrogated or removed from the zone. For most, the decision to remain silent was easily understandable, involving a modest form of betrayal that could not be helped; they recognized then, and see now, that there was no choice. What most Tengueleños find more difficult to understand is the very fact that they were presented with such a choice in the first place. How, if there were no communists, can Tengueleños understand the actions of the military, the government, the press, and local landlords, as well as the impossible choices that those actions (and inactions) forced upon the community?

Upon closer look, our original question becomes exceedingly complicated: Why have Tengueleños, including those who actively participated in the takeover of the hacienda, continued to sustain the fiction that the invasion was communist-inspired? Given the political climate and the imbalance of power, it is not particularly surprising that dominant groups succeeded in defining the invasion as communist. Efforts by elites to put a particular spin on the invasion lasted well over a year, came from powerful sources, and were relatively coherent.

Moreover, the workers were never really able to offer an alternative account that had much force or coherence; they were on the defensive from the very beginning. They did not have access to the dominant producers of history and lacked a language through which to articulate a coherent, effective, and competing history. Peasants who invaded a hacienda and talked about things such as *cooperativismo* and agrarian reform were immediately connected to Cuba, Castro, and Communism—the three "Cs" that defined the discursive boundaries through which agrarian conflict and popular uprisings were viewed during this period. Urban middle-class fears about communism and the peasantry, combined with the fact that no one seriously believed the workers could have organized themselves (it had to have been the communists), only added to their troubles. Even if all of the workers had agreed about the invasion, it would have been difficult to articulate a history in which their actions were viewed as anything but communist; they had, after all, invaded a foreign-owned plantation.

Although these factors help explain why the workers lost the larger ideological struggle over the invasion's public history, they do not help us fully understand why the workers themselves came to believe the invasion was communist. To be sure, such factors are not irrelevant. The failure of the workers to articulate an alternative history is part of the story, as is the subsequent history of failed state intervention and growing impoverishment. Workers who opposed the invasion and supported the dominant understanding of its history—either to promote their own interests or because they genuinely believed that communism was involved—were vindicated when the military rooted out the clandestine agents of communism. Similarly, the fact that United Fruit left, agrarian reform failed, and the workers were left even worse off than before has helped sustain an understanding that sees the invasion as communist (or "bad").

Nevertheless, any explanation as to how a particular history emerged instead of another, or at least one that does not conclude that the workers were collectively deluded into believing the invasion was communist, must deal with the fact that the workers were *there*. They were in Tenguel and knew, despite what sectors in the press and government were saying, that they and their friends were not communist; that the invasion, whether viewed as just or not, was led and carried out by workers who had been mistreated by both United Fruit and the state; that Russians, Cubans, and other outside agitators did not grab hold of their minds. The elites who rewrote the history of the invasion often did so from a distance and were only concerned with Tenguel inasmuch as it could be fit into arguments about agrarian reform, the virtues of a particular government, or the state of the union. That they manipulated the history of the invasion to fit their own goals should hardly be surprising. The workers, in contrast, were in Tenguel; the battles over the invasion's history necessarily included more intimate forms of betrayal.

Any explanation of why and how Tengueleños came to see the invasion as communist must not underestimate the role of coercion in securing consent.

The arrival of the military did not simply lead to the destruction of popular organizations in Tenguel; it made it virtually impossible to talk about the invasion in an intelligent and open manner. Public meetings were banned and private discussions were self-censored due to the atmosphere created by the military. Tengueleños had to say the invasion was communist, even if all of them did not believe it.

At the same time, however, it seems clear that the impossible choices that the military forced Tengueleños to make not only served to suppress alternatives accounts, but gave the communist-paranoid history of the invasion its strength. What I am suggesting is that not only did the workers have to publicly denounce the invasion and Juan Quirumbay—that is, to denounce themselves and their own role in history—but that at some point along the way they were, at least on some level, forced to believe that the invasion had been led by communists. To suggest otherwise is to break the silence and admit to themselves that the workers who were paraded around town, placed in jail, tortured, and forced from the zone were not communists, but were in fact their neighbors and friends. It is to explain what is unexplainable. It is to admit their own complicity and to revisit the humiliation of having to abandon an organization that they put their life into; the humiliation of having to join the one they had fought against; the humiliation of having to turn the other way as neighbors were carted off; and the humiliation of having to denounce their friends to save their ass. It is to remember a much more complicated history, one in which successes, failures, betrayals, and sacrifices are not forgotten, but come to replace a communist metanarrative that simplifies (and explains) everything. With communism as a backdrop, the events of 1962, and the narratives that surround them, are filled with historical errors and inconsistencies; without it, they simply make no sense.

Conclusion

I suspect that the experiences, memories, and understandings outlined above are not isolated to Tenguel, but can be found in many places where subordinate groups have seen their struggles defeated and their aspirations crushed. Failure, defeat, and their long-term consequences are central components of class struggles and histories that deserve more attention than they have received. Peasants and workers do not shape history only during those dramatic moments of revolution and "victory" when they overthrow a government; nor is their influence limited to "everyday forms of resistance," those thousands of individual, anonymous, and unorganized acts of insubordination that silently transform the socioeconomic landscape. We must, in short, continue to understand how the failed—yet conscious and organized—struggles of subordinate groups shape historical processes. Histories of partial and sometimes total defeat must be traced alongside and within what are almost always incomplete victories.

I would also argue that the very fact of subordination—of not only experiencing defeat more often than victory, but of being forced into impossible situations and choices that often involve intimate forms of betrayal—can place subalterns into antagonistic relationships to their own histories and experiences. Although this chapter cannot begin to explore the present-day political consequences of these antagonisms, it seems clear that people's memories of past experiences shape their political hopes, actions, and understandings in the present (and vice versa). Moreover, if the case at hand is at all representative, the link between experience and memory (or consciousness) is much more complicated than many Marxists have thought. Workers' experiences were not only far from uniform, and hence could not possibly produce a common (class) consciousness, but were actually *lost* through a communist-paranoid struggle over the invasion's remembered history—where workers became communists. This loss (or drastic distortion) of past experiences not only makes it difficult for some Tengueleños to live with history, but removes an important resource upon which struggles in the present must build. Understanding why, under what circumstances, and to what extent popular experiences are lost, or understood through the dominant lens of history, is a task particularly well suited to a historical anthropology of the present—where the anthropologist, by talking to people about the past, solicits their understandings and hopes for the present and future.

Ultimately, the question is not whether a particular group has formed antagonistic relationships to their history, but how, by whom, and through what processes such antagonisms were created, reproduced, and transformed—and how they have manifested themselves in the present day. When, where, and to what ends are different, often competing, histories adopted by popular groups involved in contemporary conflicts? To the extent that scholars have addressed these questions, the focus has tended to be either on "successful" struggles, where the reproduction of a glorified past is understandable, or failed struggles that have subsequently been adopted and celebrated by popular groups involved in contemporary conflicts. That our attention has been focused in these directions is not surprising—these are the struggles that often define a particular group, place, or even epoch. The manner in which history works through class struggle is most vivid in cases where a failed strike or upheaval subsequently becomes an icon, serving as an ideological tool for motivating and binding a social movement. As numerous cases suggest, memories of the past often play important roles in the political present (e.g., Sandino's enduring legacy during the Nicaraguan Revolution).

What the case of Tenguel suggests, however, is that it may be worthwhile to examine a much more common (yet less studied) type of struggle—those struggles that were not only defeated in the past, but fail to serve struggles in the present. Tenguel is instructive not because the hegemonic version of the invasion's history was partial and uneven—it clearly was, as the differing views of Tengueleños demonstrate—but that it has endured for so long. Why do certain hegemonies, however partial and changing, endure over time? Under what circumstances are failed political events—such as a strike, land invasion, or uprising—dismissed, forgotten, or denigrated by their own authors? Or, conversely, when and by whom are counter-histories resurrected and employed as a means for envisioning a different future?

There are no easy formulas for understanding the connections between visions of the past and struggles in the present (about the future). It would be (more than) a stretch to suggest that the absence of a contemporary social movement in Tenguel is due to the lack of an alternative understanding of an invasion that happened more than thirty years ago (see Vicencio, this volume). Agrarian reform, economic restructuring, military repression, state laws, and a host of other factors have gone a long way in eliminating strong popular organizations from the zone (Striffler 1999). In fact, it is more likely that the causal relationship works the other way. Alternative histories need authors, particularly politically organized groups that recognize the need to develop and utilize popular histories in order to construct and energize visions of the future. In the absence of strong political organizations or movements, the task—for activists, scholars, and other repositories of historical knowledge—is to ensure that popular histories are not permanently lost, but endure, making it possible to remember a past that is not only tolerable, but politically empowering for struggles in the present and visions of the future.

CHAPTER 9

"We Were the Strongest Ones Here"

Transformed Livelihoods in Contemporary Spain

Claudia Vicencio

In the summer of 1994, during fieldwork in the town of Abanilla in the southern region of Murcia, Spain,[1] I was invited to view a videotape of my neighbor's son's wedding. Afterward, Ruben asked if I wanted to see an old video of Abanilla, which proved to be a copy of a *"Nodo" (Noticiales documentales del estado)* or "news documentary" propaganda film made by the Franco regime during the 1950s. The film's first half is a glorifying description of productive, harmonious, industrious peasants hard at work, contributing to the Nation's economy with their local *capacho* industry.[2] Various steps in the production process are shown, while the commentary celebrates the "natural" wealth of the nation and the "natural" harmony of the town's entire population working together in the well-ordered manufacturing process. Hard-working men labor at harvesting and transporting while smiling women sit together on their doorsteps laughing and talking as the *capacho* baskets flow from their never-idle hands. The entire process is in the benign hands of the prosperous and cheery *capachero* or factory owner. Everybody has a rightful place; together they are making the town prosper and are thus exemplary Spanish citizens. The film's second half shows the happy peasants of Abanilla at play, in the collective devotional fervor of their principal religious fiesta celebrated "from time immemorial," the procession of the Holy Cross (a Francoist fabricated tradition dating from the early 1940s). My neighbors delighted in pointing out familiar faces to me (including their own), as the film shows virtually the entire population of the town. Proudly, they pointed out the young pageboy at the head of the procession: Luís Fernando, their cousin who later became a school teacher, and behind him, his sister, the Queen of the Fiestas, now an aging lady whose main activity is organizing flowers for the church. My attention was once again drawn to this film during a life history interview with one of the town's former leading *capacho* factory owners, Reinaldo and his wife, Eufemia. In fact, he is the featured *capachero* whose industry, the narrator tells us, so contributes to the prosperity of his community and to building the nation, and she is the Queen of the Fiestas of the Holy Cross, symbol of the town's Christian purity and Spain's spiritual mother.

Viewing this forty-year-old film brings into focus transformations in livelihood and social relations in Abanilla. This chapter begins with an approach to understanding the notion of local community identity in relation to historical variations in state projects, with a view to understanding how community and the state have been experienced in Abanilla. I then introduce the contemporary fieldsite and the multifarious livelihood strategies people engage in as they struggle with local contingencies and the wider forces impinging upon them. With this background, I will provide a description of the *capacho* industry, which constituted the basis of Abanilla's political economy until 1955, with a brief look at changes linked to the dismantling of Republican-era production relations. The replacement of *capacho* industry social relations by contemporary social relations will then be analyzed in terms of local collective identity. I will conclude by suggesting how current contested notions of membership in the community and the state are historically embedded and thereby impede collective action.

Throughout the chapter, I will concentrate on the fortunes of Reinaldo and Eufemia, threading their life story from the end of the Spanish Civil War until the present through the history of Abanilla and tying it to features of Spanish political and economic history. Their story, and the recollections of laborers in the *capacho* industry, illustrate significant local reconfigurations of class and community identity as they relate to state project transformations. Reinaldo and Eufemia's perceptions and explanations of their current, diminished social and economic circumstances, and their ideas about their membership in Abanilla society, are rooted in the specific, highly classed, and politicized history of the local *capacho* industry. And yet this politicized past is barely reflected in their personal narrative. I will argue that their recalled identity as *capacho* factory owners and later as entrepreneurs throughout the Franco era, continues to inform their identity now as retirees in the current context of the liberal-democratic welfare state. More specifically, while Reinaldo and Eufemia see themselves as belonging to an "active" community, and while the cohesive vision of community which they imagine and in which they make claims may be shared at the discursive level by Abanilleros, the experience of community and of successive state projects for most Abanilleros belies those discursive claims, and is reflected in their practices. I argue that the community in which local identity is rooted—the Abanilla of *capacho* production—is constructed as collective only in retrospect. The material reality of daily life and the social relations of *capacho* production (deep class divisions, back-breaking labor, and grinding poverty) deeply contradict that contemporary perception of unity and belonging, rendering it illusory. Thus, the class and politicized aspects of the past are conspicuously silent in Reinaldo and Eufemia's life story, and their claims to social membership and entitlements in community are revealed as highly ambivalent and ineffective in the current political economy. They also reveal a fundamental historical obstacle to forging collective projects.[3]

Community, Identity, and State Projects

Anthropologists with a political economy perspective have long argued that locality and community are not simply givens, but, rather, must be understood with reference to wider forces (particularly the forces of globalization) that discursively and historically construct them. Our starting point is the observation that "different states projects have led to the historical emergence of quite different ideas about what constitutes social membership and social entitlement" (Smith 1999). Looking at local ideas of belonging and entitlement in terms of state projects, including unintended consequences of ideologically motivated policies, allows us to address the interpellation of wider forces with local subjectivities and identities as an ongoing, historically and spatially specific process of mutual configuration.

A state's "project" is to produce citizens, or, more specifically, the kind of citizens that together will make up society (Smith 1999, ch. 6). This implies certain attitudes and decisions or "a particular moral ethos" (Corrigan and Sayer 1985, 1) about what society ought to be (and therefore who may be acceptably oppressed, excluded, or eliminated from it), what the state ought to do, and who has the legitimate right to insist that it do so. Who or what interests become hegemonic is in continual contestation (cf. the work of Gramsci, Williams, E. P. Thompson), so that "the civilizing script is continually being re-edited, redirected, and re-produced by an auteuriste state" (Smith 1999, 272). Whether or to what extent states actually produce, at any given time and given place, the kind of citizens their projects aim at producing (cf. Barber, Clark, Gordillo, Lem, and Striffler, this volume) is critical to understanding "place making" and "people making."

Two particular aspects of state projects interest us here: one is their operationalization in and the material consequences of state policies and legislation. The other is how the state "talks" (Corrigan and Sayer 1985, 3) about the regulation of social life, that is, the discourse that reveals a state's project. As Corrigan and Sayer remind us, however, "social integration with the nation state *is a project;* and one in constant jeopardy from the very facts of material difference" (1985, 197; emphasis mine. For a discussion of discourses of national integration, see Gupta, this volume). There are other, sometimes competing, discourses emanating from other spheres, as well as daily life experience, which may or may not fit the prevailing state project discourse or practice, but which may provide terms in which social membership and identity claims are asserted.

For the notion of "community" itself, I draw on Gupta and Ferguson's assertion that community is

> a place that sets itself apart from other places, where people share a sense of cultural similarity. . . . [However] Community is never simply the recognition of cultural similarity or local contiguity, but a categorical identity that is premised on various exclusions and constructions of otherness . . .[and] it is precisely through processes of exclusion and othering that both collective and individual subjects are formed. (Gupta and Ferguson 1997, 13)

This shared sense of cultural similarity is expressed in a "distinctive local discourse . . . [and] institutionalized practices that occur and recur mediated by local *habitus* having no immediate connection to state institutions" (Smith 1999, 264). Processes of differentiation thus give rise to local discourses and practices that may be collective for some but exclude others within communities. At the same time, modernizing state projects under capitalism imply powerful discourses of belonging that aim to construct a totality (the nation-state) through individualizing strategies:

> On the one hand, state formation is a totalizing project, representing people as members of a particular community—an "illusory community," as Marx described. This community is epitomized as the nation, which claims people's primary social identification. . . . On the other hand, as Foucault has observed, state formation equally (and no less powerfully) individualizes people in definite and specific ways. (Corrigan and Sayer, 1985, 4–5; see also Clark, Gupta, and Lem, this volume)

I wish to suggest that the general absence of "active community" identity deriving from a shared collective project, outlined by Raymond Williams (Williams 1988, 104) in Abanilla has to do with the emergence/occlusion of certain subject identities produced by the way changing state projects have configured ideas about social membership.

Abanilla

The municipality of Abanilla is located on the hilly eastern border of the extremely arid southeastern region of Murcia, Spain. Some three thousand people live in the town of Abanilla itself, and a further three thousand live in surrounding hamlets and villages. For present purposes, I situate the contemporary work experience from 1975, that is, the transition to democracy following the death of Franco, to the present. Varied rural industry and multioccupational households have characterized both region and town for generations. Unlike in much of the region, local agriculture alone has never provided households with adequate livelihoods, and intensifying drought has further restricted all but very limited production for domestic consumption (olive oil, potatoes, onions, beans, seasonal fruit). Extremely small and fragmented family land holdings do not provide sufficiently even for subsistence consumption, and harvests regularly amount to a net loss in income. Paid work tends to be highly gendered and both geographically and occupationally dispersed. Economic reforms to make the Spanish labor market more "flexible" combined with extremely high regional unemployment figures,[4] have pushed people deeply into the so-called "underground" or "informal" economy of small factories manufacturing everything from shoes to foam rubber.

Work for women is most often sewing piecework, either garments or shoe uppers, in the home. As has been amply discussed in the informal economy literature (Benton 1990; Beneria and Roldan 1987; Mingione 1991; Narotzky 1988), the work is extremely poorly paid and notoriously insecure. Nonagricultural jobs for men include manual labor, work in small local factories and some construction, but in reality, secure employment is scarce and wages are minimal. Households pursue livelihood strategies that involve different members contributing small amounts from insecure, constantly changing sources. Poverty marked by individual and household multioccupationality, mobility, and income insecurity have been the norm at least since the demise of *capacho* production some four decades ago.

The only other significant source of income available to most adults with little or no formal education or training comes from state social programs such as old age pensions, unemployment insurance, disability and veterans' pensions, and a variety of agricultural subsidies. Considerable energy is put into accessing these resources to maximum advantage, and membership in the welfare state is actively resorted to for livelihood with important implications for identity formation linked to the membership claims in the state.

The *Capacho* Industry

The *capacho* industry constituted the basis of Abanilla's political economy for at least 130 years, from approximately 1822, and probably longer (Riquelme Solar 1978). The method of manufacturing changed remarkably little since described in Pliny in 1 A.D., though the organization of production underwent significant transformations. From the end of the Civil War, when it boomed as a protected and regulated agricultural product under Franco's agro-fascist project, until its complete demise in the mid-1950s, this rural artisan industry occupied virtually the entire population of Abanilla. The vast majority of production was dominated by four family firms, all related by ties of kinship.

The production process was divided by gender. Men did the backbreaking labor of cutting, drying, and transportation. Making the *capachos,* also physically taxing, causing permanent disfigurement of the hands, was almost exclusively women's piecework, carried out in their homes. Like today's shoe homework it was compatible with domestic duties and child rearing, and is viewed positively as highly sociable work. It also provided yearlong income, a "help" to the meager seasonal returns from agriculture.

While the organization and relations of *capacho* production are too complex to elaborate fully here, it can be thought of as analogous to a multifaceted factory, with the whole town as the workplace. Schematically, the relations of production were as follows: a *capacho* factory owner purchased the raw material (esparto grass), paid men to cut and transport it, paid women on a piecework basis to transform it into commodities *(capachos),* which were sold to prearranged buyers.

Reinaldo was a *capachero,* a factory owner. He began working at fourteen and took over his father's business in 1942 at eighteen. His first concern was to locate buyers: for years he traveled to the oil presses in Andalusia to secure contracts. Real success came, however, when he "made friends" in Granada with a Civil Guard who acted locally as his *enchufe* ("contact" in the clientist slang), who recruited buyers. Having secured orders, Reinaldo would then purchase (unharvested) esparto crops. Agreeing on a price required delicate negotiation, balancing the expected price for the final product, rates for labor, competitors' offers, and the expected quality and quantity of the crop. Day laborers were hired for harvesting, as were muleteers (later, truckers) to transport the esparto to the factories/warehouses, to which women would travel, usually on foot, to collect the twelve kilogram bales of esparto and to deliver the finished product for which they were paid on the spot by the piece, at relatively standardized rates.

Because the entire community was the workplace in this production process, Reinaldo's relationship to wage laborers cannot be understood in exclusively labor/capital terms; the social relations of production are embedded in the town's social relations, including class relations, patron–client relations (between, e.g., Reinaldo and his buyers, and Reinaldo and the landowners, but also between Reinaldo and "his" workers), and gender relations. Reinaldo had as many as three to four hundred people working for him; thirty to forty in each of two factory sites, and the rest in the fields and in their homes. Recalling his position forty years later, Reinaldo insisted, "We were the strongest ones here." *He* secured the biggest orders, *he* hired the most people, and *he* paid the best wages, most reliably. "We," of course, refers to the family he headed. His wife Eufemia came from one of the largest and oldest elite families in the town. In addition to being related through her paternal great-uncle to the town's wealthiest and most powerful family, Eufemia owed her wealth and status to the family's livestock and butcher business. When she married Reinaldo, she took over management of the *capacho* enterprise, including the bookkeeping, distribution of esparto, and payments to both the undeclared women working in their homes and the registered factory workers. As *capacho* owners she and Reinaldo enjoyed a livelihood and material comforts far beyond those of the townspeople who barely scratched out a living from marginal lands and hard manual labor.

The *Nodo* nicely captures the Francoist state's dominant discourse, which configured social relations in Abanilla as both locally and nationally "collective," and allows us to situate Reinaldo and Eufemia within these constructions. Reinaldo's active life as a *capachero* lasted from 1942 until the demise of the market in 1955, that is, during the early part of the Franco era. This coincides with the existence of the falangist state, built on an ideology of the "sovereign peasantry," with state projects aimed at preserving power for the landed elite by reverting to a prerepublican agrarian social structure. According to the then dominant discourse, the countryside was the cradle and reservoir of true Spanish identity and virtue, patriotism, private property, and the Church. The state, then, configured a national collective identity rooted culturally in the local, rural community. Thus, the film depicts peasants as explicitly embodying an ideal for the Spanish state. This dual "collective" identity (i.e., at once local and national) is especially manifested in Abanilla by the post-1939 social relations of *capacho* production—with which Reinaldo and Eufemia are so closely associated—which are both historically rooted in the local and regulated by the state.

The dominant discourse of local and national identity belies the material experience of deep class divisions and processes of exclusion, which literally condemned some members of the "community" to starvation while others prospered. This contradiction, as we shall see, is expressed in daily social interactions in the present, makes present-day claims of "community" problematic, and may even obstruct current collective community undertakings.

Capacho and the Republic

To understand how community and the state were experienced locally, we must examine the brief but critical period between 1931 (birth of the Second Republic) and 1939, the end of the Civil War. In 1931, workers in Abanilla joined together to start a Capacho Workers' Cooperative (henceforth CWC). The CWC collectively took on the role hitherto reserved for the local *cacique* families: it purchased uncut esparto crops, paid for harvesting, weaving, and transportation (at set rates, disentangled from the more exploitative socially embedded relations described above), and marketed the finished product. The CWC was successful even during the war, as olive presses in Republican Jaen continued to buy capacho from Republican Abanilla. As the war advanced and the country became desperately impoverished, the cooperative was able to barter its *capacho* production into otherwise scarce basic goods and food. For a significant proportion of the town, the CWC was the basis for personal survival and the community's very existence.

With the Republican defeat in 1939, the coop's leaders were summarily jailed, and its entire inventory and capital forcefully confiscated by the newly installed provincial authorities without any opposition from local power holders. On the contrary, a "gang of Abanilla industrialists" (the four big *capacho* producers, whose prerepublican power had been undercut by the CWC) ended up with everything and then sold it back to the people of Abanilla for a profit. In his memoirs, a later falangist mayor wrote, "If these industrialists from our town had not bought those *capachos* (. . .) then there would be no black legend about the coop" (Rivera Rocamora 1992; my translation). Defeated workers were forced by dire need to buy back the fruit of their own labor, and production was immediately reorganized under the control of the four factory owners, including Reinaldo's father. The fact that all records of the coop have been lost and that only a few people would discuss it do not indicate that this episode, or the multiple experiences of oppression and exploitation of which it was a part, are lost to contemporary experience. On the contrary, Rivera Rocamora's memoir tells us that the episode has the status of (black) "legend," a story popularly remembered as part of local history. The violent and divisive end of the CWC continues to constrain present beliefs about the possibility of collective undertakings in Abanilla.

To give just one example, in 1982 a group of young women attempted but failed to form a workers' cooperative for shoe production. The failure is most often explained by statements such as, "Coops have been tried here, they never work," or, "The problem is that you can't trust anybody here," or, "People will say that they're in it for the general good of everybody, but in the end everybody is only in it for themselves." None said that a cooperative is a bad idea per se— on the contrary, they insisted, it is the people of this town you can't trust. Indeed, informants frequently offered this perception of fellow townspeople as untrustworthy as an explanation for the general lack of economic optimism in Abanilla, even beyond the futility of attempting to establish any kind of cooperative. This lack of trust can be understood in the context of the unfolding social relations engendered by local processes of capitalist development. Between 1939 and 1955, moreover, the contradictions between the ideal captured in the *Nodo* propaganda film and the realities of daily life for Abanilla's workers were in intense and bitter contrast to Republican-era livelihoods. As we shall see, the factory-owning families who betrayed their fellow Abanilleros in 1939 and then prospered under agro-fascism as *capacheros*, found themselves relocated in the town's political economy after 1955 to an increasingly equal economic footing with many former CWC workers.

After the war, the Francoist state portrayed itself as the New Spain after the chaos and degeneration of the Republic. Social integration, according to the hegemonic discourse, was not achievable through class identification but rather through "natural" spheres of action—the family, the municipality, the vertical occupational syndicate. Local municipal administrations were appointed by the traditionalist Spanish Falange party, assisted by and overlapping with the preexisting local elites. Local administrations controlled resources and were given a free hand over product control and rationing, and they exercised their powers on a clientelistic and often violent basis, with the armed support of the Civil Guard.

In Abanilla the same local elite who dictated very concretely the terms of belonging to the state (under Francoism "intercession" and "contacts" were necessary to obtain administrative "favors" such as the granting of residence permits, social benefits, housing, or commercial licences, admission to certain schools, import and export permits, etc.) also dictated the terms of local belonging through their control of the labor process. Thus, throughout the falangist period the esparto harvest was rigidly controlled, with Civil Guards monitoring workers and payment transactions. In the experience of workers, the state was present in the process of production itself: repressive, violent, and clearly there to protect the interests of the *capacho* owner: "The Civil Guard has traditionally been seen, and continues to be seen, as an instrument of the state and of the powerful classes, with the power to act against [the laborers]. . . . The repressive attitude of the Civil Guard was very intense during the first ten or fifteen postwar years" (Contreras 1991, 513; my translation). It is in this light that Reinaldo's status as a boss and his clientelistic association with his Civil Guard "friend" stand in contrast to the experience of the men and women who worked for him. Their contradictory experiences with respect to this "instrument of the state . . . which served efficiently to enforce respect for property rights" (Contreras 1991, 513; my translation) also has implications for identity claims based in the state.

Reinaldo took over the family enterprise at a time when the factory owner earned at least a comfortable livelihood, while most of the population earned starvation wages while being subjected to rigid scrutiny and control by state institutions. Social control was achieved locally largely through the regulation of the single industry that bound the town's highly differentiated social structure together, and was experienced in both the productive and reproductive spheres of daily life. This period is reconstructed today (by many) as a period of collective community identity, resonating at least in the areas of ritual and discourse with the Francoist state project's rhetoric. However, the experience of the material reality of daily life arising from the relations of *capacho* production—how locality and community were formed and lived—stand in contradiction to this reconstruction. This is the time people refer to as *la miseria*, the misery. Few owned or had access to enough land to cover subsistence needs. For most, working in the *capacho* industry was the only local source of income other than agriculture day labor, which paid even lower wages. One woman I met came from a peasant family of fifteen children—ten of whom died of starvation during this period. Reinaldo's comments about his workers reveal a less than harmonious relationship, pointing to the contradiction between the discourse of peasant sovereignty and the realities of daily life. "The men would steal everything" and the women would all "sink" manufacturers by "sucking" social security payments out of the factory owners. His emphasis on his *strength* in this context (rather than wealth or influence), speaks to the rigid enforcement of sharply experienced local differentiation and exploitation.

The Collapse of *Capacho* and the Emergence of Contemporary Social Relations

Capacho as a livelihood collapsed in 1955, with the introduction of industrial plastics. Machine-made synthetic olive-press sieves were stronger and far cheaper to produce. Reinaldo and Eufemia closed the business in 1954, only two years after their marriage. The relationship between the breakup of the *capacho* industry and the pervasive heterogeneity of contemporary livelihoods is complex. The loss of the *capacho* industry meant the loss of the single economic activity that had sustained and defined Abanilla. More importantly, the social relations of *capacho* production marked subsequent transformations in social relations in ways that contribute to the growing contradictions in local identity. Moreover, the *capacho* industry's collapse coincides with a crucial shift in the economic ideology of the Spanish state. By 1951, Spain's protectionist economy was in desperate straits, and urban labor and social unrest could not be contained; Franco responded by discarding agricultural policies favoring self-sufficiency, reducing state intervention in production, introducing measures to liberalize the market, and implementing policies that supported the private sector at the expense of the public.[5] Ideologically, "peasant sovereignty" was abandoned. Successive state projects (contained, for example, in the Plans for Social and Economic Development initiated in 1964) undermined rural elite interests in favor of urban industrialization, so that "as successive governments committed themselves to policies of 'modernization' . . . [they] relied, not on traditional landholding elites, but rather on industrial elites . . ." (Contreras 1991, 515; my translation). The official glorification of (supposedly) traditional rural values ended, and the sovereign peasant was displaced as Spain's ideal citizen.

This shift in state projects takes on a highly particular form in Abanilla. Although the rural nature of *capacho* production had identified Abanilleros with the discourse of peasant sovereignty, a local political economy based on agriculture per se was, for ecological reasons, limited. Capacho production involved manufacturing; Reinaldo was an industrialist with some capital accumulation, and thus able to make membership claims in the state on the basis of this new discourse of modernization. The ability of the town's working population to do the same was far more limited, particularly for men whose role in *capacho* production was primarily agricultural, whereas women labored in manufacturing. New development policies put pressure on landless peasants and the poorest segments of the landholding peasantry to emigrate. Between 1955 and 1975 one-half to one-third of the male population left to find work in France while women stayed in Abanilla.

The state's new industrial policies allowed the city of Elche (sixty kilometers from Abanilla) to emerge as a center for shoe manufacturing, and it is to this source of livelihood that Reinaldo and Eufemia turned after the collapse of *capacho*. By 1955 their *capacho* factory had become a small shoe factory, subcontracting from a larger firm in Elche. Reinaldo became a distributer of piecework to many of the same women he had previously employed in *capacho* production. At first Eufemia trained them, then kept the books and maintained quality control. Again, poverty for most of the population was endemic. Income from smallholdings was nonexistent. The only source of livelihood was from remittances, and the piecework. Reinaldo could no longer negotiate with his buyers: he was one node in a capitalist subcontracting network and forced to meet quotas set by his suppliers, who in turn responded to ever-changing national and international markets. In addition, he was required to make substantial capital investments in order to compete with other distributors. They stayed in business for fifteen years, but by the 1970s, due to expansion and technological changes in the manufacturing process, more shoe distributors were offering better-paid work in the area. Rather than making the costly capital investments in the shoe business, the family shifted efforts to a taxi and car sales business that grew as the road infrastructure improved and the demand for travel increased. The family business today is modest, consisting in used car sales and a fleet of five or six taxis.

Most of the couple's income now derives from his seniors' and military pensions, and from social security benefits. Eufemia receives a small monthly disability benefit, and is waiting impatiently for her pension. In 1994 she was engaged in fierce battle with social services officials about when her entitlements ought to begin, giving very concrete and personal meaning to "making claims on the state." While not poverty striken, their standard of living has dropped considerably and they are no longer considered part of the town's elite. In contrast, the current welfare state does contribute to standards of living for most Abanilleros much improved over those of the Franco era.

Reinaldo and Eufemia differ in their present attitudes to their former workers, now neighbors. He proudly emphasizes his success, business acumen, knowledge of industry, and generosity:

> Everybody likes me, because they know . . . I generated money. When there wasn't enough, I'd look for the money and pay, and I paid more. . . . There were people here who'd give out four measly bunches of esparto, and you know what for? to squeeze out every last . . . [trails off] when I'd arrive they'd say "Reinaldo's in now, now things can move." Here, everybody has liked me on that level.

In his view, he belongs in his community because he aligned himself historically against the (worst excesses of) exploitation of workers while at the same time implicitly alluding to his strength and superiority over them as their employer. He belongs, in a sense, because they owe him. His wife's attitude is more ambivalent:

> My life has always been the same, but it made you sorry for the people. Nowadays everybody dresses, everybody moves, everybody lives, but then [during the era of capacho production] we were always the same ones who ate, the same ones with clothes. . . . I like to see the young women now, how they're all the same, because they all work at their jobs. They can look good, but before the poor things used to work so hard and couldn't set foot outdoors . . . but us, the strong ones, we had farms and we ate off the farms and the butcher shop, so maybe it wasn't necessary to do all that [*capacho*] work . . .

Here she explictly recognizes the class gulf that separated her from her neighbors (though not quite linking herself to their exploitation), but she now seeks an implicit identification with them; she belongs, in this sense, because of their present equality. Despite their slightly different reconstructions, both Eufemia and Reinaldo view the social relations in which they are enmeshed and which shape their present Abanillero identity as deeply rooted in the *capacho* era.

Eufemia says nothing about the transformation of her own family's livelihood—indeed, for her, "life has always been the same." This contrasts sharply with a graphic remark made by one older woman who had worked making *capacho* and later shoes for them. When asked about her former employer she snorted, hoisted up her arm, took a deep breath and said, "She can smell my pit!" This colorful expression might mean something like, "She can kiss my ass," but the remark implies more than retrospective resentment and contempt. For what Eufemia would smell is *cleanliness*. The specific class relationship between the two women changed (one no longer works for the other), and Eufemia's star has fallen; the smell of cleanliness is *not* the smell of sweat, of *not* being forced by grinding poverty to toil "from birth until life closes."

Transformations in the local political economy have led to a comparable standard of living for working people and their former patrons/exploiters. While Reinaldo's refrain throughout our conversations was "We were the *strongest* ones here," a common refrain especially among women who made *capacho* and/or sewed shoes was, "We are the all the *same* here now," with "we" including the former boss. This "sameness" is not, however, synonymous with "collective" so much as it occludes a history of belonging marked by differentiation. First, the *capacho* industry divided the town along class lines, and then the breakup of the *capacho* industry forced a population with a more or less unified work experience (albeit highly classed and gendered) into a wide variety of livelihood responses. Within this heterogeneity there is a sense of sameness that, expressed positively, arises from nobody being elevated too high, or negatively, from generalized poverty. In neither sense, however, does this sense of general equality translate into any optimism with repect to the possibility of success for collective undertaking that would make Abanilla an "active" community in the sense discussed earlier.

A significant element in this experience of leveling is the effect of the modern welfare state, through such projects as minimum wage benefits, social security benefits, unemployment, disability, and retirement and veterans' pensions, which are vitally important to Abanilla's late capitalist political economy. The local experiences described lead to dissonant views on what constitute legitimate claims on the state. A point of some distress to Eufemia is that she will get, upon retirement, no more for the ten years she contributed social security payments than anybody else, and that Reinaldo gets the same monthly amount regardless of the twenty-eight long years he contributed to the plan. Even more distressing to her are "sick people who are collecting without having paid anything . . . no payments, and when they're sick the state helps them out." Implicit in this complaint is a belief that not all claims on the state are equal, and that some citizens (like herself), with a particular historical relation to the state, have a greater right to make such claims.

When explaining the complicated system of rotating social security payments they used to avoid contributing for all employees, Reinaldo was adamant: "Most older people in Abanilla have collected retirement pensions, medical pensions through manufacturers who would declare that they'd been working for them . . . many are collecting *from me.*" In Reinaldo's view he, personally, continues to pay these people. Thus, the common identity as experienced in encounters with neighbors—the basis of his social claims on the community—is simultaneously constructed with reference to the state's definitions of entitlement, and to former local relations of *capacho* production. In this way he is able to shift (for himself) the location of what was paid and received in both space and time.

Conclusion

I have sought to show that the implications for claims and belonging that are constitutive of identity vary significantly depending on where one stood in Abanilla's changing social relations of production. This has been an exploration of how community and state are experienced in a historically and spatially contingent manner, giving rise to locally specific ideas about social membership. I use the notion of community as a place with a shared sense of cultural similarity and local contiguity, where processes of exclusion and othering give rise to identity. In addition, I use Williams's notion of an "active" community to add a dimension of collective agency, necessary for making membership claims. My underlying concern is to explain the individuating effect of successive modernizing state projects. To do this, I suggest how certain discourses of integration emanating from a transforming Spanish state contradict the material realities of daily life, and in so doing undermine (active) community.

Reinaldo and Eufemia are discursively and historically constructed subjects who were able, in particular spatial and historical circumstances, to negotiate a shift in livelihood following the shift in Franco's modernizing state project, and reinvent themselves as entrepreneurs under liberal capitalism. Their transformation leaves them turning increasingly to the welfare state for an idiom of belonging and identity. What is absent in Reinaldo and Eufemia's narrative is any reference to the changing political context of their lives. The Francoist state's regulation of the *capacho* industry, and the way that it overwhelmingly shaped local culture and defined Abanilla as a collectivity, is glossed over in a single remark by Eufemia: "It was all very organized." Their local claims to social membership are not as enthusiastically embraced by all Abanilleros, except in cultural forums such as the annual fiestas to which Reinaldo and Eufemia are deeply connected. On a discursive level, in the arena of ritual, collective community is reimagined and expressed. On the level of practice, however, conflicting histories undermine active community.

The people of Abanilla express pessimism about the possibility of forging collective undertakings. They share, it is true, a marked sense of cultural similarity deriving from a nearly universal participation in a single production process, and they share a strong sense of belonging to that particular place. But the very internal processes of differentiation and exclusion that have configured contemporary identities carry within them a legacy of mistrust and contradiction. Following the end of the Civil War, the relations of *capacho* production in Abanilla were constructed as collective by the state's ideology of peasant sovereignty, but this ideological construct was contradicted by the material reality of most people's lives. After the collapse of the *capacho* industry, insufficiencies of water and land, combined with urban industrial policies, forced the population to either migrate or adopt highly idiosyncratic, fragmented livelihood strategies, a situation that continues and is intensified with national, regional, and local responses to global capitalist development. It remains to be seen whether current state projects will contibute to the emergence of a more (or even less) active community in Abanilla.

Notes

1. I conducted fieldwork in Abanilla from September 1993 to November 1994. Names have been changed to preserve the anonymity of these informants.

2. *Capacho* is the large, flat-bottomed basket through which raw crushed olives are pressed to produce oil. *Capachos* are handmade from *esparto,* a tough natural fiber similar to sisal.

3. See also Striffler (this volume) for a discussion of the contradictory relation of people to their history.

4. The 1995 unemployment rate for Murcia is estimated at 22.2 percent, but for this non-agricultural hinterland the figure is closer to 42 percent. (*The Economist*, Dec. 14, 1996).

5. The shift in Franco's economic policies from agriculture to industry has been extensively discussed by social historians. See for example: Payne 1962; Brandes 1976; Martinez Alier 1971; Cole 1977; and Albarracín 1987.

CHAPTER 10

The Italian Post-Communist Left and Unemployment

Finding a New Position on Labor

Michael Blim

To borrow a phrase from Eric Hobsbawm, it has been an age of extremes. Political economy, first fashioned by that doughty Scot Adam Smith and refashioned as an instrument of social change by Marx, has succumbed to the bipolar malady that seems characteristic of our times. For Soviets and Maoists, a messianic politics combined with state terror could transform economies and reform human nature. For convinced capitalist economists and politicians, economics reduced to the operation of markets could remove the need for politics. Furthermore, both parties, by their fanatical stress of one variable in the equation at the expense of the other, have left us in the sorry mess where their linkage seems an imputation rather than a necessity. Much of the political and intellectual work of progressives is now spent providing the justification for putting the two together again.

Though anthropology has shown a dismaying tendency to quit the field of political encounter in the midst of what one might call the foundational phase of the arguments by devoting its energies to empty universals (as in, it is both politics and markets) or witless empiricism (as in, that's not how they do it among the BaoBao), which Geertz (1973, 16) rightly excoriated as going around the world to count the cats in Zanzibar, there are other options available to us. I propose here to provide one from among many alternatives: namely, to analyze in some detail how progressive intellectuals and politicians are attempting to rejoin politics and economics in solving the problem of unemployment, one of the ailments most endemic to modern capitalism and most resistant to cure. The rich and varied progressive politics of contemporary Italy provides an ideal listening post for discovering how leftists of differing persuasions are refashioning a viable political economy in practice.

For the Left, treating unemployment as a function of inadequate demand, as liberals and conservative social democrats since Keynes have, is decidedly too simple a matter. As Western economies floundered from the mid-seventies onward, neither robust Keynesian pump priming nor its reactionary supply-side counterpart best represented in Thatcher-Reaganism has solved the problem of long-term unemployment. As Brenner (1998) argues, even the so-called American solution of deregulation and lower-paid, flexible service employment only "solves" the unemployment problem by creating more social inequality and a lower standard of living for the majority of American households.

Not only is the problem far from resolution, but the causes for persistent unemployment remain highly debatable. At base, as shown below, contemporary Left politicians and intellectuals, to use Italy as a sounding board, either believe that advanced capitalist economies are ineluctably tied to exploiting labor for super-profits, and thus battles should be fought to wrest more of the value workers produce from capitalists, at home as well as in lands where capitalists pursue cheaper labor, or, they believe in contrast that capitalism will no longer create full employment in advanced capitalist societies but will pick and choose those whom it rewards with increasingly scarce employment opportunities. From this perspective, the employment pie needs re-dividing so as to provide better entry prospects for economically marginalized young people and women in advanced capitalist societies such as Italy.

Thus, how one decides the causes of contemporary unemployment and what one proposes as solutions define the current reconstruction of political economy by the Left. Study and debate of these issues also reveals how the Left remains divided in practice as it tries to field solutions where it currently holds some political power. I propose here to look over the shoulders of Italian Left intellectuals and politicians and seek what can be learned about some of our common dilemmas.

These important policy issues acquired a personal dimension over the course of eighteen years of personal contact through fieldwork among shoe workers and small-scale shoe-producing firms in the Marche region of central Italy. I had become habituated to a pattern of labor deployment whose very intensity gave the region a virtual zero rate of unemployment—except, that is, when one factored in the employment prospects of anyone who had achieved the equivalent of a high school degree or better. These persons found themselves overqualified for the local labor market and unable to crack the national labor markets for skilled workers that were occupied by middle-aged, tenured, male workers. In the Marche region's largely industrial economy of the eighties, these unemployed and underemployed but educated workers merited mention, but not extensive treatment ethnographically (see Blim 1990). With the passage of time, and Italy's entrance into a more service-dominated, postindustrial economy, these workers—or nonworkers—and their plight have become a national policy preoccupation as well as a significant segment of local economies of the sort I had studied in the Marche region.

The Italian Left and Achieving Social Normality

Un paese normale, a normal country. To paraphrase Massimo D'Alema, the first postcommunist prime minister of Italy and former general secretary of Italy's *Democratici di Sinistra,* the largest party of Italy's democratic left (DS), a normal country is what Italians long for, and according to D'Alema, what the postcommunist Left should help bring to pass. Neither restorationist nor revolutionary, the call to normality actually strikes a progressive chord among constituencies of the Italian center and Left (D'Alema 1995). I intend to show that the postsocialist, postcommunist political parties in Italy confront difficult choices ahead in creating their vision of *un paese normale.* In particular, they face the hard job of fostering full employment in an economic environment that has fallen well short of the goal since the late seventies, and they must meet the equally difficult imperative of redesigning a welfare state that takes account of this new reality. It is hoped that the issues raised here can shed some light on the larger dialogue about "what's left" for the Italian Left in this time of turbulent economic and social change.

To accomplish these goals, I examine the dimensions of the unemployment problem in Italy and examine how the Italian welfare state addresses it. I also show how the discourse among the parties of the Italian Left reveals the possibilities as well as limits of the progressive imagination at this critical juncture in the social life of Italy as a Western capitalist society.

Italy, like the rest of Europe, suffers from chronic unemployment. In fact, unemployment in Italy has risen steadily since the worldwide recession of the mid-seventies, and has remained in the double digits since the mid-eighties. Throughout the nineties, it has hovered stubbornly around 12 percent, which is usually a point or two above the European average (Reyneri 1996; *New York Times,* January 4, 1999, C13).

But Italian unemployment has its peculiar characteristics. First, in contrast to the experience of other EU countries, Italy's unemployment rate varies greatly by region. Unemployment in the Italian south, for instance, has run at no less than twice the national rate since the mid-eighties; recent studies put southern youth unemployment at 60 percent (*La Repubblica,* May 28, 1998, 6; Reyneri 1997, 68–70; *Economist,* November 8, 1997, Italy Survey, 5). Second, the majority of the unemployed consists of women and young people less than twenty-nine years of age in search of their first job. Though women have higher unemployment rates in most Western European countries including Italy, Italy's generally lower rate of labor participation especially penalizes women. Unemployment among young people under the age of twenty-nine in Italy is perhaps a more unusual phenomenon: they compose 70 percent of the unemployed in Italy, as compared with 30 percent in France and 45 percent in Great Britain. Equally odd, 90 percent of Italy's young job seekers have never had any prior job experience; in contrast, only 30 percent of the young in France and 40 percent in Great Britain and Germany looking for posts lacked job experience (Reyneri 1996, 71).

The other side of the Italian employment equation is that middle-aged men have the lowest unemployment rate of any group in Italy—and with the exception of Portugal and Greece, of any group of men in Western Europe. Reyneri's analysis of unemployment by age cohorts for the European Union's eleven nations in 1991 shows that the unemployment for Italian men between the ages of forty and forty-nine drops to 1.8 percent, and rises only slightly to 2.5 percent for men aged fifty-five to fifty-nine. For the same period, 24 percent of Italian males between fourteen and twenty-four years were unemployed. No other country features so radical a discrepancy in the employment prospects of young and old men as Italy does (Reyneri 1996, 133–136).

The reasons, Reyneri argues, are several. First, new jobs in Italy are scarcer; occupants happen to be predominantly male and middle-aged. Second, because assuming personnel is a relatively rare event, firms tend to choose people with job experience based on the belief that the experienced will be more productive and trustworthy. Third, jobs in Italy in many sectors of the Italian economy are relatively secure, and thus the chances for turnover for those who are employed are slight when compared with the rest of Europe (Reyneri 1996, 137–152).

The resulting social structure is also distinctive. Households remain united much longer, and are much more reliant upon the earnings of the household head. Considerable attention has been paid to the notion of an Italian *famiglia lunga,* where 90 percent of the young between sixteen and twenty-four still live at home (Piccone Stella 1997). Comparable figures for European neighbors range from 47 percent in Great Britain and 60 percent among the French. Also, dual wage-earning couples, in contrast to other EU countries, are found less often in Italian households. Thus, given the bias in the labor market for older males, many more Italian households proportionately are largely or exclusively dependent upon incomes generated by male household heads (Reyneri 1996, 148–150; Paci 1996).

Legacies of the Italian Welfare State

If one accepts the premise that the ultimate rationale for the Italian welfare state is political reward and rule, then, sociologist Massimo Paci argues (1996, 203–214; cf. Pizzorno 1974), the process reduces to two fundamental and finally complementary logics. On the one hand, emphasis is placed upon supporting classes that acquire a more corporate rather than simply categorical awareness of themselves, and to encourage them to intertwine their destinies with the state and its political regime. In this way, segments of society such as professionals, white-collar workers, and small business people find themselves and each other through the process of demanding and benefiting from state recognition and largesse. On the other hand, since the system is by nature particularistic and discriminating in character, its rewards are rationalized as assistance rather than the fulfillment of rights, and its process is clientelistic.

The historical record would seem to support Paci's hypothesis. The Italian welfare system is not the product of progressive social reform, but instead owes its origins to the desires of the post-Unification elites at the turn of the twentieth century to secure political consensus for capitalist development and for the new Italian state. The elite objective was to enhance social and political control over workers by tying their fates to the state, while gaining cross-class allies among the rising middle classes. In 1898, the state created compulsory pensions for the work-related disabled and sponsored voluntary pensions for the elderly and the disabled. Work-related disability pensions were extended in 1917 to agricultural workers, small farmers, and sharecroppers; the same occupational categories along with industrial workers were granted the right to participate in voluntary schemes covering old age, general disability, and unemployment in 1919. Health benefits were provided through state insurance agencies, *Casse mutue,* organized once more beginning in 1929 strictly by occupational category (Ascoli 1987, 283–287).

The modern system of unemployment compensation adheres to the same pattern. When large industrial firms move to lay off large numbers of workers, managements in consultation with worker assemblies file for wage subsidy support with *La Cassa Integrazione dei Guadagni,* the state agency that provides furloughed workers with income assistance typically equivalent to 90 percent of their wages. Benefits have been extended by legislation through the eighties and nineties for periods of up to ten years, but in practice, they are unlimited in duration. These protections do not apply to workers employed in small and medium-sized enterprises who receive a maximum benefit of 25 percent of their former salaries for six months. Unlike other EU countries, no general public assistance is available to workers beyond the six-month unemployment benefit (Reyneri 1996, 209). The cumulative impact of this system on contemporary labor markets is discussed below.

Thus, Italy's welfare system, in toto, divides Italians into two kinds of social strata, and does it two times. First, there are the included and the excluded: the needs of some are amply rewarded, while the needs of others in similar settings are ignored. Second, among the included, differentiation proceeds anew: some have better pensions and benefits than others, as distinguished by their occupational and professional rank, or by virtue of the size and importance of their place of employment.

A profligate Italian welfare state might be something devoutly to be wished for, especially if one stands outside its circle of beneficence. When compared with EU partners, however, Italian social expenditures at the rate of 20 percent of gross domestic product are normal and roughly equivalent to Germany's outlay and only 3 percent behind those of France. How the money is spent, however, differs significantly. Two-thirds in Italy is spent on pensions for the widowed and the elderly. The remaining one-third supports employment benefits, but the lion's share of these funds go to those regularly employed in large industries or in the public sector. In contrast, EU counterparts spend half of their social expenditures on income maintenance and various forms of unemployment compensation (Rossi 1998, 102–104).

The Left(s) Respond(s)

For the political Left in Italy, employment has long been considered a fundamental human right.[1] But the mission of the center-Left since its victory in April 1996 has been to steer Italy into conformity with the norms necessary for continued economic and monetary integration with the European Union. Italy's budget deficits, national debt, and inflation rate ran very roughly at twice the average of its northern EU neighbors. It still has the highest unfunded pension liability in Europe.

Yet the Left found itself newly divided. Since 1991, the former Communist Party (PCI) has been split in two, becoming *Partito Democratico della Sinistra* (PDS, and later *Democratici della Sinistra* or DS) and *Rifondazione Comunista* (RF).[2] The Communist fissure reflected an unsuccessful attempt by the reformist, social democratic majority of the party to convince a minority consisting of a mix of Marxist intellectuals, traditionalists, and more pro-Soviet comrades to come along into a new postcommunist world. The majority offered new connections with reemergent social democratic parties in France, Britain, and Germany, as well as an escape from political entrapment precipitated by communist catastrophe in the East. Not incidentally, such a move would also position the PDS to become a party of government in a center-Left majority for the first time since World War II.[3]

The split in the communist movement was quite significant. By the political elections of 1992, the PDS slumped to 16 percent of the national vote, while the *Rifondazione* had picked up nearly 6 percent of the vote. In the last political elections of 1996, the PDS had bounced back to 21 percent of the national vote; *Rifondazione* under its secretary Fausto Bertinotti also improved its standing, polling nearly 9 percent of the total. Importantly, though, the PDS became a party of government and took ministerial posts in the center-Left coalition led by Romano Prodi. *Rifondazione* refused to join the government, but its external support in the Camera of Deputies in Parliament provided Prodi with his slender governing majority.

From the outset, the Prodi government was pushed to fulfill two seemingly contradictory goals. The first was to raise taxes, reduce debt, and stifle economic demand sufficiently to enable Italy to squeak by the Maastricht conditions for monetary union. The majority of the government including the PDS claimed this as the first priority. At the same time, because former Communists of both stripes comprised a significant segment of its majority, the government faced demands that it stimulate economic growth and emphasize job creation. *Rifondazione* became increasingly restive with government policies that seemed more congenial to business than to worker interests. Fiscal austerity, pension reform, privatization, and sound money caused consternation and discomfort in the ranks. With the French socialist Lionel Jospin's victory in June 1997, *Rifondazione's* position hardened: something had to be given up to justify their continued support of Prodi.

Job creation and economic development of the Italian South became the key demands, and the reduction of the working week from thirty-nine to thirty-five hours a week for the RF became the elixir that would revitalize the lethargic Italian economy. French passage of thirty-five-hour week legislation provided added incentive, though the trade union confederations and the large industrial employers represented by their trade organization, the *Confindustria,* had been discussing the possibility intermittently for several years. Even as the Prodi government took office in May 1996, with its mandate to facilitate Italian entry into the new EU monetary system at all cost, pressures from all of its Left coalition partners pressed it move ahead on job creation. In fact, Prodi, in asking for his first vote of confidence, announced his government's desire to create new jobs in cooperation with the unions and big business. Astutely at the same time, Sergio Cofferati, head of the *Confederazione Generale Italiana del Lavoro* (CGIL), the most powerful and politically progressive of the three general labor confederations, suggested that labor might trade increased flexibility in the workplace for increased jobs through work-week reductions. Cofferati envisioned a gradual and contractually negotiated process that would achieve work-week reduction over time, and the government passed a law that provided financial incentives for experimentation by firms and unions with reduced working hours. Through *concertazione*,[4] many in the unions and in the government (including the PDS) believed progress could be made (*Corriere della Sera,* May 23, 1996, 15; July 2, 1997, 18; January 18, 1998, 6).

The Prodi government's Europe-pleasing austerity program and struggles for primacy among its Left coalition partners soon transformed an issue with some corporatist appeal indeed into a political test of wills. By February 1997, the Left erupted in controversy over the government's commitment to job creation. D'Alema, then PDS general secretary, placed the employment issue squarely within the context of welfare state reform: the present system, he charged, only covered "older men who live in the north." For D'Alema, the state should be using welfare to provide opportunities for women and unemployed youth, the weakest players in Italian labor market. Furthermore, D'Alema argued that in the face of seemingly intractable problems in generating successful development in the South, national labor contracts should not preclude local negotiations for lower and more variable wages. He also challenged unions to take up the cause of unemployed youth who were excluded from the normal system of protections as workers and citizens (*Corriere della Sera,* February 11, 1997, 3).

The fallout was immediate. Bertinotti, the *Rifondazione* leader, saw it as another sign that D'Alema and the PDS supported the process of capitalist modernization with its recourse to free markets, privatization, and attacks on the welfare state (*Corriere della Sera,* February 19, 1997). Cofferati of the CGIL was more outraged: It was "humiliating," he charged at the national congress of the PDS, "to argue on the left with those who accuse you of conservatism, while they point to Ireland and Korea as shining models" of flexibility (*Corriere della Sera,* February 22, 1997, 5).

D'Alema reply is instructive. The welfare state should become "more egalitarian, less corporatist, and less based on the model of the adult male worker," and should be "inclusive so as to offer the same opportunities to all." Addressing directly Cofferati and Bertinotti, D'Alema described Italy as he saw it:

> This is a closed society in the organization of careers, in entering the professions, and in the academic world. It is a society organized against the young.
> (*Corriere della Sera,* February 23, 1997, 3)

D'Alema called for lower wages to stimulate job creation for youth in the South, and set off a firestorm of criticism from his Left—so much so that he partly retracted his position, claiming he was speaking of isolated rather than general instances in the South. Cofferati responded that wages in the *Mezzogiorno* were already 25 percent below the national average, and high unemployment persisted. Even government centrists such as Carlo Ciampi and Tiziano Treu, finance and labor ministers respectively, disavowed D'Alema's position, agreeing with Cofferati that wages in the South were already depressed, and that a solution based on wage differentials by region was simplistic (*La Repubblica,* May 28, 6; *L'Unita,* May 29, 1998, 9).

For Bertinotti, the lower Southern wage proposal was another, more dramatic instance of D'Alema's apostasy. His ideas were disastrous for the Left, for unions, and for the country. What is more, Bertinotti argued:

> The thing that strikes me the most is D'Alema's position is a complete adoption of neo-liberalism. . . . If the object is the pursuit of the lowest possible wage, explain to me why an entrepreneur would stop at Calabria or Sicilia, and not go instead to Morocco or Romania. . . . The difference between us and the DS is the same that once divided the left from the conservatives. (*La Repubblica,* May 28, 1998, 6)

With rhetoric fast rending the majority's minimal cohesion, the Prodi government moved quickly to incorporate its concessions to the *Rifondazione* into its ongoing employment policy. Following the agreement with Bertinotti, a new government agency, *Sviluppo Italia,* was created to facilitate Southern economic development and improve market access for Southern firms. In addition, finance minister Ciampi and minister for social solidarity Livia Turco of the DS announced the implementation of a two-year experimental subsidy to the poor of *Lire* 500,000 a month (approximately US$300). Because 70 percent of Italy's poor reside in the South, it was treated as part of the government's Southern development project. While a potentially interesting step toward a guaranteed annual income, the "solidarity subsidy," as it is called, also obliges recipients to participate in programs designed to facilitate reentry into everyday life and the world of work (*La Repubblica,* June 12, 1998, 29; *L'Unita,* June 13, 1998, 2).

Yet these moves failed to placate Bertinotti. His opposition to the 1999 budget alienated him from the majority and split *Rifondazione*. On October 9, 1998, with half of *Rifondazione* abstaining from support of the government, Prodi lost a vote of confidence by one vote. By October 15, he gave up all hope of forming another government. On October 21, Massimo D'Alema was sworn in as the first postcommunist premier of Italy.

As Gilbert's analysis of the DS leader's tendency to identify politics with parties, and the state with the leading role in civil society rightly suggests (1998), D'Alema was not one who could have been expected to sit by and count the blessings of government until the legislative term ran out. Once again, he launched the provocation of labor flexibility—this time as premier with less than three months in office. D'Alema called for reform of the *Statuto dei Lavoratori,* the nation's fundamental labor law passed in 1970 as the fruit of years of labor agitation up to and including the factory occupations during the "Hot Autumn" of 1969. The statute, he argued, hurt job creation in small firms, because the full legal protections due workers were invoked once a firm had assumed at least fifteen workers. He proposed adjusting upward the limit under which small firms could escape the full force of the labor law (*La Repubblica,* January 27, 1999, 4).

Again, as before, outrage. Cofferati: "The fundamental rights of working people can never be used as an instrument to encourage economic development. . . . The idea of suspending or modifying these rights is profoundly mistaken and regressive . . ." Bertinotti:"Not even an old Christian Democratic or center-right government would have risked trying this . . ." Even prominent DS parliamentarians rejected D'Alema's proposal (*La Repubblica,* January 28, 1999, 2).

D'Alema's response seems patterned by now: "We shouldn't worry only about those who are already protected. . . . When we speak of workers' rights, we often forget that many workers don't enjoy these rights. . . . I want to open the way for more jobs . . ." (*La Stampa,* January 29, 1998).

Evaluating Differing Alternatives

The historical exclusion of the communist Left from Italian governments since World War II has produced a set of conditioned responses that figure importantly in the Left's calculus of politics. On the one hand, there is the desire to rule, and to do what is necessary to govern, given that the Left by no means has the backing of a majority of the voters, nor is likely to obtain an absolute majority in the foreseeable future. On the other hand, there is the impulse for opposition bred of years in the minority, which disposes its possessors to fight and hold on to whatever gains can be gotten from the political system they are convinced is permanently tilted against the interests of the less powerful.

Good politics also requires a strategic sense of where one's society is going. What are society's prospects? How does one identify the greater good in midstream? And how does one draw society nearer the greater good over time?

In these times, at least, the Panglossian view typically belongs to the Right. For the Left, there is the preoccupation with the capitalist global economy, by turns destructive, demanding, and dismissive of peoples and societies around the world. Italian leftists see a slow-growing Italian economy, chronic high unemployment, and an expensive and inefficient state apparatus that seems to get in the way of economic growth. Taking a longer view, they would see a country with a declining birth rate, declining labor union membership, and declining labor militancy. They would see an economy that attracts less capital from the outside than any other EU country, but for Greece and Portugal. They would find a national capital class that has invested more abroad than at home every year since 1990 (*Economist,* November 8, 1997, Survey of Italy; *Financial Times,* December 16, 1998, I–X). In short, Left observers would see the same society that barely gained entrance into the European monetary union and now lives on with the sufferance of the EU minders.

It is argued here that the conflicting designs of the Italian Left, however, also reflect reactions to the deeper signs and portents of the changing world economy. Distilled in the political visions of the DS and D'Alema and the *Rifondazione* of Bertinotti are two contrasting expectations of where capitalist economies in Europe are going. To evaluate their employment programs, one needs to assess the degree to which they sensibly stack up to a reasonable diagnosis of where an Italian economy will find itself over the next quarter-century. This finding in turn rests upon a judicious assessment of the future direction of the world economy.

At the risk of some oversimplification, there are two fundamental approaches to understanding the world economy from a Left, political-economic perspective. The first is what might be called the standard view of the global capitalist economy. As richly developed most recently by Robert Brenner (1998), this view advances a Marxist theory of crisis whereby capitalist productive forces simply outrun themselves in a spree of overproduction. With some differences, David Harvey (1989) and Giovanni Arrighi (1994) stress the restless, crisis-ridden character of capitalism and its constant search for higher profits achieved through the exploitation of cheaper, proletarianized labor. The second, featured most prominently in the work of Manuel Castells (1996–1998) is an upgraded reprise of the dual economy hypothesis: namely, that capitalism organizes outposts of exploitation throughout the world economy, but excludes many more people than it involves in its work. Hence, whole populations or population segments are marginalized, rather than proletarianized in the more conventional Marxist sense implied by the first vision of world capitalism as we know it.

The two Italian Lefts reflect the different aspects of these approaches to global capitalist change. The "new" or "ex-new" Left of D'Alema in rhetoric as well as in orientation is arguing that it is the excluded—not the classically exploited—who are the future losers in the Italy of the next century. Youth and women, likely but not exclusively from the Italian South, are becoming a lost generation of nonworkers and therefore of the nonentitled.

The other Left of Bertinotti, perhaps more reliably "old" Left, views capitalist exploitation as the enemy and proletarianization the result of worker engagement with the capitalist class. Like the ex-trade unionist he is, Bertinotti sees "reform" of labor markets, "flexible" wages, contracts, and the like, as give-backs of money and rights that have been wrested from the bosses. It amounts to part of the workers' share of the surplus value; the Left should seek more, not less in the tri-cornered negotiations between state, labor, and capital.

Hence, by Bertinotti's lights, a mandatory thirty-five-hour work week signifies more value for the worker for less labor, which equals less objective exploitation. In theory, it should also lead to more jobs for the excluded. Better to push "the system" to fund public jobs in the South than allow capital to offer lower wages to the worker, and thus increase their rate of exploitation. Bertinotti may be faulted for tactics, but the *Rifondazione* advocacy for the thirty-five-hour week without pay reduction makes sense. The aggravated European economic slowdown is part of a larger secular trend of long-term deceleration of economic growth in Western capitalist societies and Japan. The United States has been the only economy over the decade to add jobs in any substantial numbers, but has done it by letting markets shift employment from manufacturing to service sectors. Because of lower productivity and lower initial wages, American workers have lost economic standing, the U.S. economic expansion notwithstanding (Brenner 1998, 137–156). So, the outlook is not terribly optimistic for a European or Italian economic reprise that would really provide full employment—without living standards decline.

Thus, the equation of less work for the same money has an appeal. Given Italian capital's tendency to invest more outside than inside the country, it probably cannot be implemented by diktat from Rome.[5] Cofferati's proposal to make thirty-five-hour weeks part of flexibility negotiations between labor and management makes more sense given the less than hopeful prognosis for full employment recovery in Europe. In this game of relative winners and absolute losers, Italian labor has a strong interest, Cofferati believes, in seeing wages and productivity increase, so that Italian industry can compete more successfully in the world arena.

D'Alema's labor flexibility notions, on closer examination, seem less than salutary. If the Brenner-Arrighi-Harvey synthesis used here is accurate,[6] that is, that the advanced capitalist economies are rapidly and irretrievably losing ground to increased labor exploitation in the developing world, then it is unlikely that regional and youth wage differentials will attract much capital investment to create new jobs. Existing jobs might become "cheaper" for capital, but personal income from wages would suffer, and thus the standard of living of Italian workers in the aggregate would suffer.

The objective of including the excluded in Italian labor markets is a fundamental challenge to the Italian economy and politics, but the matter is not addressed easily. With the onset of the European monetary union, demand management by individual states and central banks is no longer possible. An expansive fiscal policy is largely proscribed by Italy's continuing struggle to conform to European monetary system norms. Monetary policy-making authority, once the province of the Bank of Italy, is now made by the European Central Bank.

However, successive governments over the past decade have created through law and regulation new instruments and incentives to encourage employment of women, the handicapped, and younger workers (Reyneri 1996, 359–377). In addition, the "Pachetto Treu," a series of labor market measures passed by the Prodi government in June 1997, set out for the first time (and with the consent of the union confederations) legal norms for temporary, limited contractual and part-time employment. This Italian experiment in "regulated flexibility," as it was called, countenances enormous changes in Italian labor markets, and implementation has barely begun (Deaglio 1998, 155–158). D'Alema's points notwithstanding, it seems prudent at this juncture to question the degree to which new legislation is needed. Perhaps, as Cofferati suggests, the unions and management might work creatively together on a case-by-case or regional basis, to unleash the possibilities contained in the new reform measures (cf. Locke 1996).

Instead, the Italian Left might wish to speed along the normalization of Italy's employment policies, inasmuch as Italy's economy generally is being "normalized" within the framework of the European common currency and economic institutions. This means that Italy needs to devote a higher percentage of its domestic product to funds for unemployment insurance, training, and education, and to deploy those monies more universally. I would argue that it is once more the historical job of the Left to promote a set of universal guarantees, and to move the state to be the guarantor.

As noted above, the problem is not the lack of resources. The total proportion of the national product devoted to social expenditures is near the middle of the EU average (Rossi 1998, 102–104).[7] The problem is with how the monies are distributed. Democratizing unemployment insurance is an obvious starting point. Combining fairer and more universal distribution of unemployment benefits with an expansion and substantial upgrading of the "solidarity subsidy" would provide postwar Italy with its first social safety net—and one no longer reliant upon the iniquitous pension system to do the job.

Given the challenges of a crisis-ridden world economy in which Italy finds itself increasingly at competitive disadvantage, a new virtuous circle will not be easily formed. The tenuous hold on power of the succession of center-Left governments limits the capacity of the Italian Left for policy innovation. Perhaps the return to power of the social democratic Left throughout the EU can provide some support for new initiatives on the part of the Italian left. For the skeptical Bertinotti, little good can be expected: "Our center-left governments must always appear more royal than the king, more liberal than the liberals" (*La Repubblica,* February 16, 1999, 6).

In the end, though, the Italian Left can undertake reforms of the pension system, lower the government deficit, help drop inflation to a thirty year low, get Italy into the European monetary union, and even talk their allies in the unions into becoming more "flexible" in future labor contracts. It remains for footloose capital to decide to stay and participate in the Italian economy. After reviewing the government's accomplishments, an exasperated Carlo Ciampi, the centrist architect of Italy's fiscal recovery and current President of the Republic, demanded of the top industrialists in Italy: "What are you waiting for? If you don't invest now, when do you think you ever will?" (*La Repubblica,* February 2, 1999, 2)

Notes

1. The Communist Party manifesto approved at the 17th Congress, September, 1986, reported in *Tesi, Programma, Statuto: I Documenti Approvati dal 17 Congresso del PCI*

(Roma: Editrice L'Unita, 1987, 20–21), is typical: "We reaffirm the right to work as a fundamental personal right, with the knowledge that work for all, men and women, is the measure of the validity and the democratic character of every act of government in a modern society." For a brief summary of the Left's activities on behalf of employment since World War II, see Michael Salvati, "La sfida politica di una politica per l'occupazione," *Interessi e ideali: Inerventi sul programma del nuovo PCI* (Milano: Feltrinelli, 1990, 131–167).

2. The PDS became the *Democratici della Sinistra* (DS) in an attempt to reach out to former socialists and other fragments of the Left in 1998.

3. See Kertzer (1997) for an excellent analysis of the events leading to the formation of the PDS.

4. *Concertazione* describes the process whereby the state mediates management and labor conflicts for what is perceived as the greater good. It is a term that has gained currency over the past half-dozen years or so, starting with the elimination of the *scala mobile*, the mandated annual cost of living increase, through 1992 negotiations between the national labor confederations and big business conducted by the Amato government. See Braun (1995) for a thorough discussion of the reprise of corporatist consensus seeking.

5. In fact, Giorgio Fossa, president of the *Confindustria*, has already threatened to launch a referendum against a mandatory thirty-five-hour law (*La Repubblica*, February 2, 1999, 2).

6. There are significant differences in their positions, but they are being combined here for heuristic purposes.

7. OECD's (1999) data base for 1995, for instance, shows that Italy's public expenditures on education at 4.7 percent of GDP and 9 percent of government expenditures is below those of France's at 6.1 percent and 11.1 percent respectively, but are virtually identical to those of Germany at 4.8 percent and 9.5 percent respectively.

CHAPTER 11

The Language of Contention in Liberal Ecuador

A. Kim Clark

This chapter asks how, from the perspective of an anthropological political economy sensitive to material and symbolic processes, we might go about the study of "national culture" or a national "community" in a nation as deeply divided along lines of class, ethnicity, and region as Ecuador was in the early twentieth century (and, indeed, continues to be). This problem was brought home to me when, while carrying out the research for this analysis, I responded to people's questions about what I was studying with what seemed to be a convenient shortcut: I was studying the historical construction of Ecuadorian national culture. They invariably pointed out the obvious: Ecuador does not have a shared national culture, nor does its population participate in a unified national community. However, while the concept of "national community" seems to suggest shared interests or identity, there are alternative ways to conceptualize community. Gavin Smith has suggested that we rethink membership in a community as indicating not shared interests or identity, but rather, the process of "being engaged in the same argument" (1991, 195). While he refers to the contentious production of culture in a Peruvian peasant community, I have found it useful to extend this notion to the analysis of a national community. Thus, this chapter aims not to establish the common cultural characteristics of Ecuadorians, but rather to analyze common participation by Ecuadorians in a series of national cultural processes, in their material context. The concept of hegemony is central to understanding these processes.

Roseberry has proposed that rather than equate hegemony with ideological consensus, we should use the concept of hegemonic process:

> *not* to understand consent but to understand struggle, the ways in which the words, images, symbols, forms, organizations, institutions, and movements used by subordinate populations to talk about, understand, confront, accommodate themselves to, or resist their domination are shaped by the process of domination itself. What hegemony constructs, then, is not a shared ideology but a common material and meaningful framework for living through, talking about, and acting upon social orders characterized by domination. That

common material and meaningful framework is, in part, discursive, a common language or way of talking about social relationships that sets out the central terms around which and in terms of which contestation and struggle can occur. (Roseberry 1994, 360–361)

Roseberry refers to hegemonic process, then, as involving the emergence of an accepted language of contention.[1]

In this chapter I use the concept of a language of contention to examine the development of a shared but contested discursive framework in liberal Ecuador, during the thirty-year period following the Liberal Revolution of 1895. The processes examined below are simultaneously material and symbolic. The emphasis on language does not imply a focus on mere words: rather, it involves the analysis of a discursive formation constituted through material practices, including forms of communication and well-defined—almost ritualized—ways of addressing the state. Overall, I see the relations between different social groups as constituting what E. P. Thompson called a "field-of-force" (1978, 151) in which all social groups in the field were at least partially constrained by the actions, interests, and historically constituted expectations and perceptions of other groups. One of the ways that the room for maneuvering of each group was limited was precisely by their common participation in constituting the shared language of contention, which made certain things possible but at the same time eliminated other possibilities. By analyzing these political and cultural processes in terms of hegemonic projects rather than achievements, our attention is directed both to their successes, always temporary, and to their points of frailty and rupture (see also Roseberry 1994, 365). The following discussion is rooted in class analysis, but with an understanding that the class interests of various groups are not automatically dictated by their relation to the means of production, but rather that these interests, and people's perceptions of their interests, are forged and modified in their relations with other social groups, suggesting the importance of history, politics, and culture for the analysis of class.

The concept of a language of contention directs us to some of the subtleties through which domination occurred in early-twentieth-century Ecuador, a domination that drew Indians into legitimizing the central state, precisely because the state provided them with tools to deal with some of their most pressing everyday problems (although some of those problems were themselves intensified by state actions; see below). It also points to and explains something that has often been seen by Ecuadorianists as a weakness: the inability of the coastal liberal elite to impose a "pure" and "radical" liberal project, crushing the power of more "traditional" highland landowners and thoroughly transforming society. I see the processes explored below in rather different terms: as the expression of the strength of a hegemonic project that nourished itself on its ability to incorporate the aspirations of other social groups.

In exploring these issues in early-twentieth-century Ecuador, I examine first the processes by which the two main regionally based elite groups came to a tentative agreement on some aspects of a project of national modernization. This fragile consensus was based on an agreement on the importance of "movement" and "connection" for improving Ecuador's economic situation and modernizing the country. Movement and connection became key words in liberal discourse, in the sense that Raymond Williams (1983) uses this term, pointing us toward conflicts over meaning that are obscured through the use of a common term. The meanings of key words are not set, but are articulated and transformed through struggles over specific political-economic and cultural projects. Thus, key words give the appearance of consensus, although they may well evoke different things for different people. Indeed, we will see that movement and connection meant different things to the two dominant groups, reflecting their different social locations, especially in terms of class and region. After exploring elite projects, I go on to examine the ways that this language was adopted and transformed at the local level (based on research in the region of Alausí in the central highland province of Chimborazo). Throughout, we will see that on the one hand, the development of this shared language implied the channeling of conflict in certain directions, but on the other, this certainly did not imply the elimination of conflict.

In Ecuador in the late nineteenth century there were two strong, regionally based dominant classes: one in the highlands, associated with *haciendas* (large estates) producing for local markets and the other on the coast, producing cocoa for the world market on plantations. The coastal elite tended to be liberal, while the highland elite tended to be conservative. Throughout the nineteenth century political power in Ecuador had been concentrated in the highlands, in the hands of large landowners closely linked to the Catholic Church. In 1895, coastal liberals, whose economic power had been growing for some time, based on the expansion of coastal cocoa exports and the declining importance of highland textile production in the late colonial period and the nineteenth century, finally seized political power in the Liberal Revolution. In some sense, different political ideologies were "naturally" rooted in the distinct economic and social terrain of the coast and the highlands. Liberal coastal elites were involved in the import-export trade and production for the world market; thus, they sought fewer barriers to trade. In addition, the coast was much less influenced by the conservative ideology of the Catholic Church: not only did the church own few rural properties on the coast (reducing its economic and political power in the region), but the coast had relatively few churches and even fewer convents or monasteries. Anticlericalism on the coast was also due to the increasing proportion of coastal contributions to church revenues during the nineteenth century, through the payment of tithes that amounted to 10 percent of gross production, which was seen as reducing the competitiveness of Ecuadorian cocoa in international markets (not to mention the profits of coastal planters). In contrast, the highlands tended to favor more protectionist policies, given that the textile industry, long the center of the area's economy, was undermined by British imports after independence. In addition, the Catholic Church was overwhelmingly concentrated in the highlands, where it was one of the largest landowners, where the majority of convents were located, and where members of the clergy were often elected to congress or the senate. The majority of the Ecuadorian population lived in the highlands, a center of dense indigenous population since pre-Columbian times.

While the Liberal Revolution represented the rise of the coastal elite, as they achieved political power to match their increasing economic dominance, this group was nonetheless unable to impose a project that was exclusively in its own interests during the liberal period. This was due in part to the fact that, while the liberals were able to control elections of the executive (among other things, through well-documented electoral fraud), it proved much more difficult to engineer elections to the legislative branch, where the more populous and conservative region of the highlands tended to dominate. As a result, an uneasy working relationship developed between the two dominant classes, creating an atmosphere of competition and tension that had implications for the possibilities open to subaltern groups as well, as we will see.

One of the central projects of the liberal government after 1895 was the construction of a railway between the coastal port of Guayaquil and the highland capital of Quito (the other main project was the separation of church and state). The Guayaquil-Quito Railway held a key position in the formation of a language of contention in liberal Ecuador. In discussions and debates about the railway, a discourse emerged centering on the need to transform the nation through movement and connection. While this language was developed principally in regard to the importance of a railway to stimulate the economy out of its "stagnation," it was increasingly applied to other issues: the need to eliminate "routine" in education, the need to stimulate immigration and the free flow of modern ideas, the need to break down the rigid hierarchies of society (as supported by the Catholic Church), and the need to teach criminals and vagrants the value of work and schoolchildren the value of exercise. The positive values attached to movement and connection were contrasted with stagnation, routine, and backwardness, in public discourse about a wide range of social and political issues. This discourse was developed in political speeches and debates in Congress, cabinet ministers' annual reports, newspaper articles, and scholarly writings. The fact that the railway in particular was of interest to groups in the highlands and coast allowed for the constitution of a general consensus about national renewal among elites from these two regions, and among liberals and conservatives, at the turn of the century. Indeed in general, the discourse of movement, connection, work, and energy as developed around the railway was ambiguous enough to appeal to a broad audience, various components of which could see in this discourse something of interest to them.

In general terms, the language of movement and connection developed around the railway was perfectly appropriate for a nation whose economic prosperity was linked to the movement of a primary product out to the world market. Nonetheless, this product, cocoa, was not moved by the railway; it was produced on the coast and moved to the port of Guayaquil by a system of steamboats on coastal rivers. While railway construction was one of the definitive liberal projects in Ecuador, coastal liberals in fact had some reservations about it: for instance, they objected to the fact that export earnings generated in their region (which were used to guarantee debt payments associated with the railway) were being used for a project that did not benefit their production directly. On the other hand, the agro-export elite of the coast was closely integrated with import interests, and the construction of a railway between the port and the capital did suggest the possibility of selling imported products in the country's interior, which had been very difficult to reach previously (travel between the regions was suspended for several months each year due to landslides, and at other moments was a treacherous two-week journey by mule, which greatly limited interregional trade and transport). The discourse of movement was also engaged by coastal liberals to criticize church control over education, to promote the free circulation of published works and freedom of expression in general, as well as to condemn the institution's resistance to immigration of non-Catholics and its role in reducing the competitive advantage of Ecuadorian cocoa on the international market, as the liberal state carried out a series of controversial policies to separate church and state between 1895 and 1910. However, perhaps most importantly from the perspective of coastal elites, it was hoped that movement and connection would break down the insularity of the highlands and thus stimulate a flow of workers from the highlands toward the coast, and in general the formation of a labor market in order to expand coastal export production. The movement of people, in the form of indigenous workers from the highlands (who made up half or more of the national population in this era), was very much in the interest of coastal plantation owners, since the scarce population of the coastal zone meant that wages there were much higher than in the highlands. The development of the language of movement and connection and the construction of the railway in particular were part of the broader project of coastal elites to transform the highlands to free indigenous labor from the control of highland landowners and to undermine church power, as well as to attain modernity and progress in general.

The movement of indigenous workers toward the coast was not in the interests of the highland landowning elite, whose agricultural estates had always relied on large amounts of Indian labor, working for very low wages or a subsistence plot and bound to the estates through debt peonage and strong ties of paternalism. However, another kind of movement, also to be stimulated by the railway, was very much in their interests. Highland elites were especially attracted to the possibility of forging an internal market, moving highland agricultural and livestock products to the coast by train. With the rise of the coastal cocoa economy and the rapid urban growth of Guayaquil in the late nineteenth and early twentieth centuries, an important market for food staples was created. However, due to the difficulties and high cost of transport from the highlands, the coast was provisioned through imports of food: for instance, it was cheaper to bring grains by steamer from Chile or the United States to Guayaquil than to transport them from the Ecuadorian highlands, only a few hundred kilometers away. Indeed, the lack of easy access to markets discouraged the expansion of agricultural production in the highlands, since it was difficult even to move products between neighboring highland provinces divided by transverse mountain ridges, much less up and over the Andes and down to the tropical coast. A railway would facilitate the transport of highland products, especially bulky, heavy, or perishable goods that were difficult and expensive to move by mule. While some highland landowners were engaged in incipient attempts to expand and modernize their production at the end of the nineteenth century, these efforts were necessarily limited by the lack of efficient transport routes.

Thus, in the railway project, and the broader discourse of movement associated with it, elites from both the coast and highlands could identify some—although not all—of their own interests. However, underlying this shared language were two different projects of movement and connection. While the railway would promote both the formation of a labor market and the strengthening of the internal market, at times these two projects were in fact in contradiction with one another. For instance, the intensification of highland agricultural production for the internal market usually depended precisely on increased control over labor, since mechanization was carried out only to a limited extent (for instance, in dairy production). The shared nature of this discourse masks the fact that in some ways these goals could not be pursued simultaneously.

As suggested, for coastal agro-export elites, the language of movement and connection was most closely related to the project of generating labor migrations to the coast, to lower labor costs and extend the agricultural frontier. Coastal agro-export elites looked to the new liberal administration after 1895 to stimulate labor migrations, through a loosening of labor ties in the highlands. Coastal planters saw highland landowners as "artificially" maintaining a monopoly over labor, using various noneconomic means to immobilize and control the indigenous population: paternalism, debt peonage, and the legal institutionalization of various "traditional" labor services provided to highland landowners and other local power holders. In so doing, highland elites were seen as sabotaging the prospects for national development through export production. In this context, the liberal state attempted to gain the moral upper hand over highland landowners precisely by insisting on its own role as protector of highland Indians from the abuses of both "traditional" highland landowners and the Catholic Church (which was also a large landowner). The liberal goal of generating a labor market thus involved the development of a discourse emphasizing liberty of contracts, and political measures to undermine highland landowners' control over labor (in the form of specific laws and government pronouncements), rather than the use of extra-economic coercion to generate flows of forced labor or to dispossess indigenous peasants of their lands (policies established by liberal governments in some other Latin American countries). The "freeing" of indigenous peasant labor for its employment in export production thus did not occur through a violent transformation of this sector into a proletariat or semi-proletariat, but rather through a series of legal regulations that gradually undermined the power of highland landowners as well as the church. These included the elimination of the subsidiary labor tax and of various special labor services due to clergy, as well as the establishment of measures to modify the institution of debt peonage. The latter included the requirement that indigenous laborers enter freely into their work contracts and that state officials oversee these contractual relations, and a prohibition on the heritability of debt. There were also limitations placed on local political authorities' ability to recruit indigenous labor for local public works. Together, these legal provisions contributed to the transformation of local labor relations into contractual relations agreed to by ostensibly free and equal individuals, and they indeed had the effect of stimulating labor migrations to the coast. (Railway construction itself also stimulated labor migrations, given the relatively high wages paid during construction, and the increased ease of travel to the coast following construction.)

How were these legal measures operationalized in highland areas, once they were passed as laws or executive decrees? Once the central state passed legal measures, they took effect principally due to the actions of subordinate groups, who called on the central state to limit local abuses (whether by clergy, landowners, or the local authorities closely allied with them). Indeed, in addition to national laws, many of the legal resources used by Indians to resist various claims on their labor by local political authorities, landowners, or the church were specific orders and decrees passed at the national or provincial level in response to Indians' complaints about abuses of their individual rights.[2] These complaints typically took the form of citing a specific instance in which, for example, local political authorities used the pretext of the labor recruitment system for municipal public works to illegally force Indians to work on their own agricultural properties or those of their friends and allies. Indians would cite the constitutional article that prohibited forced labor, and ask the supralocal authority to protect them from these local abuses. The supralocal authority would then send a specific order to local officials specifying fines that would be levied (or other consequences) for abusing Indians' rights. In these processes, Indians were able to call on the authority of the central state to limit abuses of local officials.[3] In the particular case of labor abuses in local public works, through a judicious combination of work evasions and well-placed petitions, Indians in the Alausí area at least managed to dismantle the existing system of labor recruitment for public works by the end of the 1910s.

Given the liberal state's emphasis on legal measures to undermine highland elites' control over labor, it is not surprising that indigenous complaints had a heavily legalistic tone during the liberal period. This has led Andrés Guerrero (1994) to propose that the liberal state promoted a "ventriloquist's" image of the Indian. New channels of communication were established between the state and Indians when laws were passed that undermined local powers in the highlands, with the rationale that these groups abused the rights of Indians; as a result, Indians parroted back to the state its image of them as requiring protection. It should be noted, however, that Indians also focused on their rights as citizens to move freely about the national territory, and to form labor contracts of their own free will. That is, they appropriated the discourse of the liberal state in order to deal, often successfully, with some of their most pressing everyday problems. The ways that Indians approached the state can be seen as a kind of performance, in which they enacted and recognized the power of the state, and adopted its forms (which does not imply that this encompassed all of their experience or interpretation of the actions of the state). The central state gained legitimacy precisely from the fact that central state projects were successful in incorporating at least some Indian aspirations.

If this is how local Indians responded to the coastal elite's project to generate a labor market, how did they respond to the highland elite's project to forge an internal market? The latter involved the intensification of agricultural production in highland areas in order to maximize the products available for transport to the coast. This project gained force during World War I, when the paralysis of international trade led to a crisis in cocoa exports, and hence the impossibility to continue importing basic food products for coastal consumption. Highland elites took advantage of this conjuncture to argue for the importance of increasing agricultural production in the highlands through a series of government incentives, which they argued was in the national interest. A group of modernizing highland agriculturalists successfully organized themselves into the *Sociedad Nacional de Agricultura* and became a consultative body for the national government on agricultural policy. One of their greatest achievements came when they designed a new law called the Law of Agricultural Development *(Ley de Fomento Agrícola)*, which they submitted to the minister of agriculture, who in turn presented it to congress. This law, passed in 1918, represented the first attempt to administer highland agricultural policy at the national level, and to expand and modernize the production of food staples. The law mandated the distribution of information about modern agricultural techniques, allowed the importation of farm machinery, seeds, and livestock free of customs duties, and through various measures facilitated the movement of products from field to national markets, drawing again on the discourse of movement.

At the local level in the highlands, a series of conflicts between haciendas and indigenous communities arose in the late 1910s and early 1920s precisely due to the efforts to expand and modernize agricultural and livestock production. In the area of Alausí in the central highlands, strategically located as the first highland *cantón* (county) on the railway's route inland from the coast, strong indigenous resistance to the intensification of labor demands in agriculture led those *hacendados* (large landowners) with access to high-altitude pasture lands to respond to new marketing opportunities by expanding labor-extensive livestock pasturing rather than labor-intensive grain production. This was accompanied by efforts both to enclose indigenous lands, and to limit indigenous peasant access to hacienda pastures for their own herds. The latter took the form of closing down paths that crossed haciendas, a strategy that became widespread in the Alausí region in the late 1910s and early 1920s. These conflicts were recorded in government archives precisely because the closure of customary paths through haciendas became the motive for repeated peasant complaints to the cantonal junta of agricultural development. Since the increased circulation of agricultural products was a central goal of the *Ley de Fomento Agrícola,* road closure had been made subject to fine under this law. Of course, the particular paths being closed by hacendados were those leading through their haciendas, rather than between hacienda and market. This distinction was not noted in the law itself, allowing local Indians to engage this legislation in their struggles with hacendados, but it made a great deal of difference to hacendados striving to modernize and expand their production: closing down internal paths allowed them to protect their investments in improved livestock breeds and pasture, precisely to take full advantage of improved external paths leading to markets. These events were also significant because indigenous peasants raised petitions to various high-level political authorities (including the nation's president) in their conflicts with hacendados. This led to an investigation that took the local police chief onto a hacienda, and into an indigenous community, in order to mediate labor disputes between the two. This was unprecedented in that era, and occurred at the instigation of indigenous peasants who argued that their freedom of movement was violated by local landowners through the closure of customary paths.

Another set of conflicts also arose at the local level in association with the efforts to move highland agricultural products to the coast, in the form of marketing disputes. These took place when merchants bought up large quantities of staple foods in local markets in the highlands, knowing that they would fetch higher prices in coastal towns and in Guayaquil. Interestingly, these disputes produced a series of conflicting statements and claims about the operation of monopoly and of the law of supply and demand, which precisely focused on the importance of the circulation of products. That is, local townspeople claimed that large merchants were "monopolizing" goods when they paid prices that were beyond the reach of local consumers. Townspeople also drew on precedents set during World War I, when price fixing had been undertaken by the national government to combat speculation in food products. Merchants, however, countered with the argument that they were simply facilitating the operation of the "natural" law of supply and demand; in contrast, they argued that when municipal authorities attempted to control the flow of goods, they were the ones promoting monopoly. In these conflicts, local townspeople attempted to use the language of contention in ways that redefined what freedom of movement should mean: they stretched liberal discourse by arguing that the draining of food products from the region was "monopoly," penalized by law. However, of the various ways that the language of movement was engaged during the liberal period, this particular argument was the least successful, possibly because it was associated with purely local interests rather than involving an alliance of local and regional or national elite interests.

Thus, during the liberal period in Ecuador, a language involving freedom of movement was engaged in many different ways. At the national level, it facilitated a tenuous consensus between two regionally based elites who could each identify some of their own interests in the language of movement and connection. While they debated what the content of this project should include, they did not debate the importance of movement as a source of progress, modernity, and economic stimulus for the country. It is in this sense that we can identify a shared but contested language: a language of contention, through which disputes could be carried out.

At the local level, the project to promote the free movement of laborers was incorporated strategically into indigenous resistance to local power holders. That is, Indians adopted the language of the central state to claim their rights before those who abused them. The particular kind of rights they were able to claim were defined for them: most importantly, these were the rights to form and dissolve individual labor contracts and to resist forced labor recruitment of various kinds. In contrast, they were quite pointedly not able to claim collective rights through this language. The project to promote greater production and circulation of staple foods, in turn, was resisted at the local level by various social groups, given that this provoked both agrarian conflicts and marketing conflicts. However, the form that resistance took was precisely to engage elements of the language of movement. In the agrarian conflicts peasants called on central government authorities to deal with landowner abuses, and claimed their rights as citizens to move freely and to enjoy constitutional guarantees. Interestingly, one of the legal resources that peasants drew on in resisting hacienda expansion was precisely part of the *Ley de Fomento Agrícola,* the same law that facilitated that expansion in the first place. This law was passed due to lobbying by large landowners, but some of its articles could also be used against them. Law and rhetoric from national sources were also appropriated in struggles over the marketing of food products: for instance, when local authorities attempted to control commerce in situations of local scarcity, drawing (unsuccessfully) on regulations that had been used to deal with national scarcity during World War I. In all of these cases, local social groups adopted the language of the liberal project precisely to resist some of its effects at the local level.

Not only did local Indians use the idiom of citizenship and claims to freedom of movement in their petitions to higher authorities, but in the 1920s they actually invited state officials into their communities to mediate labor disputes with haciendas, something that was unprecedented in previous years. In addition, during the 1920s, Indians increasingly sent delegations to provincial capitals and Quito to complain to higher authorities about the abuses of local officials and landowners. This indicates the success of the central state in positioning itself as the protector of indigenous rights against abuses by local power holders in the highlands.

Local uses of the language of contention represented efforts to stretch the boundaries of central, elite discourses, although different local social groups attempted to stretch them in different directions. These processes indicate the strength of the language of contention: its basic concepts were both shared and contested, providing the possibility of incorporating, in a restricted way, the aspirations of a wide range of social groups into a single hegemonic project. Conflict was clearly not eliminated, but the very fact that liberal discourse and law were adopted by local groups in their struggles, indicates the broad success of processes of incorporation, in terms of the development of a shared discursive framework. In the conflicts considered here, the language of contention succeeded in channeling conflict between various social groups.

The extent to which local social groups "believed" the language they adopted in their disputes is beyond the scope of the analysis carried out here. Indeed, there is no assumption that they internalized the language of the central state, or that the analysis of this language exhausts the lived reality of these groups, invading the full range of their cultural conceptions. As Asad argues, "[W]hat is shared in such situations is not 'belief,' as an interior state of mind but cultural discourses that constitute objective social conditions" (1987, 605). In fact, the central state and elite groups do not seem to have been concerned with the beliefs of local groups, as long as their resistance to elite projects remained within the limits defined by the language of contention.

In light of the above, I want to return to Antonio Gramsci's discussion of the concept of hegemony. In his "Notes on Italian History," Gramsci (1971, 44–120) analyzes hegemony as a political process that requires a ruling class to both "lead" and "dominate." In order to lead successfully, the ruling class must incorporate the aspirations of other social groups into its own political program, and to promote and defend those interests as well as its own. The achievement of consent is thus not simple manipulation, but rather involves the forging of political alliances and the development of a broad program of social change that cannot be reduced to the interests of a single group (although the interests of the dominant group will nonetheless predominate). This points us to another aspect of hegemony often forgotten: that hegemonic projects are confining, not only for subaltern groups, but also for those who design such projects.

In order to move beyond the notions of ideological consensus and false consciousness often associated with the concept of hegemony, it is useful to remember that by definition, hegemony can never be complete. Politically, there is a tension between the interests of various social groups in any alliance. Indeed, there are often lines of cleavage and conflict among elite groups, which lead to tensions within dominant cultures. That is, elite projects themselves are subject to contention among and even within dominant groups. And culturally, while the social groups who dominate a society will attempt to impose their own ideas as general ones, this runs up against limits, as Raymond Williams suggests in his concept of dominant culture (1977). Precisely because the dominant culture arises out of and is consistent with the experiences of dominant groups, the experiences of subordinate groups can only be partially represented in the dominant culture. Indeed, a dominant culture cannot be all encompassing because the members of subordinate groups continually experience the world in ways that contradict it (see also Vicencio, this volume). Some aspects of dominant culture seem to connect with people's lives, while others will be contradicted by their lived experiences. Under some conditions, the latter may be the basis for new forms of discourse and alternative meanings, only some of which the dominant culture will be capable of absorbing. Alternatively, subordinate groups may attempt to stretch the meanings drawn from dominant culture to fit their own experiences and projects. A successful hegemonic project will allow for this, and in doing so, reshape itself to include (some) interests of (some) subordinate groups. It is in this sense that subaltern groups, under some conditions, may contribute to the redefinition of elite strategies and projects.

While the expression of subaltern interests through the language of contention in liberal Ecuador indicates the strength of this hegemonic process, it should be noted that this "dialogue" was broken at both the subaltern and dominant levels toward the end of the liberal period. In the early 1920s a series of indigenous uprisings occurred that did not limit themselves to complaints and petitions to the state. And in 1922 a workers' strike ended in a government massacre of workers in Guayaquil that continues to hold a central place in the historical memory of the Left and workers' movements in Ecuador. In 1925, the liberal government was overthrown in the *Revolución Juliana* by a group of progressive military officers allied with the middle classes. The 1930s in turn saw economic crisis and profound political upheaval, with fifteen governments in that decade alone, the emergence of new political parties and urban populism, and the establishment of new forms of organization among peasants and workers. One of the results of economic and political crisis was the establishment of social policy, which represented a real achievement for the lower classes, but also provided a new legal framework within which struggles could be carried out. In this sense, a new language of contention emerged in the 1930s that gave the struggles of that era a quite different tone from those of the liberal period.

Notes

This chapter summarizes some of the arguments made at greater length in Clark (1998); see that work for a more complete bibliography relevant to the processes analyzed here. The research for this analysis was funded by the Social Sciences and Humanities Research Council of Canada and the New School for Social Research, to whom I am grateful.

1. In a similar way, Gupta (this volume, p. 177) suggests that in nation-states a public sphere emerges in which "there is general agreement on how disagreements should be framed."

2. For specific examples of indigenous strategies of resistance to local public works, see Clark (1994).

3. Rather than assuming that the state is a monolithic entity with a single set of interests, I conceptualize the state as encompassing a range of often conflicting interests among its various officials and institutions. For a later period in Ecuador where schisms among different state representatives are also evident, see Striffler's analysis (this volume) of the various state responses to mobilizations by coastal agricultural workers against the United Fruit Company in the 1960s.

PART 3

Hegemonies and Histories

CHAPTER 12

The Decline of Patriarchy?
The Political Economy of Patriarchy

Maquiladoras in Yucatan, Mexico

Marie France Labrecque

The inspiration for this chapter on the case of maquiladoras in Yucatan came from a short article written by Barbara Ehrenreich, "The Decline of Patriarchy." In the article, she convincingly argues that patriarchy is declining in the United States. She defines patriarchy as "the intimate power of men over women, a power which is historically exercised within the family by the male as breadwinner, property owner, or armed defender of women and children." She illustrates this with the rapid rise in the number of families "headed" by women, the decline in male wages, and men's declining interest in children (the proof being that 50 percent of divorced fathers are defaulting on their child support payments). Another illustration is the fact that "men no longer depend on women for physical survival" and that they are embracing the consumer culture (Ehrenreich 1995, 285–287).

For women, the decline of patriarchy does not imply liberation. Ehrenreich states, to the contrary, that this decline means the end of mutual obligations between men and women, including the protection that men were expected to provide to women. Not only do men no longer want to assume this role, in fact, they do not even want women any more. The hypocrisy linked to patriarchy having disappeared, there is a resurgence of male violence toward women who have no other option than to masculinize in order to defend themselves. Ehrenreich mentions that many American women in the suburbs are arming themselves and that there is even a magazine called *Women and Guns*. She evokes female models of the bitchy woman in movies such as *Thelma and Louise* and *Basic Instinct* to which I would add *G.I. Jane*. The author concludes that if women and men do not change in the near future, the expression "battle of the sexes" "may stop being a metaphor and become an armed struggle" (Ehrenreich 1995, 290).

Ehrenreich's analysis could easily be extended to cases outside the United States. I read her article some time before reading the May/June 1998 issue of

Ms. which included an article entitled "The Maquila Murders" (Quiñones 1998). The word *maquila* comes from *maquiladora* which is "a production facility that manufactures, assembles or produces raw materials and components that have been temporarily imported [into the country]. Products are then shipped back to the originating country for final assembly or distribution" (Raafat et al. 1992, 181). The *Ms.* article points out that 106 female maquiladora workers have been killed since 1993 in Ciudad Juarez, a city of one million located just on the other side of the Rio Grande river and near El Paso, Texas. The article suggests that maquiladoras have contributed to changing the roles of men and women as the latter become breadwinners for their families. The author writes: "The maquiladoras created a new Mexican woman—but not a new man" (Quiñones 1998, 14). Of course, we don't know to what extent the murders are linked to domestic violence that is the result of men's resentment toward women, but women's groups in Ciudad Juarez believe that forced modernization plays a role (Quiñones 1998, 14).

It is an understatement to say that this conclusion contradicts the assertions of modernization theory according to which job opportunities for women represent a protection against violence. Actually, the relation usually drawn between economic opportunities for women and the acquisition of power, especially within the family, is not that clear.

While studies of maquiladoras and their consequences for women's labor force participation in the U.S.-Mexican border region are quite abundant (Fernandez-Kelly 1997), those on maquiladoras in Yucatan are still few and far between. The fact that these maquiladoras massively hire women from the countryside—though their proportion is tending to decrease in relation to men's—provides another illustration of the way in which the sexual division of labor is being used by multinationals. It confirms that gender should lie at the center of the analysis of the global political economy and of the state.

Like the other contributors to this section, I want to understand how the state establishes its domination over its subjects and citizens. In this chapter I endeavor to show how patriarchy interweaves with the state, and how it "works," not only at an abstract level, but also in the daily lives of the people.

What I would like to do here is to reflect upon Ehrenreich's proposal regarding the decline of patriarchy and the rise of male domination in a context such as Yucatan. The point I want to make is that the concepts of patriarchy and male domination are not necessarily two different historical moments, as Ehrenreich suggests. In fact, to be anthropologically correct, patriarchy is the dominance of the extended family ruled by a patriarch, a form that was specific to precapitalist societies (Mackintosh 1984). However, a number of recent publications use the concept of patriarchy to describe the contemporary state and its social practices (Fox 1988; Connell 1990; Steans 1998). Their authors refer to discriminatory practices based on perceived sexual differences that were socially and historically constructed in the context of modernity and which still constitute one of the foundations of Western societies. In Connell's words, "'patriarchy' is a serviceable term for historically produced situations in gender relations where men's domination is *institutionalized*" (1990, 514; his emphasis).

So, patriarchy admittedly has a historical content but that is precisely what legitimizes its use in a contemporary context as a concept that belongs to a global/structural arena. The patriarchal state is complex and full of contradictions. Under the pressures of social movements, the state is responsible for contradictory measures (Connell 1990, 517). At the same time as it "handicaps the sex that bears children" (Fox 1988, 176), the state takes steps that could be interpreted as protecting women. Contrary to what Ehrenreich is suggesting, patriarchy and male domination could simply be two dimensions of the same social relations, a structural dimension and an institutional one, rather than two different historical moments. We could even speak of three dimensions if we add machismo to these concepts, machismo being exercised in the arena of individuals in the context of daily life.

The relevance of these considerations on patriarchy, male dominance, and machismo as three different dimensions of the same set of social relations will be illustrated in the specific context of Yucatan. At the same time, I will attempt to show that the contradictory transformation of gender relations is central to the economic history of the region and the global economy.

The Specifics of the Yucatan Population and Region

The region that interests me is located near the state capital of Yucatan, Mérida. For at least one century, its economy rested on the cultivation of the henequen plant, better known as sisal. It is populated by the Maya who for historical and political reasons call themselves *mestizos*.

When I did my first fieldwork in Mexico in the 1970s, rural villages in northern Yucatan were, at first sight, just as they had been described by North American anthropologists in the 1930s and 1940s. Everything contributed to an impression of homogeneity and conservatism. However, as in so many other regions of Mexico, the fate of these villages had been narrowly linked to that of distant regions of the world, especially from the end of the nineteenth century on, when its population started producing sisal on a large scale. Its fiber was used to supply the North American market with baling twine for combines. In the beginning, Yucatan was the only producer of sisal in the whole world. The landowners and producers of the precious fiber became very wealthy and were able to build luxurious mansions that can still be seen in Mérida, which now house banks and the local headquarters of multinational companies.

In the 1920s, the plant was smuggled to Tanzania and elsewhere in the world to be grown and transformed at a better price. As a result, Yucatan entered recurring periods of economic crisis. These down periods were interrupted by the two world wars and by the Korean war because of increased demand for the natural fiber. While everywhere else in the world people were praying for the end of the wars, fiber workers in Yucatan implored their saints for their continuation. I was a witness to similar circumstances in 1973–1974 with the Arab embargo on oil, a situation that was devastating for the Western world, especially the United States, but was a windfall for the sisal industry in Yucatan. With the embargo, U.S. synthetic fiber industries, which relied heavily on oil, were cut off from their supplies. At least for a while, the world again turned toward natural fibers, including sisal.

As we can see, the concept of globalization accurately describes Yucatan's integration in the world economy. Many authors, such as Wolf (1982), have demonstrated that regional economies have been interdependent at least since the Middle Ages. On the other hand, in recent decades, with the development of information technologies, there has been an acceleration of economic processes and an intensification of their effects on people at the local level. Until recently these effects could only be detected on the structural level through an analysis of the processes; they are nowadays evident in every dimension of daily life.

In the summer of 2000, I returned to a village where I have stayed many times since the 1970s. I was living, as usual, in one of the typical Mayan oval houses with a thatched roof. The women in the house still wear the traditional *huipil* (an embroidered white dress) and the men, though dressed in jeans, still wear sandals as a marker of ethnic identity. Women still cook in the backyard in a separate shelter and on the floor. From an economic point of view, the men of the family are rural workers who, until the collapse of the sisal industry and the changes in the *ejido* (a kind of communal land tenure), also worked on plantations or for local landowners. From a cultural point of view though, these men still define themselves as peasants because they cultivate a *milpa*. Many young people, both boys and girls, also live in this traditional household, but they come and go in a flurry for they—this is relatively new for the girls—definitely prefer being out wandering around the central park with their group of friends.

Since the 1980s, as a consequence of the economic crisis, young men and women have become temporary migrants to the city. Specifically, young women have become used to working in Mérida, the capital, as domestic servants. A turning point for young men came in 1980, when the government interrupted its subsidies to the henequen industry. The result was an important crisis in the countryside that caused the ruin of thousands of families who turned to temporary or daily emigration to the city in search of an income. Many communities in the region have been defined as "ghost villages" because their population works elsewhere leaving only a handful of individuals (mainly the elders) cultivating henequen (*Diario de Yucatan* 1997–10–20). In fact, this phenomenon produces a certain heterogeneity within the household, for not all of the members emigrate. It also produces changes in identities, because while the youth who emigrate may no longer be peasants, neither have they become urban.

Everywhere in Yucatan, whether in urban or rural areas, there has been a diversification in women's and men's activities. The rate of women's participation in the formal labor market was 12.6 percent in 1970, and rose to 18.2 percent in 1990, while men's rate of participation remained constant over the same period (70 percent) (INEGI 1992, 78). It is in this context that maquiladoras came to Yucatan at the end of the 1980s. It is too early to evaluate all aspects of their impact on women's participation as well as on gender relations in the 1990s. However, we can already see that women's and men's rates of participation in the formal labor market have increased. In 1995 women's participation rate was 38.9 percent, while men's was 79 percent (INEGI 1996, 833). Maquiladoras seem to make a difference, and it is worth exploring some of the tendencies of social change in relation to the phenomenon in the region.

Maquiladoras in Yucatan and the Redefinition of Gender Relations

The Mexican population in general is quite familiar with the concept of maquiladoras. However, this type of production is not exclusive to Mexico. It is a worldwide phenomenon that was initially characterized by a mixed production system located in export-processing free trade zones, sometimes combined with subcontracting firms and sweatshops. The system was first found in Asia and Central America (Ong 1991, 279), often, not surprisingly, in countries with authoritarian governments.

In considering the specific conditions of Yucatan in relation to the installation of textile maquiladoras on its territory, it is important to know that Maya women have always been associated with weaving, sewing, and embroidery. During colonization, they wove the cotton cloth that constituted the tribute that the communities had to pay to the Spanish conquistadores. According to contemporary research (*Diario de Yucatan* 1997–10–12), embroidering techniques and styles are pre-Colombian and there are projects in the countryside to salvage its diversity. Even today, thousands of rural women are involved in textile crafts. An important proportion of the income-generating projects I studied in the 1980s—such as the *Unidades agricolas e industriales para la mujer* (UAIM)—and that still exist, involve sewing and embroidery. In these circumstances, it is not surprising that clothing maquiladoras are now converging toward the Yucatecan countryside.

This is the context in which maquiladoras are spreading throughout Yucatan. It is a recent phenomenon as compared to the situation on the U.S. border.

In 1984, 90 percent of maquiladoras were located in that zone. In 1995, 70 percent were located in the border states of Mexico, and the rest were to be found elsewhere in the country (International Confederation of Free Trade Unions, n.d.). In June 1997, 897,354 Mexicans were working in 2,676 maquiladoras, that is, 16 percent more than in 1996 (Migration News 1997). As of March 1999, the number of workers in maquiladoras at the national level had increased to 1,090,042 (INEGI 1999), clearly showing that this economic model is still in its expansion phase.

In the henequen region of Yucatan, in September 2000, there are no fewer than forty-two maquiladoras, mostly garment factories. The importance of the phenomenon is apparent in the example of the Monty, a maquiladora located in the small town of Motul, thirty minutes from the capital, which produces 40,000 pairs of jeans a week and employs 4,600 workers (SEDEINCO 2000). Motul has a population of 27,755 and 44.5 percent of those above five years old still speak the Maya language at home (INEGI 1996, 112, 283).

For now, maquiladoras in the Yucatan offer more possibilities for women than for men. In September 1999, statistics indicated that there were 129 maquiladoras throughout the state of Yucatan, providing work to 29,549 workers of which 58.37 percent were women (INEGI 1999). In other regions, the feminization of the labor force has produced a redefinition of male and female roles. There is a possibility that women's wages are giving them new access to power. Some feminists think that this increasing participation in market production is "a natural, almost biological response" to poverty, drug trafficking, violence, and ecological disasters (*Diario de Yucatan* 1997–10–12). Other researchers emphasize that women are now taking on, at least partly, men's traditional roles while there is more formal wage labor for women than for men. Women end up becoming breadwinners for their families with all the ensuing social and cultural consequences (Torres Gongora and Castilla Ramos as quoted in the *Diario de Yucatan* 1997–06–01). Moreover, the working women are sometimes very young women who take their father's place as breadwinner.

What is the impact of these changes on gender? There are many ways to approach the question and a wide range of debates is going on. According to Steans, "feminists are broadly divided amongst those who insist that gender can be understood in terms of social structures, and those who emphasize the importance of discourse in understanding how gender is constructed" (Steans 1998, 160). I would say that from a feminist political economy standpoint, it is possible, methodologically, to be on both sides of the fence, depending on the arenas that are being discussed. In the global/structural arena, gender can be understood in terms of social structures. In the local arena and the one of individuals, it seems more appropriate to take into account the experiences and practices of social actors in order to understand the construction of gender. In an area such as the northern part of Yucatan, the global social structure is translated into multiple social hierarchies, experienced in daily life by men and women, that have the effect of diversifying the construction of gender. If gender is a constituent part of the global political economy and if we want to elucidate its processes, it is therefore important to be able to consider simultaneously all the social arenas in which men and women are involved.

Globalization (which in the case of Yucatan takes the form of an encroachment of maquiladoras in the countryside) and gender can therefore be approached from the same theoretical perspective. Gender and its construction are both necessary dimensions of the globalization process and ongoing results of it. In this sense, production in the context of globalization becomes more than ever a gendered production and a necessary condition to the reproduction of the process. In this process, the production of profits depends on multiple hierarchies in general; on their specific sociocultural combination, such as in the case of Yucatan; and on actual gender hierarchies at the level of social actors. Maquiladoras, with their preference for a docile, female labor force, clearly illustrate a convergence of globalization and the gendering of production, resulting in rapid social changes.

These changes manifest themselves in various social arenas. Generally, these changes have been observed in the structural arena, but as Catherine Scott has pointed out, the fact that theories have concentrated on this arena has greatly contributed to the invisibility of women (Scott 1995). Moreover, a reconsideration of the process of development (of which maquiladoras are a part) should begin with a study of the household (Scott 1995, 133).

In the Yucatan, thus far, there has been no systematic study of the changes brought about by the integration of women into the maquiladoras in rural areas. However, an exploratory study was undertaken by Lucie Lortie in Motul in 1997. She selected a small sample of twelve households, including women working in the maquiladora. In all cases, these women's incomes were important to the well-being of the household. In half the cases, women's wages represented the principal financial contribution to the household, whether they be the wages of the wife or daughter of the family "head." Out of the twelve cases, only three women said they used their wages exclusively for their own needs (Lortie 1999, 164).

In Motul, the fact that women are now able to earn wages from the industrial sector is a change in itself. That some of them earn more money than their fathers or husbands, as reported by Lortie, constitutes a radical change over such a short period of time. However, are these spectacular changes in the domain of production likely to produce other changes, for example, in the domain of domestic work? Again, in Motul, Lortie found that in every household in her study, the main part of domestic work was executed by adult and young women who did not have a remunerated job outside the home. She also realized that in spite of the fact that a few men participated in certain domestic tasks, their contribution clearly remained inferior to that of women, as much in quantitative as in qualitative terms (Lortie 1999, 178).

In my own recent (Summer 2000) fieldwork in a neighboring village (Tixkokob),where there is a maquiladora much of the same type as in Motul, in response to a question about how her husband dealt with the fact that she worked outside her home, a young worker answered: "It's very difficult because he doesn't like that I work. He says my work keeps me away from my house, from my tasks, from my children, that I don't take care of them properly. We have problems because of my work, there's a lot of discussion because he doesn't like that I work" (woman aged 30, mother of 3, July 2000).

This woman's husband is an itinerant hammock dealer who only returns home once a week, so the daily domestic tasks which in his opinion are not properly undertaken certainly do not "fall back" on him. On this subject, my informant told me that she relies on her mother who lives nearby to take care of the house and her children. My interview with this informant, and the preliminary results of my research in five other villages with dozens of informants in the region, combined with Lortie's findings, confirm those of many other scholars. Although women have less time for domestic chores, men are still very reluctant to take over the responsibility for such tasks. Moreover, men's growing involvement in household labor does not necessarily lead to an egalitarian redistribution of tasks. So, men do not play their traditional role anymore, but even when a man is no longer a breadwinner, he still enjoys certain privileges. The question seems to be: What are the factors that protect those privileges? In her book *The Myth of the Male Breadwinner*, Helen Safa points toward the role of public structures in this phenomenon. The book deals with women and the industrialization of the Dominican Republic, Cuba, and Puerto Rico. Safa states that "the myth of the male breadwinner is preserved by public forms of patriarchy, which continue to profit from women's subordination" (Safa 1995, 185). Therefore, the issue might not be the decline or the durability of patriarchy. Instead, it seems to be the contradictions within the state itself. In the next section, I will deal with these contradictions and demonstrate that the process of globalization exacerbates them while weakening local states.

The Contradictory Role of the State in Development

The spreading of maquiladoras in Mexico away from the northern border is partly the result of a certain saturation of the area. Especially in the garment industry, competition is fierce. So the Yucatan government is clearly advertising that one of the main advantages for productive investment is the abundant labor force and the low wages that are being paid in the region (*Diario de Yucatan* 5/29/97). In fact, the Mexican garment industry is expanding. In 1996, exports increased by 22 percent. Mexico has outdone China as the main cloth exporter to the United States. The Mexican clothing sector employs some 435,000 workers, and in the first quarter of 1997, four out of ten industrial jobs were created in the garment field (Migration News 1997). Without a doubt, the competition is fierce, encouraging the spread of capital in Yucatan, always in search of cheap and docile labor. In fact, the website produced by the Yucatan government highlights the comparative advantages of production costs in the state (Gobierno de Yucatan 1998). Although the Yucatan government is trying to attract maquiladoras (even advertising on the Web to do so), it is evident that the real power has slipped from the hands of local and regional governments. In fact, the very definition of power is changing. It has become delocalized.

Very clearly, economic development has not resulted in the prosperity NAFTA had promised to the working classes in Mexico. The Interamerican Bank for Development stated that for this year, this country has the most unequal distribution of income in all Latin America: 40 percent of the people live in poverty, a situation that is constantly deteriorating (Migration News 1997). Once more, Mexico has had to turn to international World Bank programs to alleviate poverty. After President Salinas de Gortari's Solidaridad program, comes President Zedillo's program El Progreso (Migration News 1997), probably also conceived and paid for by the World Bank. But, as power is being delocalized, no single state or institution can be "blamed" for the situation. It is not surprising that so-called "civil society"—at least in the case of Mexico—has so much difficulty finding alternatives to neoliberalism . . . even with a little help from the neo-Zapatistas.

For the time being, the youth in Yucatan is being targeted and trained for the type of tasks to be accomplished. As I mentioned earlier, there is a tendency in Yucatan and elsewhere to integrate more men in the maquiladoras. Currently, young inexperienced men increasingly fit the definition of the ideal worker in the maquiladora, which is a docile worker. This is even true in the garment sector, which is traditionally female. In fact, in some maquiladoras, the individual sex is unimportant to the extent that certain men (such as young Maya men in Yucatan) correspond to the dominant culture's stereotypes of women—that is, docile and quiet. In this way, the definition of the genders may change without challenging inequalities between actual men and women. Behind all this lie cultural forms, such as the myth of the male breadwinner, that influence hiring even though it is far from certain that the recruited men will actually take care of their families.

If we consider patriarchy as a set of institutionalized gender relations (as in Connell 1990), what is happening in Mexico is not so much a decline of patriarchy as a decline of the state itself, which can no longer manage to attenuate the more blatant contradictions between classes, ethnic groups, genders, and the different social categories in general. From now on in Mexico, as in many other places in the world, the power traditionally exercised by the state is being replaced by the rules of neoliberalism. In the structural arena, this system undermines state patriarchy but not necessarily patriarchy itself. As a consequence of the undermining of state patriarchy, male domination, understood as a set of sociocultural and localized practices between social categories such as men and women, is reinforced so the competition between genders continues to secure basic economic processes locally. The field has now been left open for the exercise of new forms of violence against women.

In the maquiladoras where women are hired, structural violence (henceforth uncontrolled by the state) combines with male domination in Mexican society as a whole and with machismo in everyday life leading to total contempt for women's basic human rights and dignity. In many maquiladoras, women have to prove that they are not pregnant to get a job. In the most degrading cases, each month women must show their used sanitary napkins to their supervisor (*Globe and Mail* 10/14/97). As we can see, women's biological specificity is still used against them. There are both striking similarities and differences between the domination transnational corporations exercise over workers in general, and the gendered violence that seems to have been exercised against the maquiladora women as individuals, and not against maquiladora men, in Ciudad Juarez. The daily violence other women are enduring is perhaps less spectacular than such murders, but there certainly is a continuity between the way violence is exercised in the structural arena and in the one of individuals.

Conclusion

Patriarchy has multiple dimensions. The maquiladora case shows that in the structural arena, the Mexican state has more or less yielded a part of its power to multinationals and international institutions. This does not mean that patriarchy has disappeared. Nor does it mean that inequalities between men and women are in the process of disappearing in that country. It simply means that the Mexican state is no longer in a position to exercise this kind of power over women as a social category; international institutions have taken over that position. But the way they exercise power is another story.

To understand patriarchy, its continuity and its decline, we have to consider the dimensions of male domination in the context of specific situations and locations. We also have to consider the individuals and be prepared to identify machismo as another dimension of patriarchy. Although this type of research at the level of social actors has been undertaken by a number of academics in the north of Mexico and in other regions, there is still a real need for this type of research in Yucatan. This will permit a more precise grasp of the local dimensions of the gendering of production and its effects on men and women in their daily life, and also of the way they reinterpret social change.

There also is a need to clarify the methodologies that are being used to study gender. When Ehrenreich, for example, writes about the decline of patriarchy as a set of relations between men and women instead of as a structural phenomenon, she takes a methodological shortcut that could lead to some unwarranted general conclusions about U.S. society. To do the same thing in the case of Mexico could even result in increased prejudices against the country as a whole and against certain sectors of the population.

This has been the case, for example, of issues concerning poverty. It has been said that, in the context of the economic crisis and structural adjustment programs, "poverty in Mexico has the face of a woman" (*Diario de Yucatan* 8/6/96). This affirmation suggests that all women in Mexico are poor and that they are all powerless victims of neoliberalism. Such a comment eventually contributes to maintaining a truncated image of the country as a whole and of women as a social category. There is some room for refinement and the definition of poverty that varies from one household to another and even within a particular household. I would argue that the generalizations we are able to make in the structural arena both for poverty and for violence and gender have to be verified and redefined in different social arenas. Because of the multiple hierarchies facing social actors in daily life, the picture could be quite different.

The same phenomenon occurs in the case of machismo. It is not because patriarchy is a structural feature of neoliberalism and because male domination seems to characterize Mexican culture and organizations that all male individuals in Mexico are machos. This is what Gutmann brilliantly discussed in his book (1996). At the level of social actors and individuals, he showed that there is much space for heterogeneity, difference, and change.

Preliminary data collected in the area of Motul in northern Yucatan, and elsewhere in the region, as in Tixkokob, tend to suggest that new ways of integrating social actors into maquiladoras are emerging in spite of structural similarities between this region and the northern border. The availability of a cheap labor force, and therefore an increased possibility for reducing production costs, seems to be more important than the proximity of the U.S. consumer market. Because the maquiladoras are built within the confines of the villages, they are not as much an abstract concept for people as they could be for the population of the interior of the Republic who send their members to the border.

Maquiladoras in Yucatan are now part of the landscape, the neighborhood, and perhaps even the family. Therefore, one could expect a constant flow of workers linked less to one another than to a specific maquiladora. This could even stop, or at least slow down, the desertion so typical of the border. Perhaps the Yucatecan people will be able to fit the new concept of their maquiladoras into old ones, and even establish fictitious kinship relations with the managers and supervisors, as they used to do with their *hacendado* (large landowners for whom the local population worked). These thoughts are only speculations, but it is to be expected that the population of the northern part of Yucatan will offer both a certain form of resistance to the new production system, and a certain form of reinterpretation as well. We still do not know how and when it will happen but it is a story worth following.

As the other chapters in this section show, much of the strength of the state rests on hegemonic processes, which take on different forms through history, and which also contribute to shaping places. There is no doubt that patriarchy—in all of its dimensions—is a fundamental part of these processes.

Note

This chapter is a reworked and updated version of a paper presented in the joint conference of CASCA/AES, at the University of Toronto, May 8, 1998, in the session entitled: "Political Economy and the Production of Culture." The English was revised by Mary Richardson. The author wishes to thank two master's students from the Department of Anthropology at Laval University, Lucie Lortie and Mireille Ménard, who carried out fieldwork in the northern region of Yucatan during the summer of 1997, and with whom she was able to verify some of her ideas. The update is based on fieldwork done in the summer of 2000 through a SSHRC grant entitled "Perspective sur le changement social au Yucatan (Mexique) au temps des maquiladoras."

CHAPTER 13

Remembering "The Ancient Ones"

Memory, Hegemony, and the Shadows of State Terror in the Argentinean Chaco

Gastón Gordillo

In March 1917, two regiments of cavalry of the Argentinean army arrived on the banks of the middle course of the Pilcomayo River, the borderline with Bolivia and Paraguay and the last region in Argentina where there were still indigenous groups not totally "pacified" by the army. The troops had been called to curb an uprising of the Tobas of the area, who—according to local reports—had killed a Criollo settler, burned down his house, and stolen his cattle. The military clashed with the Tobas twice, first in Laguna Martín and then in Sombrero Negro. According to several historical accounts (Torres 1975, 53–55; Rodas 1991, 59; Mendoza and Maldonado 1995), in spite of the Tobas' fierce resistance the troops caused havoc among them. Having suffered heavy casualties, the Tobas abandoned their villages and fled to the Bolivian—today Paraguayan—bank of the river.[1] Eighty years later, in the mid and late 1990s, many Tobas living in this area of the Pilcomayo had a vivid recollection of these clashes with the army.[2] Most adult men had heard accounts about them from their parents and grandparents and, even though they were not participants in these events, they talked about them in bursting flashes of images. Each person emphasized some details over others, but almost everybody agreed on one crucial aspect: the Toba warriors defeated the army, killed numerous soldiers, and suffered almost no casualties.

The Tobas' memory of this battle, its semantic density, and especially its unambiguous forcefulness stand in a tension with the contradictory way they often remember their ancestors. For the current social memory of most Tobas is ambiguously molded by hegemonic values about the virtues of their conversion to Christianity and their incorporation into the Argentinean nation-state, a process whose most violent expression was that encounter with the army in 1917. The aim of this chapter is to analyze the overall ambiguity that pervades Toba social memory and, simultaneously, the acts of remembrance that momentarily overcome it, such as those involving their clashes with the military. Even though many features of this social memory are shared by men and women alike, the accounts presented here were produced by Toba men; they often involve strong markers of masculinity: warfare, physical strength, bravery, or hunting skills, and as a result I will analyze these memories as part of a male discourse.

Social memory is a representation that is deeply shaped by experiences and hegemonic fields contemporary to the act of remembering. Thus, the collective memory of subaltern actors, even though based on their own lived experiences, does not escape the influence of state discourses, in a process in which people internalize hegemonic narratives of remembrance, reformulate them, or construct memories critical to them. Social memory then becomes a contested arena in which different actors produce competing yet intertwined versions of the past, especially in regard to experiences of violence and social suffering (Swedenburg 1991; Trouillot 1995; Hale 1997; Sider and Smith 1997; Warren 2000; see also Menzies, this volume). As part of this process, the meanings that members of a group associate with past experiences are crucial in the production of their memories about them (Fentress and Wickham 1992, 58–59). In other words, memory becomes part of social debates on the meaningfulness of the past for the present, in a process that not only commemorates but also silences historical events (Trouillot 1995; Sider and Smith 1997). This perspective implies that rather than attempting to establish whether certain memories are "true" or "false" it is important to unravel the fields of force and collective experiences lying behind their production. Fentress and Wickham (1992, xi) have rightly argued that the issue of the factual truth of memory is interesting insofar as it sheds light on how social memory itself works. And this necessarily takes us to the complex connections between remembering, historical experience, and hegemonic formations. In this chapter, I will explore this unfolding by analyzing how members of a subaltern, indigenous group internalize, reformulate, and challenge hegemonic narratives about their "savage" past and how in this process they cope with the burden of past experiences of terror.

Remembering the Ancient Ones

Until the late nineteenth century, the indigenous groups of the Gran Chaco—a mostly semiarid plain covering a good part of northern Argentina, western Paraguay, and southeastern Bolivia—had been able to resist and even undermine the advance of the Spanish and then Creole frontiers. Because of this situation, in the 1880s the Argentinean nation-state organized large military campaigns to accomplish the final "pacification" of the region. By the turn of the century, most indigenous groups in southern and eastern Chaco had been militarily defeated. The middle course of the Pilcomayo River, however, was still in the hands of indigenous groups, and in the 1910s skirmishes between the first Criollo settlers and Toba, Pilagá, and Wichí groups were not rare. The battles that involved the Tobas in 1917 were part of the final military assault on this region, and in the 1920s and early 1930s troops stationed on the Pilcomayo were still committing massacres of indigenous groups. In 1928, looking for protection from the army and the settlers, the Tobas asked British missionaries who had recently arrived in the area to establish a mission in their lands. Two years later, the missionaries founded a station among them on the Pilcomayo River.

When in the mid and late 1990s Toba men and women looked at their past, they saw the foundation of the Anglican mission in 1930 as the most clear turning point in their history. People refer to their ancestors living before the arrival of the missionaries as *yagaiki'pí*, the "old ones" or "ancient ones" (*los antiguos* in Spanish). Most Tobas view the ancient ones with an ambiguous mixture of proximity and distance. The *yagaiki'pí* were certainly their own ancestors, their own people; but they were also part of a very different and definitively gone world. People usually talk about their grandparents as "them," "the ancient ones," as if the few generations that separate them formed an insurmountable gap. As part of this sense of break with the past, the current generations of Tobas call themselves *dalagaik'pí*, "the new ones," *los nuevos*. The distinction between *yagaiki'pí* and *dalagaik'pí* is part of a single movement, in which the features of one group are defined in contrast to the other. As a result, when people talk about the ancient ones they usually contrast them to themselves, the new ones, and vice versa. This dialectical construction of the past is inescapable to the social memory of any social group. But among the Tobas, as well as among other indigenous groups of the Chaco (Arengo 1996), this memory has been shaped by its immersion within hegemonic imageries about the intrinsic backwardness of *los indios* ("the Indians") and by their own experience of missionization, labor exploitation, and state domination.

When the Anglican missionaries arrived in their lands in 1930, many Tobas of the Pilcomayo (men, women, and children) had been migrating for about three decades, but at first only sporadically, as seasonal wage laborers to the sugar plantations of northwest Argentina, in Salta and Jujuy. These migrations continued until the late 1960s, when the plantations mechanized much of their labor processes and Toba men and women began to be recruited by other capitalist sectors. This experience of exploitation has been molded by the hierarchical segmentation of the labor force along ethnic lines imposed by the plantations' administration, which located the Tobas and the rest of the *aborígenes* (the local term used to refer to the indigenous groups of the Chaco) at the bottom of the scale in terms of wages and working conditions. Through this experience of labor, many Tobas acquired the sense of being less valuable than other workers because of their aboriginality. This experience was for decades parallel to the missionization at home, through which the British missionaries condemned the practices of their ancestors as heathen, diabolical, or sinful and banned most of their public rituals and festivities (such as dancing or drinking fermented beverages). In the 1980s—after the 1982 Malvinas (Falklands) War between Argentina and Great Britain—the missionaries diminished their presence in the region, and the Tobas increased their interaction with institutions of the Argentinean state, favored by the return of democracy to the country at the end of 1983. This growing interaction with state institutions brought public-sector jobs and other state resources in their villages, where most households combine foraging and horticulture with petty commodity production and seasonal wage labor. The growing presence of state agencies in the area further immersed the Tobas into discourses that celebrate the European heritage of the nation over their own identity as *aborígenes*. These experiences, the Tobas' attempt to gain recognition and resources from the state, and their simultaneous attempt to give positive meaning to their ethnic identity, have made them produce memories of the ancient ones that are highly dynamic and contradictory.

Current generations of Tobas imagine the times previous to the Anglican missionization as a distant, somewhat dazzling landscape: "the time of the ancient ones." Indeed, people remember this time as a different place: a world of open grasslands and scattered patches of forest (which came to an end with the arrival of the Criollos' cattle, which decimated the grasslands and contributed to the decimation of the bush); furthermore, they remember it as a place without any trace of Criollos, cattle, missionaries, soldiers, or towns. Felipe, a man in his late sixties, defined (like many others) those times through a dialectic between an absolute negativity of markers of the present and an equally absolute presence of *aborígenes:* "In the past there was nothing, absolutely nothing. There was no Juárez [a nearby town], there were no Criollos . . . only the poor *aborígenes*."[3]

In the 1990s, many Toba men remembered those times "when there was nothing" in negative terms, both in a moral sense and in the sense of absences, and as part of narratives that incorporate hegemonic views about the savagery of "uncivilized Indians." Hence, they portray the ancient ones as violent and merciless people who were permanently at war with other indigenous groups (especially the Chulupíes and Wichís), collected the scalps of their slain enemies, were fond of "vices" such as drinking and dancing, and were ignorant of the material goods, manners, and religious values that define the current generations of Tobas. Along the same lines, people talk about themselves, "the new ones," in a positive light: as people who have dropped the heathen rituals of the past, have learned "the message of Jesus Christ," and enjoy many of the valuable material goods and practices of civilization. The Tobas' recurrent emphasis on the "ignorance" of the *yagaiki'pí* often creates a grim image of their past. For instance, Emiliano, a man in his late fifties, presented the opposition between "ancient ones" and "new ones" in terms of the current use by the latter of markers of civility such as "beds" and "chairs":

The *aborígenes* were fighting just among them, among all the poor. Poor ancient ones. . . . There was no bed, just the floor, just the leather of a wild pig [*rosillo*]. They slept there; there was no blanket. . . . The water was pouring into the hut. People were sad . . . I was sad, thinking, very bad the ancient ones. They suffered when it rained. . . . We, the new ones, we know chairs, we know something. The ancient ones didn't. They were bored, very bored. They were sad. Since we're new ones we know beds, we know public health, we know chairs. Not in the past. We knew nothing.

Segundo, a man who was born in the 1920s, told me how "silly" their ancestors were along similar lines: "The ancient ones knew nothing about dates, days, nothing. Silly. People had the ears pierced with a hole like this, big. . . . Not anymore. . . . They didn't know what a shotgun was, they didn't know anything." When men remember their ancestors' first migrations to the sugar plantations at the beginning of the twentieth century, they usually emphasize their estrangement with commodities they had never seen before. For instance, many argue that the *yagaiki'pí* tried to "cook" sugar by pouring it into boiling water. Others tell stories of how they threw away the *yerba mate* (a type of "tea" that is popular in Argentina) because they thought that it was "animal dung." When people recall these stories, they usually cannot avoid laughing, with a sort of tender compassion, at the "ignorance" of the ancient ones.

On other occasions, however, this emphasis on the ignorance of the *yagaiki'pí* acquires a different tone. In these cases, people turn the attributed ignorance of the ancient ones into a naiveté that allows them to justify some of the actions that the Criollos blamed them for. For instance, some men argue that the *yagaiki'pí* "didn't know" that the cattle that began roaming in their lands in the 1910s, brought by the Criollos, "had an owner." Consequently, they go on, they just killed those cows for their meat as they did with any other wild animal. Referring to this attitude, Patricio, a man in his seventies, told me: "Poor people, ignorant, they knew nothing. They didn't know there are believers; they didn't know there are cows." I asked Mariano, a man in his late fifties, why the military came to attack the Tobas in 1917, and he gave me a reply similar to that of many others, emphasizing the *yagaiki'pí's* naïve ignorance of the rules of private property: "They denounced that the ancient one, when there was a cow, when he saw it, he killed it right away. That's why. The ancient one thought that they were from the country, from the bush. But there was an owner. There was an owner." In these cases, the remembered ignorance of the ancient ones triggers an attitude of implicit understanding and complicity; for this unawareness outlines the novelty of the new property rules brought by the settlers and, by doing so, denaturalizes them in relation with the Tobas' own, collective relations of production. And this memory is also politically significant, for it is informed by conflicts over the use of the land with the settlers that continue in the present.

Consequently, when in people's accounts the memory of what the *yagaiki'pí* "lacked" resonates with current experiences of exclusion, the ironies and laughs about them tend to dissipate. Moreover, when men point, directly or indirectly, to their current experience of domination and poverty, they often turn upside down the terms of the opposition between "ancient" and "new" people. This time, those who are portrayed negatively in terms of ignorance and absences—as people who "don't know"—are the new generations of Tobas. Thus, in tension with the characterization of new ones and ancient ones just outlined, it is very common to hear men complain that "the new ones" are *cholagaik'pí,* "flabby" *(flojos):* mediocre hunters and gatherers who are "forgetting" the "bush food" (honey, fish, wild fruits, game meat) and are becoming increasingly dependent on store-bought food (pasta, rice, corn meal, *yerba mate,* sugar). Everybody agrees that this situation makes them physically weak and prone to diseases. As part of the same characterization, many men inevitably compare themselves negatively with their ancestors. For the ancient ones, everybody agrees, were the epitome of health, physical strength, and bravery. This contrast usually hinges upon the opposition between bush food and store-bought food. Teodoro, a nurse in his thirties, told me:

> What's ruining us is the pasta, the rice. In the past, it wasn't at all like this. People used their own food: for instance, algarroba [a wild fruit], honey, fish. Now we're very weak because of the *yerba,* because of the sugar. Our life has already changed, pop drink, juice. Very weak the people. Maybe they're going to have even more diseases. We don't have the energy that we had in the past.

This sense of loss also includes forms of knowledge and skills that in the past defined the practice of the *yagaiki'pí*. These include the shamanic knowledge to communicate with animals and birds, which people agree that current shamans have lost, or the knowledge to use medicinal plants from the bush. In this regard, the memory of the strength, health, and knowledge of the ancient ones informs a critical appraisal of current social conditions. And the complaints on people's diminishing knowledge of the bush or their dependence on *mercadería* (store-bought food) become metaphors for a situation of domination that was alien to the *yagaiki'pí*. Eduardo, a man in his early forties who is now a committed lay member of the Anglican church and used to be active in politics, told me emphatically: "We're new ones, we're useless! The ancient ones didn't grieve about *mercadería*. Now we're new ones, we have to ask to the storekeeper. There's food in the bush, but we're already used to store-bought food. We're drugged already." In this regard, the memory of the autonomy and health of the ancient ones enhances the value of a type of food that, unlike store-bought food, many Tobas still produce through their own labor practices. Hence, bush food becomes a symbol of both a practice over which they still exert relative control and a past free from domination, when their ancestors were full-time foragers who were not dependent on the commodified resources of the *do'okohé* (the whites).

Many Toba men intertwine these contradictory references—the emphasis on the gains of the present and the ignorance of the past, on the abundance of the past and the losses of the present—almost permanently, depending on the circumstances in which they speak. And these shifts create a recurrent ambiguity in their social memory. Javier, a nurse and also an Anglican priest in his sixties, emphasized in a Sunday service: "We're civilized already. We have electric light, we have houses; we know how to read. In the past we knew nothing. We didn't know how to read; we didn't use tables, we didn't use spoons. . . . Now we're like men, we're not like animals." A few months earlier, however, Javier was telling me about a flu epidemic that was affecting many children, and at that time he had given me a strikingly different portrayal of the difference between "new ones" and "ancient ones": "People are very flabby now. The ancient ones ate a lot of proteins, honey. . . . Now people eat carbohydrates only. . . . Now we have no idea how to fight. The ancient ones cut the head of the Chulupíes and drank *aloja* with it, like a plate. I'm not brave enough to do that [laughs]. . . . The ancient ones were very good at running. They didn't get tired."

This unresolved tension between contrasting memories is significant because it informs current political practices, although in a selective and contradictory fashion. Currently, one of the things Toba men value most is having public-sector jobs, and in the 1990s this triggered mobilizations based on the demand for *trabajo* (jobs) in state-run institutions. As part of these demands, men often produce memories that emphasize the need to overcome the sufferings, poverty, and backwardness of the foraging practices of their ancestors through the acquisition of public-sector jobs (even though fishing, hunting, and gathering are still important for the subsistence of most Toba households). Simultaneously, in tension with these memories and the valorization of *trabajo*, most Toba men often exalt "the bush" and foraging as domains of relative autonomy from capitalist exploitation and state control (Gordillo 1999). Furthermore, in the 1980s these meanings were at the core of their successful land claims vis-à-vis the provincial government. In their land struggle and in current complaints about forms of state domination, many men invoke the memory of the ancient ones to outline the health and well-being associated with the use of their lands through foraging, and consequently they emphasize the positive aspects of their ancestors' practices. These oscillations remind us, first, that the production of memory is intrinsically bound to experiences and agendas contemporary to the act of remembering. Secondly, this situation shows how social memory is tied to the definition of values that may have political implications in the definition of hegemonic fields, and how in turn hegemonic values are always negotiated and reconstituted (cf. Williams 1977; see also Lem, this volume).

The memory of the warlike practices of the ancient ones occupies a particular place in this complex unfolding. Even men committed to an Anglican morality (as was Javier's case) are caught up in an admiration not only of their ancestors' strength but also of their practices as warriors. Even though many people argue that one of the most important values "the new ones" learned from the missionaries was "to live in peace" and "love our brothers," and even though they assert that the *yagaiki'pí* were cruel and merciless, they often show a subtle fascination at the fighting skills of their grandparents. This fascination for a warlike pride often creates more or less open expressions of nostalgia. Gervacio, a man in his forties actively involved in local politics, told me in 1996, intertwining some of the contradictory views on the "ancient ones" I have referred to:

> They didn't have a place where to stay for good, poor things. They were mean, the ancient ones, they only thought about war. So many men died in this land where we live! So many were those who died! Here, they defended the land, they defended it, defended it. That's the history of the ancient ones. Now, it's peaceful around here; in the past it wasn't. Now, we don't endure anything. Not the old ones, they were tough, they had their spirit. That's why they knew when somebody was coming, through the birds. But who knows how to do that now? Nobody, I think. Not even the *pioGonáq* [shamans] Now, the *pioGonáq* have no knowledge whatsoever; they aren't like the ancient ones. . . . In the past, there were spirits which were strong, which helped the people [*el pueblo*]. What a strength that people had! I think that now there's nothing left of that.

Despite the tensions permeating this account, by outlining their ancestors' knowledgeable boldness Gervacio ended up emphasizing the positive features of the *yagaiki'pí* ("they had their spirit," "what a strength!") over the negative ones ("poor things," "mean," "only thinking about war"). The production of nostalgic memories such as this one are particularly clear when men remember their ancestors' most important display of bravery: their fighting against the army.

"It's Them Who Died!"

Many adult men can give long, detailed accounts of the clashes of 1917, and many among them clearly enjoy recalling those events, as if this memory was a confirmation of the boldness and strength not only of the ancient ones but also of "the Tobas" as a single people. In their remembrance of these battles, men focus on gestures, images, and actions that usually merge the two clashes in Laguna Martín and Sombrero Negro into the narrative of a single fight. This narrative articulates events relatively independent from each other: the "birds" telling the shamans that the military were coming; the headman wounded "in the leg"; the two "girls" (some say "boys") kidnapped by the military; the capture by the Tobas of a wagon carried by the soldiers; the leading presence of a warrior and shaman named *Yogodíñik* who proclaimed that bullets would not wound him and that all the settlers were to be expelled from their lands; the moment when a Toba headman, with a precise shot from his Winchester rifle, killed the officer in charge of the troops: the hated "Teniente Videla," who was the second in command of one of the regiments involved (Torres 1975, 53; Rodas 1991, 59).[4]

Beyond these details, what I always found most striking in these accounts was the depiction of the outcome of the fighting, totally at odds with the version of the battle that has become dominant in the historiography of the region. Rodas (1991, 59), a regional historian, quoted a Criollo who joined the advancing troops and noted that many Tobas fled across the river to avoid extermination: "For a moment the Indians resisted the attack, but since they saw that they were dying by the score, they started fleeing to the river, which was four hundred meters away from the village. . . . Many got to reach the other side of the Pilcomayo, but those who fell in the fight were much more." In the 1990s, however, most Toba men claimed—with startling conviction—that their grandparents killed an enormous number of soldiers and defeated the army, suffering almost no casualties. Take, for instance, these three men in their sixties and seventies, whom I talked to about the clashes independently of one another:

> *Did any ancient one die?* Nothing, nothing! Sixty military died. *Aborigen,* nothing. One was injured, shot here [he pointed to his leg]. But it healed. (Segundo)
>
> More than two hundred of the army died . . . *What about the Tobas?* Not even one Toba died. [The soldiers] almost caught a little old man. But they didn't see him, because he was beside a large *yuchán* tree. . . . (Mariano)
>
> Many soldiers died. Like one thousand, or fifteen hundred. *What about the Tobas?* Nobody died. Only a very old woman; she couldn't escape from the hut. The Criollos say that like two thousand *aborígenes* died, but no, nothing. It's them who died! (Agustín)

Many Tobas acknowledge that the "ancient ones" had to cross the Pilcomayo River to Bolivia. But they did so, most agree, only because they ran out of ammunition. Moreover, their retreat did not change the status of their victory. After Mariano told me that the Tobas crossed the river, I asked him: "So, who won then?" He looked a bit surprised at my question and said: "The Tobas won." Ernesto, a schoolteacher in his thirties, told me about the retreat across the river, and when I asked him whether many Tobas died in the clashes, he replied: "No. Very few, they say."

These confident reconstructions of the battles of 1917 were always a sort of a puzzle for me in terms of the complex conjunction of memory, historical experience, and the blurry contours of "truth." And they provide a sharp contrast to the memory of other indigenous groups living in the same region, such as the Wichís. Even though Wichí men have also produced heroic accounts of partial victories over the army, most of them remember in an open fashion the death and terror that the military caused among them (see VV.AA. 1994, 12, 18–20, 36). By contrast, the social memory that most Toba men have produced about those times of violence does not include a memory of terror. It is not a memory about soldiers murdering Toba men, women, and children. Rather, it is about Toba warriors killing soldiers, and plenty of them.

The importance of this memory does not lie merely in the fact that it contradicts the "official history." It is certainly tempting to emphasize the subjective components of memory when the narrative includes what seem to be improbable events (Smith 1994). But memory is always a cultural construction made from the concerns of the present, a representation of past events that hinges on clusters of meaning important for those who remember. And being the Tobas' last armed demonstration of defiance to the state, the memory of the battle conjures for current generations of men clear meanings of pride and resistance. Since the nineteenth century, explorers and missionaries have argued that one of the defining "cultural attributes" of the Tobas of the Pilcomayo, especially in contrast to the Wichís, was their "insolence" and "arrogance" (cf. Campos 1888, 153; Leake 1970, 13). This "arrogance"—in addition to being an ideological construction by white observers—was an expression of the fact that until the early twentieth century warfare was central in the socialization of Toba men. Their conversion to Christianity and the social control imposed by the missionaries implied not only the end of the warriors' practices and rituals but also a deep reconfiguration of this "Toba pride." When in the 1990s Toba men remembered their grandparents defying the settlers and the army, this pride gained new, different meanings, reformulated by an experience of oppression. This experience, although sharp, has not been long enough to blur the memory of a past of independence that, as such, denaturalizes the life conditions of the present. Hence, when remembering the fighting with the army the contrast with the past gains a semantic momentum of its own, and people put momentarily aside the negative and condescending features they attach to the *yagaiki'pí*. Their ancestors are no longer "poor things," ignorant, and heathen; this time they are simply brave, skillful, unbeatable warriors who were doing something no Toba man would dare doing today: to face, arms in hand, the institutions of the Argentinean state.

Memory, Hegemony, and the Shadows of State Terror

Ted Swedenburg (1991, 156) has argued that social memory is "one front in the battle over hegemony." Along similar lines, the Toba men's memory of their ancestors is part of an attempt to put forward a particular version of their past, molded by a silent, unconscious tension between contrasting views on the *aborígenes* that result from their immersion within processes of construction of hegemony by the state. Thus, most Tobas produce memories about the ancient ones trying to partially adapt to discourses about the negative features of indigenous groups living outside Christianity and civilization while at the same time partially challenging these discourses, by trying to give positive meaning to their own identity as *aborígenes*. As part of this process, their memory becomes part of what defines them as a social subject. As argued by Michel-Rolph Trouillot (1995, 16), the collective subjects who remember their past did not exist as such at the time of the events they claim to remember: "Rather, their constitution as subjects goes hand in hand with the continuous creation of the past. As such, they do not succeed such a past: they are its contemporaries."

The Toba men's recollection of their violent experience with the army in 1917 is part of what makes their past contemporary to their present, and it provides a counterpoint to the ambiguity that permeates their memory of "the ancient ones." This is a memory produced by generations that did not experience the violence of the army in a direct way and have reformulated its significance in terms of their own, more recent social experiences. More so than in other areas of their social memory, the recollection of the battle conjures up values of defiance to state authority that challenge dominant accounts on the positive character of their incorporation into the Argentinean nation-state. Yet this memory evokes meanings of pride and resistance from a deeply paradoxical and in the end politically weakening position, which downplays the amount of social suffering unleashed among them by the military. All over Latin America, the public memory of terror has become politically important as a form of social healing and as a condemnation of state repression. Among the Tobas of this area of the Pilcomayo, this critical dimension of memory is relatively absent; but this does not mean that terror is not inscribed in other domains of their social memory.

In the 1990s, I often noticed that in the confident memory of the events of 1917 it was possible to unearth some of the social scars left on the Tobas by those turbulent times; for the emphatic, unambiguous stress on their grandparents' victory and the negation of their status as victims of state violence ("It's them who died!") expresses one of the features of memory as a social construction: that the smoother the story is remembered the more evident it is that it has been considerably "reworked" (Lambek 1996, 246). And when in the 1990s men remembered the events that followed the clashes, they revealed—usually unaware of contradicting their previous accounts of the battle—some threads of the terror that in those years their grandparents may have experienced.

Many Tobas agree that after running out of ammunition and retreating across the Pilcomayo the ancient ones had to move farther to the east, could not return to their territories for several years, and temporarily stopped migrating to the *ingenios* (sugar plantations). Some men argue that the *yagaiki'pí* returned to their homelands and reassumed labor migrations only because the owners of a particular sugar plantation, San Martín del Tabacal, sent *mayordomos* (contractors) to their lands again. As if not talking directly about the battle made them more willing to acknowledge the power of the army, they agree that the contractors asked the military "not to kill the Tobas" and that in that moment the *yagaiki'pí* were terrified at the sight of soldiers. Patricio had just told me about the clashes of 1917 in detail and emphasized that whereas scores of soldiers were left dead on the ground "not even one Toba died." Yet a few minutes later, when recalling the arrival of the *mayordomos,* he told me, to my amazement at his capacity to shift with undisturbed grace between contradictory statements:

> If it wasn't for the *ingenio* San Martín, there would be no Toba left. Ingenio San Martín defended the people. . . . In the year 1919, Patrón Costas remembered the Tobas: "Very hard-working," he said. So, he sent a *mayordomo* to look for the Tobas. . . . And the people went with the *mayordomo*. They were most scared. Poor Toba people, they were most scared at the military. *Why?* Because maybe the military didn't forget and wanted to fight. But the people already had a *mayordomo,* and he told the commander that they had to stop screwing around, that they had to stop killing people, that the people had to work so that Argentina keeps growing.

On the one hand, accounts such as this bring to light the complex ways in which class and nationhood were then being amalgamated in the Tobas' traumatic incorporation into a new political economy. It is also suggestive of the way in which people in the 1990s traced back their own inclusion into the "imagined community" of Argentina. On the other hand, and most importantly for our narrative, this account shows that the *yagaiki'pí* indeed seemed to have been terrified by the military. Along similar lines, other men clearly remember the intense fear that the ancient ones felt at the sugar plantations when, several times in the 1920s, the administration threatened "to kill them all" due to violent incidents with foremen. Thus, people remember that fear was a recurrent aspect of the experience of the *yagaiki'pí* after the repression of the army, and this experience most probably played a major role in their request for the protection of the British missionaries in 1928.

These blurred, indirect expressions of earlier experiences of state violence are also connected, in mediated ways, with the wave of state terrorism that swept Argentina during the military dictatorship of 1976–1983. In those years, the Tobas of the mid-Pilcomayo were not the target of organic forms of repression, for this area of the Chaco was relatively marginal in terms of previous political activism. Still, during the Malvinas War between Argentina and Britain of 1982, and after the British missionaries left the country, the *gendarmes* (military police of border areas) regarded the Tobas as potential allies of *los ingleses* (the English). Thus, they made several searches in their villages looking for weapons and interrogating people. In 1995, Eduardo told me that in those days of 1982 his old aunt in her eighties (now deceased) thought that the army would arrive in their lands scorching the earth as it did in the late 1910s. He remembered: "One day she was crying, the old woman, because she was scared. . . . She was very scared, the old woman, for she knew. She had seen that, when she was young . . . when the military came."

The fact that the person who felt terrified at the prospect of repeating the experience of 1917 was a woman is certainly a sign of the gendered forms of memory created by Toba men in the 1990s. Yet among the generation of men who participated in these clashes, in the following decades terror seems to have been similarly present in their social memory. It was only after dozens of interviews and informal chats on this issue in the mid-1990s that I began to gather bits and pieces of what that previous generation of Toba men, by then long gone, may have remembered of 1917. For instance, Esteban, a man in his late thirties, told me that when his father was alive he did not like to remember the fighting with the army: "Now people like to talk about it, but the old people didn't." When I asked him why, he did not elaborate much on that; he simply added that this memory made his father "sad." In my experience among the Tobas, only once did a man talk openly and explicitly of the horror and death brought by the army. And it was almost by chance that I heard him. One morning in May 1996, I was chatting with Eduardo in his household and he was telling me that "the day of the *aborígenes*" (a holiday celebrated in some provinces of Argentina on April 25) should not be a day of "joy" but rather one of "pain." A few meters away from us Julián, a man in his fifties, was listening in silence. All of a sudden, he started talking. It took me a few seconds to realize he was referring to the battles of 1917. Eduardo and I turned, and we listened to a version of the outcome of the fighting totally opposed to the one that has become dominant among Toba men, and openly critical of it:

> There's a place, *kodagi lakaegó* ["the head of the *majana* wild pig"], it has no name in Spanish. My old man used to say that there, the military reached the ancient people, where they used to hide. There, it seems that the military got the people. There, a lot of people of our ancient ones died. There are other old men who say that the ancient people didn't die. But that's a lie. Many died, when the military came.

The complexity of the production of social memory certainly defies a dualistic opposition between "true" and "false" accounts. But Julián's memory, triggered by a reference to the pain of the *aborígenes*, points to a critical component that is absent in the dominant recollection of the battle among most Toba men. On the one hand, this dominant narrative provides a counterpoint to the ambiguity that characterizes much of their social memory; it highlights the historical contradictions underlying their own experience of domination and brings to the fore values of resistance, defiance, and pride that state terror aims at suppressing. But on the other hand, by downplaying horror this memory undermines its own potential to turn pain into a critical political force. That morning, Julián brought to light that counteracting domination requires, aside from pride, the collective remembrance of the suffering unleashed by state terror.

Notes

I presented an earlier version of this chapter in the American Ethnological Society/CASCA Meeting held in May 1998 in Toronto. My analysis of the Tobas' social memory has benefited enormously from the challenging incentive of Gavin Smith and Richard Lee. I am also grateful to John Comaroff, Andrew Martindale, Michael Lambek, Robin Oakley, Celia Rothenberg, Heike Schimkat, Andrew Walsh, and in particular Anke Schwittay for their critical insights on some of the topics here discussed. Winnie Lem's and Belinda Leach's comments greatly contributed to improving this chapter. Kari Jones read one of its final versions with her always caring and sharp eye. My deepest gratitude goes to the Tobas, who over the years have generously shared with me their experiences, concerns, and memories. My fieldwork was funded, at different stages, by The Wenner Gren Foundation for Anthropological Research (Pre-doctoral grant 6053), the Secretaría de Ciencia y Técnica, Universidad de Buenos Aires, and the Ministry of Education and Training of Ontario.

1. After the Chaco War between Paraguay and Bolivia (1932–1935), most of the Chaco boreal, north of the Pilcomayo, became Paraguayan territory.

2. This Toba group forms a subgroup of the Argentinean Tobas and today encompasses about 1,500 people living in the northwest of Formosa province. The Tobas belong to the Guaycurú linguistic family and encompass a total population of circa 30,000 in Argentina, most of whom fall into subgroupings that inhabit the mid-east of Chaco and Formosa provinces.

3. All the names mentioned in the text are pseudonyms.

4. However, Lieutenant Videla's personal file in the Archivo General del Ejército (The Army General Archives) in Buenos Aires shows that he survived the battle with the Tobas. He retired in 1953 and died in 1967. A.G.E. *Legajo 14775. Legajo personal original del Teniente Coronel Videla, Luis H.*

CHAPTER 14

Class, Discipline, and the Politics of Opposition in Ontario

Belinda Leach

> No mass action is possible if the masses themselves are not convinced of the goals they want to achieve and of the methods that need to be applied. In order to be able to become a governing class, the proletariat must rid itself of every residue of corporatism, every syndicalist prejudice and incrustation. What does this mean? It means that the distinctions that exist between one trade and another must be overcome. But not only: in order to win the trust and the consent of the peasants and of some semi-proletarian urban categories, it is also necessary to overcome certain prejudices and to defeat certain forms of egoism that can and do subsist within the working class as such, even after the disappearance of narrow craft distinctions.
>
> —Antonio Gramsci

On Saturday, October 24, 1996, about a quarter of a million people rallied at the Ontario legislature to protest the policies of the provincial government. It was the largest demonstration in Canadian history. In the warmth of sun and solidarity I demonstrated with friends and family in Toronto, as we had done a few months earlier at a similar event in Hamilton. For many of us these events were especially powerful and vital because, under the banners of student, labor, women's, First Nations, antiracist, and disability groups, the day brought together a broad-based coalition of popular organizations, promising a progressive political movement in response to restructuring policies. Yet the thrill was accompanied in the weeks that followed by nagging questions concerning research and politics. If this event signaled the possibility for a regeneration of the Left in Ontario politics, how could one explain the withdrawal of active support by a number of Ontario unions during the preceding months, severing the fragile but critical relationship with a broad-based coalition of community organizations? At the same time these moves held an ominous resonance with things I had heard in my conversations with steelworkers a couple of years earlier—their shift away from labor militancy toward more right-wing political parties and their frustration with policies such as employment equity, welfare, and immigration.

While such questions may be construed as emerging from the particular historical conjuncture that unions in Canada face, and to an extent they are, the issue of the goals of labor unions is far from being a new one for politically engaged analysts on the Left. Marx and Engels, as well as Lenin, while arguing that working-class consciousness would emerge from formal organization (the union or the party), recognized that there were limitations to the kind of consciousness that would emerge from daily shopfloor experiences. For Lenin, "trade union consciousness" limited workers' attention to day-to-day instrumentalist issues and narrow goals, but social transformation could only occur with the development of concern for broader issues (Hobsbawm 1984, 27). Lenin's solution to the political problem thrown up by this was to import socialist consciousness from outside, via the party vanguard.

Gramsci began from a Leninist position, and in his earlier writings was concerned about the potential of the older, established unions in Italy to nurture a socialist consciousness in workers. He set up parallel "factory councils" to which all workers could belong regardless of party or union membership, where workers would develop consciousness of their adversarial relation to the factory owners, since, as a contemporary of Gramsci wrote, "until this consciousness is universally affirmed in the work place, it is futile to talk about the founding of a new state" (Togliatti cited in Gramsci 1979, 442). The councils were eventually supposed to take over the role of the unions, where they could address problems of "discipline," training workers to act appropriately in their political actions. The factory councils failed, however, and Gramsci's attention shifted to a much more cultural and historical analysis, discarding Lenin's solution and developing his ideas in two key directions. First, through the concept of hegemony, which helped explain the contradictory consciousness of the working classes, and second, through the idea of the organic intellectual, as a political strategy for uncovering hegemonic processes and by connecting individual experience to broader social processes (Eagleton 1991, 119).

This chapter attempts to reveal the roots of the failure of the attempted coalition of labor and community groups that staged the Days of Action in Ontario. Understanding this is crucial to resolving a key strategic problem for Left intellectuals and politicians, and for the labor movement, how to revitalize a Left political agenda while incorporating diverse constituencies that do not make class-based identity their priority, and ultimately to the central political goal of social transformation itself. To piece together an understanding of the dissent that undermined the coalition, the chapter explores four lines of inquiry. Part one talks about the Days of Action and class issues; the second part looks at the industrial relations framework, in which discipline is a key issue; the third draws on my field research with steelworkers in Hamilton, members of the United Steelworkers of America (USWA), one of the unions that withdrew from the coalition, to reveal the cultural configurations that underpin steel work in Hamilton; and the fourth part builds on that cultural analysis to shed light on the actions of the union leadership, actions that were key to the split in the coalition. The paper draws on ideas from Gramsci for the analysis of trade unions, discipline, and the constitution of the Fordist worker.

Local union politics and solidarity, together with a prosperous steel industry, made the USWA Local 1005 at the Stelco steel company in Hamilton strong and powerful within the Canadian labor movement (Freeman 1982). But the potential for transformation through these kinds of class politics has been muted by the accommodating tendencies of Fordism, which brought organized labor, business, and the state into uneasy equilibrium. The chapter draws out the ways in which the discipline of organized labor operates to constrain political action, and the role taken by organic intellectuals both within the labor movement and outside of it, within a specific cultural and historical configuration. Discipline emerges as an especially important keyword here, for while it is crucial for the development of a working class movement, paradoxically, in the specific form it has taken through the industrial relations system in Ontario, it constrains rather than facilitates counterhegemonic consciousness.

Using my research with Hamilton steelworkers to shed light on the actions of the union's leadership, I show that the local politics of class, historically constituted and always gendered and racialized, include the everyday experiences of workers, the organizational forms with political potential that emerge, and the regulatory framework within which organizations and individuals operate. Together, these strands result in a particular kind of labor leadership that influences the potential or otherwise of broad-based political mobilization. The questions that emerged following the Days of Action become especially important in understanding present processes of economic restructuring (in which the provincial government is actively engaged) as not simply economic, but also building upon and shaping other aspects of social life. In this process political actors are reconstituted, inhibiting some forms of mobilization while they facilitate others, demanding a rethinking of strategies for the Left.

The Days of Action and Its Class Basis

The political landscape in Ontario at the turn of the century is dominated by a conservative government, elected in 1995, just a year after my fieldwork, which has relentlessly pursued policies that erode economic security for most working people.[1] Immediately after the election, a series of demonstrations began in cities around the province to protest the political agenda of the government. These demonstrations developed into more organized protests including local general strikes in London, Hamilton, and eventually Toronto. At first organized by the Ontario Federation of Labour (OFL), they gradually incorporated more and more community-based organizations. But the relationship between the two kinds of groups was always difficult. Of the London strike in November 1995, one community activist commented, "It is a labor defined thing. Either you sit with it or you don't," and a journalist noted that flyers circulated by the unions that day targeted the new "right-to-work" legislation, with no attention to community issues (Ziedenberg 1996a, 7). The unions were protesting fairly narrowly defined workplace issues, rather than broader social issues such as health, education, and welfare cuts.

Unlike the London and Hamilton protests, which were clearly labor led, in an important symbolic move the coordinating committee for the Toronto Days of Action was co-chaired by two women, one from the labor movement, the other from the social justice community. The process of building toward the October events involved teach-ins and rallies around child care, public education, and health care, as well as interfaith vigils, First Nations rallies, and cross-cultural events (Ziedenberg 1997, 8). The labor movement seconded seventy staff to help organize community groups, as well as providing infrastructural funding.

The first day of the action in Toronto was a citywide shutdown, the second a march and demonstration, at which thousands marched under union banners representing many different kinds of workplaces. Yet even as their members marched, the leadership of some of the unions was distancing itself from the campaign. As his union brothers and sisters picketed Toronto workplaces, the president of the OFL was photographed raking leaves in his garden (Ziedenberg 1997, 10). The Pink Paper group,[2] which included the steelworkers' union, objected to the organizers' refusal to provide special status at the rally to the New Democratic Party (NDP). This refusal was due to the anger many unions felt toward the NDP, which, while in office, had suspended collective bargaining for government workers. The unions held, in contrast, that the only route for successfully opposing the Tory agenda was through support for the NDP. During a post-protest executive meeting of the OFL, the leaders of the steelworkers and powerworkers unions announced to the press that they would replace the Days of Action with "militant, targeted actions against employers who ignore workers' rights by using scabs and locking out workers" (Ziedenberg 1997, 10).

Making class central to understanding what is happening here is an unpopular position to take, on at least two counts. First, many contemporary cultural theorists argue that Marxism's preoccupation with class has been displaced in political significance. Noting, for example, the resurgence of neofascist groups, racially motivated violence, and racialized discourses around citizenship, such theorists focus on these, rather than class-based discourses and practices, as ways people deal with deepening economic instability and cultural dislocation. Winant argues that "[t]he increasing significance of race (and gender as well) is in part caused by the declining significance of class. Class politics, class struggle, are preponderantly white, male politics. . . ." (Winant 1994, 275). The more fashionable analysis of the events above would be a fairly simplistic one—that labor organizations are now irrelevant and out of touch with the majority of people—women, people of color, students, the disabled, First Nations people, and so on. While such criticism cannot be disregarded, it is not sufficient reason to discard class as irrelevant. Beverley Skeggs (1997, 6) has argued:

> To abandon class as a theoretical tool does not mean it doesn't exist any more, only that some theorists don't value it. It does not mean the women [in her study] would experience inequality any differently; rather it would make it more difficult for them to identify and challenge the basis of the inequality which they experience.

This last point is, of course, the critical political one.

This analysis begins from the premise that economic, social, political, and cultural restructuring is driven by economic imperatives that benefit the rich (as indeed were historical restructuring processes such as colonialism) and result in economic insecurity and precarious livelihoods for a majority of working people. Both historically and in its contemporary forms, Western capitalism is characterized by relations of exploitation. The sharpening of inequalities resulting from the most recent round of transformation of the underlying structural forces in capitalist countries, would force the conclusion that class politics are of crucial rather than marginal importance. Yet, as I show below, class relations are always conditioned by relations of gender, race, region, and the rights of citizenship, among other factors.

The class basis of both the restructuring policies and of the protest emerges quite clearly. The policies of the provincial government support business interests, by removing tough labor and environmental standards, and loosening regulations and laying off workers to pave the way for the entry of for-profit enterprises into previously government-controlled sectors. This kind of restructuring in the public sector accounts for the large numbers of teachers and nurses and their organizations in the protests, as the health care and education sectors are primary targets for privatization. In response to the restructuring initiatives, the protest organizers made the symbols and realities of corporate class power their target during the Days of Action. The one-day general strikes hit employers where they knew it would hurt most, halting production and provision of services. In a symbolic act of class war, a demonstration organized by steelworkers during the Toronto Days of Action besieged traders at the Toronto Stock Exchange (Ziedenberg 1997, 8).

The second reason that my argument is unpopular concerns the dynamic of class politics itself. Many Marxist analysts of organized labor have tended to examine labor exclusively in terms of its conflict with capital. The result of this has been to neglect, or at least overlook, the ways in which labor's economic interests have been historically linked to corporate interests. At a local level, the relationship between corporate success and everyday stability for workers has often led workers to pursue fairly narrowly conceived, instrumentalist goals. There are obvious political reasons for analysts' own rather circumscribed focus. These concern the role of class struggle and labor in the process of social transformation, and the more difficult issue of the role of the analyst in facilitating or impeding social change. Yet a narrow analysis that fails to pay attention to the complexity of the relationship between workers and their employers renders the events under scrutiny here difficult to understand, and impossible to deal with in practical, strategic terms. Other analysts have pointed out similar problems in specific contexts. David Harvey, looking at a fight to keep a car factory open in Oxford (Harvey 1995) and Gerry Sider (1996), in a rethinking of the Massachusetts Bread and Roses Strike, have pointed out how, in quite different ways, concentrating on the local political project and workers' immediate interests obscures larger political questions, complexities, and strategies.

Gramsci's insights permit an analysis that keeps the Left political project central, while pointing to the complexity and contradiction within processes of hegemony and consequent political alignments. Stuart Hall has pointed out Gramsci's conception of the wider social character of class, which, rather than reducing it to "a struggle between two, apparently simple and homogenous class blocs" (Hall 1996, 425), posits a system of alliances, where the strategic political questions concern the mechanisms through which the support of different segments of working people is won through consent rather than compulsion.

Gramsci argued that group consciousness unfolded through three phases or "moments" (Gramsci 1971, 179). The most difficult transition, but essential to social transformation, was to the third phase where workers would recognize their shared interests with all subordinate groups. He argued that trade unionism is an impediment to reaching this third moment because of its disdain for party politics, precisely the ability to be concerned with broader issues. To be "convinced of the goals they want to achieve" (Gramsci 1971, 557), as the opening quotation suggests, is critical to mass action. Labor unions need to make the shift from concern solely with their own narrowly conceived economic well-being, and this requires leadership and discipline, as hegemony is not simply economic, but operates in the cultural, moral, ethical, and intellectual domains as well (Hall 1996, 426). It is precisely this shift that many labor leaders in Ontario (and elsewhere) have been reluctant to bring about. They have been unable, or unwilling, to draw out an understanding beyond the local, and to guide their members so that they come to see "the historical problems flashing on the screen as connected to my own" (Smith 1999, 51). The inability to broaden beyond instrumentalist goals is attributable at least in part to the particular forms that discipline and reward, leadership and organization have taken in this specific locality.

Industrial Relations, Discipline, and Reward

In his early work Gramsci was concerned with discipline which he saw as crucial to the capacity of organizations to develop socialist consciousness in workers. The factory councils were set up because although industrial work had the effect of disciplining workers, Gramsci felt this still to be inadequate to the job of overcoming bourgeois influence (Smith 1999, 49–50). Discipline is an important factor in the the state's capacity to maintain its hegemony (Eagleton 1991, 116), thus counterhegemonic groups must develop their own discipline through conscious intellectual leadership, which Gramsci saw explicitly as going hand-in-hand (Gramsci 1971, 49). It is useful, then, to assess the ways leadership, discipline, and reward have played out in this segment of the Ontario labor movement, and to examine the specific outcomes of this.

In his essay *Americanism and Fordism* Gramsci pointed to the effects of Fordism on the labor movement. He anticipated the emergence of a neocorporatist productivist bloc between industrial workers and management, which would ease the way for further economic development (1971, 291). This has occurred in Ontario in two ways. First, through the institutionalization of the industrial relations system generally, and the collective bargaining process in particular, struggles between labor and capital have been disciplined and constrained by the developing framework for industrial relations, which paradoxically sought to defuse class conflict even as it recognized its existence (Krahn and Lowe 1998, ch. 7). One of the effects of this system has been to divide the leadership from the rank and file by making the leadership responsible for ensuring that members stick to the rules. This puts labor leaders in the position of having to discipline their members to conform to the system, or face penalties themselves. Examples of the kinds of dilemmas for unions that this legislation produces abound in recent Canadian labor history. At least two examples exist in the social memory at the Stelco steelworker local. In one case, the so-called Left Wing Group, which gained power during the late 1960s, objected to the bureaucratization of the industrial relations system and the co-optation of the union staff within that system. The group tried, unsuccessfully, to work against the union staff (Freeman 1982). This paradox within the system also led to a situation where, during a wildcat strike at the steel plant in 1966, management could rely on the leadership to plead with their members to return to the job (Freeman 1982, 103). Thus, under the industrial relations system, the union leadership has to align with the company against the rank and file to ensure the continued production that is protected by the union contract in its "no strike" clause. Moreover, and ultimately more important, the leadership takes an active role in quelling the spontaneous eruption of working-class protest. It is not simply that spontaneous protest is not accommodated by the system, the system is in place to prevent it.

The institutionalization of industrial relations, with concomitant tradeoffs that circumscribe workers' rights even as they enshrine them, was an important step in securing the consent of workers in the actions of capital. Another important step in this process involved the drumming out of the communist elements in the unions, which took place in Canada during the 1950s. In her work on the closure of the General Electric company facility in Pittsfield, Massachusetts, June Nash argues that the demise of the communist unions in the United States in the 1920s and 1930s signaled the ascendence of a corporate hegemony that subsequently set the agenda for labor (Nash 1989). Later, McCarthyism repressed the development of critical political consciousness (Nash 1994). Similarly, in Canada the communist elements in the prewar unions were expelled by less radical unionists working together with the Cooperative Commonwealth Federation (CCF), the predecessor to the NDP, the party then and now most closely linked to the interests of workers. This particular struggle was played out in Hamilton in the steelworkers local as the CCF fought and won supremacy over the communist party leadership (Freeman 1982). Subsequent relations between the union and other communist-identified unions became not simply strained, but politically dangerous.

A similar process took place again in the late 1960s, when a leftist and determinedly nationalist wing of the NDP threatened the party, demanding new agendas and challenging the labor hierarchy within the party. The Waffle aligned itself with rank and file union members, while the mainstream party supported the union leaders. After years of acrimonious fighting, the Waffle was expelled, exposing what Palmer calls "the pragmatic and non-radical nature of the party" (Palmer 1992, 335).

The key issue here is that both communist organizers and members of the Waffle were explicitly interested in broader social issues (for the communists, no less than overturning capitalism), while the business unionists who prevailed were more narrowly interested in serving their members, within the existing system. These historical developments had consequences for the capacity of the labor movement to take a broader, social justice approach.

Under the collective bargaining system the interests of workers are directly linked to the economic well-being of the company. Workers will make gains only if the company is itself healthy, and circularly, this may be constructed as dependent on workers' willingness to work harder and take lesser rewards to allow the company to make capital reinvestment. This apparently mutual dependency is then publicly played out through the incorporation of union representatives on government boards and tribunals. Yet in exchange for the relatively high wages and organizational security that unionized workers enjoy, it can be argued that they have paid a high price. Real power remains concentrated in management's hands, while unions act as advocates for workers in a legalistic and bureaucratic system. As one analyst contends, "[T]he unintended consequence of the establishment of unions has been to legitimize an existing political and economic system in the eyes of the rank and file" (Freeman 1982, 239). Labor politics in this system become circumscribed and curtailed, the potential for transformation effectively removed.

Cultural Configurations: Fordism and Steel Work in Hamilton

In the context of organizational priorities and constraints Gramsci was concerned also with the cultural expressions of ordinary people and the ways in which these two aspects operate together. As Smith (1999, 48) insists, analytically it is crucial to keep these two together, since hegemonic power is pervasively and often obscurely imbricated in daily cultural practices and experience (Eagleton 1991, 114).

In *Americanism and Fordism,* Gramsci reflects on the historic conjuncture that brought about Fordism. He notes the characteristics of Fordism, frequently referred to by recent analysts, to include mass production, carried out by semiskilled workers, commanding high wages through collective bargaining (which also protects corporate interests); the encouragement, through advertising, of mass consumption of mass produced commodities; and the provision by the state of a welfare system designed to protect workers and families from economic downturns. Of course, as it developed, Fordism became a lived reality for only a minority of workers. Even in an affluent country such as Canada entire regions, as well as significant groups of workers in industrial areas, were excluded from the social and economic benefits that it brought. The beneficiaries, people such as the steelworkers I am concerned with here, however, enjoyed a high standard of living, allowing them to participate actively in consuming the commodities they and some of their neighbors made. For steelworkers the rewards of Fordism meant they owned their own homes, most of them far from the working-class neighborhoods around the steel plant built in the early decades of the century to house the workers. Families frequently ran two cars, and their homes exhibited the electronic equipment that signals success in the 1990s.

A striking feature of the steel workforce in Hamilton is that through most of the century it has been almost entirely "white" and male. This is not of course simply a historical accident. The workforce was constituted over generations through discriminatory hiring practices that favored "white" men (Livingstone and Mangan 1996). Various categories of "ethnic" labor, including new migrants, were used by the company in the early decades of the century to keep wages low and profits high. The transience of many of these workers, often willing to work long hours for low pay as they looked for alternative permanent employment elsewhere, resulted in a segmentation of the labor force along ethnic lines, as workers from different backgrounds maintained their "completely separate social worlds" (Heron and Storey 1986, 220–225). Roediger's (1991) evocative phrase "the wages of whiteness" thus has resonance here. In the 1970s, the Women into Stelco campaign, a local protest stimulated by the company's unwillingness to hire women into the well-paying steelmill jobs (see Corman et al. 1993, ch. 4), succeeded in placing women in the plant. Government-initiated antidiscrimination and affirmative action policies in the 1980s also had an effect on the composition of the steel labor force. All of this came to little, however, as the seniority-driven layoffs of the late 1980s and early 1990s led to an almost entirely "white," male workforce by the mid-1990s.

Unlike many subsequent analysts, Gramsci was clear about the cultural implications of Fordism. He persuasively argued that Fordism needed a worker specifically suited to the new processes of production, one who was physically capable (hence the need eventually for the welfare state, anticipated by Gramsci), and psychologically adapted to perform routinized work tasks. Gramsci linked the new methods of work to cultural and ideological shifts concerning sexuality and family life. Prohibition, with its puritanical underpinnings and resultant sober, disciplined worker, was part of the hegemonic project of constituting the Fordist subject. These shifts can also be construed as forms of discipline.

The development of the breadwinner family under these conditions generally, and among Hamilton steelworkers specifically (Livingstone and Luxton 1996; Leach 1997) confirms Gramsci's point. Women who married steelworkers until the early 1980s were expected to stay at home to care for children and husband. Indeed, women's labor force participation rates in Hamilton remained relatively low compared to other parts of the country through the 1970s (Livingstone and Luxton 1996, 112), reflecting the dominance of the breadwinner family form. Women did take part-time work as a short-term solution to financial difficulties during a long strike or layoff. More recently, steelworkers and their families have experienced the effects of restructuring in the industry. At Stelco the workforce has diminished by two-thirds, and a sense of economic instability and job insecurity, even among those still fortunate enough to have their jobs, has become a feature of everyday strategies for getting by. As a result, in the past decade women have entered the labor force more permanently, but often with reluctance and resentment.

I have argued elsewhere (Leach 1997) that steelworkers and their wives showed a marked preoccupation with family issues. By this I mean that conversations seemed inevitably to drift toward a discussion of family issues. This included not only the dynamics of their own families, although these were often foremost in their minds, but included as well the ways family issues were being dealt with by government and the broader society. Members of steelworker families were quick to take conservative positions on contemporary social issues such as lesbian and gay rights, abortion, childcare, and families on welfare. They were frequently outspoken in condemning the effects of feminist and antiracist activism on Canadian society. Resentment was also directed toward immigrant workers competing for "Canadian" jobs, and employment equity policies that would disadvantage their sons' labor market chances (Leach 1998). Their support for such positions, and their recent and unprecedented experience of economic vulnerability, combined with their own demographic composition, hardly drew Hamilton steelworkers to the kinds of community groups represented in the Days of Action coalition.

Connolly (1981, ch. 3) has provided a convincing rationale for such conservative views among the working class. He argues, following Sennett and Cobb, that white working-class males consider the work they do to be justifiable in terms of a sacrifice necessary to ensure their children's futures. The conduct of welfare recipients, student dissidents, feminists, and intellectuals, among others, is viewed negatively because it threatens the ideology of sacrifice upon which working-class life is based. As he argues, "The denial of the grievances of Blacks and welfare recipients is part of the process by which those in marginally more secure circumstances subvert questions about their own dignity, integrity and freedom" (Connolly 1981, 74). He shows how this ideology of sacrifice then supports beliefs in the background about the necessity and desirability of the institutional structures against which the ideology has been developed, in the process giving legitimacy to the dominant institutions and support to their priorities (Connolly 1981, 69), yet at the same time providing a sense of individual agency.

Political Opportunities: The High Stakes of Labor Leadership in the 1990s

The conservative working-class views identified above unconsciously provide the underpinning for a certain kind of administrative power in the labor movement. This in turn underlies the schism that developed within the Ontario labor movement around the Days of Action, which superficially appears to be no more than a difference in political strategy. One analyst argues that the steelworkers' union, the USWA, is the "historic voice" of part of the labor movement where bargaining for local economic issues was primary, and political action was confined to facilitating the election of the NDP. On the other side of the divide are the public sector unions and the Canadian Auto Workers

(CAW), fighting to keep the social, political and economic interests of labor closely linked (Palmer 1996, 23). The struggle between these factions is a struggle over the direction for labor in the province, with critical consequences for social justice and social transformation. The president of one of the public sector unions told a newspaper, "[T]here's no question the Pink Group is trying to take over Ontario's labor movement . . . they are old style labor bosses who think the world begins and ends in their office" (Ziedenberg 1996a, 8).

A senior staff person of the USWA, David Mackenzie, was profiled in a journal article a month after the Toronto Days of Action. He is quoted in confidential internal memos in which he describes his members as unconcerned about the equality issues that drove the lesbian, gay, native, and women activists to protest (Ziedenberg 1996b, 17). He apparently wrote: "'The dirty secret that many choose to evade is just how distant the political, social, and equality views of union leadership are from those of the 'members'" (quoted in Ziedenberg 1996b, 18). In another memo he argued that his members find affirmative action politics and social programs to be "wasteful and unjust," and that his own members have bought into the Tory message on welfare and employment equity (Ziedenberg 1996b, 18; see also Leach 1998). These tendencies are reflected in a move by a CAW local in 1993 that voted to terminate its funding to the New Democratic Party, appealing to its members as "property owners," "whites," "males," and "taxpayers," whose "jobs come from the 'corporate agenda' and investment in Ontario" (quoted in Ziedenberg 1996b, 19). As far as the Days of Action were concerned, for some of the unions, "their members had *voted* for Harris—so there wasn't any point in asking them to protest" (Ziedenberg 1996b, 20). As one union leader summed it up, "We believe that a majority of our members have not yet been directly affected by this government and therefore there is little support for action of this kind" (quoted in Ziedenberg 1996b, 20).

Whereas a Gramscian strategy, and that suggested by the journalist writing the article, would be to attempt to change these ways of thinking, mend the schism, and build toward a socialist transformation, Mackenzie, along with other leaders, derives considerable power from the division. He has used it politically to secure his leadership of the Pink Paper group and to work single-mindedly to elect the NDP (Ziedenberg 1996b, 18).

The leadership on the other side of the issue clearly saw the broader political goals as central to the protests, and there was cautious optimism about the desire of unions to work in coalition with community groups, as well as a new sense of solidarity between labor and community organizations that had not existed before (Ritchie and Bain 1997; Munro 1997). One USWA local vice-president was quite clear about the impact of the protest: "It's the visual message to everybody, not just the government. In fact it did have an impact. The protests educated a lot of people who don't have the privilege of being part of the union" (quoted in Kuitenbrouwer 1997, 17).

Industrial Workers in a Post-Fordist Era

I do not argue that Fordist methods of production have disappeared with the end of the Fordist regime, yet to the extent that the bargain struck between labor, business, and the state, which permitted the relative well-being of certain segments of the working class, has been broken in the last two decades, it seems clear that we are now in a post-Fordist era, and that it is necessary to take the cultural and social implications of that very seriously (Hall 1996, 225). Hamilton steelworkers have seen their workforce shrink, watched their former coworkers and neighbors struggle with unemployment, and confronted job insecurity themselves, all the while aware that the social safety net is unraveling beneath them (Leach 1998). Wives have entered the workforce more permanently to offset the declining standard of living, and provide insurance against job loss. Children and their parents fear for a future without the security an employer such as the steel industry used to provide.

Despite Hamilton's history as one of Canada's oldest industrial cities and a center for labor militancy for well over a century, my research shows a shift away from older, working-class-based identities and identifications with organized labor and the political party designed to represent it. Indeed, at the time of my field research in 1994, when the NDP had been in power in Ontario for three years, even those who said they had always voted for the NDP were leaning toward the parties of the Right. There is little doubt that many I spoke to, along with their brothers in the union, voted for the Harris government the following year, and again when it was reelected in 1999 as this chapter was being written, despite the government's rigid adherence to its right wing agenda. Talking about restructuring at Stelco, several articulated the prevailing political ideology, linking their welfare to that of the company: "The fewer and fewer people, the more competitive we are going to become, the cheaper we'll be able to sell our steel."

These workers now question the relevance of labor organizations and collective bargaining in changing times, and they question especially the wisdom of sustaining an antagonistic relationship with the employer, favoring rather a conciliatory approach in the hope of protecting the company's future and saving jobs, as indicated by the inclusive "we" in the quote above. Comments from the steelworkers, such as "I think the day of ranting and raving and standing outside with a placard is over" and "unions have run their course," support these ideas.

This is in marked contrast to the continued militancy of workers in Cape Breton who face restructuring initiatives (see Barber this volume), a difference I take to be the result of their very different experiences of Fordism. The positions taken by steelworkers above are not taken without reflection and a degree of awareness, and are certainly colored, complicated, and slowed by local labor history and labor ideology (Leach 1998). Moreover, actions at the local level are not necessarily consistent with those of the leadership. The vice-president of one USWA local (not a steelworker) firmly stated that despite the USWA leadership's position that it would not be involved in future protests, his local "would definitely get a bus and go down" (quoted in Kuitenbrouwer 1997, 17). This suggests that space exists for counterhegemonic struggle within the leadership of the labor movement.

These workers are fighting on a number of fronts to defend the way of life that Fordism promised them, and they do it constrained by their history, their everyday experience, their leadership, and the regulatory framework. As Alf Lüdtke (1995) has shown in trying to understand the shift of a strong, Left union movement toward fascism in Germany after 1919, it is the combination of everyday life experience and the institutional framework in which these take place that leads to particular political positions. For steelworkers these factors get in the way of their wholehearted involvement in the kind of popular protest represented by the Days of Action.

A useful way to understand this is to consider the idea of the strike, the ultimate bargaining tool of workers historically, and a cornerstone of the Days of Action strategy. Within the contemporary Canadian industrial relations system, the strike is the final stage in a controlled, bureaucratic process, and can only be used when all other routes for dispute resolution have been exhausted. This protects employers from unanticipated work stoppages, ensuring continuous production for the duration of a union contract. Labor staff and leaders, as well as workers more generally, have been socialized into this bureaucratized system and leaders made to police their members if they transgress, as noted earlier regarding the wildcat strike at the steel plant in 1966. Discipline is clearly an important aspect of the strike tool within this system.

Within this framework, the local general strikes attempted through the Days of Action in each city are illegal acts, with those participating subject to fines or imprisonment. I remarked earlier that the Pink Paper union leaders stated that they preferred to target "employers who ignore workers' rights by using scabs and locking out workers" (cited in Ziedenberg 1997, 10). They wanted to maintain their protest within the existing framework, protesting employers not honoring the principles laid down over decades. Indeed, faced with the demand to close their own workplace, the Stelco plant, during the Hamilton Days of Action, the steelworkers' union preferred to negotiate with their employer to substitute that day for a later statutory holiday. They chose to arrange to get the day off with pay, within the terms of their collective agreement, rather than to strike illegally. They even refused to set up a symbolic picket line around the steel plant (Palmer 1996, 23).

In the weeks preceding the Toronto protest the mainstream press published numerous articles outlining the disruption that would be caused by the Days of Action, and the potential for chaos, violence, and even riot. There seemed to be a profound fear and anticipation of an undisciplined mass protest. Yet the responses to the actual events are equally interesting. As one left-wing commentator put it, "When the well-organized, disciplined work stoppage took place without violence, with little confrontation and with no suffering that anyone could discover, some of the media declared it a failure" (Rebick 1996, 26). While the mainstream newpapers could apparently only yawn in the aftermath, the left-wing press exhibited considerable relief that events had proceeded without significant incident, variously describing it as "well organized" and "peaceful." Discipline was a concern across the political spectrum.

Yet the general strike is the most powerful weapon the working class has because, as one editorial stated, "[T]here are no limits to the uncertainty it raises (investors hate uncertainty) and the economic damage it does to the capitalists (they hate that even more)" (*Canadian Dimension* Jan.–Feb. 1997, 3). The general strike is the popular expression of the only real power the working class has, to withdraw its labor collectively and strategically. Palmer argues that the strikers were "sacrificing the material reward of days of pay, risking state wrath by insisting that the political strike is a right of the workers movement, rather than an illegal act" (Palmer 1996, 23), in other words, demanding a historic right of citizenship. Apparently in agreement, the Ontario courts ruled in 1998 that the Days of Action were not an illegal strike, but rather a political protest.

It seems ironic that the workers who might be expected to lead such a general strike are those for whom the experience of Fordism in the postwar period has produced a very circumscribed notion of class struggle. While the union leadership is constrained by a narrowly conceived range of action consistent with the industrial relations aspects of the Fordist regime, the membership, because of the historical construction of steel work, community, and family life, find their interests lie closer to those of the company and a neoconservative government than to the organizations forming the loose Days of Action coalition. Clearly, the capacity to lead the popular movement from a position of industrial strength (Gill 1997) is also a factor inhibiting the role these workers take. These would seem to be key issues in developing and sustaining an alternative politics in opposition to the neoconservative agendas dominating most world polities.

Notes

1. Such policies include a 22 percent cut to welfare benefits, repeal of progressive labor legislation, elimination of equity policies, and cuts of $1.7 billion from health and $1.3 billion from education.

2. The Pink Paper Group emerged in response to the move by public sector unions to cut their ties to the NDP. The private sector unions dissented with a statement printed on pink paper.

CHAPTER 15

Militant Particularism and Cultural Struggles as Cape Breton Burns Again

Pauline Gardiner Barber

This chapter examines how industrial workers in Cape Breton, Nova Scotia, known for their volatile labor and cultural politics, are faring under the socially fractious neoliberal regimes at the turn of the century. The priorities of globally mobile capital have turned from coal and steel, the mainstays of Cape Breton's economy for more than 150 years. These industries, often unstable, are in the final stages of a long and socially painful demise. Theories of uneven development suggest such a scenario is historically predictable. Things are, however, more confusing from the standpoint of many workers who continue, with militant particularism, to contest plant closures, privatization, and the terms of settlement for layoffs. This is particularly true in Cape Breton's industrial "heartland" made up of the old coal towns and Sydney, the regional center. Sydney harbors what was once a major steel plant, now a costly white elephant and major ecological disaster.[1] Although processes of deindustrialization are essentially complete, many still contest the role of industry in local development. They also challenge the reductions in federal government social spending which, as budget slashing intensified during the 1990s, were widely interpreted in Cape Breton as a refusal to honor previously struck bargains between employers, the state, and laid-off workers who, to use a Cape Breton cultural idiom, are "down on their luck."

The ethnographic material in this chapter includes two moments of transformation in Cape Breton's political economy. First, I discuss the many layers of meaning, material and symbolic, surrounding the torching of a construction site during a labor rally in Sydney in February 1997, ostensibly because nonunion labor had been hired. Such defiance can be related to class practices, which are imbricated with ideas about community. In Cape Breton, forceful labor militancy has historical antecedents (Barber 1992) but in the late 1990s it seems out of step with the newly valorized entrepreneurial livelihoods and flexible subjectivity, the hallmark of neoliberal "development" policies.

My second example considers responses to the "death throes" of Cape

Breton's mining industry. This discussion takes us forward to January 1999 and the federal government's announcement of the pending closure of the two remaining Cape Breton collieries managed by the Canadian crown corporation, Devco. The Phalen mine was slated for closure, the Prince mine for privatization. Because the mining scenarios remain unresolved, particularly with regards to layoff protocols and pension settlements, the industrial "riot" will receive greater attention. The struggles described here engage ideas about community and livelihoods as key issues of contention in the period under discussion (February 1997 to March 1999). Why this is so and who comprises the "us" and "them" of Cape Breton community/ies are central to this chapter.

The "Industrial Riot" and Its Aftermath

On February 24, 1997, a crowd of approximately one thousand people, reportedly composed of unionized workers and their supporters, ran "amok" in industrial Cape Breton. Angered by the hiring of nonunion labor at a construction site in Sydney, a large crowd assembled early in the morning. The gathering included some two hundred tradesmen employed at the area's largest construction project, Stora Forest Industries, located at Port Hawkesbury, forty-five minutes' drive from Sydney. These workers called in sick in a remarkable display of union solidarity causing the company to halt construction for the day. In Sydney, the morning brought chaos as tempers flared and some nonunion men were "roughed up." The building on the picketed site—a seniors' apartment complex of fifty-one units—was then set alight, along with a worker's truck and a security vehicle. Firefighters were turned away by the crowd, and police and firefighters were pelted with ice.

As the crowd dispersed around ten in the morning, one woman turned to television cameras and shouted, to the accompaniment of loud cheers: "We're alive and well in Cape Breton!" This challenge resonates with ideas about livelihood, identity, and community, and speaks to the widespread concern of Cape Breton working people about their fears for loss of their "way of life." Stora workers were also somewhat redeemed in the recriminations surrounding the incident when a company spokesperson publicly praised their work and reported the union guarantee that absent employees would make up the lost time (*Mail Star,* 28 February 1997). Here, a politics of resistance and accommodation, their double face, is revealed. In avoiding reprimand, union militancy was seemingly vindicated. On the other hand, union concerns with company production schedules could be portrayed as cooperation (rather than complicity)—precisely the mode of unionism called for by Cape Breton business leaders.

In the days following the riots police were criticized for not taking a more aggressive stance. They were, however, more successful than members of the media (forced to retreat to the periphery) in recording the events on video. Police chief MacLeod later defended the reaction of his force, insisting that "intervention at that time would have led to an escalation of violence and bloodshed" (*Mail Star*, 26 February 1997). Eventually this defense was accepted by the most vocal critics, the Cape Breton Board of Trade, who were appeased by police accounts of their ongoing investigations. Interestingly, the Nova Scotia provincial minister of labor, a Cape Bretoner from Sydney, refused to define the events within the purview of the Trade Union Act. Instead, he discursively repositioned the event as "an act of violence," a matter of law and order not a labor dispute. Yet, in the numerous public conversations about these unlawful events, ideas about economic development priorities and the character and needs of Cape Breton labor were both prominent and contradictory. Class and cultural struggles loomed in the aftermath of the riot.

Police investigations were publicly scrutinized as the media focused upon a perceived threat to business. For example, Sydney's mayor, Coady, summed up local business interests, calling labor leaders to task for failing to apologize for the riot: "We're talking about business and business development in the region. Many companies are refusing to provide [insurance] coverage and others are including rioting clauses in the policies stating that only unionized workers can be hired" (*Mail Star*, 9 May 1997). This could be read as a union victory, but hardly any pro-union voices entered the public debate and police and politicians were closely monitored for any suggestion that workers' frustrations were justified.

One month after the riot, a team of twelve investigators reported interviewing three hundred suspects and 130 eyewitnesses, many of whom were members of the large union, the Cape Breton Island Building and Construction Trades Council. This union's offices were raided by police early in their inquiry. Soon after, ten men were charged with rioting, weapons offenses, and property damage. When police work was concluded, fourteen union members were charged. By July, the intransigent Cape Breton Island Building and Construction Trades Council had accepted responsibility for the riot and agreed to compensate the developer. In return, the developer turned construction at the site over to the trades council for completion.

As the incident concluded, in a most dramatic contradiction, the terrain of struggle for containment of the riot's meaning was re-framed by the lawyer representing the developer whose property was damaged. At a press conference on July 16, the labor conflict was strategically re-situated within the terrain of Nova Scotia labor law, changed in 1994 to allow for open tendering and the hiring of nonunion labor at construction sites.[2] The developer's lawyer said: "This agreement does not speak to the broader policy issue of union and nonunion working together. . . . That's left on the table. . . . The open tendering process gives the developer the right to develop the project in the most cost-effective and efficient manner possible" (*Mail Star,* 16 July 1997). Union leader Cliff Murphy pointed to the conflict's double meaning—law and order versus labor politics: "Business should proceed as normal. . . . As far as victories go, we're just happy the job is going union, and people are paid a good wage to do the work there" (*Mail Star,* 16 July 1997).

In the end, fifteen men were arrested and charged with various offenses including rioting and arson. The trades council held a fund-raising drive that netted the $1.2 million required for the damage settlement and the men's legal charges. Victor Tomiczek, local president of the powerful Canadian Auto Workers Union said: "Labor is getting painted with the black eye on this and I think it makes sense for anybody that works in labor or who is involved with labor to try to at least erase some of that tainted image. We can't be held responsible for the action of a few but we can at times make things right." He continued defiantly: "People should not forget that the message has been sent and the message was noted by entrepreneurs, that they can't come in here and rub our faces in their anti-union activities and expect to get away with it" (*Mail Star,* 8 July 1997).

At this moment, even Mayor Coady retreated to a pro-union stand, likely a necessity for his political future. Praising the fund-raising drive he said: "It just indicates the strength of the union and unionism and brotherhood, and obviously that's a laudable thing." He continued: "We can't forever blame unions for our problems" (*Mail Star,* 8 July 1997). Here, the politically delicate reconfiguration of Cape Breton class relations surrounding this incident completed its cycle. Unions, equated with brotherhood and through symbolic extension, ties of kin, were again accorded a central position in projections of "community" for development purposes. The incident and its aftermath, however, revealed the boundaries of tolerance for union militancy and suggested that transgressions exact penalties from capital, both monetary and ideological.

As Raymond Williams and other interpreters of Gramsci suggest, in moments like this, where oppositional culture is appropriated by those in power, coercion is always a possibility. Sayer, for example, maintains that "it is the exercise of power pure and simple that authorizes and legitimates; and it does this less by the manipulation of beliefs than by defining of the boundaries of the possible" (1994, 375). While Sayer's argument is compelling inasmuch as the riot and what followed suggest state and business collusion, it also rings true in the politics of that moment for the union. For both sides, extended conflict and overt coercion could exact a high price, materially and symbolically. Both sides tolerated conflict, but as the resolution revealed, such tolerance has limits. More routinely, "economic development" in Cape Breton relies, however inefficiently, upon what Williams (see 1991) calls "social training" to achieve "saturations" of consciousness; a sense-making of the riot that allows a conclusion which fits local cultural practices. Local cultural and labor practices rework a historical dialectic entailing militancy, coercion, and conciliation. This was the strategic accomplishment of both sides in this dispute, so artfully described by the mayor.

Law, Order, and Unions in Their Place

Deliberate efforts to reforge workers' politics and identities take various forms. Most salient to these struggles is an official discourse about development that poses an economically pressing need for unions to become more flexible, to set aside their historically adversarial stance. In other words, the story goes, what is good for the economy is also in the best interests of working people. The contesting of Cape Breton development priorities is usefully discussed in terms of Gramscian hegemony. The idea of "social training" draws attention to the everyday practices where hegemony is played out in ways that are not so obviously socially fractious. Social training occurs in education, public policy, and media discourses that reinforce attitudes and practices favorable to the interests of dominant groups. These directives are normalizing and comprise Gramsci's notion of quotidian "common sense." Common sense is not to be confused with Gramscian "good sense," namely, alternative or oppositional viewpoints that might be construed as in the best interests of the workers and their families. As Williams notes, social training serves to "incorporate" dominant agendas into everyday understandings and may include the selective reworking of cultural practices deemed inappropriate to new dominant priorities. When social training is challenged, the forms of contestation may provide the social ground and language for further struggle (Roseberry 1996). In Cape Breton, the language of community, its varying meanings, is key to hegemonic negotiation, the reworking and challenging of "tradition."

At issue is the selective reworking of identities associated with industrial employment, that is, matters of class and community and historically developed commitments to trade unions. Community loyalty, defined differently (in sociospatial terms) for different purposes, matters more than usual because union and other collective political expressions have historically relied upon social practices surrounding "community." Community in Cape Breton cultural politics may refer to particular named locations such as the historically formed pithead neighborhoods, the coal towns themselves, the industrial region, discrete rural villages, or the whole island. As the Stora scenario reveals, recruitment for the Sydney demonstration drew upon a broad notion of "community" more tied to union loyalty than to geography. Official discourses of community and economic development aim to recast these variously articulated claims as out of step with the new, so-called globalized economy where collective identities and local loyalties are not only anachronistic but actually dysfunctional.

No matter that these new priorities for individuated economic subjects and their promised flexibility also portend the loss of hard-won wage levels, job security, and benefits, and perhaps most significant to Cape Bretoners in these examples, a legitimate collective voice, both union and community-based. Admittedly the voice is exclusionary from the point of view of "outsiders" hired at the construction site; Cape Breton union politics can be strongly held and at times bloody. Nonetheless, to unionized Cape Bretoners who hold one of the highest rate of union membership in Canada, unions matter, as does their loss of power. "Common sense" here suggests that capital's agendas should predominate; Cape Breton livelihoods depend upon new forms of employment, certainly if livelihood is narrowly construed as waged employment. "Good sense" may be, somewhat stubbornly, that it is not in the interests of workers to relinquish previously struck bargains with employers and the state. Later, the discussion of militant particularism will return to this seeming dilemma.

Contemporary Cape Breton labor militancy also stands in stark contrast to the nonmilitant responses of working people discussed by Dunk and Leach in this volume, also in Nash's (1989) study of capital flight in Pittsfield, Massachusetts. These comparisons suggest the defiance of Cape Bretoners is worthy of closer scrutiny. Alternatively, David Harvey (1995) suggests that old-style labor politics such as those in Cape Breton, or in Oxford (Hayter and Harvey 1993), are laced with contradictions concerning community and environment. He takes issue with "workerist" efforts to conserve industrial employment and views their protectionist politics as anachronistic to a viable generalizable contemporary socialist politics. Is this helpful in understanding the circumstances in Cape Breton? Certainly, the tensions between protecting what was laid out in the past and looking ahead to differently configured political and economic futures now dominates conversations in most social niches in Cape Breton society. But this has likely been the case for most of this century, as it was when I commenced ethnographic fieldwork on working class cultural politics in the late 1980s. In the remainder of the chapter I explore these contradictions associated with livelihood, identities, and cultural politics in collision (and collusion?) with capital and state agendas. Raymond Williams outlined what was at stake in the British mining conflicts of the mid-1980s. He said:

> For what is at issue, in the struggles about the rights of management, about alternative economic policies, and about the conditions of communities, is in a profound way a matter of order: not of command or authority but of a way of *life* chosen by a substantial majority of its citizens. Instead of being defensive about disorder, socialists should take every opportunity to show what is now really happening: the dislocation of our habitual social order and the destruction of specific communities, in a combined political and economic offensive. (1989, 126)

The parallels with Cape Breton are compelling. What more can be said of the elision of social and economic processes through this discourse?

Labor, Livelihoods, and Structures of Feeling

Williams and Harvey both accord close attention to the politics of class and ideas about community resulting from the "embeddedness" of large-scale industrial production in particular locales. Williams's ideas about class rootedness in historically configured communities have been somewhat contentious (Dworkin and Roman 1993; Eagleton 1989). His discussion of community continuity is seen by some as exclusionary, for example in lending legitimacy to arguments that conflate identities with place in ways that privilege claims made by white workers seeking to exclude im/migrants in competitive labor markets. Moreover, Williams's depiction of working-class men has been characterized by some feminist critics as insensitive to gendered social reproduction (Swindells and Jardine 1990). Harvey's reworking of Williams's argument concedes these limitations but praises Williams's rendering of the dialectical articulation between culture and political economy. Harvey looks to Williams's novels for resolution to some contradictions expressed through the political sensibilities of various key protagonists.

In Cape Breton cultural politics, notions of community have always been socially and spatially bounded to make particular arguments for particular audiences. Invariably, this conjures up social inequities through the privileging of some claims over others. In my earlier research, people's reliance upon place and patronage networks for jobs and access to other essential economic resources relied upon competing claims. These networks represented forms of cultivated social capital that were typically longstanding and thereby exclusionary. Inequities also characterized employment structures, which relied upon gendered skills and were apparent in the sex-typing of industrial jobs and labor process controls. However, what I have always found compelling in expressions of a generic Cape Breton identity is the consistent theme of a shared identity of place. Many Cape Bretoners speak of a shared identity that entails greater sociability (across various social differences) than is found elsewhere, particularly in larger urban centers. Idioms of community in Cape Breton, however, are not solely romanticized, or by turn inclusive and exclusive. Elsewhere I have argued for the historical origins of Cape Breton sociability and its social capital and that these condition political expressions of both accommodation and resistance. In the current political struggles, the social language of community in class contestation, an "us/we-ness," is politically charged precisely because corporate interests seek more vigorously than in the past to discredit and disentangle these various commitments. As Williams demonstrates and the political actions described here confirm, "community" is made and remade through social practices. Community is now and has been historically, albeit it in different ways, the terrain of struggle in contemporary Cape Breton politics. It is not that there is a consistently held, universal sense of community shared by all working-class

Cape Bretoners, but that in the current crisis with its looming threat of the loss of upward of 1,500 more industrial jobs, the appeal of a common class-based community is both widespread and potent.

Furthermore, struggles such as those in Cape Breton are about workers' identities in the broadest sense. This is well captured by a Marxian concept of livelihood that extends the definition of labor to embrace the social relations of sustaining life, and the subjectivity and cultural politics that this gives rise to. Class politics are thereby located some distance from the shop floor in community and cultural practices with their particularized forms of social differentiation and power differences. In this sense, the political expressions of Cape Breton workers and their families are about ways of *living,* their daily making and remaking over time.

Historically, how the coal and steel industries took hold in Cape Breton—their social and cultural articulation—defined the social relations of livelihood. The significance of livelihood in daily life is what Williams (1977) referred to rather abstractly as "structures of feeling," in his attempt to grasp the processural, dialectical engagement of material and symbolic aspects of livelihood. Or, as Harvey (1995) says, "how space is turned into place." In large measure, these ideas help explain the tenor of Cape Breton's labor conflicts, taking them beyond what is usually meant by labor relations, into the realm of community and cultural politics. For Cape Breton, cultural struggles still coincide with structures of capital, perhaps more visibly than in most other North American urban industrial locations.

But more than demonstrating the continuing relevance of material approaches to the study of culture, I now question political responses to the assault on livelihood and varied commitments to place being exacted by the priorities of late-twentieth-century capitalism. Cape Breton is usefully discussed through Williams's concept of "militant particularism," further developed by Harvey. Let me revisit my earlier conclusions about the double-faced character of historically articulated accommodation and resistance. How resilient are such practices and how forceful are the new hegemonic social training and "ideological apparatuses" in compelling different views of livelihood and culture, more in step with the individuated economic subjects represented in development discourses as prerequisite to the successful global positioning of Cape Bretoners?

In keeping with Harvey's reading of Williams on "militant particularism," the issue becomes whether the expressions of localized class interests can be construed as productive collective political action. Or, in local politics, are the issues too easily re-framed? For example, the law and order advocates render militancy as individuated acts of "thuggery." In this vein, business and community leaders argue that expressions of union volatility will fuel old debates about testy Cape Breton workers. This in turn, such critics caution, provides further excuse for the intransigence of capital (usually foreign) about relocation in Cape

Breton, despite the attractive conditions provided by state subsidies. Here we see the point at which local political struggles might be converted into a wider political field. This gets to Harvey's concern with militant particularism, namely, whether a shift in political register from the local to "universal," from the experiential to the abstracted, is possible given that the political questions arise within, are limited by, the production politics of particular industries. For Harvey, appeals to maintain such an industrial framework are suspect through

> the perpetuation of patterns of social relations and community solidarities—loyalties—achieved under a certain kind of oppressive and uncaring industrial order. While ownership may change (through nationalization, for example), the mines and assembly lines must be kept going, for these are the material bases for the ways of social relation and mechanisms of class solidarity embedded in particular places and communities. Socialist politics acquired its conservative edge because it cannot easily be about the radical transformation and overthrow of old modes of working and living—it must in the first instance be about keeping the coal mines open and the assembly lines moving at any cost . . . (1995, 91)

However, another competing discourse, less present in public discussion and much more evident in everyday social exchanges, that of "loss of way of life," posed by Williams above, provides further complexity to these contradictions and their attendant political questions.

"Community Service" and the Locus of Militant Particularism

After the riots, the disciplinary measures exacted by the courts proved milder than the initial outrage might have suggested. In three separate trials concluding at the end of June 1998, the men pleaded guilty to lesser charges of unlawful assembly, mischief, and causing a disturbance. Ironically, the court sentences for these crimes, essentially of class and property, called for one hundred hours of "community service." Some probationary terms were also required. This "punishment" was apparently seen to fit "the crime"—it provoked no media commentary. Appeals of the sentences were also not forthcoming.

"Community service," however, is precisely what these workers might argue was their mission and that of their union; such are the cultural politics of place in this region. This is idiomatically presented in everyday discourses of livelihood where ideas of class and the social content of community are conjoined. For example, my conversations with people about the content of their daily routines typically included remarks about "looking out for one's own," "standing together," and "helping others to get by" as priorities that are partially resolved through the practices of community and of class. Such practices are both social and economic, and are related to ideas about the precariousness of working-class lives, hence my use of the trope "making do" to characterize local culture. Local culture is constituted (discursively and materially), both oppositionally and when romanticized, in a dialectical relationship between something Williams (1991) calls "experience" and "practice, or "practical consciousness" (1977, 131). In part, this dialectic is more pronounced in Cape Breton coal towns because life there has been so marked by economic hardship. As is true almost everywhere, women in Cape Breton households are more expressive than men about the complexities and dailiness of their livelihood practices, hence the quotidian "culture of making do" trope incorporates a gendered livelihood sensibility.

In arguments about how gendered livelihood practices are implicated in community and cultural politics it thus becomes particularly important that class practices are viewed in social locations beyond shop floor politics. Otherwise, for masculinized industries such as coal mining, women's extensive contributions to livelihood remain invisible or the subject of inference. Women's political expressions may also be silenced, or defined only in terms of their deliberate and strategic actions, such as on February 14, 1999, discussed below. Women's social capital work, their maintenance of social and other resources at the community level, is necessary to livelihood, as critical as the labor expended for wages and in the "informal sector." Hence, gendered cultural practices are crucial in articulations of community and political consciousness.

The spatially articulated social practices of neighborliness are also relevant to Cape Breton idioms of community and, therefore, to the local significance of "community service." The neighborhoods of coal towns such as Glace Bay bear the scars of coal extraction both physically and symbolically. Names of neighborhoods carry the identity of long-closed pit heads into the present and people in these neighborhoods may rally to help each other in times of need, regardless of affiliations with the present-day industry. In everyday social interaction, people locate themselves with reference to these neighborhoods as they communicate various stereotypical notions of the character of people who live here and there. Curious about the negative account of residents in one particular neighborhood (their greater disposition toward crime), described to me by some residents of an adjacent neighborhood, I checked on crime rates with the Glace Bay police. Not surprisingly, there were no factual grounds for neighborhood-based rivalry. On the other hand, there was plenty of evidence that Glace Bay people rally across neighborhood boundaries to collectively confront what they perceive to be larger threats to their community and way of life. The riots in Sydney provide a clear recent example of the shifting boundaries of community and class. Given these understandings, the idea of sentencing militant unionists to perform community service is deeply ironic, particularly when the Gramscian contradictions of common sense are considered.

Despite media's pro-business reports of the industrial strife, to be "down on your luck" in Cape Breton continues to garner sympathy. The relatively sympathetic court sentences suggests that union militancy remains a viable mode of political action, as it has been historically. This is so even when it takes a criminal turn, and even in the late 1990s when many forms of criminality, but particularly those associated with the unemployed, reserve, or urban underclass are viewed with increasing harshness. But also historically important is the kind of disciplined union action that can prevent workers' riots in the face of extreme, militarized provocation, such as that turned against severely hard-pressed striking miners in the 1920s. Such discipline lay behind the initial organization of the Sydney riot. In the long historical vista, however, neither of these two modes of response have proven particularly effective for Cape Breton workers; not for such short-term gains as halting layoffs, nor for longer-term goals of socialist politics.

For Cape Breton workers in the 1920s and in the 1990s, the problem of translation between the strictly local, or particularized viewpoint, and a transformative generalized vision for socialism poses difficulties. Again, this is Harvey's concern with "militant particularism." I now turn to the moment of closure for Cape Breton coal mining to further explore whether Harvey's argument about conservatism is conclusive.

Discourses of the Heart; the Resignation of Coal Miners

In further events leading up to the 1999 announcement of mine closures, the union and community leaders agreed to put the matter of union militancy aside. However, soon after these agreements were reached in 1997, 450 miners were laid off from the troubled Phalen Colliery. Since it first assumed a significant role in the submarine coal fields, after the distastrous closure of Colliery No. 26 in 1984 (laying off 1,750 men), the Phalen mine's production has routinely been interrupted because of technical difficulties and, to a lesser extent, problems with markets. Nonetheless, it was recourse to the familiar "solution" of creating more industrial jobs that fueled the rhetoric of local politicians as they dealt with the 1997 layoffs. In an appeal to the Cape Breton Development Corporation to expand production into a third mining operation, Councillor Gerard Burke of Glace Bay said: "Somebody has to get off their fanny and do something. With the amount of suicides, marriage breakups and vandalism, Glace Bay is starting to look like Tombstone—the town depicted in old western movies" (*Mail Star,* January 22, 1998).

Moving ahead to February 1999, a few weeks after the federal government had announced the pending permanent closure of the Phalen mine and the sale of the Prince mine, there was a Valentine's Day rally in Glace Bay. At this rally a nationally renowned miners' choir, Men of the Deeps, sang about the mining way of life, as did a miner's daughter whose father had recently died of cancer. These performances moved many in the overflow audience to tears. A leading headline was: "'For Love of Cape Breton' . . . Valentine's Day was celebrated much differently this year in Cape Breton but the love of family and of island is as strong as ever" (*Mail Star,* February 16, 1999). The organizers of this event adopted the identity of United Families. Some went on to call themselves "Cape Breton Miners' Wives." After their initial success they continued to present concern over the loss of mining employment, giving an invited lecture to students in Halifax on International Women's Day in March. In a more confrontational mood, twenty of them visited the legislature to hear the Nova Scotian premier discuss plans for Cape Breton. The women remained sceptical about the contents of the premier's address and one shouted that he was "playing with the lives of our families" (*Mail Star,* March 25, 1999).

A primary concern for these women (and many others who joined larger public demonstrations) is the severance payments and pensions for laid-off miners. A significant number of the approximately 1,600 people who will lose their jobs are in their forties and ineligible to receive pensions. At the time of writing, various competing strategies are proposed by different interest groups but the plan endorsed by the major union, the United Mine Workers' Union (UMW) is that the government maintain ownership to keep the Prince mine in production for twelve years to cover the pension eligibility period for the younger miners. This point was made by another protest group, approximately sixty miners, who showed up at Devco's office with a trailer load of horse manure "to raise a stink" (*Mail Star,* March 18, 1999).

Various protests—ranging in size from thousands of miners and their families, down to small groups of between two to twenty miners' wives—articulate fears of job loss in a language of community. As Gwen MacDonald, a miner's wife, explained to a reporter during her turn at an information picket at a Marine Atlantic ferry terminal: "A lot of these people have small children and if they leave Cape Breton and take their children . . . what's going to happen to the schools? What's going to happen to the business community? Its not a small group of people who are going to be affected . . ." (*Mail Star,* March 6, 1999). In an address to one of the larger rallies in Sydney, retired steelworker Nelson Muise recalled protests that he had participated in with seven of his nine children in tow, during earlier moments of threats to the steel and coal industries in the 1960s. He mused about the temptations of migration at that time and his decision not to leave: "Cape Breton salt water is in my veins. I was born here, and I hope to die and be planted here" (*Mail Star,* March 8, 1999). Metaphors of commitment of this order characterize much of the public discussions of development in Cape Breton.

In comparison with the bitterness at the construction site, what is striking about the various miners' rallies and protests is that the language of contention is community and way of life, more so than militant challenge. Of course, events are still unfolding with mine closure projected for some two years hence. However, with the exception of the increasingly politicized feisty miners' wives who have traveled to the provincial and national capital to state their case, there is an emergent tone of resignation and a muting of class arguments in the shift to acceptance of the closure. The UMW has not been particularly vocal but has reprimanded the miners' wives for interfering in their bargaining over dates and pensions. Some voices, more strident, attack provincial politicians for favoring Halifax as a business and development center. Others call for Cape Breton–based initiatives, including a plan for a cooperative to purchase the Prince mine, an idea soundly criticized by the UMW president. In sum, protest efforts are articulated through familial idioms and community effort commencing from but not remaining within union control.

Conclusion

Class claims that come to the fore in moments of workers' collective action, usually through their unions, may be more readily nudged aside than those of community. Appeals to community and way of life have material, symbolic, and experiential dimensions in the social memories that translate historical periods of Cape Breton labor militancy into the present. Resistance in Cape Breton has always been fueled by appeals to community-based solidarities and practices, some of which predate the relatively short history of the industrialized coal industry. Glace Bay was incorporated early in this century when it was a jumble of makeshift company-built houses, inadequate for the burgeoning migrant labor population. Labor migrants came with their families from rural areas in Nova Scotia, and a little later from Europe. Both waves of migrants brought with them cultural practices (of livelihood) and political predispositions. Above all, they knew the necessity of maintaining social networks and political alliances. Their survival depended upon it because life in the coal towns was as desperate as it could be in Canada; Glace Bay in the 1920s had the highest rate of infant mortality in the country and the highest incidence of infectious disease. By the 1920s union politics and socialist ideals held sway, for which miners were severely punished. Even in a series of strikes attended by the Canadian Armed Forces, union discipline held until the last moment when the company store was burned and looted.

The historical parallels with the present examples are interesting. Similar cultural practices underlie workers' resistance and resignation. Interpretations of courses of action and the consequences that flow from them are not entirely predictable, rather, they are struggled over, usually with contradictory outcomes. Resistance to capital and state agendas, along with various accommodations, are made possible through livelihood and community practices, as much as through production politics. Flexible livelihoods have mitigated against the worst effects of political and economic instabilities. Familial and community idioms have also substituted for political analysis, as can be seen in some of the contradictory discourses described here. In these ways, conservatism is certainly present in Cape Breton cultural politics.

On the other hand, the two moments presented here are not what they seem. The first action is seemingly anarchic but more likely it was a calculated intervention based on class sentiments. The Valentine's Day rally has the surface appearance of resignation, an expression of loss, valorizing familial and community relations over those of class. But here again, the rally may be an expression of class action in another form; articulated through idioms of family and community. Given these interpretive possibilities, it is difficult to accept that for Cape Breton communities a more generalizable socialist politics are improbable. For as Williams wrote:

> A new theory of socialism must now centrally involve place. Remember the argument was that the proletariat had no country, the factor which differentiated it from the property-owning classes. But place has been shown to be a crucial element in the bonding process—more so perhaps for the working class than the capital owning class—by the explosion of the international economy and the destructive effects of deindustrialization upon old communities. *When capital has moved on, the importance of place is more clearly revealed.* (1989, 242)

Surely, the cultural practices—those that affirm places as community—within which class is expressed, might yet continue their dialectical refashioning of political struggles and redirect these onto another, more abstracted spatial plane. All political struggles require complex, multisited forms of collective consciousness, one of which may be a socially articulated community identity. Cape Breton, is indeed the "derelict" town of the Tombstone metaphor; how could it not be, given its past? Harvey's work on militant particularism and the difficulties of articulating from the local to a more abstract vision for socialism combines with a Marxian notion of livelihood to direct his praxis toward a materialist concept of production and environment. This is a long-overdue corrective to some of the romanticized, undertheorized work on environmental politics that leaves cultural and class politics aside in variants of determinism. For sure, the appeals to a retooling of Cape Breton coal mining disregard the industry's environmental degradation, and the human risks of underground mining. In this and other ways, expressions of militant particularism in Cape Breton cultural politics are riddled with blind spots from localized orientations. On the other hand as Harvey, in Gramscian mode, writes:

The relevant place and range of political action . . . cannot get resolved outside of a particularly dialectical way of defining loyalties to place across space. And within such loyalties we will always find a peculiar tension between resistance and complicity. (1995, 82)

Here he moves beyond a productionist logic but still equivocates. Surely, what happens when class practices are located in the broader space and place of community must mean that the struggles, over class and commitments to community for workers in "places" such as Cape Breton, will continue. They are neither fundamentally conservative, nor progressive. As I have attempted to show they are more often a mix, laced with contradictions. Sometimes the struggles will bear fruit, usually not. As Smith suggests in this volume, it is not the politics of the workplace, or shop floor, that should engage our attention. Rather it is the politics of the place of work in daily life that matters. Seen in this light, industrial communities still have much to teach us about the cultural politics of place and the spatial scope of political action: "Alive and well in Cape Breton," indeed. For all the difficulties that flow from Williams's ideas of "community," this chapter suggests the continuing relevance of his work to the articulation of culture and political economy in particular places, and to theorists who remain concerned about questions of class and identity.

Notes

The trope of fire aptly references historical volatility and hardship in Cape Breton's cultural and class politics. During the 1920s striking miners burned the company store. Just prior to my fieldwork in 1987 two major fires occurred. Colliery 26 was closed after a fatal explosion, and a major fish plant burned to the ground. The rebuilt plant became the venue for labor struggles discussed in my doctoral thesis.

1. In February 1997 approximately seven hundred steel workers were laid off midst concerns about plant privatization.

2. Union statistics show that the unemployment rate among unionized construction workers in Nova Scotia increased from 30 to 75 percent as a result of the 1994 decision (*Mail Star,* February 25, 1998). In 1998, official unemployment in Cape Breton was 26 percent, the highest level in Canada. These statistics do not fully capture seasonal unemployment.

CHAPTER 16

Acquiescence and Quiescence

Gender and Politics in Rural Languedoc

Winnie Lem

During the first half of the twentieth century, women were a familiar presence in the political struggles that were initiated by the small holders and laborers of rural Languedoc. In a region noted for the militancy of its inhabitants, rural women were not merely swept up in the current of the struggles that prevailed at the time, but they also emerged at the forefront of challenges to forces that were undermining livelihoods at that time. As the Languedoc rural economy was coming to be increasingly oriented toward the commercial production of wine, the overriding political concern of Languedoc farmers was to defend a rural livelihood derived from family farming combined with wage work on wine-growing estates. Indeed over the past one hundred years or so, this concern has come to be established as the predominant political project in an era of capitalist transformation. In the period before World War II, women who worked as agricultural laborers on local estates participated routinely in acts of defiance against landowners who sought to rationalize their estates and to apply principles of cost effectiveness in organizing production. Also, women who worked on their own family holdings played key roles in organizing demonstrations, rallies, and marches as well as initiating a series of local actions to contest state interventions which promoted the restructuring of agriculture into modern profit-oriented enterprises. In the era before World War II and briefly after it, rural women engaged with their political worlds. They conceived of themselves as political subjects, acted as political agents, and, by challenging their efforts toward contesting the practices imposed by landowners and policies imposed by the state, they acquiesced to a project around which the political life of the region pivoted—the defense of rural livelihoods.

In recent decades, however, the presence of women in the political life of rural Languedoc has become much diminished in a region still noted for the political aggressiveness of its inhabitants. Fewer and fewer women tend to participate in the strikes, demonstrations, rallies, and marches that continue to punctuate the public political arena of Languedoc. Still fewer women engage in the clandestine expressions of disaffection that erupt from time to time in the more secluded and local political arenas.[1] In recent decades, women tend to have withdrawn from the political world and have become relatively politically quiescent. Noting this transformation, many Languedoc people attribute it to an egoism and selfish mentality that has come to prevail, particularly among younger village women, in contrast to their elders. For example, when I asked Marcelle, an eighty-five-year-old inhabitant of the village of Broussan[2] why women no longer get involved in political activity, she replied: "Young women only think of themselves and their families. They are selfish *(Elles sont egoïstes)*." When these sorts of comments are made, people are often acutely aware of the paradox presented by the contemporary quiescence of women who inhabit a politically volatile region. Marcelle concluded her commentary by uttering: "So they don't bother with politics. Yet we are the *Midi Rouge*.[3] I don't understand it. Do you?"

This chapter therefore is an attempt to address the question posed by Marcelle and to explain the paradox, which many inhabitants of rural Languedoc find perplexing. I suggest that the shifts in women's political engagement are linked to the changes in the division of labor that have accompanied capitalist transformation and the modernization of Languedoc viticulture. Specifically, I argue that these changes have resulted in increasingly differentiated spheres of women's and men's work. Men have come to control the production of vines, the facet of the economy most central to rural livelihoods, while women have become alienated from it. Power asymmetries between women and men have become more manifest and gender hierarchy more intense. Moreover, I suggest that capitalist transformation and modernization have not only promoted changes in the organization of the production of Languedoc vines, but they have also been accompanied by changes in local culture, subjectivity, and the meanings attached to political struggle and work in its different forms. In contemporary rural Languedoc, the meaning of the key political project of defending rural livelihoods has shifted. While the defense of a livelihood has become validated as the single most legitimate form of political expression in rural Languedoc, it has become one that sustains power imbalances between women and men that have emerged from changes in the division of labor. At the same time, this political project has become part of the commonsense reality of everyday political life in rural Languedoc, so much so that to challenge its primacy or to contest some of the terms of the struggle appears to go against nature. Because it is a project that defends institutions that sustain gender hierarchy, women's relationship to that project is one of ambivalence. Their ambivalence is expressed through political passivity and quiescence rather than acquiescence to a struggle that in many respects fails to articulate with the interest of women qua women. As the questions I propose to examine here revolve around politics, economy, culture, power, subjectivity, acquiescence, and consent, my approach to understanding the question of women's political agency draws on Gramsci's concept of hegemony.

Hegemony

The concept of hegemony has been used by different scholars to explain situations of domination and the exercise of power, not as brute force but as an invitation to acquiescence.[4] The most quoted characterization of the term comes from his *Prison Notebooks* and according to Gramsci, hegemony is:

> the "spontaneous" consent given by the great masses of the population to the general direction imposed on social life by the dominant fundamental group; this consent is "historically" caused by the prestige (and consequent confidence) which the dominant group enjoys because of its position and function in the world of production. (Gramsci 1971, 12)

Many writers have emphasized that hegemony is a process that permits an understanding of how groups in the social world establish their domination over others by achieving consent and also by defining the boundaries of a commonsense reality (see, for example, Jackson Lears 1985; also see Leach, Clark, this volume). As a process, it is located in the institutions of power in civil society such as schools, churches, and the family, where those in positions of power aim to shape and form the world view and collective wills. Through hegemonic processes, the legitimacy of the power wielded by certain groups in society is established and the primacy of their political visions and their projects is accepted.

The concept of hegemony is particularly apposite for my purposes here for it allows us to view a social world as made up of fields of power. The social world of rural Languedoc, in this light, then, is constituted in terms of a variety of fields of power. It is made up of the institutions of the family, the community, the farm, and the estate, and each is characterized by a particular configuration of power, where certain subject categories rule and others are ruled. References to dominant groups in Gramsci's work largely apply to political elites, and dominant classes. However, as I explain below, I extend his notion of dominant groups to include the social category of men because men in a variety of contexts wield power as a group and, as I shall argue, through the exercise of that power, the visions and projects of male subjects become defined as commonsense reality and established as legitimate.

The concept of hegemony is particularly apposite for another reason. Gramsci uses the concept of hegemony to try to move away from the economism of Marxism. He does this by shifting to the cultural sphere. However, as many writers have noted, he never repudiates materialism. As Bocock argues, Gramsci "sees the relationship between the material, productive base, and the cultural sphere as being a complex, reciprocal one in which human beings mediate between the two zones"(1986, 79). Therefore, any usage of Gramsci's concept must be materially grounded. This is particularly significant for my purposes here for I argue that it is only possible to understand the changes in the subjectivities and political agency of women (and also men) by understanding the role of the "world of production." The cultural sphere must be linked to the material conditions that provide the everyday context of changes in agency and subjectivity, that is to say, historical changes in the division of labor in which their lives give shape to the identity of subjects and meaning to the political projects of the day.

Divisions of Labor and Livelihood Struggles

> We were strong. We were united. Women were always involved in political struggle. When I worked on the estates, we [women day laborers *(journalières)*] could bring the owners [*propriétaires*] to their knees. When the *propriétaires* got out of control again, we *journalières* and *journaliers* [male day laborers] would rise up again and again and put them in their place. (Collette Castre, eighty-nine)

> I make banners and paint them with political slogans. But this isn't real politics. I do for my husband. He does all the political stuff. I do this as a favor for him. Women don't tend to get involved in politics. Politics is for men. (Eliane Mas, forty-five)

Collette Castre is a retired agricultural laborer who worked on a wine-growing estate during the 1930s. She identifies herself as *journalière* and a women wine grower *(viticultrice)*. Eliane is married to one of the most militant inhabitants of Broussan and identifies herself as a housewife *(femme au foyer)*. The contrasts in the two statements encapsulate the differences in the political sentiments and identities of women whose lives have been shaped by different experiences of work in different periods of time.

Collette labored on large agricultural estates during a period when Languedoc viticulture was becoming transformed into commercial monoculture. From the mid-1800s to the pre–World War II period, Languedoc growers, large and small alike, geared the cultivation of grapes toward the manufacture of wines for the expanding market for cheap low-grade wines. Large landowners increasingly rationalized production on estates and small growers rapidly converted their fields into vineyards. As a commodity, Languedoc wines and viticulture itself became increasingly susceptible to market fluctuations and cycles of boom and bust that characterized the wine market.[5] Downturns in the market, particularly, were periods when conflicts erupted in the Languedoc countryside. Large landowners tended to respond to downturns in the market by laying off workers, implementing wage cuts, and rescinding customary entitlements, such as gleaning and rendering payments in kind. Agricultural laborers, such as Collette, continuously challenged the implementation of such practices and responded to such actions with intense defiance. In these periods, *journalières* joined *journaliers* to organize work disruptions and boycotts. They threatened to ravage vineyards and destroy agricultural instruments if landowners persisted in taking what they saw as exploitative measures to ensure their own profit levels.

The fact that women participated in such forms of political struggle reflected their direct involvement in the production of vines. In pre–World War II Languedoc, women and men both worked on large rural estates and also on small family holdings. On both the large- and smallholding, a gendered division of labor prevailed. Tasks that were considered by owners and stewards as the lighter and less skilled were assigned women. These included the collection of vine shoots, hoeing, and weeding. Frequently, however, jobs normally designated as men's work were allocated to women. They included such tasks as ploughing, pruning, and treating vines with sprays. These tasks were thought to be heavier and skilled, and thus were defined as men's work. On smallholdings, women often simply undertook these tasks as a matter of routine.

As Collette's statement indicates, women in the pre–World War II period were key participants in building a tradition of militancy that involved class struggle and also struggles against the state. From the late nineteenth century to the immediate postwar period, local oppositional politics were foregrounded by the defense of class interests as rural women and men struggled against local landlords. Working directly on both smallholdings and local estates in the process of vine cultivation as laborers shaped the sensibilities of both women and men. Women identified with men as workers and wine growers. In many elderly women's ontological narratives,[6] the terms *ouvrières* and *viticultrices* were used in self-definitional statements such as Collette's earlier statement. Used in recounting the past, they indicate the ways in which women and men were subsumed within an identity as "worker." Such statements and such narratives established unity in the political identity of women and men—their unity in terms of class. Livelihood claims and economic interests were asserted in terms of the defense of class interests. In the context of rural Languedoc, such livelihood interests and class interests came also to be asserted as the defense of a region, Occitania, its culture, language, and smallhold farming as a way of life against the modernizing impulses of the state. As livelihoods were obtained predominantly through work on small family holdings and as laborers on large estates in the region of Lower Languedoc, the defense of the regional interests against the cultural and economic imperatives emanating from outside incorporated class interests. The defense of Occitan as a language expressed class interests, for Occitan was considered the language of work, spoken by the laborers and small-scale farmers. French, on the other hand, was the language of the landowners, who were members of the local bourgeoisie and either belonged to or aspired to belong to the national bourgeoisie. In the post–World War II decades, the era of the consolidation of capitalism in Languedoc agriculture, Occitan culture and what became nationalist themes acquired a renewed immediacy as state interventions designed to modernize the rural economy involved the introduction of Malthusian policies and measures that promoted a cost-efficient, market-oriented, fully rationalized commodity-producing agriculture by eliminating the small-scale farming. So from World War II through to the 1980s, winegrowers' protests and acts of political confrontation came more and more to incorporate Occitan discourses, symbols, and images that emphasized a "traditional" language and a "traditional" way of life of small-scale farming. This form of expression became particularly prevalent in the postsocialist climate of the 1980s and 1990s, when claims and interests articulated so obviously in terms of class were discouraged. As Occitan political discourses became more salient, women withdrew more and more from the political landscape. Men tended to act more as the agents asserting Occitan interests in regional struggles.

To understand how this developed, it is important to focus on the ways in which economic imperatives formed under the modernizing agendas of the state are gendered. Economic and cultural modernization has different objectives, consequences, and implications for women and men. In the context of the development of capitalism in rural Languedoc, relations are gendered in the sense that the creation of cost effective, capital intensive agriculture that is competitive in contemporary global markets implies changing and reconstituting the gender division of labor, altering power relations between women and men and ideas that inform gender identity.

Modernization, Work, and Identity

Changes in work organization and the division of labor have been taking place gradually from the mid-nineteenth century to the present with the capitalist transformation of Languedoc viticulture. The state through its modernizing agenda introduced policies to restructure vine cultivation, which intensified in the postwar period, accelerated by the mechanization of farming following the introduction of tractors. The technological transformations of farming, initiated in the period of postwar economic reconstruction of France was a process that in fact encouraged the masculinization of farming.

Farming came to be a masculine occupation as the technologies that were introduced tended to be addressed toward men rather than women. Support and financing of the purchase of machinery was offered to men. Training for the use of these machines was extended to men. The consequence of this was that men tended to control the machines, thereby controlling production and ultimately capital. Machines, in many respects, were the embodiment of capital, and men's control over machines and other means of production allowed them to occupy a privileged and socially valued position in the world of production. Men not only controlled production of the primary source of livelihood but these activities were accorded high economic value and social prestige in an increasingly commodified economy. In these respects, the modernization of viticulture reinforced male power and supremacy in the livelihood sphere.

Mechanization also resulted in the rapid elimination of women from sustained involvement in the cultivation of grapes. They lost their jobs on local estates and became redundant on household enterprises, which too became increasingly geared toward market production and the production of competitive product. Women were subjected to a process of domestication, assigned to the task of maintaining the household as their primary, and to some extent, exclusive responsibility. Women were both constituted as marginal and construed as marginal to the economy of vine cultivation. By contrast, in an earlier era, when they labored on estates and smallholdings alongside men, they were central to production both on estates and on family farms. Their presence and direct involvement in the process of vine cultivation testified to the significance of their role in the production of the most socially valued good in rural Languedoc. In contemporary rural Languedoc, by contrast, their invisibility and absence from direct production demonstrates their marginality. Men came to control and exercise authority over the activities related to the masculine world of farming. Men assumed the identity of "*viticulteurs*" virtually exclusively.

Women assumed the identity of "housewife" *(femme au foyer)* and this identity became galvanized as a part of the collective consciousness of women. The primacy of "housewife" in women's subjective definitions was the result of the success of one aspect of the modernity project of the state. That project was to create a nation of French citizens with a modern subjectivity. The identity as housewife, then, has come to be hegemonic. It is seen as natural, part of the commonsense structuring of the role and position of women in Languedoc rural life. Indeed, many women, similar to Eliane, seldom position themselves in the occupational universe using terms other than that of housewife. Women seldom self-identify in terms that reflect the concrete work and occupations in which they are engaged, either in the informal economy or in the formal economy. For although women's labor was rendered redundant and superfluous to viticulture, many, in fact, participated in maintaining the household and farm by securing paid work in many different work settings as factory workers, servants, cleaners, and clerks in both the formal and underground economy. None of the kinds of work and occupations held by women were valued as highly or seen as significant as farming in this context where vine cultivation and the production of wine represented the economic mainstay. Therefore, other work and occupational identities tended to be submerged, effaced by the hegemonic construction of housewife, an identity that has been encouraged and reinforced by the state, market, and media. It is also an identity that fits well in a context where work in viticulture is considered the most important economic activity of Languedoc villages.

In the past, then, the political project of defending a livelihood based on the cultivation of grapes presented and represented the interests of both women and men from worker/peasant households as the source of their livelihoods. A political project of contesting wage cuts on estates during periods of economic duress, resisting the mechanization of estate agriculture, contesting unfavorable work conditions as well as the restructuring of family farms forged a unity between women and men mirrored in the united and less differentiated experiences of work. This unity was forged despite political and economic differences that were evident between women and men. For example, as I said earlier women and men often performed the same work on the estates. Yet women were regularly paid one-fifth to one-third less than men workers. Yet, neither women nor men for that matter contested the lower wages paid to women. This appeared as part of the natural order of things, that women's work was of less value. A unity between men and women established a division of labor that effaced these differences as women and men struggled together as *"ouvriers"* and *"viticulteurs."*

In this fashion, men, acting as a dominant group, were able to establish their hegemony over and the primacy of their priorities over women in the past. Women consented to the naturalness of this order. They did not contest it. While Gramsci tends to use hegemony largely in relation to class (though not exclusively), it can also be instructively applied to analyzing relations between men as a group and women as a group. According to Sassoon, the "hegemony of a class consists in its ability to represent the universal interests of the whole society and to unite to itself a group of allies"(1982, 111). Similarly, men as a group were able to present the interests of men, the defense of the family farm and worker's struggles as if they represented the interests of both women and men. They were thus able to forge alliances between women and men and act upon them in livelihood struggles, and women acquiesced to the terms of the political struggle.

By contrast, in the more contemporary period, the hegemony of men and their vision has become less secure in the political field. To understand this we need to refer again to the material conditions of the production of livelihoods and explore the ways in which women and men mediate between the cultural and material zones. As I said earlier, in post–World War II France, women have become displaced in the fields and the concrete day-to-day processes of making a livelihood are less immediately tied to vine cultivation, a masculine occupation and preoccupation. Men assumed and asserted the identity of wine growers, whereas women identify themselves as housewives performing work both in the home and outside as socially and symbolically of less value. Women tend now to be less at the forefront of livelihood struggles, and the arena of both public and political practice is occupied by men. This can be explained to some extent by the simple observation that as women have become marginalized in the economy of vine cultivation and their relationship to viticulture has become mediated through men, they have become marginal in the political struggles to defend viticulture. However necessary this explanation is, it must be pointed out that it falls into the economistic and deterministic trap of an orthodoxy that fails to account for the fact that political interests seldom reflect economic interests in a simple and direct way. For example, a good proportion of the working class in Britain tends to be anti-union and espouse conservative politics. It can be argued further that the unity of interests can no longer be forged nor sustained. In the absence of material conditions to support this unity, women refuse to participate in struggles to defend a livelihood, for to do so would be to lend their support to the defense of an institution—the household—now predominantly a woman's domain in which women are subordinate if not subordinated. They would also lend it to economic practices where the power differences between women and men have been thrown into stark relief. To speak of this political inactivity, indeed, passivity as an act of resistance or defiance, as it might be tempting to do using a particular framework of political analysis (Scott 1985), would grant women a measure of agency and consciousness that is not evidenced by their actions. Again, the processes of hegemony and how they work may help to explore what this act of quiescence may signify.

Williams (1977, 107), among others, has pointed out that hegemony is never total. It captures some and not others. This proposition allows us a way to explain this in relation to the state and its modernizing agenda. As I have said earlier, part of the program of the state in its program to build a nation has been to create a modern subject and citizen and this subject is French speaking. The construction of a French national identity has involved a concerted campaign since World War II to divest subjects of their primordial characteristics. This has involved shaking off the cultures and traditions that have shackled the present to the past, to transform peasants into Frenchmen (Weber 1976). In France this has involved producing a French subjectivity and sensibility against regional subjectivities, not only through the promotion of the French language through systems of rewards and punishments in systems of education, but also by promoting modern ideals in economic as well as cultural practices. The economic ideal in agriculture has been to restructure farming, as I said earlier, into a cost-effective, profit-making, capital-intensive technologically driven agriculture resulting in the masculinization of farming. Modernity has also meant the symbolic domestication of women and the assumption of an identity as housewife, in spite of the concrete experiences of work that fashion women's lives. For a woman to still work in the vines is not only a symbol of want, economic necessity, and poverty, but also of being harnessed to a premodern past, that is, to "tradition." For women to identify themselves as housewives is a statement of being economically secure and modern, in effect liberated. In this respect, the modernity project of the state has been internalized by women. The state has established its hegemony over women and women have become assimilated to the nationalist ideal of the modern French bourgeois woman, a consumer of industrial capitalism's commodities and not a producer.

Modernity also implies a subject who has repudiated "patois" by speaking French. Indeed, the issue of language illustrates how men have failed to maintain their hegemony over women in contemporary Languedoc. It also reflects, in fact paradoxically, the success of the hegemony of modernizing practices. In their livelihood struggles, men employ the symbols and representation of regional and traditional culture—Occitan political discourses. In fact, many men are devoted to speaking and maintaining Occitan as a living language as part of their political project. In this respect, men seem to be acting as the guardians of tradition, a role that is normally attributed to women (cf. Yuval Davis 1997). Moreover, many of the practices, patterns of sociability, and institutions that are central to regional culture are also male bastions. They include playing rugby football (called the national sport of Occitania), participating in bar life where men seek out and enjoy the company of other men, and reaffirming the Mediterranean family where men by and large exercise authority and control. Occitan language and struggles are used to contest the modernizing projects of the state and to ensure the even distribution of power and resources and the process of unequal development of regional powers. Women then are drawn into the modernizing project and have by and large assimilated the identity of the modern French women. Men on the other hand have resisted these terms of the modernity project and many have clung to their Occitan identity, wielding it as a political weapon. Women reject this, do not feel part of this, and have withdrawn themselves from Occitan struggles and livelihood struggles, occupying a space of quiescence in the political domain. This quiescence is reinforced by the hegemonic space occupied by viticultural politics. In a vine-cultivating milieu, where livelihoods rest first and foremost on the cultivation of vines and where wine represents the mainstay of the regional economy, it seems natural that any form of political activity must focus on viticulture and its livelihoods. Other political priorities are less important and marginal. This is part of the commonsense reality of living in a viticultural milieu with a strong tradition of militancy. To overtly resist or challenge the agents of this political project or to contest the objectives and interests of defending the institutions of Occitan culture and practice is to defy common sense and go against the natural order of things. So women experience some sense of dissonance and unease with respect to a political project that not only does not resonate with their experiences of domination, but in fact reinforces them, so they remain politically detached.

So, in the postwar period, women's participation in the many forms of political activity that characterize a region still noted for it militancy has become diminished. This shift is reflected in the many oral accounts and photo representations in family archives of local demonstrations and conflicts. Rural men and women alike tended to portray women as peripheral to the contemporary world of political action, as Eliane's earlier statement indicates. Similarly, in the stories that women tell to define themselves, to make sense of and act in their lives, in what Somers (1994) refers to as "ontological narratives," work in the private sphere of the household has become a key defining feature of women's identity. Eliane's statement and identification of herself as a "housewife" tends to be itself hegemonic.

Conclusion

I have argued that the political quiescence of contemporary Languedoc women is related to contests between different but related hegemonic projects, each attempting to establish itself as normal, that is, to become established as a regime.[7] For the sake of simplicity, one might be called a traditional regime, the other a modernizing regime. Despite the differing agendas, what is common to both is that the combination of economic, political, and cultural conditions upholds the power and the interests of men. What makes them different is that under a traditional regime, differences in interests and power are effaced. In a modernizing regime, those differences are exposed.

In a traditional regime, then, power differences were obliterated to the extent that men are able to establish their hegemony over women, and women's political and economic interests were seen by both women and men alike to be indistinguishable from the interests of men. These distinctions were eclipsed by a unity of interests that was forged by a division of labor in which both women and men worked on estates as agricultural laborers and smallholdings as vine cultivators. The subjectivities of both women and men were formed and informed by their immediate involvement in the production of vines. Therefore, in the past, women threw their lot in with men in political campaigns of the late nineteenth and twentieth century. Rural women identified with rural men as *viticulteurs* and *viticultrices,* as well as *ouvriers* and *ouvrières*. In turn, these forces shaped their agency. Women vociferously expressed their interests and vigorously displayed their defiance to landlords, the state, and capital in the class-based politics of the era. They acquiesced to a political project dedicated to the defense of rural livelihoods. In so doing, however, they also in fact lent their support to the defense of key institutions in rural Languedoc and economic practices that implied gender hierarchies and the subordination of women. In the past as in the present, women did not contest the structures of power and the hegemony of men.

In contemporary rural Languedoc, the modernizing regime, whose main agent is the state, in fact challenged the ability of men to sustain their hegemony over women. Changes in the material conditions of their lives and work have resulted in the differentiation and dissociation of women from men in their worlds of work and subjectivities. Women tended to identify themselves in domestic terms as housewives and no longer identify themselves with their husbands, brothers, or fathers as wine growers or agricultural laborers. Changes in the material conditions of work and the division of labor are reflected in the fact that the political project of defending a rural livelihood based on farming has come not only to embody and represent masculine interests more overtly, but to reinforce male power and privilege in the hegemonic institution of the household and in Languedoc society at large. The economic, political, and cultural forces of modernization exposed rather than concealed the differences of interests and power between women and men. The contemporary context changes in the division of labor have resulted in a more differentiated sphere of work and different experiences of control and domination. This has shattered the political unity of women and men. Women's subjectivity came to be defined less through the imperatives of men but instead through the ideas and ideals of modernity that were linked to the process of modernization of agriculture set into motion by the post-1949 French state. So, one of the consequences of the advent of modernization and of the economic and cultural transformation was that ideas and ideals governing women's identity and agency also changed. In contemporary rural Languedoc, women were both withdrawn and withdrew themselves from the realm of the traditional. They were withdrawn from vine cultivation as the forces of modernization ended a tradition of women working in the vines and they withdrew from a tradition of engaging in political struggle in a context where struggles to defend the livelihood of wine production had been long established as the hegemonic political project within a tradition of militancy. They identified less with men as political agents.

In contemporary rural Languedoc, then, women have become ambivalent to the contemporary political struggles of smallholders because they fail to articulate the interests of women who have been displaced from farm work and redeployed to labor in a series of different workplaces by the processes of capitalist restructuring. Yet no idioms of political discourse have yet emerged to regalvanize the political agency of women or articulate that with the complexity of women's experiences of domination and subordination in the home and in the many different contexts in which women work. While the political quiescence of women in contemporary rural Languedoc may be lamentable in the light of a rich tradition of women's contentiousness, it can nonetheless be salutary. Those moments of quiescence provide a hiatus, indeed an opportunity, for what Gramsci refers to as "organic intellectuals"[8] to dedicate their efforts to the reconstitution and establishment of a politics and practice that speaks to the interests of rural women in Languedoc and also in other contexts. But this project must be sensitive to the complexity of the conditions of women's lives and attentive to the dynamics of gender relations in each specific context, and this requires careful study and reflection on the interplay between culture, economy, gender, history, and politics. In this chapter, I have proposed some possibilities for apprehending that complexity through employing Gramsci's concept of hegemony in analyzing the political, economic, and cultural processes that give shape to women's political dispositions. The failure of what might be called "feminist politics" to establish a hegemony in many rural contexts in Languedoc, France, Europe, and elsewhere testifies to the fact that such work is needed. Indeed, it is necessary in order to constitute and reconstitute women as political subjects, with a specific subjectivity that enables the prosaic political objective of challenging the forms and overturning practices that result in the subordination of women. In the absence of nuanced contextually sensitive work of organic intellectuals, the women of Languedoc and also elsewhere will remain withdrawn from the political sphere in silent consent and acquiescence to the practices and processes that establish the supremacy of the subject categories of men as husbands, fathers, brothers, and sons.

Notes

The research upon which this paper is based was generously supported by grants from the Social Sciences and Humanities Research Council of Canada, the Wenner Gren Foundation for Anthropological Research and Trent University.

1. Forms of political struggle and expression are described in Lem 1999.

2. This is a pseudonym for one of the villages in the regions of Languedoc where I have been conducting fieldwork since 1984.

3. *Midi* refers in a general sense to the south of France, where the sun soaks the landscape as it does at midday. *Rouge* (red) refers to the tradition of radical and Left politics that prevails in the south of France.

4. For recent discussions on hegemony see Smith 1999, Kurtz 1996, and Roseberry 1994.

5. The reasons for this are explored in Lem 1999.

6. For a discussion of this concept see Somers 1994.

7. By hegemonic regimes, I mean simply a specific combination of political, economic, and cultural forces that characterize specific institutions and fields of power. Struggles between hegemonic regimes involve the attempt by the agents of each regime to assert their own visions of the normal in a contest to establish legitimacy.

8. For a discussion of "organic intellectuals" and the role they play in politics see Smith 1999.

CHAPTER 17

Red Flags and Lace Coiffes

Identity, Livelihood, and the Politics of Survival in the Bigoudennie, France

Charles R. Menzies

Small- to medium-scale commercial fishing persists despite capitalism's dominant economic trend toward concentration, despite the attempts of resource managers to "rationalize" production, and despite the apparent economic inefficiencies that plague such fisheries. This chapter is about why: Why do family-based fishing enterprises continue in the face of what seem to be overwhelming odds? Why do fishing communities continue their struggle? While this chapter takes as its social field all fishers in the Bigouden region of France—deckhands and skippers—the primary focus is upon boat owners (skippers) and is motivated by the following question: How are the memories of past struggles constructed and then mobilized by boat owners, to advance their own economic interests? Ultimately, this chapter is about how a melange of traditional peasant and militant working-class identities—identities that emerged out of the region's recent industrial past—have been used by boat-owning skippers to mobilize their crews and local communities in a struggle to defend the skippers' livelihoods.

The Place and the People

The Bigouden region of Brittany is located in the Department of Finistere, on the westernmost tip of France, south of the military port of Brest and near the departmental capital, Quimper. The region is characterized by intense cultural particularities, the most notable of which are the tall lace coiffe worn by its womenfolk (more on this later) and the persistence of Breton as a living language.

For most of the past century, the driving force behind the local economy has been a family-based commercial fishery, first tied to industrial canners and then, post–World War II, to a system of fresh fish auctions. Prior to the rise of an industrial capitalist fishery in the late nineteenth century, the region was an isolated, rural backwater, all but forgotten on the edge of the French metropolitan world. The extent to which this region has been "isolated" has varied throughout the preceding centuries.

The contemporary Bigouden fishing fleet consists of approximately 450 capital intensive and technologically sophisticated vessels. The typical boat is a 12–24-meter offshore dragger with a crew of between two and six men. With the exception of two limited companies (who own about twenty 24-meter boats between themselves), each of the boats is individually owned by its skipper and his immediate family. The early fishery was directly tied to vertically integrated, industrial canners. The contemporary fishery is predominately oriented toward the fresh fish market. The large processing firms of the early twentieth century have all but disappeared and have been replaced by government-supported fish auctions.

Commercial Fishing and Class Struggle

The world of commercial fisheries seems to sustain only one thing: crisis. This has been especially true since the application of industrial relations of production to the harvesting and processing of fish. Fisheries crises are often popularized in ecological terms—decline of a fish stock, destruction of the environment, etc. The symptoms of crisis are declining incomes, rising debt and bankruptcy, and the economic collapse of coastal communities. The underlying cause is to be found in the inherent tendency of capitalism toward accumulation and expansion. This has led to fisheries management schemes aimed at preserving and maintaining "acceptable" rates of return on investment, not the social well-being of fisheries-dependent communities.

How fishers respond to their particular crises can vary from resigned acceptance, passive resistance, to open revolt. In the Bigoudennie, a detailed history of active resistance can be traced back from the social protests of the 1990s to the revolutionary trade unionism of the early twentieth century and the even more remote, antifeudal peasant revolt of 1675. Each of these moments of struggle has left its imprint in the collective memory and, for better or worse, has laid the pathways to resistance for the contemporary period of neoliberal globalization.

Skippers and Crews: Together in Struggle?

The fishers' protests of the early 1990s were steeped in local symbols that invoked memories of early-twentieth-century industrial strikes and seventeenth-century peasant revolts. In so doing, the respective class contradictions of earlier moments of struggle (peasant-landlord, worker-capitalist) were reconfigured as Bigouden versus outsider. Thus, the memories of past struggles informed the present struggle in such a fashion as to silence both past and present internal contradictions.

The protest organizers eschewed a discourse of class, apparently as a mobilization tactic, emphasizing instead a strong sense of local solidarity and community (Leach's account, this volume, of the politics of opposition highlights the importance of placing class at the center of analysis in the face of social movements that deny or suppress class in their construction of identity. See also Smith and Barber, this volume, for discussions of class and community as interlinked identities.) This reflects the reorganization of production in late-twentieth-century capitalism in which the state has, to a large extent, replaced capitalist firms as the primary pole of struggle vis-à-vis boat owners and hired crews. This is so in two senses. First, the state plays a fundamental role in the regulation of the fisheries—a role compounded in France by the Common Fisheries Policy (CFP) of the European Union which governs all fishing outside of a twelve-mile coastal strip. Second, the state (again at both the national and European Union level) finances and, through a variety of provisions, controls crucial economic structures such as boat loans, marketing, and processing facilities, in addition to setting the minimum prices for species of fish.

On February 22, 1993, the day before Breton fishers stormed the Rungis fish market and destroyed nearly $4 million worth of fish, four thousand demonstrators marched through the streets of Le Guilvinec. The newspaper *Ouest-France* declared: "In the memory of the Bigoudennie, we haven't seen so many people demonstrating in Le Guilvinec since May '68." Survival Committee organizers declared the demonstration a success: "Here, everyone understood that if the fishery crashes, everyone will crash along with it," the organizers said. The exasperation and anger of the demonstrators was reflected in the slogans on their placards: "Briezh[Breton] fish inside, American fish outside, Brussels-watch the cauliflower and leave us the fish, Fish unsold, Fishermen in rags, US Go Home."

The visible signs of Bigouden identity, from the flag to the coiffe, were everywhere in the demonstration. The speakers stood upon a makeshift platform draped in the black and white of the Breton flag and the orange and yellow of the Bigouden flag. Mothers and grandmothers of the striking fishers joined in the demonstration wearing the tall lace coiffe of the region's traditional costume. Speaker after speaker emphasized the region's unique identity, its history of struggle, and the need to defend the life of the community by preserving an economically viable fishery.

As the protest movement developed and expanded, it was clear that the Bigoudennie was at the epicenter. Roving bands of fishers entered grocery stores and cold storage facilities and destroyed thousands of kilos of imported fish. Trucks loaded with imported fish were held up on local highways and their contents dumped out. The national government tried to put out the flames of protest with the promise of a 225 million French Franc "emergency plan" and an offer to review government fisheries policy (*Le Telegramme,* Feb. 24, 1993). The protests continued unabated.

The protests were organized by a coalition of boat owners who were able to mobilize support from their crews through a careful manipulation of the symbols of past struggles and local identity. The crucial point is that underlying the shroud of identity politics are the class interests of a group of petty capitalists struggling to maintain their socioeconomic location within a rapidly shifting field. That their movement took on the aura of local identity and the struggle against "outsiders" reflects the particularities of their local history. That it was grounded in the political and economic power of the boat owners reveals the contemporary economic structure of late-twentieth-century capitalism.

With few exceptions, all of the Bigouden skippers participated in the strikes and direct actions which rocked Brittany and France in 1993 and 1994. The membership of the strike organizing committees was dominated by skippers. In fact, the two leading members of the survival committee were skipper-owners of vessels in the 24m class.

Most crew members I interviewed said they had supported and participated in the protests. However, they did so under conditions in which their absence would be clearly noted by their skippers. This is a critical feature of the intense and intimate working conditions of small-scale fishers. Crews and skippers are divided in functional terms in the process of fishing (skipper in the wheelhouse, crew on deck) and economically (skippers own the boat or means of production, the crew "sell" their labor power to him). However, they are also united in the pursuit of fish as co-adventurers and must rely upon each other for their own safety and well-being at sea. Skippers and crew members often share in the sociability of male-centered cultural activities in their off-duty time onshore. There are, therefore, no neat class cleavages that pit these men one against the other. Yet the very conditions that make for close working relationships also mute the expression of crew members' opposition. Ultimately, the skipper can fire a crew member, and in the close-knit community of Bigouden fishers being fired off one boat may well ensure that a deckhand doesn't fish on a local boat again.

In 1993, the skippers had been at the forefront of the struggle. In 1994, crew members tried, without much success, to push their demands on working conditions and pay into the limelight. A call for a general strike following a meeting of Le Guilvinec fishers led to a coastwide shutdown of France's Atlantic fishery. As in 1993, the fishers organized roving bands of "commandos" whose task it was to destroy imported fish wherever it was found. Other units went into the local markets to publicize the differences between the price paid to fishermen at the dock and the price charged by the retailer.

The national government acted quickly to forestall an escalation of the protest. In answer to the strike organizers' demands, a meeting was set up in Rennes, the capital of Brittany, between then prime minister Eduard Balladur and elected representatives from the government-mandated local fishers' committees. On the day of the meeting, several thousand fishers, their families, and supporters demonstrated in the streets. While the minister talked with the fishers, riot police chased demonstrators through the streets of the city using tear gas, rubber bullets, and clubs. The fishers fought back with distress flares, one of which landed on the roof of the historic former parliament building of Brittany.

Early the next morning demonstrators returned home to pictures of the burning parliament building and fishers with bloody and beaten faces in the local newspapers. The fishers continued their protests until the government eventually promised more subsidies to help boat owners in difficulty. Crew members, however, received little attention. Social cleavages at the local level between skipper and crew widened and made subsequent solidarity more difficult. One manifestation of this was the growth of a union new to the Bigoudennie, *Force Ouvier*—Workers Force—on the 24m class vessels based in the Bigouden port of Loctudy.

The national government's response to two years of protest was to introduce additional funding programs for boat owners and regulatory changes that improved the economic conditions of the owner-operator fishing enterprises. Four years after the last major confrontation, the majority of the fishing skippers were back on an even keel. The outlook for their crews, however, was not rosy. For the crews, the lackluster conclusion of the 1994 phase of the social protest reflected the internal contradictions of the fishing community itself. The divergent solidarities of crew and skipper were revealed in the willingness of the national government to address the interests of boat-owning skippers while ignoring the plight of the crews. In promoting their own social and economic interests, the boat owners simultaneously relied upon the support and the subordination of their crews (a similar point is raised by Barber in her discussion of community and class in Cape Breton concerning the suppression of internal class conflicts in the face of external threats).

The Sardine Years

Throughout the period of protest in the 1990s fishers explained their involvement in the struggle in historical terms. Boat owners located their protest within the narrative structure of a radical working-class history in which their grandparents had battled against the big bosses and had won. The militant tactics of their grandparents were invoked both as an explanation of their own militancy and as providing the groundwork for effective struggle in the present. In this section I explore the region's history of struggle as expressed in oral interviews and archival sources, and its implications in the creation of a militant local identity.

During the early period of industrial transformation in the Bigoudennie—The Sardine Years (roughly 1880–1936)—local resistance was expressed as class struggle. It was represented symbolically in the red flag and the singing of the *International*. Following the mid-twentieth-century shift from an industrial sardine canning fishery to a fresh fish auction system, a local Bigouden identity superseded that of being a "worker." This shift serves to conceal, or displace, the underlying class dynamics of the artisanal fishery in which the economic survival of boat owners is, to some extent, dependent upon their ability to exploit the social labor of their own kin and fellow community members.

Industrial capitalism arrived in the backcountry of Brittany in much the same manner as it was implanted in Europe's overseas colonies. "Foreign" capitalists expropriated local labor and resources and, in the process, undermined local forms of production. The particular form of struggle that emerged in the Bigoudennie reflects this colonial context. This is not to say that the local struggles that emerged were explicitly or necessarily nationalist in nature. Rather, local expressions of class solidarity were more easily cultivated when the cannery owners and managers were French speaking and the working class were Breton speaking. The result was a legacy of militant trade unionism accustomed to employing the tactics of direct action in pursuit of its aims.

It is important to emphasize that this was not a revolutionary militantism, though the representatives of the state and local business feared it was part of a "red wave washing over Brittany." Despite the involvement of noted Socialist Party and trade union militants (clearly documented in police informer reports), the local expressions of militancy rarely moved beyond the narrow economism of a trade union perspective. However, in the pursuit of their economic interests, striking fishers and fishworkers did not hesitate in destroying the industrialists' property nor did they restrain themselves from physically confronting police, strike breakers, or the cannery owners and managers.

The strikes that shook the Bigouden region during the Sardine years (1880–1936) were not isolated events. They occurred within a context of expanding working-class militancy on the national stage (Noiriel 1990, 88–95). Union membership, "still under 200,000 in 1890, had risen to around 1 million in 1914" (Magraw 1992, 99). The average length of strikes increased from seven days in 1875 to twenty-one in 1902 (Noiriel 1990, 89). The decade and one-half immediately prior to World War I was a time of struggle and misery for working people in general and for Breton fisherfolk in particular. In the Bigoudennie, the wave of national strikes coincided with collapsing fish prices and declining fish stocks. The following account is drawn from archival sources and contemporary oral accounts. While singular in its particularities, it is emblematic of the strikes and protests referred to by contemporary fishers during the social protests of the early 1990s.

Trashing Fish in St. Guenole-Penmarc'h, 1909

In the early morning hours of September 7, 1909, a group of about sixty St. Guenole fishers stopped three wagons of tuna on its way to a nearby cannery. The fishers were protesting the canner's refusal to buy their sardines. First the police and then the town mayor asked the fishers to step aside. According to the police report, the fishers calmly refused to move.[1] Shortly thereafter, the demonstrating fishers were joined by another 150 from a nearby port, one of whom was carrying the tricolor (the national flag of France). The police report continues: "They rolled up the blue and the white onto the pole and, in this way, made a red flag. Next they pushed over one of the transport cars and took hold of the other two. Despite our presence, they continued their strike and threw the tuna into the sea."

The police reports focus on the "over-excitement" of the crowd and the specific physical acts they observed. The local cannery owner, Landais, saw the fishers' actions as an infringement on his property rights and his ability to conduct business untrammelled by "violence." For the fishers, however, the issue was their very ability to survive.

The fishers argued that the price for fish was too low to be able to support their families and that a local-first fish purchasing policy should be implemented. The fishers fought for a price for their fish that would allow them to survive and feed their families. They were desperate times. The situation was so severe that, in 1905, the bakers in St. Guenole threatened to go on strike and close their shops if the prefecture did not provide aid to the fishers. In a letter to the prefect, the bakers' committee said they could no longer afford to extend credit to the fishers and their families. They said, "The people will undoubtedly starve without government support."

Fishers also tried to control which boats could sell fish where. Home port fleets argued that their fish should have priority over visiting boats and that the local canners should buy all of the local boat's fish before they either imported fish or purchased fish from the nonlocal fleets. Understandably, this was a key source of conflict between fishers from different ports, even between ports in what is now called the Bigouden region.

These interport conflicts highlight the contradictory notion of a single Bigouden identity. Over the course of the twentieth century the "local" has been progressively enlarged to incorporate not just a particular village, but an entire region that incorporated a half-dozen or so small communities and fishing ports. During the Sardine Years, fishers fought both the canners and each other, alternatively employing a class, then a local identity. Control over sales in the local port led to intraclass conflict, struggles between groups of fishers based in different ports such as St. Guenole or Le Guilvinec. The struggles with the canners, however, relied upon interport solidarity and employed a language of class struggle that was able to transcend differences between villages in order to unite and fight against the canners.

In order to protect their livelihood at the local level, fishers wanted the canners to agree not to import fish from other ports or to buy from boats based in a different port. That is, a Penmarc'h cannery was to buy only from boats that habitually sold their fish and hired their crews in Penmarc'h. Landais and the other cannery owners saw this as a direct infringement on their rights to free enterprise and thus many of them refused to buy the local sardines and chose, instead, to bring in fish from outside the region.

Despite the "local" aspect of the demonstration against Landais, it encapsulates two central features of conflict within the fishery at that point: the struggle over fish prices and the question of who could sell fish where. Globally, these two points of leverage—the price of fish and the control over who can sell where—have been the most critical points of struggle between fishers and capital throughout most of the twentieth century. However, as systems of marketing, transportation, and processing became more and more integrated into a single world economy, the ability of fishers to affect change through strikes or direct actions at the local level has diminished considerably.

Red Flags and Memories of Struggle

The social struggles of the Sardine Years brought people together in an industrial setting who, until that point, had primarily thought of themselves as villagers, as opposed to seeing themselves as embodying more abstract identities such as French, Breton, or worker. In the struggle against the "bosses" of the late nineteenth and early twentieth centuries, a collective identity, manifest in a class idiom, emerged. Though not evident at the time, this early proletarian identity contained within it the seeds of a "local" identity. Subsequent changes in the local political economy—primarily the collapse of the industrial canning industry—stripped away the unambiguous class basis of their collective identity and opened the path for the emergence of a Bigouden identity, which the fishing skippers of the 1990s manipulated in order to advance their own specific set of class interests (see Gordillo this volume on the role of memory in social struggle).

A common theme linking the strikes and political actions during the Sardine Years is their reference point in a language of class and struggle and their invocation of highly symbolic markers such as the red flag. And, during the social protests of the 1990s, the strikes of the Sardine Years themselves became symbolic markers of struggle. This is not to deny the abject poverty and the real sociopolitical issues that gave birth to these particular struggles, but rather to point out, to prefigure, the underlying multiplicity of meanings and the ambivalence with which people entering periods of crisis "conjure up the spirits of the past to their service and borrow from them names, battle cries and costumes in order to present the new scene of world history in this time-honored disguise and this borrowed language" (Marx 1969, 398). In the retelling of the earlier strikes, two symbols of struggle repeatedly appear: the red flag and the singing of the *International*. The flag preceded the processions. Singing was a ritualized way of opening both socialist and union meetings—duly recorded by police spies in and among the strikers and observing from the sides.

The red flag is fraught with a double nature: simultaneously "national" in its invocation of the French Revolution and international as the flag of workers' revolution. In both cases the flag symbolizes a threat and provocation to the state. It is a reminder of the rights of citizenship within the Republic. But more fundamentally, it is part of a collective project engaged in creating "something that has never yet existed" (Marx 1969, 398). And, as Noiriel, points out: "[T]he red flag became the badge of highest honor; it became the late nineteenth century's rallying emblem for workers and their struggle everywhere, to the detriment of the tricolour flag symbolizing the Republic" (1990, 94).

The singing of the *International* can be read (as indeed metropolitan based academics have sometimes done) as a misreading of the French by Breton speakers: "*en terre nationale*" as opposed to "*internationale.*" While it is more likely that this is a contemporary misreading, it points to the social and economic violence being enacted upon the Breton people. The gibe at their singing in French fails to acknowledge that their first language, Breton, was actively being erased by the national state. Clearly, the symbolic power of the singing and the waving of flags were read by the state as provocative and, in one instance, all flags but the tricolor were banned from a public parade.

As the passage of time separates the present from its past, the rough edges of memory are rounded off. One's political perspective is no antidote. Both Left and Right (re)construct romantic images of the past with which to fight their battles for the future. As Sider argues in "Cleansing History" (1996), historical renderings have simplified the past in such a way as to paper over real processes of differentiation and struggle. For contemporary Bigoudens, the period of social protest and struggle during "*L'Epopee de la Sardine*" (see Boulard 1991 and Tillion 1971, 64–82, 84–85) was a potent symbol of solidarity mobilized in the context of the protests of the 1990s.

The period between 1905 and 1936, a time when "*on chantait rouge*" (Tillion 1977), is reworked in the context of the contemporary protests as a romantic period in which the "community" was united in opposition to an exploitative class of owners. The contemporary view of these strikes is part critique of the present and part longing for the past. The past is here constructed as a time in which familial ties were strong and community solidarities important. The contemporary rendering of the Sardine Years evokes the importance of community and kin-based networks of mutual support and solidarity while acknowledging their decisive opposition to the industrial "outsiders," represented by the cannery owners and managers.

Lace Coiffes and Industrial Work

The tall, cylindrical coiffe of the Bigoudennie has become the primary symbol (if not caricature) of the region (Segalen 1991, 2). From tourist brochures to union banners, the Bigouden coiffe marks out an important domain of local identity. The fetishization of the coiffe, both as emblem of the contemporary and marker of the exotic, reveals the intimate link between the processes of the everyday and the violence of capital.

The origin of the coiffe is a subject of some debate (Duigou 1990; Cornou 1993; Cousine-Kervennic 1994). One particularly robust local story roots it in a peasant uprising in 1675, "*La Revolte des Bonnets Rouges.*" The historical evidence, such as it is, suggests a far more recent origin (Duigou 1990, 12). Nonetheless, the origin of the coiffe is linked in popular memory with local sentiments of resistance and struggle. Beyond issues of truth or myth, the crucial point concerns how the social violence of capitalism is etched into the cultural matrix through popular costume and memory.

The Coiffe in Its Present Form

The contemporary coiffe has the appearance of a tall white-lace cylinder worn on top of a woman's head. It is actually a rather elaborate headdress comprised of a bonnet plus a lace cylinder. The hair is first pulled up into a tight bun on the back of the head upon which a small black cloth bonnet is secured. The lace cylinder is then attached to the bonnet by use of hairpins and two lace ribbons tied under the women's chin.

The coiffe appears in three specific social-symbolic contexts: (1) as a regular item of clothing worn by a dwindling number of elderly women; (2) as a tourist and marketing image; and (3) as worn by young women at special "cultural" events. Given the extent of tourism during the summer months, the dividing line between these three specific contexts can at times become blurred, as everyday life is transformed into performance.

It is not uncommon, for example, to see several elderly women with coiffes in Pont L'Abbé on market day. During the height of the tourist season, one may witness the rather surreal sight of an elderly Bigouden moving slowly through the market, stopping here and there as she makes her weekly purchases. Her coiffe, visible above the crowds, stands like a lighthouse attracting the turned gaze of tourists, the boldest of whom are busy taking her photo as she passes by. A similar scene replays itself in the heart of the rainy Breton winter, except the cast of thousands is reduced to the local inhabitants who take no notice of the "old Bigouden" as she passes by with her coiffe encased in a special clear plastic bag to protect it from the rain.

Up until the late 1950s most of the women in the Bigoudennie wore a coiffe for all manner of occasions ranging from work in the canneries and work in the home to important public occasions and events. Few, if any, young women coming of age in the 1960s wore the coiffe. Coincident with the wider processes of "modernization," the coiffe was seen as retrogressive, traditional in a negative sense, and as a marker of inferior social class. Emulation of aristocratic costume was replaced by an emulation of "bourgeois" costume with its attendant understatement and neutrality. Though modeled on an aristocratic costume, the coiffe is every bit as much a product of the twentieth century as are automobiles or assembly-line production. In the late 1980s, young women whose mothers stopped wearing the coiffe in the 1950s joined folk groups in which they wore the local costume and performed "traditional" folk dances. At the dawn of the twenty-first century, a growing number of young women are choosing to be married in traditional costume and/or have their wedding pictures taken in a coiffe.

The phenomenal development and elaboration of the coiffe occurred at the hands of the young women who worked in the new canneries starting from the late 1800s. In the mid-1800s the distinctive coiffe was little more than a suggestion, a slight peak at the front of an otherwise unremarkable bonnet. The coiffe rose (both literally and figuratively) out of the flux and disruption initiated by the fishery during the early years of this century.

Coincidentally, although by no means causally linked, the decline of the coiffe as an item of everyday attire occurred along with the withdrawal of the canning industry from the region. As the canneries left, job opportunities for women shifted into the service sector (retail and government). In the 1980s and 1990s the coiffe reemerged in folk festivals, pan-Celtic cultural events, and as a marketing icon in the tourist trade. The contemporary coiffe has lost it link to the everyday and, with the exception of a dwindling group of elderly women, is now worn only as a costume. It is an extravagant marker of local identity symbolically linked with an imagined past.

The Coiffe's Political Context

The coiffe emerged within a period of intense social strife in the Bigoudennie which culminated in the election of the United Front government of 1936.

The mass working-class movement was also part of an inescapable process of proletarianization in which a rural peasantry was transformed into a semi-urban proletariat. The seemingly anachronistic, even paradoxical, expression of "tradition" as manifested in the elaboration of the locally distinct lace coiffe must be placed in the context of these processes of social dislocation. As Brian Palmer points out: "Capitalism does not so much come to the countryside. The backcountry is itself the site of historical transformation, generating social (gender/racial) relations, protoindustrialization, demographic convulsions, and market forms pivotal in the transition to capitalism" (1994, 15). The Bigoudennie was one space within a wider field of industrialization and social strife which, in terms of the fishery in 1900, included 10,000 fishers and 30,000 workers in more than one hundred canneries, plus several thousands more in support industries such as net making and boat building.

It is crucial to note that the elaboration of a "traditional" costume was not isolated to the Bigoudennie. Similar processes can be identified throughout the region. In practically all cases these examples of "cultural innovation" stem first and foremost from young women entering waged employment in industrial food processing plants: thus simultaneously maintaining and severing their connections with the agricultural-based networks of kin, reciprocity, and exploitation. As Sider notes, such examples of intensifying cultural particularism are directly associated with the elaboration and intensification of locally specific forms of inequality, both within and between communities (1997).

The origins of the coiffe, as a symbol of local identity, emerged at a key moment of socioeconomic transition from peasant agriculture to industrial capitalism in the Bigouden region. While men, working on fish boats, experienced this transition as part of kin-ordered fishing crews, women's experience was shaped by wage labor in the canneries and family ties to men on the fishing boats. This different and gendered experience of the transition to industrial capitalism created the backdrop against which the coiffe emerged as a distinctly modern symbol of locality.

Stories of the coiffe's origin are rooted in stories of resistance dating back to a peasant revolt of the 1600s yet the actual development of the coiffe is fully "modern" in that it emerges (quite literally takes off) out of the process whereby young peasant women are incorporated into an industrial working class while their husbands and fathers become commercial fishers. The origin of the coiffe can be found in the episode of industrialization between the 1890s and the 1930s.

The crucially different gendered experiences of industrialization are critical to the process out of which the coiffe emerges. As Lem (this volume) points out, the specific experience of women or men within the relations of production have important consequences in terms of, for example, men or women's relative levels of political activity. In the Bigouden region men were incorporated into the industrial capitalist economy via the sociability of small, intimate all-male working groups of between eight and twelve men working for a skipper and sharing in both risks and profits as sharesmen. Women, however, were inserted into a fully capitalist form of wage labor and subjected to the discipline of factory-regulated work in which machinery (not the vicissitudes of nature, wind, rain, and fish) drove the pace of work. For our purposes here, it is sufficient to simply highlight that the importance of a gender's location in the relations of production can influence the development of cultural particularities such as the Bigouden coiffe (see Labrecque this volume for an expanded discussion of three key arenas that shaped gendered experiences of work).

Conclusion

What are the implications for struggle? Essentially, the contemporary struggle was a form of conservative populism manipulated discursively and directly by a class of independent boat owners in transition from a state-created form of peasant ownership into a fully capitalist form of production.

Two important conclusions emerge from this study. The first details the specific ways in which the development of the welfare state reconfigured the social-spatial dimensions of class struggle. The second concerns the issue of custom, struggle, and invention. Here, I am specifically referring to the manner in which a unique cultural particularity emerged out of the imposition of industrial social relations: specifically, the development the local Bigouden coiffe. The crucial issue concerns the manner in which a seemingly archaic custom was in fact a direct product of the experience of proletarianization even as it became entangled in the present within a social protest rooted in the productive middle classes.

State and Social Class

One of the primary functions of the welfare state has been to contain the demands of the working and petty bourgeois classes within the confines of a capitalist state. The welfare state is the hidden side of Fordism—the part of social peace and stability that the state underwrites. With respect to the fishing communities of the Bigoudennie, the development of the welfare state coincided with the decline of the industrial sardine canning industry and the rise of an artisanal fishery of skipper/boat owners. While it is prudent to caution against drawing too hasty a conclusion, neither should one underestimate the role of state intervention in this change. The archival evidence is clear: Capital and state did in fact combine to: (1) undermine relations of social solidarity within the fishers' communities and (2) pull certain classes of fishers into the orbit of the propertied classes. Here it is important to emphasize that the form of state intervention was neither limited to nor uniquely focused on the use of coercive force. A key area of state intervention involved the development of state-funded financial instruments (i.e., *Credit Maritime,* a credit union–like agency) that deliberately targeted segments of the fishing communities (specifically boat skippers) in order to incorporate them into the capitalist economy through the device of ownership.

Local Custom and Social Struggle

The question of how local customs fit into social struggle is particularly important. In the Bigoudennie the lace coiffe emerged as a symbol of local identity at precisely the moment in which the local society was undergoing a transition from a peasant to an industrial capitalist economy. The structure of social inequality changed from one in which the primary lines of control over labor were located within the family, to an industrial waged economy in which the previous kin-based forms of control were disrupted. The old paternalism of the father was replaced by a new paternalism in which the manager or owner of the cannery now appropriated the labor power of household members.

This new form of social inequality had different meanings for the genders. Men working on the fish boats were nominally independent of the direct control of industrial capital over their labor. They experienced a work setting in which the idiom of companionship and equality predominated. As pointed out in the body of the chapter, the control of a skipper over the labor of crew throughout the twentieth century has been less pronounced or brutal than the control of a factory boss over a wage laborer. Women, however, worked under the direct control of capital. They were paid wages based upon their hours of work and, for the most part worked in an assembly-line-type setting. Thus, the experiences of industrial capitalism varied dramatically according to one's gender (see also Lem and Labrecque this volume).

In the changes engendered by the rise of an industrial capitalist fishery, three features are crucial to note: 1) the language of the local or the construction of a local identity is part of a structure of conflicting class antagonisms that crosscut families; 2) the symbolism of struggle in the 1990s is local but the arena of struggle is not—struggle is located in a de-spatialized context of the universalization of production and exchange; and 3) the speakers, the storytellers, are the boat owners who, through their skilful use of local identity and the shared memory of struggle (see also, Barber, Gordillo, and Smith, all this volume) have been able to forge an effective political coalition with their crews, the crews' families, and with a national "liberal"/social democratic agenda that has primarily benefited the most successful of boatowners.

The struggles during the Sardine Years at the beginning of the twentieth century centered around the extension of capitalist relations of production into a previously agrarian society. Between then and the 1990s yet another, potentially more fundamental shift, has occurred. This shift is not epochal, nor is it a harbinger of some new stage of the world economy. Rather, it represents the universalization of capitalist relations of production. In this context, fisheries are subordinated to an economic logic that extends far beyond the local fish port, auction, or fishing ground. It is in this newly emerging global capitalist system (as opposed to a world economic system based only on trade and exchange) that the local identity "Bigouden" has emerged as part of a tactical program for political struggle in the global arena. Thus, the boat owners attempt to strategically place themselves within an intensely local construction while simultaneously orienting or locating their field of struggle within a global frame. This struggle emerges out of the antagonisms within a family-based form of petty capitalism that it is no longer critical in the reproduction of local capital. Thus, the boat owners are forced to either transform themselves utterly and completely into the raw unadulterated relations of exploitation and appropriation of a capitalist social formation or disappear into the mists of memory.

Notes

My thanks to Gerald Sider who has been a supportive mentor and stalwart intellectual guide during my time as a student at the City University of New York and beyond. Thanks also to Michael Blim and Jane Schneider whose comments, suggestions, and advice have always been appreciated. The core research this paper draws on was funded in part by a Wenner Gren Foundation Doctoral Research Grant and a Social Sciences and Humanities Research Council Doctoral Fellowship. Additional support was provided by a UBC Humanities and Social Science Research Grant.

1. Archives departmentales, Quimper: File, 4S 358, Rapport du Brigadier Vivier sur les incident survena le 7 courant à St. Guenole.

CHAPTER 18

Out of Site

The Horizons of Collective Identity

Gavin Smith

It is perhaps ironic that while in the corridors of power everybody wants to be associated with neoliberalism, among our colleagues everybody wants to assert their "political economy" credentials. It is *de rigeur* for any self-respecting postmodernist or postcolonialist to decry postmodernism and assert how bogus postcolonial critiques really are, while asserting that they themselves have long been political economists[1] and, while acknowledging the arrogance and myopia of Marx, are profoundly influenced by the acuteness of his processes of thought (Eagleton, 1999).[2] But we don't have to go quite so far onto the strobe lit dance floor of these kinds of high-powered cultural theorists to encounter an albeit less extreme but similar discourse. Self-described post-Marxists, it turns out, have moved on from their own early days and are now truer to the vision of Marx than ever. Laclau's hegemony goes well beyond Gramsci's; Touraine's social movements make class obsolete; and Castells, whose brilliant early work reshaped urban studies, has discovered that our world is no longer as dependent on the material production of food, bricks, and bombs as it is on "information."

It is within this context that it has become fashionable to talk of "the end of work" and of the need to recognize the significance of transnational populations disconnected from place. No doubt such expressions are not intended to be taken entirely literally; rather, they come as part of a package that wishes to call to our attention the fact that work and locality now play a very small part in people's sense of collective identity. Such assertions carry with them the idea that there is something radically new and different about the world we live in, because traditionally in classical social and political analysis place and work have been taken to be two of the most fundamental determinants of social identity and political practice. But if we want to assess the degree to which there is something new about the sources of our collective identity, we will need to go beyond simply placing words such as *work, labor, region,* or *community* in front of "social identity," find other determinants to be vitally important too, such as gender, ethnicity, and religion, and then toss out the older assumptions for being materialist, overly essentialist, and so on. Instead, we need to ask what *particular elements* of people's embeddedness in a place and a regime of work were being alluded to. We need to ask, in other words, not why place and work-regime were so obviously important to older generations of social thinkers, but rather how they saw these two notions as condensations of very particular social forces, relationships, and experiences at different historical moments and in various geographical settings. Only then can we interrogate the present and only when, having done so, we find no such forces, relationships, and experiences to be especially salient, can we speak of the end of work and place as determinants of social subjectivity.

I do this by looking at two bodies of literature, one revolving around factory regimes and the other, more recent, around "flexible" regional regimes. Part of my argument is that insofar as they become authoritative accounts of reality the selectivity of these often very powerful bodies of theory itself plays a major part in the way people understand the way their collective identities are formed. I argue too that, when theoretical understandings become translated into policy—means for directing the processes of change and development in a given society—then selections at the level of ideas play a major part, through history, in the way the material world gets to be built over time. Understanding how these processes of selectivity occur therefore is important—as much for bodies of knowledge that gripped people's minds in the past, as for the trends that appeal to us today.

In fact, if we begin with contemporary debates and discussions about the role of work and place in our social identities, as we might expect, the situation is not clear-cut. In 1985 Ernesto Laclau remarked that terms such as *working class* or *petit bourgeois* were no longer especially meaningful "as ways of understanding the overall identity of social agents" (Laclau 1985, 27). An older generation of scholars was associated with the idea that a collection of people might have quite salient concerns, perceptions, and interests in common as a result of the kind of work they did—the industrial worker with his [sic] experience of the factory, the small shopkeeper, with a quite different experience—yet people such as Gorz (1982), Touraine (1992), or Laclau argued that this was by no means as salient today as it once was.[3] Then writers especially committed to the cultural determination of social subjectivity, such as Clifford (1995) and Appadurai (1991), wrote a similar epitaph for the role of physical place. Transnationalism, the mobility of people and the global flows of capital, have made membership in a physical locale a far less powerful factor in people's sense of collective identity than before.

In a sense these epiphanies were discipline-specific. The worm turned differently as sociological assumptions about the links between labor and (class) identity were interrogated in one guild, while anthropological assumptions about the links between (ethnographic) site and (cultural) identity were questioned in another. Yet once we shift the glass to catch a different refraction, we find that the crossing of disciplinary boundaries has produced reassertions of place and work though now in a different register. Harvey's (1982) sustained attack on the role of time in social theorizing and the subordinate relegation of space was taken up by Giddens (1985) who increasingly sought to embrace spatial criteria in his social theorizing, plus a spate of work by a new generation of geographers. In cultural anthropology too, along with the advocacy of multisited ethnography, and the growing importance of transnational populations whose relationship to place is complex and problematic, there has been a return to a concern with the importance of locality as a source of collective identity. Appadurai's interest in the production of locality (1995) has recently been joined by Gupta and Ferguson's (1997) collection on locations.

Then, in writings more directly tied to policy, unsurprisingly the role of work in the economy has been far from abandoned, and indeed the ways in which certain kinds of work and certain kinds of place relate to one another become especially salient as *flexible* work is now seen to offer a crucial fix for capitalism. Though the way in which this (supposedly) new kind of work relates specifically to social identity has not been at the forefront of this literature, flexible work has crucially been associated with the way in which certain kinds of (regional and urban) space are constituted. A further feature of this work on "regional economy" is that places are not only seen to be reinscribed by new forms of labor, but by global *capital* too. Sassen persuasively argues against the rhetoric "in which place is seen as neutralized by global communications and the hypermobility of capital" (1998, xxi), suggesting instead that "place is central to many circuits through which economic globalization is constituted" (1998, xix).

One might argue that these are very different understandings of work and place than had gone before. But to argue thus is only to expose the point I wish to make: that we can only say this if we have already established just what did lie beneath older assumptions. The idea here, then, is to sensitize ourselves to the thought processes that underlie on the one hand the proposition that *shared experiences of place* give rise to collective identity, and on the other the idea that *shared experiences of work* give rise to collective identity. At a time when many anthropologists were condensing the peculiar features of small-scale places in the term *community*, for example, the mass-production factory was becoming an especially powerful condensed shorthand in other social sciences, for the idea that work played a powerful role in collective identity. Each of these ideas was empowered by the commonsense ideas we all might have about a small village on the one hand or a large factory on the other, ideas deriving from our attention to the appearance of life as experienced every day. Yet we need too to remind ourselves of the two sets of relationships that underlie these two powerful tropes: the first having to do with proximity/distance, the second with appropriation/

expropriation. By persistently investing our interest in everyday experience with these *relational* features of place and work, we may be able to interrogate more acutely the great variety of ways in which place and work are mutually constitutive.

The Mass Production of Categories

Elsewhere I have tried to examine the ways in which we, as anthropologists, might try to rethink the role of face-to-face relations in the context of what Gramsci called "the ethical state" (Smith, 1999, 133–166, 195–227); here I will take as my point of departure the mass-production factory and its influence on the way "work" has become reified. Where once work was seen preeminently to take place in the mass-production factory or in the rows of desks of the modern office, more recently this concentration of "work" is said to give way to images of its dispersion. Sites of work are envisaged as being networked through spaces of greater or lesser regional coherence. This would appear to provide us with a nice opportunity to reintroduce more critical acuity into the way in which sites of productive activity and the silhouette of other sites influence one another. Yet we do *not* get a deconstruction of these dense condensations (of "work" and "locality"). Rather, the taken-for-granted assumptions of an older selective tradition remain uninterrogated. Instead of "work" and "economy" being rethought, further hypostasizations called "the social" (as in "the social economy" and "social capital") and "culture" (as in "a distinct regional culture of work and saving") are simply grafted on to existing ones (Smith 1999, ch. 4).

I have used the expression *selective tradition* here intentionally. The fact that so little critical attention is directed to terms like *economy, work,* and *social* capital in policy-oriented literature serves well to make the point that authoritative assessments about social reality—whether grandly called theory or more pragmatically called policy-driven problem solving—arise out of political purposes. The process of selecting from reality what is or is not relevant to the discussion at hand is a function of the protagonists' purposes—their personal, social, and political goals. When this kind of selection is closely linked to policy, to programs of governance and the ordering of development, this selection in the realm of ideas is translated into the material order of things. Selective representations in one generation condition concrete conditions in another. The blueprints for the myriads of failed development projects that were imposed on the Soviet Union by Stalin and his successors, as well as those that were foisted on the dependent countries of the post–World War II era by the Western powers, were drawn by use of a highly selective historiography of the Industrial Revolution whose narrative culls from less than a hundred years in just one county in England.

Thus the model of the mass-production factory was necessarily that—a model, a model moreover that arose to serve quite identifiable purposes, on the one side, of management and, on the other side, of labor. These led to quite specific political goals that involved, to give a very obvious example, a very specific imagery of the nature of "the working class" and its role in society, in contrast, for example, to images of the peasantry and *its* role in society (Hobsbawm 1971; 1973; Wolf 1969). There were many rich complexities left out, both with respect to the extent to which mass production monopolized the experience of working people even at its height, and with respect to the extent of mass production even in the heartlands of the factory system, as we shall see.

To forget that other experiences *were* kept in shows a myopic rereading of an earlier selective tradition. But it provides the basis for a rising master narrative in which older forms of collective movements are replaced by *new* "social" movements. The new Ernesto Laclau, as well as Touraine and Melucci, would argue that we should reverse our thinking about the relationship between the social identity we acquire as we make our way from one day to the next in addressing the practical matters of our lives and collective praxis. Rather than seeking out factors in the former, in the mundane world of the quotidian, which might precede and then lead to a movement expressing some collective version of this experience—close proximity in the workplace, similar experiences of deprivation and alienation, and so on—people's engagement in collective struggles, they argue, *themselves give rise to their self-conscious identity,* their social subjectivity. Once again, before hastening to decide who might be right or wrong in this kind of name calling, we need first to ask what is characteristic about this newer kind of selective tradition. We might note, for example, that *this* kind of selectivity shifts attention away from the sites where social relations of production occur toward the primacy of "enculturated" politics as the source of individual and collective self-consciousness; a kind of culture and politics cut loose from the historical necessities of any particular process of social reproduction.

Whether or not "everyday life" is a more sharply honed intellectual instrument than "work" or "place" need not detain us here; we need instead to note that when an earlier generation of social analysts talked of the role of the factory whistle or urban slum in ordinary people's lives, or when the anthropologist engaged in the face-to-face world of a small community, both *thought* they were addressing precisely issues of everyday life. Moreover, whatever else it involves, everyday life is always about situated getting-by, that is, a place to work. To stress the newness of its observations this literature needs to be overselective of what was already a selective model—overemphasising the past image of the urban factory, which, as I have said, selected criteria from a much more complex social reality, a selection that took place through a whole series of shifting political conjunctures, interpretations of those conjunctures, and broader understandings of how history would unfold; in other words, an array of situated practices that accumulated through an epoch into a patterned structure of feeling (Williams 1988).

So if we are to examine the ways in which "sites of work" were understood to act as important bases for people's overall sense of social identity, we need to go well beyond these kinds of career-motivated intentional misreadings of an earlier literature. The question we need to answer is whether what we are seeing is the disappearance of the class basis of identity to be replaced by "new social movements," or whether the task isn't a great deal more challenging and difficult. If instead we set out to try to understand a whole series of different kinds of relationships between livelihood and identity so as to enrich and redraw our understanding of class and political engagement, then we are directed to a quite different and possibly quite extensive set of questions about a given place and historical period than is possible if we take the view that collective expression is an entirely deracinated *cultural* matter, a series of colorful choices to be made by life's consumers.

To answer such questions, we need to deconstruct the process of thought that led earlier thinkers to link membership in the working class to a particular way of thinking about oneself as a person and as a member of society. We can do so by postponing for a moment the tempting calls of "everyday life" and "experience" and suggest that what was at issue then (what might possibly be at issue now) are precisely issues of proximity and distance and of appropriation and exploitation that have already been mentioned. With the advance of industrial society in Europe, discussions of the sociology of working people's lives were premised on the proposition that matters of experience and of the everyday arose out of a pivotal relationship without which it was increasingly difficult to engage in work; that the profits on which the reproduction of the system depended were based on the difference between the value produced by workers-in-combination-with-machinery and the wage advanced to the workforce. It was the "rationalization" of this process that gave rise to a selective image of the conditions that class of people most existentially faced. Primary among these was the observation that working people who may have once made a living working the land were now living together in close proximity in urban areas largely cut off (distanced) from this countryside and working at jobs whose draconian discipline and routine was greatly enhanced by the fact that the workplace was itself sharply cut off (distanced) from the home. In other words the conditions of regimented humiliation at work and indignity and division in society at large, were themselves the product of a formulaic set of cultural categories. Whether different kinds of people *experienced* all this preeminently as non-freedom, as humiliation, regimentation, as the forceful casting off of the skills they had been taught by their mothers and fathers are all matters that should be of extensive concern to cultural analysts. But we need to recognize that this fascinating rhythm of exploitation, though pounding upon the awful dance of experience, is not reducible to experience alone; rather, it is a concrete abstraction. Exploitation may have been experienced as such, yet it was (and is) a relationship that existed irrespective of whether or not it was experienced.

Contained within this imagery are real and imagined notions of proximity and likeness, distance and alienation, and appropriation and exploitation. It became increasingly clear that regimentation and discipline in the factory would require a war on working people's persistent (and often, successful) attempts to retain other sources of livelihood in and around the home. This meant that the earlier distance and separation—from their rural backgrounds and from their cultural and traditional village ways of life—had to be matched by another; a conceptual distance between their "work" in the factory and the rest of their waking hours, supposedly devoted to nonwork. Getting by at home, in the evenings, on the weekends, back at Uncle Archie's farm; it was not that these things didn't happen. It's that there came a time when the tension between owners seeking means to regulate work in the factory and workers seeking some form of counterstrength in the collective withdrawal of work, gave rise to the hardening of categories. Categories became both a weapon in the political struggle and an outcome of those struggles.

Alongside this very powerful image of industrial society we might juxtapose a more recent image of supposedly "post-industrial" society—the model of the "regional economy" which appears to combine nicely the two determinants of collective identity I have been referring to: work and geographical place. As we would expect, this too is a highly selective image of reality serving specific political goals. As we might also expect the political leverage of this discourse (one that is profoundly tied to policy and to the goals of better governance) derives its authority from assertions that the reality it addresses represents a radical break with the past. And again such authority derives less from the interrogation of specific historical material, more from a selective reading of earlier *models* that were themselves selective. Then, in a further development, these compounded processes of selection from "history" and prioritizations in the present produce the conditions—the processes of thought, the policies, the visions of the future—that frame contemporary material reality.[4]

Regional Economies and the Inflexibility of Categories

There is now a burgeoning literature in studies of contemporary capitalism, which focuses on the growing importance of "regions" for the organization of supposedly flexible kinds of social and economic institutions. Drawing on the evidence from such highly "successful" regional economies as the Third Italy, Baden Wurtemburg, or Silicon Valley, these studies have sought to identify the factors that might account for such success and, of course also, might account for what we could call "deficient regionality."

Seeking a term that would capture the sine qua non of a regional economy, Arnaldo Bagnasco (1977) resorted to the notion of the *social* market. The market per se induces images of the self-seeking individual, of competition, of parties to a deal indifferent to one another as identifiable social persons—a friend, a father, etc. But in the *social* market regionally clustered firms and production sites relying on a workforce characterized by its flexibility in working hours, career patterns, and skills are so intricately and thoroughly networked with one another that the economic rationality of decision making needs to be studied less in terms of any one unit, and more in terms of its embeddedness within these networks. Of course, just as the market here becomes social, so too (regional) society becomes market-like, marketable. This new modernity might be seen as rather like the kind of transposing of forms we now watch with fascination on TV science fiction programs—economic X-files. As the large, physically concentrated factory has given way to a dispersed production process that looks more like an entire district, so the region increasingly takes on the characteristics of a factory without walls, a firm with profit margins, whose "success" or "failure" must be measured with appropriate criteria (Hirst and Zeitlin 1989; Pike et al. 1992). From a regional perspective old people can be a resource (if they do free child care) or a deficit (if they themselves require care). Charles Sabel (1989) suggests that in the Third Italy the use of child labor might better be seen as the training of apprentices than as the exploitation of cheap family labor.

The cogs and levers of such a social system cannot work, of course without the oil of an appropriate cultural disposition. Every social market requires too a "regional culture." For example, a pervasive argument about "the Third Italy," Europe's most famous regional success story, is that cultural predispositions in this area explain much of its success—commercially oriented sharecroppers in a region of rural manufacture developed an entrepreneurial culture and a propensity to shift flexibly between occupations, as well as a culture of trust and cooperation (Bagnasco 1977; Becattini 1992). Though rejecting this rather saccharine version of history Charles Sabel (1989, 29f) does, then, reject the importance of culture. Rather, he proposes that cultural predispositions can be mined to provide gold for the future. Through first becoming aware of local cultural mores and values (in a way that the previous generation of [non-anthropological] analysts had not) and then through treating them with instrumental selectivity, such cultures can themselves be rendered "flexible" for the purposes of "development."

What we need to note here is that the term *culture* is sucked out from the rest of social practices and placed in a laboratory vial precisely so that terms such as work, economy, social capital, and so on do *not* have to be understood as historically quite specific sets of relationships dialectically constitutive and profoundly cultural from the outset. The problem lies in the fact that the very element that is used as a decisive feature of a particular region becomes its "culture," yet what makes this "culture" visible—identifiable as a set of practices distinct from "normal" economic behavior outside the region—is that it cannot be embraced by the terms of the *logic of interests*. The muddle in this empirically derived model, then, is that in shifting toward an understanding of economic practices that relies on elements of the social world called "culture," analysts are in fact simply grafting on to an older tradition of work and interests whatever new gargoyles they hope will enhance the architecture (Granovetter 1985). They are not exploring sets of relationships and the dialectical process by which these categories are historically constituted.

Marginalia

It is important not to misread what I am arguing here. I *am* arguing that both "models" of the role of place and work in the forming of people's sense of themselves are selective. But I am *not* thereby arguing that they are necessarily "wrong." Rather, I have argued that all descriptions of social reality are selective; we need to know what the criteria are for that selectivity. We may not always be able to find out, but making ourselves aware of possibilities gives us a critical edge for disentangling what is being said. Few would be shocked at the suggestion that writings on industrial work were formed in a world in which workers and business managers were arguing over the right course of history. In engaging in this argument they selected what they took to be the especially salient features of social reality for that historical process. It doesn't seem unreasonable therefore to ask about the analogous selection process that goes into the more recent studies of flexible entrepreneurial workers, and regions characterized by especially advantageous economic arrangements. These too are likely to carry with them an underlying assumption about the best way in which history should unfold.

It is hardly likely that Gorz believes in "the end of work," or that those who argue that we are in a postindustrial "information society" (Bell 1976, Castells 1998) really believe that there is nobody in Korea, China, Mexico, or Indonesia making those steel plates, axial cables, running shoes, and oil tankers. They just don't think those things are important in the future history of the world. This historical vision is a profoundly political matter and it sets the criteria for the way in which such people select what is significant about the past. A series of distinctions and separations need to be made—postcolonial/colonial; postmodern/modern, and so on. And irrespective of how fuzzy people might be in the employment of such terms, their mere use gives rise to sets of distinguishing characteristics. This is no less true of the mass production and regional models I have been talking about here. And one way to make ourselves aware of this is to create noise so as to muddle the clarity of their distinctions.

Baumann (1982) likes to locate the origins of the factory in its predecessor the poor house where "routinization and surveillance developed as means of, simultaneously, punishment and moral education, with physical labor serving both" (1982, 114). He goes on to argue how crucial the continuity of this moral control was later in the factories: "It meant . . . a decisive crackdown on all and any residue of indigenous folk culture and a determined effort to exterminate all its manifestations" (115–116). Here Baumann is alluding to two separations, one to do with punishing factory work versus the rewards of another kind of life, the other to do with a new world arising out of the extermination of the old. He notes that both of these were not some "natural" process of modernization that created these conditions, but the energetic intervention of factory owners, yet Baumann appears to regard the outcome of their determined efforts as a foregone conclusion—it suits his and our ideas about the modern world. Yet, citing E. P. Thompson, Pollert notes how long and hard was the job of making rigid the working day, of building a wall between what was work and what wasn't. This was the job of destroying alternative sources of income to generate reliance on the wage. In the process there was a long debate between advocates of regular employed work versus "taken work" (1988). In other words, processes of selection took place once more and these processes then became inscribed on participants' views of reality. But not without workers struggling.

One kind of struggle was preeminently a public affair and was directed at the owners themselves, of course. William Reddy has noted that an early use of the expression *faire la grève* which today would be translated as "to go on strike" in fact involved the punishing of employers or possible a whole town by actively *seeking work* elsewhere (1984, 129). Referring to textile workers in Reims as late as the 1880s, he reflects:

> These demands suggest how closely weavers continued to associate the justice of pay with output instead of effort, and the extent to which they wished to be left to their own devices at the machine, to make their own decisions about when to start, when to stop, when to fix, when to set up, when to lubricate, when to stare out of the window. (1984, 333)

Another kind of struggle was less out there in the open to be seen—less public—and involved getting the family by. Thus, John Benson writes that

> few families were dependent simply upon a single, regular, weekly wage. Much employment was seasonal or casual in nature and most families derived their income from a whole cluster of different sources: from work done by the wife and children, from begging, from the Poor Law, and from petty crime such as coal picking or poaching. (Benson 1983, 3–4)

And even here, the writer is lapsing into a retrospective view of "petty crime": just five pages later he is telling us that coal picking was regarded as late as 1921 much like gleaning in rural society, mine owners "not saying anything about [their employees] fetching a bag or barrowful for their own use" (1983, 9–10). Indeed the picking was part of the wage in many workers' eyes.

We can go back a long way in the history of industry to find a tradition that workers would have a share in the product of their labor. Thus, the line separating "established rights" from "barefaced robbery" was difficult to draw; there was a close connection between "long pay" and the embezzlement of materials (Berg et al. 1983, 2). Referring to the period "before the factory," Berg et al. conclude:

> There was . . . a long tradition of acquiring portions of income in ways other than the wage. The failure to keep time and to respond to wages was associated with the need to engage in a whole series of extra-curricular activities yielding up various forms of non-monetary and monetary income. Industrial discipline could only succeed as these other sources of income started to dry up. Thus the importance of the emergence of restrictions on gleaning, poaching and gathering wood. (1983, 9)

Indeed, what terminated such practices was the need on the part of owners to give bite to the lockout: to force dependence on the wage and the wage alone. It was the need to control labor, not just in the factory, but beyond it, then, that put an end to this symbiotic linkage in livelihood practices (Benson 1983, 2). As a result, workers "had to accept the categories of their employers and learned to fight back within them" (Berg 1988, 86).

Yet it was not just workers who were pressed into this mould. Social analysts' increasing reliance on statistics acted as an especially powerful form of selectivity vis-à-vis social reality (Hacking 1990). Occupational classifications useful for the collection of statistics generated a bounded notion of the working person, which can ensnare the historical sociologist. Pollert talks of their confused understanding of what ever constituted "employment" in the ideal period. "This has been further complicated by an historical 'discovery' of insecurity," she says, "as though it were radically new, and the calling of this a 'flexible' trend" (1988, 51). We have already noted Reddy's observation that *la grève* referred less to idleness than to the active pursuit of alternative work, and the same holds true for any radical line statistics has encouraged us to draw between employment and unemployment. Factory workers may not have been *just* factory workers, and even when they were, they may not have had the job for their entire working lives. Many nineteenth-century workers were more like Jacks (or Janes)-of-all-trades, and one reason why the term *worker* replaced "artisan" was that the latter, almost as part of its definition, escapes statistical classification.

This makes it hard to understand the *artisanat* in occupational terms. There was always an ad hoc-ness, an approximation about such a life spent looking for opportunities (Zdatny 1990, 184). For many of these people, then, the broader term *livelihood* would have been more appropriate. We see this again and again. Even in the heart of industrial capitalism the single wage as the sole and precarious source of household income was not at all common until the very end of the nineteenth century (Kumar 1988, 151; Chambers 1963; Berg 1994, 205).

Thus, if we were to turn from the individual worker or artisan to the household subsistence enterprise, we would find multi-occupationality and job seeking to be pervasive.

> Factory experience was of course a fact of experience for only a minority of nineteenth century workers, and least of all for adult males. The persistence of the family economy was naturally even more evident in the small-scale domestic and outwork industries which, far from being extinguished by industrialization, actually expanded enormously as a result. . . .It was the continuation of domestic and outwork industry . . . that was mainly responsible for concealing from contemporary census enumerators—and later historians—a good deal of the remunerative work actually done . . . especially by women. (Kumar 1988, 158)

If an adult man's working life often involved almost as much time and mental agility seeking work as doing it, this was vastly more true of women (Alexander 1976, 65). Meanwhile, children made an important contribution to the family economy. "It was not until as late as the 1920s that wealth flowed from parents to children instead of the reverse . . ." (Berg 1988, 66). We can find early evidence of the kind of attitude to children learning to be good workers that Sabel highlighted in his view of the Third Italy, when Dorothy George points out that it was only when work was associated with the factory system that the idea of child labor was taken to be an outrage rather than something to be admired and emulated by other families. "It was the sense of something monstrous in the factory system which directed attention to the yet more monstrous exploitation of the labor of young children" (quoted in Berg 1988, 66). Work in the home then, as now, need not be romanticized for us to acknowledge that the idea of "work" shifts from its role in the organic interlinkages, skills, and inventiveness of household members to a place where its discipline and drudgery are alienated.

So we see first a process of struggle between workers and owners producing divisions, distinctions, and categorizations, and we see further how the gathering of "knowledge" through statistics served to give still more heightened resolution to these features. But the selective process I am talking about also produced as a byproduct, a particular idea of the rural community. One of the things Krishan Kumar (1988) notes in his reflections on the changing ideas of work and "unemployment" in England from the Elizabethan Poor Laws of 1597 and 1601 to the height of the industrial factory in the 1920s, is that the villages the proletariat left behind were by no means noncommodified subsistence agricultural places but multioccupational industrial and agricultural communities. We have just seen a somewhat more "enterprising" kind of family household in England's nineteenth-century towns than the idea of the proletarian often conjures up, but in rural settings too people were packaging together fragmentary, flexible, and varied physical tasks and social services that were often necessarily fixed in particular geographical sites. These have often been glossed as "community." But, partly as a result of the way it was marginalized as a focus of historical sociology, the rural community has suffered both from a powerful romanticism and, more importantly, from precisely the kind of selective compartmentalization built into the industrialization model, becoming simply the mirror image of everything to be found in the industrial city. Berg (1988, 85) complains that "[k]inship and community have been equated with notions of mutuality. . . . By extension it has also been assumed that the cohesiveness of the local community and with this the social and organizational role of women was broken by the advance of capitalist competition and the market."

One particular effect of this—one for which anthropologists need to take much of the blame—is the assumption that a sense of community arises positively and obviously from intimacy and various kinds of nonmarket relationships, thus obviating the need to ask how people themselves had to fight for such collective solidarity just as self-consciously as did unionized workers. Indeed, Berg notes that in the West Country of England, "[t]rade consciousness was . . . synonymous with community consciousness" (1988, 87; see Lem 1999 for the same observation about French wine growers). Williams (1973) has made a very similar point about Tysoe, a village in the Midlands.

> In Tysoe there was a revival of community, as the village came together in the nineteenth century, to fight for its rights of allotment in the Town Lands. In many parts of rural Britain, a new kind of community emerged as an aspect of struggle, against the dominant landowners or, as in the laborers revolts . . . against the whole class-system of rural capitalism.

The important point here is that "community" did not arise out of some inherent features of rural life, nor was it the result of a convenient opposition to all that sociologists, romantic novelists, and reformers found bad about industrial cities. Often community didn't exist very much at all, and when it did it was likely the result of quite self-conscious agency on the part of participants—making it not so very different perhaps from the kind of "movement" Melucci, Touraine, and Castells want to call distinctively "new."

Once we accept this we are relieved of much of the baggage that comes with notions of rural settlement and its radical difference from market capitalism. We may be relieved too of the idea that there was little movement or information flow between these two sites. Writing of North Yorkshire in the early part of this century, Donadjgrodski comments, "Although [rural people] shared a distinctive culture, they were members of the 20th century" (1989, 431). "[F]armers of small acreages . . . almost wholly dependent on family labor, generally poorly capitalized and often involved in the dual economy . . . were not subsistence farmers. Most human food and some animal food as well as other commodities like clothes, shoes, most fuel and household goods had to be bought" (1989, 430). "On many holdings it was essential that at least one member of the family had another job. *Attitudes to work were versatile and flexible.* . . . There was no rigid boundary between farming and other types of work, except among the most prosperous" (1989, 434; Italics mine). As one informant remembered it, "I used to do the cows and then go to work . . ." (1989, 431). Speaking of nineteenth-century New England, Laurie (1989, 21) comments, "Change came in the early stages of the industrial revolution, which opened up employment for rural women as operatives in textile mills and outworkers in the shoe and clothing mills. Outworkers far outnumbered operatives and stayed at home doing industrial work and farm chores." It is of course precisely these characteristics of livelihood—the fragmentary and flexible nature of work in production and services—that are now used as the hallmark of regional economies. I want to turn now to the historical backdrop of one such region.

Workers as Agents

Earlier I have argued that we need to attend to the important relationships that underlie the experience of everyday life in different settings—in this case of the urban factory characteristic of "high capitalism," and of the regional economies that form an important part of today's capitalism. I suggested that underlying sociological understandings of the new industrial classes were ideas about space (proximity/distance) and the relations that characterized the new labor process (appropriation/exploitation). I then reviewed the decisive features identified by students of contemporary regional economies. These, I noted, are, at the present stage at least, rather empirically driven and descriptive. They fail to conduct detailed historical studies that might help us to understand the dynamic and mutually constitutive nature of sets of relationships. Rather, they tend to highlight desocialized key features—the entrepreneurial worker, regional culture, or "networks" (a shorthand word in this case for a wide variety of relationships).

I then used evidence from England, conventionally taken to be the baseline case for the Industrial Revolution, to suggest that we tend to arrive at the distinctive features of industrialism through a process of selection that is not always helpful. That evidence provides the same check on the supposedly distinctive characteristics of flexible capitalism. In both cases, rather than sharp historical breaks, or radically distinct kinds of societies, we are faced with a more uneven and fractured dividing line. An older generation of rural workers may indeed have been rather different from their urban offspring, but not always, and not necessarily in the ways we might expect. And of course if this is so, then it means also that today's regional worker may not be as sharply distinctive as we are led to believe.

Moreover, as these historical processes become more complex, so too do the sets of relationships on which we base our conceptualizations. In arguing for or against the role of work in the constitution of social identity, we can no longer take older notions of work as our starting point. In dismissing the role of place in a particular people's sense of who they are, or in making an argument that place is especially important, we need to attend to the ways in which demands of a certain kind of livelihood and the composition of the household family play upon one another. We need, too, to try to situate the pressures and possibilities of livelihood and the features of different kinds of household-families[5] within the ongoing production and reproduction of the wider social field of what is likely to be a socially and culturally differentiated relevant collectivity (often glossed as "community").

Part of the problem lies with the fact that most of the people we study have themselves absorbed the rigid categories invoked by social science. This can have the paradoxical effect of removing their own usages of key terms—such as work, home town, etc.—from the *interpretive* element of our work. Rather than being stopped in our tracks by the limits of our linguistic competence, the texture of a term allows it to slip too easily into what we take for granted. We need to pause over the term *pegujalero,* so we listen to how people use it, we note how its sense is negotiated among different sets of people, we ask questions. In short, our attention is attuned to interpretive work. But when people say, "Work is hell" one minute and, "Thank God I've got work" the next; or perhaps "I've never left Cape Breton" or "We're stuck in Bigoudennie" or "People here in Murviel have a different *mentalité* from people [10 km away] in Magalas," it is frequently difficult to oblige ourselves to defamiliarize what is meant by "work" or in what sense one "comes from," "leaves," or "gets stuck in" a place. One suspects that this would be less of an issue for Gordillo (chapter 13) precisely because of the degree to which the Toba are removed from the discourses of social science. On the other hand it may well be a fascinating lever into women's subjectivities in the *maquiladoras* that Labrecque discusses (chapter 12).

On the other hand, our practice of doing ethnography, coupled with our respect for certain kinds of revindicative collective politics, may well effectively draw our attention to the disjuncture between terms rendered hegemonic through the authority of social science (and adoption thereby into "policy") and the counterassertions made effective through resistance. Struggles themselves are especially forceful ways of asserting meaning or shattering classifications, as we see in the chapters of Leach, Barber, Lem, and Menzies. We simply need to steel ourselves against the kind of teleology of our hopes (socialist, feminist, environmentalist) and thereby too quickly drawing conclusions as to what a struggle is about, or what might be its best outcome or a setback. Unfortunately, because of the self-confident modernism of the era when such concepts were set in their moulds, their use does not always enhance these kinds of sensitivities.

This has not been a subject amenable to conclusions. Instead I have tried to give some sense of what I mean by seeking out the mutually constitutive nature of relationships between practices and people. We need to evoke the texture of "work" and the way it is threaded through emergent ideas of locality or place by trying to explore the multiplex ways in which work and place mutually constitute one another. An intricate dialectic arises in which the characteristic features of work arrangements, the household family, and the field of the socially and culturally differentiated community reciprocally give form to one another. So a way to start this kind of inquiry would be to examine the different ways in which work for securing an income, the form of the household-family, and local interpersonal relations are variously integrated with one another. If we were to think for example of "work for securing income" in more specific terms such as the kind of work being done, its organization, the materials, tools, and skills needed, and the characteristic kinds of workplace relationships, then we might ask what the interplay was between this setting and the site of the family household and thence the world of the local community. We may, as a result, be led to a far more complex understanding of the ways in which social identity is formed, apparently abandoned, and reformed. We may also be able to grasp more realistically the balance between the choice and construction of social identity and its more embedded "given-ness."

Notes

1. It is partly for this reason that I prefer the term *historical realism*. See Smith 1999, 15.

2. Eagleton comments dryly:
> The idea of the post-colonial has taken such a battering from post-colonial theorists that to use the word unreservedly of oneself would be rather like calling oneself Fatso, or confessing to a furtive interest in coprophilia. (1999, 3)

3. It has become fashionable to associate this kind of thinking uniquely with Marx and with Marxian social inquiry, but both Weber and Durkheim made very similar kinds of connections between, for example, the entrepreneurial spirit, or the division of labor,

and certain kinds of social subjectivity, though of course the nature of these linkages were not necessarily supposed to be the same.

4. To a certain extent, Piore, Sabel, and Zeitlin are exceptions to this tendency (Piore and Sabel 1984; Sabel and Zeitlin 1985). But once Sabel turns to contemporary regions, his attention to their historical specificity becomes shallow and formulaic, relying on a culturalist version of regional history, a constructed past arising from the strategizing of agents apparently themselves outside and beyond the mould of historical formation and able to invent their own politics of memory (Sabel 1989).

5. The use of this expression "household–family" is cumbersome but intentional. I do not employ either term as a sharp analytic category but as actors' necessary constructions—ideological work that needs to be done to retain ideas of "family" and or a common "household project" under a wide variety of livelihood conditions and pressures from a wider social environment, which, in turn, give specific character to a household family.

References

Aguirre Beltrán, G. 1952. *Problemas de la población indígena en la cuenca del Tepalcaltepec.* Mexico City: Instituto Nacional Indigenista.

———. 1967. *Regiones de refugio.* Mexico City: Instituto Indigenista Interamericano.

Ahmad, A. 1992. *In Theory.* London and New York: Verso.

Albarracín, J. 1987. *La onda larga del capitalismo español.* Madrid: Libros Economistas.

Alexander, S. 1976. Women's work in nineteenth century London: A study of the years 1820–1850. In *The rights and wrongs of women,* ed. J. Mitchell and A. Oakley. Harmondsworth: Penguin.

Alonso, A. M. 1988. The effects of truth: Re-presentations of Past and the imagining of community. *Journal of Historical Sociology* 1, 1: 33–57.

Alonso, J., ed. 1980. *Lucha urbana y acumulación de capital.* Mexico City: Ediciones de la Casa Chata.

Anderson, P. 1979. *Lineages of the absolutist state.* London: Verso.

Appadurai, A. 1991. Global ethnoscapes: Notes and queries for a transnational anthropology. In *Recapturing anthropology: Working in the present,* ed. R. Fox. Santa Fe, NM.: School of American Research Press

———. 1995. The production of locality. In *Counterworks: Managing the diversity of knowledge,* ed. R. Fardon. London: Routledge.

———. 1996. *Modernity at large: Cultural dimensions of globalization.* Minneapolis: University of Minnesota Press.

Arengo, E. 1996. *"Civilization and its discontents": History and aboriginal identity in the Argentine Chaco.* Ph.D. Dissertation, Department of Anthropology, New School for Social Research.

Arguedas, J. M. 1987. *Las comunidades de España y del Perú.* Madrid: M° de Agricultura, Pesca y Alimentación.

Arizpe, L. 1980. *La migración por relevos y la reproducción social del campes inado.* . Cuadernos del CES, El Colegio de México, 28. (English version: *Relay migration and survival of the peasant household.* In *Towards a political economy of urbanization in Third World countries,* ed. H. Safa. Delhi: Oxford University Press).

Arrighi, G. 1994. *The long twentieth century.* London: Verso.

Asad, T., ed. 1973. *Anthropology and the colonial encounter.* London: Ithaca Press.

———. 1987. Are there histories of peoples without Europe? *Comparative Studies of Society and History* 29(3): 594–607.

ASA (Association of Social Anthropologists of the Commonwealth). 1998. *Annals,* Volume 18. Canterbury: Centre for Social Anthropology and Computing and London: ASA.

Ascoli, U. 1987. Il sistema italiano di welfare tra ridimensionamento e riforma. In *La societa Italiana degli anni ottanta,* ed. U. Ascoli and R. Catanzaro. Bari: Laterza, 283–312.

Bagnasco, A. 1977. *Tre Italie: la problematica territoriale dello sviluppo italiano.* Bologna: Il Mulino.

Barber, P. G. 1992. Working through the crisis: Resistance and resignation in the culture of a de-industrialized community. In *Workers' expressions: Accommodation and resistance on the margins of capitalism,* ed. J. Calagione, D. Nugent, and D. Francis. Albany: State University of New York Press, 146–163.

Bartra, R. 1987. *La jaula de la melancolía.* Mexico City: Grijalbo.

Basave Benítez, A. 1992. *México mestizo. Análisis del nacionalismo mexicano en torno a la mestizofilia de Andrés Molina Enríquez.* Mexico City: Fondo de Cultura Económica.

Bauman, Z. 1982. *Memories of class. The pre-history and after-life of class.* Boston: Routledge and Kegan Paul.

Becattini, G. 1992. The marshallian district as a socio-econ notion. In *Industrial districts and inter-firm cooperation in Italy,* ed. F. Pyke, G.Becattini, and W. Sengenberger. Geneva: International Institute for Labour Studies.

Behar, R. 1986. *Santa María del Monte. The presence of the past in a Spanish village.* Princeton: Princeton University Press.

Bell, D. 1976. *The coming of post-industrial society.* New York: Basic Books.

Beneria, L., and M. Roldan. 1987. *The crossroads of class and gender: Industrial homework, subcontracting, and households in Mexico City.* Chicago: University of Chicago Press.

Benson, J. 1983. *The penny capitalists: A study of nineteenth-century working-class entrepreneurs.* Dublin: Gill and MacMillan.

Benton, L. 1990. *Invisible factories: The informal economy and industrial development in Spain.* Albany: State University of New York Press.

Berg, M. 1988. Women's work, mechanization, and the early phases of industrialization in England. In *On work,* ed. R. Pahl. Oxford: Blackwell.

———. 1994. *The age of manufactures, 1700–1820: Industry, innovation, and work in Britain.* 2nd Ed. London: Routledge.

Berg, M., P. Huson, and M. Sonenscher. 1983. *Manufacture in town and country before the factory*. Cambridge: Cambridge University Press.

Bhabha, H. 1990. Introduction: Narrating the Nation. In *Nation and narration*, ed. H. Bhabha. London: Routledge.

Blim, M. 1990. *Made in Italy: Small-scale industrialization and its consequences*. New York: Praeger.

Bloch, M., ed. 1985. *Marxism and anthropology*. Oxford: Oxford University Press.

Bocock, R. 1986. *Hegemony*. London: Tavistock.

Boehm de Lameiras, B. 1986. *Formación del Estado en el México prehispánico*. Zamora: El Colegio de Michoacán.

Bonfil, G. 1970. El concepto de Indio en América: Una categoría de la situación colonial, In *Anales de Antropología*, Universidad Nacional Autónoma de México, vol. VII.

———. 1989. *México profundo. Una civilización negada*. Mexico City: Consejo Nacional para la Cultura y las Artes. (English version: *México profundo*. Austin: University of Texas Press, 1996).

Boulard, J. 1991. *L'Epopee de la sardine: Un siècle d'histoires de pêche*. Paris, Brest: Editions Ouest-France, IFREMER.

Bourdieu, P. 1984a. *Distinction: A social critique of the judgement of taste*. Cambridge: Harvard University Press.

———. 1984b. *Homo academicus*. Paris: Editions de Minuit.

———. 1989. La ilusión biográfica. In *Historia y Fuente Oral*, 2.

Bourdieu, P. and L. J. D. Wacquant. 1992. *An invitation to reflexive sociology*. Chicago: University of Chicago Press.

Brandes, S. 1976. The impact of emigration on a Castillian mountain village. In J. B. Aceves and W. Douglass, *The changing face of rural Spain*. Cambridge, Mass.: Schenkman.

Braun, M. 1995. The confederated trade unions and the Dini government: The grand return to neo-corporatism? In *Italian politics: The stalled transition*, ed. M. Caciagli and D. Kertzer. Boulder, Co.: Westview, 205–221.

Brenner, R. 1998. The economies of global turbulence: A special report on the world economy, 1850–1998. *New Left Review*, 229, 1–264.

Burnet, J. R., and H. Palmer. 1988. *"Coming Canadians": An introduction to a history of Canada's peoples*. Toronto: McClelland and Stewart in association with the Multiculturalism Program, Department of the Secretary of State and the Canadian Government Publishing Centre, Supply and Services, Canada.

Campos, D. 1888. *De Tarija a la Asunción: expedición boliviana, 1883.* Buenos Aires: Imprenta Peuser.

Cardesín, J. M. 1992. *Tierra, trabajo y reproducción social en una aldea gallega (s.XVIII–XX): Muerte de unos vida de otros.* Madrid, M° Agricultura, Pesca y Alimentación.

Carrasco, P. 1976. La sociedad mexicana antes de la conquista. In *Historia General de México,* vol. I. Mexico City: El Colegio de México.

Castells, M. 1998. *The rise of network society.* Vol I of *The information age: economy, society, and culture.* Oxford: Blackwell.

Chambers, J. D. 1963. *The workshop of the world.* Oxford: Oxford University Press.

Clark, A. K. 1994. Indians, the state and law: Public works and the struggle to control labor in liberal Ecuador. *Journal of Historical Sociology* 7(1): 49–72.

———. 1998. *The redemptive work: Railway and nation in Ecuador, 1895–1930.* Wilmington, Del.: SR Books.

Clifford, J. 1983. On ethnographic authority. *Representations* I: 118–146.

———. 1995. Diasporas. *Cultural Anthropology* 9, no.3: 302–338.

Clifford, J.C., and G. E. Marcus, eds. 1986. *Writing Culture.* Berkeley and Los Angeles: University of California Press.

Cole, J. 1977. Anthropology comes partway home: Community studies in Europe. *Annual Review of Anthropology* 6: 349–378.

Collier, G. A. 1987. *Socialists of rural Andalusia. Unacknowledged revolutionaries of the Second Republic.* Stanford: Stanford University Press.

Connell, R. W. 1990. The state, gender, and sexual politics. *Theory and Society* 19.

Connolly, W. E. 1981 *Appearance and reality in politics.* Cambridge: Cambridge University Press.

Contreras, J. 1987. Introducción en Arguedas, J.M. *Las comunidades de España y del Perú,* Madrid, M.° de Agricultura, Pesca y Alimentación.

———. 1991a. Los grupos domésticos: Estrategias de producción y de reproducción. En *Antropología de los Pueblos de España,* ed. J. Prat, U. Martínez, J. Contreras, and I. Moreno. Madrid: Taurus.

———. 1991b. Estratificacion social y relaciones de poder. In *Antroplogia de los Pueblos de España,* ed. J. Contreras et al. Madrid: Taurus.

Cooper, F. 1994. Conflict and connection: rethinking colonial African history. *American Historical Review* 99: 1516–1545.

Corman, J., M. Luxton, D. W. Livingstone, and W. Seccombe. 1993. *Recasting steel labour: The Stelco story.* Toronto: Garamond.

Cornou, J. 1993. *La coiffe Bigouden: Histoire d'une estrange parure.* Pont L'Abbe: SKED.

Corrigan, P. and D. Sayer. 1985. *The great arch. English state formation as cultural revolution.* Oxford: Basil Blackwell.

Cousine-Kervennic, N. 1994. *Le pays Bigouden.* Rennes: Editions Ouest-France.

Cox, O. C. 1970. *Caste, class, and race: A study in social dynamics.* New York: Monthly Review.

Cruces, C. 1994. Navaceros, 'Nuevos agricultores' y viñistas. *Las estrategias cambiantes de la agricultura familiar en Sanlúcar de Barrameda.* Sevilla: Fundación Blas Infante.

Cueva, A. 1982. *The process of political domination.* Piscataway, N.J.: Transaction Books.

D'Alema, M. 1995. *Un paese normale: La sinistra e il futuro dell'Italia.* Milano: Mondadori.

Darnell, R. 1997. Changing patterns of ethnography in Canadian anthropology: A comparison of themes. *The Canadian Review of Sociology and Anthropology* 34(3): 269–296.

Dawson, A. 1998. From models for the nation to model citizens: Indigenismo and the 'revindication' of the Mexican Indian. *Journal of Latin American Studies* 30:279–308.

Deaglio, M. 1998. *L'Italia paga il conto.* Milano: Vitale Borghesi.

de la Peña, G. 1986. Poder local, poder regional: perspectivas socioantropológicas. In *Poder local, poder regional,* ed. J. Padua and A. Vanneph. Mexico City: El Colegio de México. (English version: Local and regional power in Mexico. In Texas Papers on Mexico, 88–01, University of Texas at Austin, ILAS, 1988).

———. 1997. Anthropology. In *Encyclopaedia of Mexico,* ed. Michael Werner. Chicago: Fitzroy Dearborn Publishers, vol. I, 54–60.

———. 1998. Educación y cultura en el México del siglo XX. In *Un siglo de educación mexicana,* ed. P. Latapí. Mexico City: Fondo de Cultura Económica/Consejo Nacional para la Cultura y las Artes.

de la Torre, C. 1993. *La seducción velasquista.* Quito: Ediciones Libri Mundi.

DiGiacomo, S. 1997. The new internal colonialism. *Critique of Anthropology* 17(1): 91–97.

di Leonardo, M., ed. 1991. *Gender at the crossroads of knowledge: Feminist anthropology in the postmodern era.* Berkeley: University of California Press.

Donajgrodzki, A. P. 1989. 20th century rural England: A case for peasant studies. *Journal of Peasant Studies* 16, no. 3 (Apr.): 425–442.

Donham, D. L. 1990. *History, power, ideology: Central issues in Marxism and anthropology.* New York: Cambridge University Press.

Douglas, M. 1995. Forgotten knowledge. In *Shifting contexts: Transformations in anthropological knowledge,* ed. M. Strathern. London: Routledge.

Drache, D. 1995. Celebrating Innis: The man, the legacy and our future. In *Harold A. Innis, Staples, Markets, and Cultural Change,* ed. D. Drache. Montreal: McGill-Queen's University Press.

Drucker-Brown, S., ed., 1980. *Malinowski in Mexico.* London: Routledge and Kegan Paul.

Duigou, S. 1990. *Les Bigoudens (et surtout les Bigoudenes).* Quimper: Editions RESSAC.

Dworkin, D., and L. Roman, eds. 1993. *Views beyond the border country.* New York: Routledge.

Dyck, N., and J. B. Waldram, eds. 1993. *Anthropology, public policy, and native peoples in Canada.* Montreal: McGill-Queen's University Press.

Eagleton, T., ed. 1989. *Raymond Williams: Critical perspectives.* Cambridge: Polity.

———. 1991. *Ideology: An introduction.* London: Verso.

———. 1999. In the gaudy supermarket. *London Review of Books* 21, no. 10 (13 May), 3–6.

Editorial Board, *Critique of Anthropology.* 1979. Editorial. *Critique of Anthropology* 13/14: 3–6.

Ehrenreich, B. 1995. The decline of patriarchy. In *Constructing masculinity,* ed. M. Berger, B. Wallis, and S. Watson. London and New York: Routledge.

Engels, F. 1958. *The condition of the working class in England.* Ed. W. O. Henderson and W. H. Chaloner. New York: Macmillan.

Escobar, A. 1998. The place of nature and the nature of place: Globalization or postdevelopment? *Social Text* [Forthcoming].

Escobar, A., M. González de la Rocha, and B. Roberts. 1987. Migration, labour markets, and the international economy: Jalisco, Mexico and the United States. In *Migrants, workers, and the social order,* ed. J. Eades. London: Tavistock.

ESRC (Economic and Social Research Council). 1998a. *ESRC Postgraduate training news.* August 1998. Swindon: ESRC.

———1998b. *Research themes: An introduction to ESRC's thematic priorities.* Swindon: ESRC.

Fabila, A. [1940] 1978. *Las tribus yaquis de Sonora,* Mexico City: Instituto Nacional Indigenistas (Colección Clásicos de la Antropología Mexicana).

Fentress, J., and C. Wickham. 1992. *Social memory.* London: Blackwell.

Fernandez-Kelly, M. P. 1997. Maquiladoras: The view from the inside. In *The Women, Gender, and Development Reader,* N. Visvanathan, co-ordinator. London and New Jersey: Zed Books.

Foucault, M. 1980. *Power/Knowledge.* New York: Pantheon.

Fox, B. J. 1988. Conceptualizing patriarchy. *Revue canadienne de sociologie et d'anthropologie/Canadian Review of Sociology and Anthropology* 25(2).

Freeman, B. 1982. *1005: Political life in a union local.* Toronto: Lorimer.

Frigolé, J. 1975a. Algunas consideraciones sobre las unidades de análisis cultural. En *Primera reunión de antropólogos españoles,* ed. Jimenez. Sevilla: Universidad de Sevilla.

———. 1975b. Creación y evolución de una cooperativa agrícola en la vega alta del Segura. *Revista de Estudios Sociales* no.14–15.

———. 1983. Religión y política en un pueblo murciano entre 1966–1976: La crisis del nacionalcatolicismo desde la perspectiva local en Revista Española de Investigaciones. *Sociológicas*, 23.

———. 1984. *Llevarse a la novia: Matrimonios consuetudinarios en Murcia y Andalucía*. Bellaterra: Universidad Autónoma Barcelona.

———. 1991. Ser cacique' y 'ser hombre' o la negación de las relaciones de patronazgo en un pueblo de la Vega Alta del Segura. En *Antropología de los Pueblos de España*, ed. J. Prat, U. Martínez, J. Contreras, and I. Moreno. Madrid: Taurus.

———. 1998. *Un hombre*. Barcelona: Muchnick Editores.

Galván, A. 1980. *Taganana. Un estudio antropológico social*. Tenerife: Aula de Cultura de Tenerife.

Gamio, M. [1935] 1987. *Hacia un México nuevo*. Mexico City: Instituto Nacional Indigenista.

———. 1922. *La población del valle de Teotihuacán*. 3 vols. Mexico City: Talleres Gráficos de la Nación.

García Canclini, N. 1990. *Culturas híbridas*. Mexico City: Grijalbo.

Geertz, C. 1973. *The interpretation of cultures*. New York: Basic Books.

Giddens, A. 1985. Time, space and regionalization. In *Social relations and spatial structures*, ed. D. Gregory and J. Urry. London: Macmillan, 265–294.

———. 1990. *The consequences of modernity*. Cambridge: Polity.

Gilbert, M. 1998. "In search of normality: The politcal strategy of Massimo D'Alema." *Journal of Modern Italian Studies*. 3 (3) 307–317.

Gill, L. 1997. Relocating class: Ex-miners and neoliberalism in Bolivia. *Critique of Anthropology* 17(3): 293–312.

Gobierno de Yucatan. 1998. Web Page, *http://www.yucatan.gob.mx/*

Godelier, M. 1972. *Rationality and irrationality in economics*. New York: Monthly Review Press.

———. 1977. *Perspectives in Marxist anthropology*. New York and Cambridge: Cambridge University Press.

González de la Rocha, M. 1986. Lo público y lo privado: El grupo doméstico frente al mercado de trabajo urgano. In *Cambio regional, mercado de trabajo y vida obrera en Jalisco*, ed. G. de la Peña and A. Escobar. Guadalajara: El Colegio de Jalisco.

Gordillo, G. 1999. *The bush, the plantations, and "the devils": Culture and historical experience in the Argentinean Chaco*. Ph.D. Dissertation, Department of Anthropology, University of Toronto.

Gorz, A. 1982. *Farewell to the working-class: An essay in post-industrial socialism*. London: Pluto.

Gough, K. 1968. World revolution and the science of man. In *The Dissenting Academy*, ed. T. Roszak. New York: Pantheon Books, 135–159.

Gramsci, A. 1971 (1929–1935). *Selections from the prison notebooks*. Ed. and trans. Q. Hoare and G. N. Smith. New York: International Publishers.

Granovetter, M. 1985. Economic action and social structure: the problem of embeddedness. *American Journal of Sociology* 91, no. 3:481–510.

Guerrero, A. 1994. Una imagen ventrílocua: El discurso liberal de la 'desgraciada raza indígena.' In *Imágenes e imagineros: Representaciones de los indígenas Ecuatorianos, Siglos XIX y XX*, ed. B. Muratorio. Quito: FLACSO, 197–252.

Gupta, A., and J. Ferguson. 1997. *Culture. Power. Place. Explorations in critical anthropology*. Durham and London: Duke University Press.

———. 1997. "Discipline and practice: The field as site, method, and location in anthropology." In *Anthropological locations: Boundaries and grounds for a field science*, ed. A. Gupta and J. Ferguson. Berkeley: University of California Press.

Gupta, D. 1996. *The context of ethnicity: Sikh identity in a comparative perspective*. Delhi: Oxford University Press.

Gutmann, M. C. 1996. *The meanings of macho. Being a man in Mexico City*. Berkeley: University of California Press.

Habermas, J. 1984. *The theory of communicative action (in two volumes)*. Volume one: *Reason and rationalization in society;* Volume 2: *Lifeworld and system—A critique of functionalist reason*. Boston: Beacon Press.

Hacking, I. 1990. *The taming of chance*. Cambridge: Cambridge University Press.

Hale, C. 1997. Consciousness, violence, and the politics of memory in Guatemala. *Current Anthropology* 38 (5): 817–838.

Hall, S. 1994. Cultural studies: two paradigms. In *Culture/Power/History*, ed. N. Dirks, G. Eley, and S. Ortner. Princeton: Princeton University Press, 520–538.

———. 1996. *Transnational connections: Culture, people, places*. London and New York: Routledge.

———. 1996. Gramsci's relevance for the study of race and ethnicity. In *Stuart Hall: Critical Dialogues in Cultural Studies*, ed. D. Morley and K. H. Chen. London: Routledge, 411–440.

Hannerz, U. 1996. *Transnational connections: Culture, people, places*. London: Routledge.

Hansen, E. 1977. *Rural Catalonia under the Franco regime*. London: Cambridge University Press.

Harding, S. 1984. *Remaking Ibieca. Rural life in Aragon under Franco.* Chapel Hill: University of North Carolina Press.

Harries-Jones, P. 1997. Canadian anthropology in an international context. *Canadian Review of Sociology and Anthropology* 34(3): 249–267.

Harris, M. 1964. *Patterns of race in the Americas.* New York: Norton.

Harvey, D. 1982. *The limits to capital.* Chicago: University of Chicago Press.

———. 1989. *The condition of postmodernity.* Oxford: Basil Blackwell.

———. 1995. Militant particularism and global ambition: The conceptual politics of place, space, and environment in the work of Raymond Williams. *Social Text* 42: 69–98.

Hayter, T., and D. Harvey, eds. 1993. *The factory and the city: The story of the Cowley automobile workers in Oxford.* Brighton: Mansell.

HEFCE (Higher Education Funding Council for England). 1995. QO 13/95 Subject Overview Report—Anthropology. Bristol: Higher Education Funding Council for England.

———. 1996. QO 8/96 Subject Overview Report—Sociology. Bristol: Higher Education Funding Council for England.

Heron, C., and R. Storey. 1986. Work and struggle in the Canadian steel industry, 1900–1950. In: *On the job: Confronting the labour process in Canada,* ed. C. Heron and R. Storey. Montreal and Kingston: McGill-Queen's University Press, 210–244.

Hirst, P., and J. Zeitlin, eds. 1989. *Reversing industrial decline? Industrial structure and policy in Britain and her competitors.* Oxford: Berg.

Hobsbawm, E. 1971. Class consciousness in history. In *Aspects of history and class consciousness,* ed. I. Mezaros. London: Routledge and Kegan Paul.

———. 1973. Peasants and politics. *Journal of Peasant Studies* 1, no. 1.

———. 1984. *Worlds of labour.* London: Wiedenfeld and Nicolson.

Hobsbawm, E., and T. Ranger, eds. 1983. *The invention of tradition.* Cambridge: Cambridge University Press.

Howes, D. 1992. What is good for anthropology in Canada? In *Fragile truths: Twenty-five years of sociology and anthropology in Canada,* ed. W. K. Carroll et al. Ottawa: Carleton University Press, 155–169.

INEGI. 1992. *Yucatán: perfil sociodemográfico. XI Censo general de población y vivienda, 1990.* México: INEGI.

INEGI. 1996. Yucatán. Tomo 1 y Tomo 2. *Conteo de Población y Vivienda 1995. Resultados definitivos. Tabulados básicos.* México: INEGI.

INEGI. 1999. *Industría maquiladora y de exportación. Mayo 1999.* Yucatán, México.

Innis, H. A. (1956) 1995. *Staples, markets and cultural change: Selected essays.* Ed. D. Drache. Montreal: McGill-Queen's University Press.

International Confederation of Free Trade Unions, n.d. *Behind the wire: Anti-union repression in the export processing zones* (consulted on August 24th, 1998). http://www.icftu.org/

Iturra, R. 1988. *Antropología económica de la Galicia rural.* Santiago de Compostela: Xunta de Galicia.

Jackson Lears, T. J. 1985. The concept of cultural hegemony: Problems and possibilities. *American Historical Review* 90, no. 3.

Jameson, F. 1991. *Postmodernism, or, the cultural logic of late capitalism.* Durham: Duke University Press.

Kahn, J., and J. Llobera, eds. 1981. *The anthropology of pre-capitalist societies.* Atlantic Highlands, N.J.: Humanities Press.

Kasmir, S. 1996. *The myth of Mondragón. Cooperatives, politics, and working-class life in a Basque town.* Albany: State University of New York Press.

Kearney, M. 1996. *Reconceptualizing the peasantry: Anthropology in global perspective.* Boulder: Westview Press.

Kennedy, J. C. 1997. At the crossroads: Newfoundland and Labrador communities in a changing international context. *Canadian Review of Sociology and Anthropology* 34(3): 297–318.

Kertzer, D. 1997. *Politics and Symbols: The Italian Communist Party and the Fall of Communism.* New Haven: Yale University Press.

Kluckhohn, C. 1962. *Culture and behavior.* New York: The Free Press.

Knauft, B. M. 1994. Pushing anthropology past the posts: Critical notes on cultural anthropology and cultural studies as influenced by postmodernism and existentialism. *Critique of Anthropology* 14(2): 117–152.

Krahn, H., and G. Lowe. 1998. *Work, industry, and Canadian society.* Toronto: Nelson.

Kuitenbrouwer, P. 1997. Days of factions. *Canadian Forum* 87(856): 14–18.

Kumar, K. 1988. From work to employment and unemployment: The English experience. In *On Work,* ed. R. E. Pahl. Oxford: Blackwell, 138–164.

Kurtz, D. V. 1996. Hegemony and anthropology: Gramsci, exegeses and reinterpretations. *Critique of Anthropology* 16(2): 103–135.

Kymlicka, W. 1995. *Multicultural citizenship: A liberal theory of minority rights.* Oxford: Clarendon Press.

Labrecque, M. F. 1998. Women and gendered production in rural Yucatan: Some local features of globalization. *Urban Anthropology and Studies of Cultural Systems and*

World Economic Development, Special Issue : Local Expressions of Global Culture, 27, no. 2.

Laclau, E. 1985. The new social movements and the plurality of the social. In *New social movements and the state in Latin America,* ed. D. Slater. Amsterdam: CEDLA.

Laclau, E., and C. Mouffe. 1985. *Hegemony and socialist strategy: Towards a radical democratic politics.* London: Verso

Lambek, M. 1996. The past imperfect: Remembering as moral practice. In *Tense past: Cultural essays on trauma and memory,* ed. P. Antze and M. Lambek. New York and London: Routledge, 235–254.

Lamont, M. 1987. How to become a dominant French philosopher: The case of Jacques Derrida. *American Journal of Sociology* 93(3): 584–622.

Lamphere, L., H. Ragoné, and P. Zavella, eds. 1997. *Situated lives: Gender and culture in everyday life.* New York: Routledge.

Lamphere, L. 1997. Work and the production of silence. In *Between history and histories: The making of silences and commemorations,* ed. G. Sider and G. Smith. Toronto: The University of Toronto Press.

Lancaster, R., and M. di Leonardo, eds. 1997. *The gender sexuality reader: Culture, history, political economy.* New York: Routledge.

Lash, S., and J. Urry. 1987. *The end of organized capitalism.* London: Polity Press.

Laurie, B. 1989. *Artisans into workers: labor in nineteenth-century America.* New York: Noonday Press.

Leach, B. 1997. The New Right and the politics of work and family in Hamilton. *Atlantis* 21(2): 35–46.

———. 1998. Citizenship and the politics of exclusion in a "post"-Fordist industriality. *Critique of Anthropology* 18(2): 181–204.

Leake, A. 1970. When the warfare ended. *Sent* (February): 11–14.

Lebovics, H. 1992. *True France: Wars over cultural identity, 1900–1945.* Ithaca: Cornell University Press.

LeClair, E. E., and H. K. Schneider. 1968. *Economic anthropology: Readings in theory and analysis.* New York: Holt, Rinehart, and Winston.

Lem, W. 1999. *Cultivating dissent: work and politics in Languedoc.* Albany: State University of New York Press.

Levine, S. K. 1979. Marxist anthropology and the critique of everyday life. In *Toward a Marxist anthropology,* ed. S. Diamond. The Hague: Mouton.

Lipset, S. M. 1990. *Continental divide: The values and institutions of the United States and Canada.* New York: Routledge.

Livingstone, D., and M. Luxton. 1996. Gender consciousness at work: Rethinking the breadwinner norm. In *Recast dreams: Class and gender consciousness in Steeltown,* ed. D. Livingstone and J. M. Mangan. Toronto: Garamond Press.

Livingstone, D., and M. Mangan. 1996. Introduction: The changing context of class and gender relations in contemporary Canada. In *Recast dreams: Class and gender consciousness in Steeltown,* ed. D. Livingstone and J. M. Mangan. Toronto: Garamond Press.

Locke, R. 1996. *Remaking the Italian economy.* Ithaca: Cornell University Press.

Lomnitz, L. 1994. *Redes sociales, cultura y poder. Ensayos de antropología latinoamericana.* México: Miguel Angel Porrúa/FLACSO.

Lortie, L. 1999. *La mondialisation de la production et le travail des femmes: l'intégration des paysannes à l'industrie du vêtement de la municipalité de Motul, Yucatan, Mexique.* Québec: Université Laval. M.A. thesis.

Lüdtke, A. 1986. Cash, coffee-breaks, horseplay: Eigensinn and politics among factory workers in Germany circa 1900. In *Confrontation, class consciousness, and the labour process. Studies in proletarian class formation,* ed. M. Hanagan, and C. Stephenson. New York: Greenwood Press.

———. 1995. What happened to the "Fiery Red Glow"? Workers' experiences and German Fascism. In *The history of everyday life: Reconstructing historical experiences and ways of Life,* ed. A. Lüdtke. Princeton: Princeton University Press.

Luhmann, N. 1990. *Essays in self reference.* New York: Columbia University Press.

Mackintosh, M. 1984. Gender and economics : The sexual division of labour and the subordination of women. In *Of marriage and the market: Women's subordination internationally and its lessons,* ed. K. Young, C. Wolkowitz, and R. McCullagh. London: Routledge and Kegan Paul.

Magraw, R. 1992. *A history of the French working class.* Oxford; Cambridge, MA.: Blackwell.

Manners, R. 1960. Methods of community analysis in the Caribbean. In *Caribbean Studies: A Symposium,* ed. V. Rubin. Seattle: University of Washington Press, 80–92.

Maranda, P. 1983. International posture and tradition of Canadian ethnology. In *Consciousness and inquiry: Ethnology and Canadian realities,* ed. F. Manning. Ottawa: National Museums of Canada, Canadian Ethnology Service Paper No. 89E, 114–129.

Marcus, G. E. 1986. Contemporary problems of ethnography in the modern world system. In *Writing Culture,* ed. J. C. Clifford and G. E. Marcus. Berkeley and Los Angeles: University of California Press, 165–93.

———. 1995. Ethnography in/of the world system: the emergence of multi-sited ethnography. *Annual Review of Anthropology* 24: 95–117.

Marcus, G. E., and M. M. J. Fischer. 1986. *Anthropology as cultural critique.* Chicago: University of Chicago Press.

Marroquín, A. 1957. *La ciudad mercado*. Mexico City: Universidad Nacional Autónoma de México.

Marshall, T. H. 1963. *Sociology at the crossroads and other essays*. London: Heinemann.

Martin, M.1997. *Communication and mass media: Culture, domination, and opposition*. Scarborough: Prentice-Hall.

Martínez-Alier, J. 1968. *La estabilidad del latifundismo*. Vesoul: Ediciones Ruedo Ibérico.

———. 1971. *Labourers and landowners in Southern Spain*. London: George Allen and Unwin.

Martínez, U. 1997. *La integracíon social de los immigrantes extranjeros en España*. Madrid: Editorial Trotta.

Marx, K. 1969. *Selected works in three volumes*, Vol. 1. Moscow: Progress Publishers.

Marx, K., and F. Engels. *Archives of Marx and Engels, Vol I*. Quoted in Ulyanovsky, R., and V. Pavlov. *Asian Dilemma*. Moscow: Progress.

Meillassoux, C. 1981. *Maidens, meal, and money*. Cambridge and New York: Cambridge University Press.

Melucci, A. 1996. *Challenging codes: Collective action in the information age*. Cambridge and New York: Cambridge University Press.

Mendoza, M., and M. E. Maldonado. 1995. Poblamiento y colonización criolla del noroeste del Territorio Nacional de Formosa entre los años 1875 y 1925. M.S.

Migration News. 1997. 4 (11), http://migration.ucdavis.edu.

Mingione, E. 1991. *Fragmented societies: A sociology of economic life beyond the market paradigm*. Trans. P. Goodrich. Oxford: Blackwell.

Mintz, S. W. 1959. The plantation as a socio-cultural type. In *Plantation systems of the New World*, ed. A. Palerm and V. Rubin. Washington: Pan American Union, 42–49.

———. 1974. *Caribbean transformations*. Chicago: Aldine.

Mintz, S. W., and E. R. Wolf. 1950. An analysis of ritual coparenthood (compadrazgo). *Southwestern Journal of Anthropology* 6: 341–368.

Mitchell, K. 1993. Multiculturalism, or the United Colors of Capitalism? *Antipode* 25, no, 4: 263–294.

Molina Enríquez, A. [1906]1981. *Los grandes problemas nacionales*. Mexico City: Editorial Era.

Moodley, K. 1983. Canadian multiculturalism as ideology. *Ethnic and Racial Studies* 6(3): 320–331.

Moreno, I. 1971. *La antropología en andalucía*. Desarrollo histórico y estado actual de las investigaciones en Ethnica, no.1.

———. 1975. La investigación antropológica en España. In *Primera reunión de antropólogos españoles,* ed. Jimenez. Sevilla: Universidad de Sevilla.

———. 1984. La doble colonització de l'antropologia andalusa i perspectives de futur. *Quaderns de l'ICA* 5.

Moreno, P. 1994. Cerraduras de sombra: Racismo, heterofobia y nacionalismo. En Contreras, J. (De.) *Los retos de la inmigración.* Madrid: Talasa.

———. 1998. La contaminación moderna: Pureza de sangre y exterminio. *Archipiélago* no. 33.

Munro, M. 1997. Ontario's "Days of Action" and strategic choices for the Left in Canada. *Studies in Political Economy* 53: 125–140.

Nader, L. 1997. The phantom factor: impact of the Cold War on anthropology. In N. Chomsky et al., *The Cold War and the university: Toward an intellectual history of the postwar years.* New York: New Press, 107–146.

Narotzky, S. 1988. *Trabajar en familia. Familias, mujeres, hogares y talleres.* Valencia: Eds. Alfons el Magnanim.

———. 1990. Not to be a burden: Ideologies of the domestic group and women's work in rural Catalonia. In *Work without wages: Comparative studies of domestic labour and self-employment,* ed. J. L. Collins, and M. Giménez. Albany: State University of New York Press.

Nash, J. 1989. *From tank town to high tech: The clash of community and corporate cycles.* New York: Columbia University Press.

———. 1994. Global integration and subsistence insecurity. *American Anthropologist* 96(1): 7–30.

———. 1997. When isms become wasms: Structural functionalism, Marxism, feminism, and postmodernism. *Critique of Anthropology* 17, no. 1: 11–32.

Noiriel, G. 1990. *Workers in French society in the 19th and 20th centuries.* Trans. from the French by H. McPhail. New York: Berg.

Ong, A. 1991. The gender and politics of postmodernity. *Annual Review of Anthropology* 20: 279–309.

Ortner, S. 1995. Resistance and the problem of ethnographic refusal. *Comparative Studies in Society and History* 37: 173–193.

———. 1998. Distinguished Lecture. Annual Meeting of the American Ethnological Society, with the Canadian Anthropological Society/Society Canadienne d'Anthropologie, Toronto, Ontario, Canada.

Paci, M. 1996. *Welfare state.* Roma: Ediesse.

Palerm, A. 1980. *Antropología y marxismo.* Mexico City: CIS-INAH/Nueva Imagen.

Palmer, B. D. 1992. *Working class experience: Rethinking the history of Canadian labour, 1800–1991*. Toronto: McClelland and Stewart.

———. 1994. *Capitalism comes to the backcountry: The Goodyear invasion of Napanee*. Toronto: Between the Lines.

———. 1996. Showdown in Ontario: Build the general strike. *Canadian Dimension* 30(3): 21–25.

Panitch, L. 1981. Dependency and class in Canadian political economy. *Studies in Political Economy* 6: 7–33.

Parekh, B. 1995. Cultural diversity and liberal democracy. In *Defining and measuring democracy*, ed. D. Beetham. London: Sage.

Passerini, L. 1992. Lacerations in the memory: Women in the Italian underground organizations. *International Social Movement Research* 4: 161–212.

Pastor, R. 1973a. La lana en Castilla y León antes de la organización de la Mesta. In *Conflictos sociales y estancamiento económico en la España medieval*. Barcelona: Ariel.

———. 1973b. En los comienzos de una economía deformada: Castilla. In *Conflictos sociales y estancamiento económico en la España medieval*. Barcelona: Ariel.

Patten, S. 1996. Preston Manning's populism: Constructing the common sense of the common people. *Studies in Political Economy* 50: 95–132.

Payne, S. 1962. *Falange: A history of Spanish fascism*. Stanford: Stanford University Press.

Piccone Stella, S. 1997. I giovani in gamiglia. In *Lo stato delle famiglie in Italia*, ed. M. Barbagli and C. Saraceno. Bologna: Il Mulino, 151–162.

Pike, F., G. Becattinee, and W. Sengenberger, eds. 1992. *Industrial districts and inter-firm cooperation in Italy*. Geneva: International Institute for Labor Studies.

Piore, M., and C. Sabel. 1984. *The second industrial divide*. New York: Basic Books.

Pi-Sunyer, O. 1985. Elites and noncorporate groups in the European Mediterranean: A reconsideration of the Catalan Case. *Comparative Studies in Society and History* 16.

Pitt-Rivers, J. A. 1971 [1954]. *The people of the Sierra*. Chicago: The University of Chicago Press.

Pizzorno, A. 1974. I ceti medi nel meccanismo del consenso. In *Il caso italiano*, ed. A. Cavazza and F. Graubard. Milano: Garzanti.

Plancarte, F. 1954. *El problema Indígena Tarahumara*. México: Instituto Nacional Indigenista.

Pollert, A. 1988. Dismantling flexibility. *Capital and Class* no. 34:42–75.

Portelli, A. 1989. Historia y memoria. La muerte de Luigi Trastulli. *Historia y Fuente Oral* 1.

———. 1991. *The death of Luigi Trastulli and other stories*. Albany: State University of New York Press.

Prat, J. 1991. Teoría. Metodología. Estudio introductorio. In *Antropología de los Pueblos de España,* ed. J. Prat, U. Martínez, J. Contreras, and I. Moreno. Madrid: Taurus.

Pred, A., and M. Watts. 1992. *Reworking modernity: Capitalisms and symbolic discontent.* New Brunswick: Rutgers University Press.

Preston, R. J., and M. Adelard-Tremblay. 1988. Anthropology. In *The Canadian Encyclopedia.* Edmonton: Hurtig, 80–83.

Price, D. H. 1998. Cold war anthropology: Collaborators and victims of the national security state. *Identities* 4(3–4): 1–42.

Quiñones, S. 1998. The maquila murders. *Ms.* May/June 1998, 10–16.

Raafat Feraidoon, F., M. M. Saghafi, R. J. Schlesinger, and K. Kiyota. 1992. Training and technology transfer: Efforts of Japanese, Mexican, and American Maquiladora companies in Mexico. *Socio-economic Planning Sciences* 26 (3).

Rabinow, P. 1996. *Essays on the anthropology of reason.* Princeton: Princeton University Press.

Rebick, J. 1996. The times they are achangin'. *Canadian Forum* 75(855): 26.

Reddy, W. 1984. *The rise of market culture: the textile trade and French society, 1750–1900.* Cambridge: Cambridge University Press.

Reitz, J., and R. Breton. 1994. *The illusion of difference: Realities of ethnicity in Canada and the United States.* Toronto: C.D. Howe Institute.

Reyneri, E. 1996. *Sociologia del mercao del lavoro.* Bologna: Il Mulino.

Riquelme Solar, J. 1978. *Historia de Abanilla.* Alicante: Editorial Villa.

Ritchie, A., and B. Bain. 1997. Metro Days of Action in Toronto: Where do we go next? *Kinesis* (Dec.–Jan.), 13,16.

Rivera Rocamora, P.-A. 1992. *Escritos y recuerdos de Pedro Rivera Gaona 1919–1982.*Unpublished manuscript.

Rodas, F. 1991. *El pueblo de Ingeniero Juárez (Formosa): Sus antecedentes, su historia y la de sus instituciones y pioneros.* Córdoba: ABC Publishing.

Roediger, D. R. 1991. *The wages of whiteness: Race and the making of the American working class.* London and New York: Verso.

Romaní, O. 1996. Che ci faccio qui? Studio degli usi della droga nella Spagna contemporanea: biografia, etnografia e storia. In *I fogli di Oriss* 6.

Roseberry, W. 1988. Political Economy. *Annual Review of Anthropology* 17.

———. 1994. Hegemony and the language of contention. In *Everyday forms of state formation: Revolution and the negotiation of modern rule in modern Mexico,* ed. G. M. Joseph, and D. Nugent. New Brunswick: Rutgers University Press.

———. 1995. Latin American peasant studies in a postcolonial era. *Journal of Latin American Anthropology* 1(1).

———. 1996. The unbearable lightness of anthropology. *Radical History Review* 65: 5–25.

———. 1997. Marx and anthropology. *Annual Review of Anthropology* 26: 25–46.

Rossi, S. 1998. *La Politica economica italiana, 1968–1998.* Bari: Laterza.

Ruiz Martín, F., and A. García Sanz, eds. 1998. *Mesta, trashumancia y lana en la España moderna.* Barcelona: Crítica.

Sabel, C. F. 1989. Flexible specialization and the re-mergence of regional economies. In *Reversing industrial decline? Industrial structure and policy in Britain and her competitors,* ed. P. Hirst and J. Zeitlin. Oxford: Berg.

Sabel, C. F., and J. Zeitlin. 1985. Historical alternatives to mass production: Politics, markets, and technology in nineteenth century industrialization. *Past and Present* no. 108.

Sacks, K. B. 1994. How did Jews become white folks. In *Race,* ed. S. Gregory and R. Sanjek. New Brunswick: Rutgers University Press.

Sáenz, M. 1936. *Carapan. Bosquejo de una experiencia.* Lima: Librería e imprenta Gil.

———. [1939] 1976. *México íntegro,* Mexico City: Secretaría de Educación Pública.

Safa, H. I. 1995. *The myth of the male breadwinner. Women and industrialization in the Caribbean.* Boulder: Westview Press.

Said, E. 1978. *Orientalism.* New York: Pantheon.

———. 1994. *Culture and imperialism.* New York: Knopf.

Sassen, S. 1998. *Globalization and its discontents.* New York: New Press.

Sassoon, A. 1982. *Approaches to Gramsci.* London: Writers and Readers Publishing Cooperative Society.

Sayer, D. 1987. *The violence of abstraction: The analytic foundations of historical materialism.* Oxford: Blackwell.

———. 1991. *Capitalism and modernity: an excursus on Marx and Weber.* London: Routledge.

———. 1994. Everyday forms of state formation: Some dissident remarks on hegemony. In *Everyday forms of state formation: Revolution and the negotiation of rule in modern Mexico,* ed. G. Joseph and D. Nugent. Durham: Duke University Press.

Scheper-Hughes, N. 1995. The primacy of the ethical: Propositions for a militant anthropology. *Current Anthropology* 36(3): 409–20.

Schneider, J. 1997. Exotic England: Benefactors as anthropological subjects. *American Anthropologist* 99 (4):713–730.

Schutz, A. 1978. Phenomenology and the social sciences. In *Phenomenology and sociology: Selected readings,* ed. T. Luckmann. Harmondsworth: Penguin.

Scott, J. 1985. *Weapons of the weak: Everyday forms of peasant resistance.* New Haven: Yale University Press.

Scott, C. V. 1995. *Gender and development. Rethinking modernization and dependency theory.* Boulder and London: Lynne Rienner.

SEDEINCO (Secretaría de Desarrollo Industrial y Comercio). 2000. *Datos sobre la maquiladora en el Estado de Yucatán.* Julio 2000. Manuscript.

Segalen, M. 1991. *Fifteen generations of Bretons: Kinship and society in lower Brittany, 1720–1980.* Cambridge: Cambridge University Press.

Sider, G. M. 1996. Cleansing history: Lawrence, Massachusetts, the strike for four loaves of bread and no roses, and the anthropology of working class consciousness. *Radical History Review* 65: 48–83.

———. 1997. The making of peculiar local cultures: Producing and surviving history. In *Peasant and tribal societies, Was Bleibt von marxistischen Perspektiven in der Geschichtsforschung?* ed. A. Lüdtke. Göttingen: Vandehoeck and Ruprecht.

Sider, G., and G. Smith, eds. 1997. *Between history and histories: The making of silences and commemorations.* Toronto: The University of Toronto Press.

Skeggs, B. 1997. *Formations of class and gender.* London: Sage.

Smart, B. 1993. *Postmodernity.* London: Routledge.

Smith, D. 1990. *The conceptual practices of power: A feminist sociology of knowledge.* Toronto: University of Toronto Press.

Smith, G. 1990. Negotiating neighbors: Livelihood and domestic politics in central Peru and the Pais Valenciano (Spain). In *Work without wages: Comparative studies of domestic labour and self-employment,* ed. J. Collins and M. Gimenez. Albany: State University of New York Press.

———. 1991. The production of culture in local rebellion. In *Golden ages, dark ages: Imagining the past in anthropology and history,* ed. J. O'Brien and W. Roseberry. Berkeley: University of California Press.

———. 1994. Social anthropology and history: Reflections on some recent forays. M.S.

———. 1999. *Confronting the present: Towards a politically engaged anthropology.* Oxford: Berg.

Soja, E. W. 1989. *Postmodern geographies: The reassertion of space in critical social theory.* London and New York: Verso.

Somers, M. 1994. The narrative construction of identity: A relational and network approach. *Theory and Society* 23.

Spivak, G. C. 1988. Can the subaltern speak? In *Marxism and the interpretation of cultures*, ed. C. Nelson and L. Grossberg. Urbana: University of Illinois Press, 271–316.

Stasiulus, D., and R. Jhappan. 1995. The fractious politics of a settler society: Canada. In *Unsettling settler societies: Articulations of gender, race, ethnicity, and class*. Thousand Oaks: Sage, 95–131.

Steans, J. 1998. *Gender and international relations. An introduction*. New Brunswick: Rutgers University Press.

Steinberg, S. 1989. *The ethnic myth: Race, ethnicity, and class in America*. Boston: Beacon Press.

Steward, J. 1955. *Theory of culture change*. Urbana: University of Illinois Press.

Steward, Julian, et al. 1956. *The people of Puerto Rico*. Urbana: University of Illinois Press.

Stolcke, V. 1993a. Madres para la nueva patria. *En pie de paz*, no. 28.

———. 1993b. El 'problema' de la inmigración en Europa: El fundamentalismo cultural como nueva retórica de exclusión. *Mientras Tanto*, no. 55.

———. 1995. Talking culture: new boundaries, new rhetorics of exclusion in Europe. *Current Anthropology* 36, no. 1.

Striffler, S. 1999. Wedded to work: Class struggles and gendered identities in the restructuring of the Ecuadorian banana industry. *Identities: Global Studies in Culture and Power* 6(1): 99–120.

Swedenburg, T. 1991. Popular memory and the Palestinian national past. In *Golden ages, dark ages: Imagining the past in anthropology and history*, ed. J. O'Brien and W. Roseberry. Berkeley: The University of California Press, 152–179.

Swift, J. 1995. *Wheel of fortune: Work and life in the age of falling expectations*. Toronto: Between the Lines Press.

Swindells, J., and L. Jardine. 1990. *What's left: Women in culture and the labour movement*. London: Routledge.

Tamir, Y. 1993. *Liberal nationalism*, Princeton: Princeton University Press.

Terradas, I. 1984a. Àngel Palerm: darrera el mètode. In *Història i Antropologia a la Memoria d'Àngel Palerm*, ed. N. Escandell and I. Terradas. Barcelona: Pub. Abadia de Montserrat.

———. 1984b. *El món històric de les masies*, Barcelona: Curial.

———. 1992. *Eliza Kendall. Reflexiones sobre una antibiografía*. Barcelona: Universidad Autónoma de Barcelona.

———. 1995 [1979]. *La qüestió de les colònies industrials. L'exemple de L'AMETLLA de Merola*. Manresa: Centre d'Estudis del Bage.

Terray, E. 1971. *Marxism and "primitive" societies*. New York: Monthly Review Press.

Thompson, E. P. 1966. *The making of the English working class.* New York: Vintage.

———. ed. 1970. *Warwick University Ltd: Industry, management, and the universities.* Harmondsworth: Penguin Books.

———. 1978. Eighteenth-century English society: Class struggle without class? *Social History* 3, no. 2: 133–165.

———. 1993. *Customs in common: Studies in traditional popular culture.* New York: New Press.

Tillion, C. 1971. *On Chantait Rouge.* Paris: Editions Robert Laffont.

Torres, M. I. 1975. *Ingeniero Guillermo Nicasio Juárez y los parajes del Oeste de Formosa.* Buenos Aires: Ediciones Tiempo de Hoy.

Touraine, A.1992. *Une critique de la modernite.* Paris: Fayard.

Trouillot, M.-R. 1995. *Silencing the past: Power and the production of history.* Boston: Beacon Press.

———. 1997. Silencing the past: Layers of meaning in the Haitian Revolution. In *Between history and histories: The making of silence and commemorations,* ed. G. Sider and G. Smith. New York: International Publishers.

Turner, V. 1974. *Dramas, fields, and metaphors: Symbolic action in human society.* Ithaca: Cornell University Press.

Valverde, M. 1991. *The age of light, soap, and water: Moral reform in English Canada, 1885–1925.* Toronto: McLelland and Stewart.

Vasconcelos, J. [1925] 1960. *La raza cósmica. Misión de la raza iberoamericana.* Argentina y Brasil, Mexico City: Espasa-Calpe Mexicana.

Villa Rojas, A. 1955. *Los mazatecos y el problema Indígena de la cuenca del Papaloapan.* Mexico City: Instituto Nacional Indigenista.

Vincent, J. 1985. Anthropology and Marxism: Past and present. *American Ethnologist* 12: 137–147.

———. 1990. *Anthropology and politics: Visions, traditions, and trends.* Tucson: University of Arizona Press.

VV.AA. 1994. *Memorias del Gran Chaco Vol. 5b: Pero, todavía existimos (Wichís).* Reconquista: INCUPO-Ecuentro Interconfesional de Misioneros.

Wade, R. 1990. *Governing the market: Economic theory and the role of government in East Asian industrialization.* Princeton: Princeton University Press.

Walzer, M. 1983. *Spheres of Justice: Defense of Pluralism and Equality.* Oxford: Blackwell.

Ward, W. P. 1978. *White Canada forever: Popular attitudes and public policy towards Orientals in British Columbia.* Montreal: McGill-Queen's University Press.

Warman, A. 1972. *Los Campesinos: hijos predilictos des regimen*. Mexico: Editorial Nuestro Tiempo.

———. 1976. *. . . .y venimos a contradecir. Los campesinos de Morelos y el Estado*. Mexico City: Ediciones de la Casa Chata. (English version: *We come to object*. Baltimore: Johns Hopkins University Press, 1980).

Warman, A., et al. 1970. *De eso que llaman antropología mexicana*. México: Nuestro Tiempo.

Warren, K. 2000. Mayan multiculturalism and the violence of memories. In *Violence and Subjectivity*, ed. V. Dal et al. Berkeley: The University of California Press, 296–314.

Weber, E. 1976. *Peasants into Frenchmen: The modernization of rural France 1870–1914*. Stanford: Stanford University Press.

Wernick, A. 1993. American popular culture in Canada: Trends and reflections. In *The beaver bites back?: American popular culture in Canada*, ed. D. H. Flaherty and F. E. Manning. Montreal: McGill-Queen's University Press.

Wessman, J. 1981. *Anthropology and Marxism*. Cambridge: Shenkman.

Williams, R. 1973. *The country and the city*. London: Hogarth.

———. 1977. *Marxism and literature*. Oxford: Oxford University Press.

———. 1983. *Keywords*. London: Fontana Press.

———. 1988. *Keywords: a vocabulary of culture and society*. Revised edition. London: Fontana.

———. 1989. *What I came to say*. London: Hutchinson Radius.

———. 1989. *Resources of hope*. London: Verso.

———. 1991. Base and superstructure in Marxist cultural theory. In *Rethinking popular culture: Contemporary perspectives in cultural studies*, ed. C. Mukerji and M. Schudson. Berkeley: University of California Press, 407–423.

Winant, H. 1994. Racial formation and hegemony: Global and local developments. In *Racism, modernity, identity: On the Western front*, ed. A. Rattansi and S. Westwood. London: Polity, 266–289.

Wolf, E. R. 1955. Types of Latin American peasantry: a preliminary discussion. *American Anthropologist* 57: 452–471.

———. 1956. Aspects of group relations in a complex society: Mexico. *American Anthropologist* 58: 1065–1078.

———. 1957. Closed corporate communities in Mesoamerica and central Java. *Southwestern Journal of Anthropology* 13: 1–18.

———. 1959. Specific aspects of plantation systems in the New World: community subcultures and social class. In *Plantation Systems of the New World*, ed. A. Palerm and V. Rubin. Washington: Pan American Union, 136–147.

———. 1969. *Peasant wars of the twentieth century.* New York: Harper & Row.

———. 1982. *Europe and the people without history.* Berkeley : University of California Press.

Wolf, E. R., and J. Jorgensen. 1970. Anthropologists on the warpath. *New York Review of Books* 15(9): 26–36.

Wolf, E. R., and S. W. Mintz. 1957. Haciendas and plantations in Middle America and the Antilles. *Social and Economic Studies* 6: 380–412.

Yuval Davis, N. 1997. *Gender and nation.* London: Sage.

Zdatny, S. M. 1990. *The politics of survival: Artisans of 20th century France.* New York: Oxford University Press.

Ziedenberg, J. 1996a. The counter revolution: Is Mike Harris helping regenerate the Ontario Left? *Canadian Dimension* 30(2): 6–8.

———. 1996b. Labour's dirty secret. *This Magazine* (Nov./Dec.) 17–21.

———. 1997. The Metro Toronto Days of Action: The Hogtown shutdown. *Canadian Dimension* 31(1) (Jan.–Feb.) 8–11.

Žižek, S. 1997. Multiculturalism, or, the cultural logic of multinational capitalism. *New Left Review* 225: 28–51.

Contributors

Pauline Gardiner Barber is associate professor of social anthropology at Dalhousie University. She is currently preparing a manuscript on the discursive and social class implications of Philippine gendered labor migration, transnationalism, and diaspora. Her latest Cape Breton research focuses upon local struggles over global priorities and the reworked economic subjectivities these give rise to.

Michael Blim teaches at the Graduate Center of the City University of New York. He has authored *Made in Italy: Small-Scale Industrialization and Its Consequences* (1990), co-edited (with Frances Rothstein) *Anthropology and the Global Factory* (1992), and has written numerous articles for *Critique of Anthropology*.

Kim Clark is associate professor of anthropology at the University of Western Ontario. She has published articles in the *Journal of Latin American Studies*, the *Journal of Historical Sociology, Anthropologica*, and various Ecuadorean journals. Her book *The Redemptive Work: Railway and Nation in Ecuador* (1998) won a Choice Outstanding Academic Book Award.

Guillermo de la Pena received his Ph.D. from the University of Manchester in 1977. He is Research Professor at Centro de Investigaciones y Estudios Superiores en Antropologia Social (CIESAS). He has written *A Legacy of Promises. Agriculture, Politics and Ritual in the Morelos Highlands of Mexico* (1981) and co-edited *Crisis, Conflicto y Sobrevivencia. Estudios sobre la Sociedad* (1990). He has also published articles in a number of books and in *Estudios Sociologicos* and *The Cambridge History of Latin America* series.

Thomas Dunk teaches anthropology and sociology at Lakehead University. He is the author of *It's a Working Man's Town: Male Working-Class Culture in Northwestern Ontario* (1991) and several articles on class, masculinity, and whiteness. His current research examines the politics and culture of hunting in the constitution of contemporary white identity.

John Gledhill is Max Gluckman Professor of Social Anthropology at the University of Manchester and co-managing editor of *Critique of Anthropology*. He has carried out research on indigenous and non-indigenous communities in Mexico, with a focus on social movements, politics, political economy, and transnational migration. He is the author of *Casi Nada: Agrarian Reform in the Homeland of Cardenismo* (Texas), also published in Spanish by El Colegio de Michoacán; *Neoliberalism, Transnationalization and Rural Poverty: A Case Study of Michoacán, Mexico*, and *Power and Its Disguises: Anthropological Perspectives on Politics*, the second English edition of which appeared in 2000, along with a first Spanish Edition published by Edicions Bellaterra.

Gastón Gordillo completed his Ph.D. in anthropology at the University of Toronto in 1999. He has been a visiting fellow in the Program in Agrarian Studies at Yale University and is currently a visiting scholar in the David Rockefeller Center for Latin American Studies at Harvard University. In addition to writing a dozen refereed journal articles in Spanish, he is the co-author of *Capitalismo y grupos indÌgenas en el Chaco centro-Occidental* (1992, Buenos Aires-CEAL) and *El río y la frontera: aborígenes, obras públicas y Mercosur en el Pilcomayo* (forthcoming, Buenos Aires-Eudeba).

Dipankar Gupta teaches at Jawaharlal Nehru University in New Delhi. His publications include *Nativism in a Metropolis: The Shiv Sena in Bombay* (1982); *The Context of Ethnicity: Sikh Identity in a Comparative Perspective* (1986); *Rivalry and Brotherhood: Politics in the Life of Farmers of North India* (1997); *Political Sociology in India* (1997); *Interrogating Caste* (2000); *Mistaken Modernity: India Between Worlds* (2000); and *Culture, Space and the Nation-State: From Sentiment to Structure* (2000). He is currently working on the idea of the public and private and how these concepts are understood in the context of modernity.

Marie France Labrecque received her Ph.D. from City University of New York. She is professor of anthropology at Laval University. Her particular interest is in economic anthropology and the study of peasantry in Mexico and Colombia. Her recent work deals with the critique of the "women and development" approach in the area of international development, including income-generating projects and participatory methodologies. She is currently carrying out research dealing with the gendering of production and the expansion of the maquiladoras in the rural areas of the state of Yucatan, Mexico. She has published in *Anthropologie et Sociétés*, *Anthropologica*, *Revue canadienne d'Études du développement/Canadian Journal of Development Studies*, and *Recherches féministes*. She coordinated *L'égalité devant soi: rapports sociaux de sexe et développement international* (1994) and in 1997 published *Sortir du labyrinthe: femmes, développement et vie quotidienne en Colombie andine*. Her recent work in English includes a chapter in Parvin Ghorayshi and Claire Bélanger (eds.), *Women, Work, and Gender Relations in Developing Countries. A Global Perspective* (1996); an article in *Urban Anthropology and Studies of Cultural Systems and World Economic Development* (2000); and a chapter in Jim Freedman (ed.), *Transforming Development. Foreign Aid for a Changing World*. She has a chapter forthcoming in Ueli Hostettler and Matthew Restall (eds.) *Maya Survivalism*. She currently is the guest editor for a special issue of the journal *Anthropologie et Sociétés* on feminist political economy in anthropology (2001) as well as guest editor with Gavin Smith of a special issue of the journal *Anthropologica* on Mexico.

Belinda Leach is an associate professor in the Department of Sociology and Anthropology at the University of Guelph. Her research on livelihoods and capitalist restructuring in Ontario has been published in *Canadian Review of Sociology and Anthropology, Labour/Le Travail, Critique of Anthropology* and a number of books. She is co-author (with Tony Winson) of *Contingent Work, Disrupted Lives: Labour and Community in the New Rural Economy* (2002).

Winnie Lem has a Ph.D. in anthropology and is an associate professor in the Comparative Development Studies and Women's Studies Programmes at Trent University. She has publications in many international journals including *Ethnologie francaise, Critique of Anthropology* and *Journal of Historical Sociology*. Her most recent book, *Cultivating Dissent: Work, Identity and Praxis* (1999), is based on fieldwork in rural France. She is currently undertaking research on migration between China and France.

Charles Menzies is an assistant professor of anthropology in the department of Anthropology and Sociology at UBC. He has published on conflicts between Euro-Canadians and First Nations in the context of land claims, on issues of resource allocation, and alliances between First Nations and the green movement. In addition, he has recently completed an ethnographic field project on the impact of social and ecological crisis on fisherfolk in Le Guilvinec, France. Menzies' primary interests are contemporary First Nations' issues, the ethnology and ethnography of Western Europe, maritime anthropology, resource management, and political economy.

Susana Narotzky is Professor Titular of Anthropology at the Universitat de Barcelona, Spain. She got her Ph.D. at the New School for Social Research, N.Y. She is the author of several books and articles on anthropology, among them *New Directions in Economic Anthropology*. She has done fieldwork in rural Catalonia and southern Alicante, Spain.

William Roseberry was professor of Latin American History at New York University. He is the author of *Coffee and Capitalism in the Venezuelan Andes* (1983) and *Anthropologies and Histories* (1989) as well as numerous journal and book articles in critical historical anthropology. He had recently been working on the impacts of nineteenth century liberal reform on indigenous communities in Mexico. He died in August 2000 at the age of 50.

Gavin Smith has taught at the University of Toronto since he received his D.Phil. from the University of Sussex in 1975. He has been doing research and writing about the relationship between different kinds of livelihood and different forms of political expression both in South America and Europe. Vaguely suspicious of the ubiquity of the term 'political economy,' he prefers to call his particular approach to anthropology 'historical realism.' He has edited a book with Gerald Sider entitled *Between History and Histories: The Making of Silences and Commemorations* (1997). His other publications include *Livelihood and Resistance: Peasants and the Politics of Land in Peru* (1989) and *Confronting the Present: Towards a Politically Engaged Anthropology* (1999).

Steve Striffler teaches anthropology and Latin American Studies at the University of Arkansas. His book on the Ecuadorian banana industry is forthcoming from Duke University Press. He is currently working on a second manuscript entitled *Mucho Trabajo, Poco Dinero: Poultry Processing, Transnational Migration, and the Transformation of Class in the U.S. South*.

Claudia Vicencio is currently completing a doctoral dissertation in social anthropology at the University of Toronto. In addition to doing fieldwork in India and Spain, she has since 1989 been a union organizer, professional grievance officer, and contract negotiator for different professional unions.

Index

Abanilla, 121–35 passim
aboriginal peoples. (*See* First Nations.)
academy, the. (*See* universities.)
Africa, 100, 101, 102
agency, 44–45, 134, 201, 222, 224, 229, 231, 262
agrarian conflict, 117, 158–59
agrarian reform. (*See* land reform.)
agrarian society, 249, 127. (*See also* agriculture.)
agribusiness, 38, 40
agriculture, 40, 125. (*See also* wine production.)
  commercial, 38
  development of. (*See also* modernization, of agriculture.)
  export, 154, 155
  family, 38. (*See also* farming.)
  and markets, 155
  subsistence, 125
Ahmad, Ajaz, 64–65, 67, 72
alienation, 255–56
Althusser, Luis, 34, 69, 70
America. (*See* United States.)
American, 43, 137
  culture and society, 21, 22, 28, 98, 137
American Anthropological Association (AAA), 65, 66
anarchism, 113
Andalusia, 34, 36, 38, 40, 126
Anglo-Canadian. (*See* English Canada.)
Anglophone, 21, 24, 31
Annales School, 34, 36
anthropology, 91, 119, 167, 251–52
  American, 4, 5, 20, 27–28, 33, 51, 59–72, 75

anglophone, 33, 34, 39, 42, 43, 45
  applied, 29, 30, 85
  British, 4, 5, 79–83, 84–85
  Canadian, 4, 19–30
  and colonialism, 5, 59, 73, 79, 84, 29
  departments of, 27–28. (*See also* universities, departments of anthropology in.)
  English-Canadian, 19–32
  European, 43, 45
  left, 59–72 passim
  Mexican, 5, 47–58
  practical, 71
  social-cultural, 19–30
  Spanish, 3–4, 33–46
anti-racist activism, 191, 201
Appadurai, A., 62, 102, 251
Argentina, 8, 177–90
Asad, Talal, 5, 73, 160
Asia, 76, 77, 100, 101, 169
Authority. (*See* power.)

bananas, 107, 109, 111. (*See also* United Fruit Company.)
Bangladesh, 96
Barber, Pauline Gardner, 8, 10, 12, 13, 203, 206, 237, 239, 248
Basque Country, 34, 40
Berg, M., 260, 261, 262
bicentrism, 19–25, 30
bilingualism, 21, 22, 24
Bigouden region, 9, 235–49
Blim, Michael, 7, 13, 93, 136–49, 249n.
Boas, Franz, 49, 57, 59
Bolivia, 178, 185
Bonfil, Guillermo, 47, 55, 56

Bourdieu, Pierre, 45, 69, 72n.2, 73–74
bourgoisie, 22, 197, 226
Brenner, R., 137, 145, 147
Breton language, 235, 240, 243
Britain, 4, 39, 73–87 passim, 141, 180, 188, 211
  and colonialism, 5
  as founding nation, 19
  history of, 30, 43, 94–95, 262
  industrial revolution in, 252, 263
British
  empiricism, 28
  missionaries, 179–80, 188
Brittany, 9, 13, 235–49 passim

Cacique, caciquismo, 50, 53, 127
Canada, 4, 10, 17–30 passim, 100, 101, 199–205 passim, 211
  anthropology in. (*See* anthropology, Canadian.)
  culture and identity in, 19–25, 26
  economy of, 25, 26
  history of, 20, 21, 23, 26, 191, 197, 198
  labor movement in, 193
  regions in, 199
  social issues in, 201
Canadian Anthropological Association/*Société d'Anthropologie Canadienne* (CASCA), 2, 3, 58, 176, 190
Canadian Auto Workers (CAW), 201–2, 209
Capacho, 8, 121–35 passim
Cape Breton, 9, 203, 206–20, 239
capital, 23, 146, 209, 231
  concentration of, 13
  control of, 227
  international/foreign/global, 22, 145, 206, 213, 252
  and labor, theoretical relationship between, 38, 126, 197, 146. (*See also* class conflict.)
  mobility of, 211
  private, 77, 148
  social, 212
  symbolic, 28

capitalism, 1–15, 51–55 passim, 59, 61, 68–69, 86, 95–96
  advanced (contemporary, late), 3, 8, 10, 12, 133, 137, 147, 213, 237, 238, 252, 263
  analysis of, 3, 9–12, 37, 62
  development of, 14, 95, 97, 226
  gendered nature of, 10, 226
  global, 9, 22, 23, 26, 146, 249
  historical changes in, 4, 14, 5, 76, 77, 226. (*See also* capitalist transformations.)
  modern, 134, 136
  peripheral, 57
  societies under, 137, 146, 147
  transition to, 12
  western, 195
capitalist
  accumulation, 5, 77, 131, 236
  development, 14, 128, 134, 140
  economies, 12, 62, 95, 131–33, 137, 145–47
  economists, 136
  exploitation. (*See* exploitation.)
  interests, 78
  investments, 145–47, 198, 131
  modernization. (*See* modernization, capitalist.)
  pre- , 166
  social relations, 23
  transformations, 9, 10, 195, 221, 222, 232, 246. (*See also* capitalism, historical changes in.)
capitalists, 95, 137, 198, 205
  foreign, 27, 240
  indigenous, 27
  local, 109, 131
  merchant, 23
  petty, 9, 238
caste, 91, 92, 93, 97
Castells, M., 146, 250, 258, 262
Castro, Fidel, 114, 117
Catalan region, 34, 38, 39, 44
  identity, 36
  nationalist project, 36
Catholic church, 152, 154, 156

Central America, 169
Chaco, el, 177–79 passim, 188–90 passim
change. (*See* social change.)
Chile, 155
China, 100, 101, 173
Christianity, 92, 177, 186, 187
citizenship, 143, 166. (*See also* rights, citizenship.)
  discourses concerning, 55, 130, 194
  membership claims based on, 133, 160
  and the nation-state, 101–6, 121
  production of (citizens), 5, 51, 123, 227, 229
  pursuit of, 56
ciudad Juarez, 166, 174
civil rights, 63, 99
civil society, 55, 104, 144, 177, 223
civilization, 43, 61, 180, 183, 187
Clark, Kim, 6, 12, 13, 94, 124, 150–62, 223
class, 3, 5, 8, 13, 14, 59, 60, 69, 103, 150, 188, 192–97, 221–34, 250. (*See also* community, and class.)
  alliances, 140, 153, 228
  analysis, 24, 151, 194–95. (*See also* Marxist analysis.)
  basis for identity, 9, 38, 70, 129, 192, 203, 210, 220, 238, 242, 255
  capitalist, corporate, 145
  configurations, 3, 122, 208
  conflict, 1, 137, 173, 192, 195, 197, 224–25, 239, 248
  consciousness, 54, 119, 139–40, 192
  culture. (*See* culture, working class.)
  divisions, 7, 22, 93 127
  dominant, 23, 108, 129, 152, 160–61, 191, 223
  emancipation, 57
  formation, 7, 52–55
  and gender, 60, 193, 194, 195. (*See also* Lem, W.)
  and inequality, 60
  interests, 7, 9, 23, 213
  lower, 162
  middle, 24, 52, 140, 161
  petty bourgeois, 247, 251
  positions, 93, 131, 133
  practices, 206
  projects, 3
  property owning. (*See* landowners.)
  and race, 97, 193, 194, 195
  relations, 27, 68, 126, 131, 209
  ruling. (*See* dominant.)
  solidarity, 214
  subaltern, 56
  upper, 24
  working. (*See* working class.)
class politics, 13, 27, 64, 193, 195, 196, 219, 231
  and social transformation, 193
class struggle, 27, 118, 119, 194, 196, 197, 208, 212, 225, 236–39, 240, 247, 262. (*See also* political change; social, change.)
clientelism, 54–55, 126, 129, 140. (*See also* patron-client relations.)
coal (industry), 206, 207, 213, 215, 217, 218, 219
collieries
  Phalen, 207, 216
  Prince, 207, 216, 217, 218
  miners, 9, 206–20
  union. (*See* UMW.)
cocoa production, 152, 154, 155, 157
Cold War, the, 62, 75
colonialism, 101. (*See also* anthropology, and colonialism.)
  anti-, 73, 93
  Ecuadoran, 152
  internal, 52
  Mexican, 47, 51, 52–53, 55
  neo-, 29, 31
  post-, 57, 73, 86
    critique, 74
  as a socio-historical force, 59–60, 195
coloniality, 60, 86
collective action, 3, 8, 12–15 passim, 213, 218
  lack of, 122–23, 134, 127

collective bargaining, 199, 201, 203. (*See also* industrial relations.)
commodification, 227
commodities, 27, 181, 199, 224, 226
　market, 236
communal organization, 48, 168
communism, 111, 112, 113, 116, 117
　post-, 136–49
communist organizations, 63–64
communist party, 34, 35, 114, 141
　leadership, 198
　post-, 138, 144
communist politics, 7, 107–19, 142, 145
communist and unions, 198
community, 223, 235, 246, 265, 158, 160, 168, 169
　as a collective grouping, 92, 101, 158, 168, 169
　class basis of, 213, 214, 239. (*See also* Barber.)
　fishing, 247
　ideas about, 38, 56, 122, 123–24, 127, 134, 150, 206–20, 261–62
　idiom of, 9, 219, 237
　imagined. (*See* nation.)
　maintenance of, 236
　meaning of, 252
　as place, 108, 116, 122, 124, 160. (*See also* place.)
　rural, 261
　service, 214–16
　studies, 37, 40–41, 51
　supralocal, 96
　values, 49
community-based organizations, 191, 192, 194, 202
concentricity, 20, 21, 30
Connell, R.W., 166, 167, 173
consciousness, 13, 44–5, 119, 196, 209
　and action, 196, 229
　class. (*See* class consciousness.)
　collective, 15, 219, 227, 262
　contradictory, 192
　counter-hegemonic, 193
　false, 161
　political, 12, 198, 215

consent, 8, 9, 161, 196, 198, 223
constitutions, 22, 24, 93, 159
consumption, 2, 199, 230
contradiction
　(historical), 53, 127, 134, 183, 186, 188, 190, 211, 214, 220
　between experience and dominant discourse, 109, 127, 129, 161, 177
contradictory practices, 122, 183, 211, 214, 220
contracts, 156, 157, 159, 198, 204
Contreras, Jesús, 36–7, 45, 46n.3, 129, 130
cooperatives, 40, 48, 112–16, 127–28, 218
critique, 1, 11, 59, 65, 73, 84
Cuba, 111, 113, 114, 117, 172
　Revolution, 107
Cultural. (*See also* identity, cultural; struggles, cultural.)
　change, transformation, 10, 49, 195, 232
　diversity, 93, 95–98
　forces, 29, 232
　particularities, 186, 235
　politics, 206, 210, 211, 212, 213, 219
　practices, 94, 97, 174, 199, 210, 218, 229
　　gendered, 215
　processes, 151
　production, 3, 8, 38, 87
　projects, 3, 1 52
　relativism, 49, 57, 58
　spaces, 91–2, 94, 96–97, 99–103, 105–6
　spheres, 104, 223
　studies, 4, 29, 44, 69
　subordination, 50
Cultural Missions (Mexico), 49
culture(s), 2, 15, 25, 59, 60, 151, 233, 254–55. (*See also* regional, culture.)
　global, 20, 28
　hegemonic, 28, 43. (*See also* dominant, culture.)
　ideas about, 55–57
　indigenous, 55–57
　local, 44, 45, 55, 134
　national, 5, 19–21, 24, 47, 55, 56, 57, 58, 150

oppositional, 209
popular (mass), 27, 28, 55
theorists, 194, 255
working class, 54, 55, 199–201. (*See also* working class.)
culture historians, 62, 98
Culture and Personality School, 36, 37

Days of Action. (*See* Ontario Days of Action.)
deindustrialization, 10, 27, 29, 206, 219
de la Peña, Guillermo, 5, 22, 30, 34, 47, 58n.3, 82
democratic institutions, 52
democracy, 94, 100, 180
development, 27, 52, 95, 171, 172, 206, 257. (*See also* discourse, development; economic development.)
  dependency theory of, 27, 36, 37, 47, 68
  policy, elaboration of, 253
  staple theory of, 25, 26
  uneven, theory of, 206
dialectic, 11, 212, 214, 257–58, 265
diasporas, 10, 100, 101
differentiation, 6, 14, 54, 124, 133, 140, 243
  social, 38, 129, 213
discipline (of labor), 8, 192, 193, 197–99, 204–5, 216, 247, 255–56, 260
discourse, 123, 170, 256
  class-based, 194, 214, 237
  development, 213
  dominant, 70, 117, 127, 129
  media, 210, 213–14
  modernization, 52, 131
  nationalist, 48–52, 159
  neoliberal, 83, 84
  official. (*See* state, discourse.)
  political, 78, 138, 232
  racialized, 194
  regional, 229
discrimination, 100
distribution, 10, 25
dominant
  classes. (*See* class, dominant.)

culture, 161, 173
  discourse. (*See* discourse, dominant.)
  groups, 7, 23, 108, 116, 210, 223, 228
  nations, 29
  values and norms, 21, 210, 177, 183. (*See also* hegemony.)
domination, 3, 14, 150, 151
  experience of, 182–83, 190
  forms of, 3
  intellectual, 5, 28
  male, 166, 174. (*See also* men.)
  political, 52
  processes of, 14, 150, 151, 223
  state, 6, 166
Dominican Republic, 172
Dunk, Tom, 4, 5, 19–32, 85, 211

Eagleton, Terry, 192, 196, 199, 250, 265n.2
Eastern Europe. (*See* Europe.)
ecology. (*See* environment.)
economic
  crisis, 9, 55, 76, 161–62, 168, 175
  forces, 3, 4, 29, 31, 232
  institutions, 71, 148, 256
  opportunities, 24, 37
  policies, 2, 5, 25, 47, 130, 131, 134, 153
  position, 9
  processes, 11, 168, 174, 211
  projects, 9, 152
  security, erosion of, 81, 138, 193, 195, 199, 219
  spheres, 103
economic development, 52, 142, 144, 172–74, 197, 206–10 passim. (*See also* development.)
economy, 14, 93, 136, 233
  agrarian, 9
  agroforest, 26
  industrial, 137
  informal, 54, 125, 215, 227
  local, 95
  pulp and paper, 26
  regional, 137, 168, 172, 251, 252, 256–58, 263
  service-dominated, 137

economy *(continued)*
  staples, 26, 28, 31
  timber, 26
  wheat, 26
  world. (*See* global economy.)
Ecuador, 107–20, 150–62
  history of, 151, 152–3, 161
Ecuadorean Indians, 7, 151, 157, 159.
  (*See also* indigenous people.)
Ecuadoran peasants, 7. (*See also* peasants.)
education, 5, 6, 47, 48, 125, 137, 148,
    149n.7, 153, 154
  and employment, 81, 125, 137
  government action concerning, 47
  and ideology, 5–6, 48, 77, 153, 210, 229
  state funding for, 76–77, 80, 148, 194
  working class access to, 77, 137
Ehrenreich, Barbara, 165, 166, 167, 175
Eighteenth Brumaire, The, 14
elections, 6, 141, 153
elites, 127, 130, 152–59, 160
empiricism, 59, 60, 70, 136
employment. (*See* work.)
Engels, Frederick, 36, 43, 192
England. (*See* Britain.)
English. (*See* British.)
English Canada, 22, 24, 28
English-speaking. (*See* Anglophone.)
environment, 25, 26, 84, 170, 206, 211,
    219, 236
ethnic groups, 22, 173
ethnic movements, 55, 56
ethnicity
  differences/divisions of, 5, 6, 85, 97,
    100, 150, 179. (*See also* inequality.)
  and gender, 60
  and identity, 22–23, 56, 57, 70, 87, 168,
    180, 100–101
  and labor, 200
  and pluralism, 6, 100, 101
  racialized forms of, 8, 22
  and solidarity, 56, 57
ethnographic studies, 10, 11, 60, 62, 264
ethnography, 3, 6, 70, 71, 252
Europe, 25, 28, 33, 40, 47, 74, 94, 218,
    255

European Union (EU), 138–48 passim, 237
European monetary union, 141, 142, 145, 147 148
exchange, 10, 27
experience, 44–45, 215
  of defeat, 118–19, 128, 185–86
  of domination/control, 39, 128–29, 179, 186–87
  everyday, 40, 123, 171, 193, 204, 252–53
  gendered, of domination, 231, 232
  individual, 192
  local, 214, 170, 130
  and memory, 178–80, 186
  of place, 252. (*See also* place.)
  political, 24, 34, 63
  shopfloor, 192
  of work, 13, 133, 179, 224, 228, 229–30, 248, 251, 252, 255–56, 261, 262. (*See also* exploitation.)
exploitation, 3, 14, 47, 127, 132, 136, 146, 147, 179, 183, 256
  as a characteristic of capitalism, 54, 137, 146, 249
  gendered, of family labor, 257
  by the state, 8

factories, 170, 247, 252–54, 256, 259, 262, 263. (*See also* industries, canning, *maquiladoras.*)
  "without walls," 126, 257
factory regimes, 250
Falange Party (Spain), 127, 129
Falklands war. (*See* Malvinas.)
family, 165, 166, 170, 175, 223, 230. (*See also* household.)
  control over labor, 248
  gender relations within the, 139, 165, 166, 230
  issues, 201
  survival of the, as an ideology, 217, 219, 241, 259
  ties of solidarity, 244
  as unit of livelihood, 54, 170, 264
farmers, 9, 140, 221

farming, 10, 90, 110, 223, 225, 226. (*See also* agriculture.)
family, 221, 263
masculinzation of, 226–29
fascism, 4, 33, 93, 104, 125, 204
neo-, 194
fieldwork, 38, 68, 69, 102, 109, 167, 172, 176, 193, 211, 233
First Nations. (*See also* indigenous peoples.)
peoples, 19, 21, 26, 29, 31, 101–2, 195
and popular protest, 191, 194
studies, 19
fishery, 9, 25
commercial, 9, 235–49 passim
Newfoundland, 25
flexibility, 210, 252
of culture, 257
of the labor market, 81, 125, 143
workplace, 77, 257
fordism, 5, 193, 197, 199–205, 247
post-, 12, 203–05
fordist worker. (*See* worker, fordist.)
Foucault, Michel, 1, 6, 69, 70, 71, 72n.2, 79, 124
France, 9, 28, 31, 221–33 passim, 235–49 passim
imperialism of, 22, 29
politics in, 142
unemployment in, 138–39, 141
Franco, General Francisco, 4, 38, 121, 122, 124, 125, 134. (*See also* fascism.)
anti-Franco dissent, 36, 38
Spanish state under. (*See* Spain, fascist.)
Francophone, 21, 24, 31, 229
free trade, 169, 170
agreement. (*See* NAFTA.)
Freeman, B., 193, 197, 198
French in Canada, 21, 26
French language, 226, 229, 230, 240
French speaking. (*See* Francophone.)
Frigolé, Joan, 35–36, 38, 35–6, 38, 45, 45n.

Galicia (Spain), 39, 40
Gamio, M., 49, 51, 57, 59

gender. (*See also* capitalism, gendered nature of; class, and gender; family, gender relations within the; farming, masculinization of; globalization, and gender; hierarchy, gendered; labor, and gender; gendered market, men; patriarchy; poverty, gendered; power, relations, gendered; production, gendered; wages, gender differentials of, women's.)
analysis, 8, 9, 22, 170
cultural construction of, 38, 70, 165, 170–72
and identity, 226, 229
and political struggle, 141, 215, 217–18, 221–34, 191
relations, 9, 59, 165, 166, 167, 169, 173
stereotypes, 173
Germany, 28, 76, 94, 97, 100, 110, 139, 141
Glace Bay (Canada), 215–18
Gledhill, John, 4, 6, 31n.4, 45, 63
global culture. (*See* culture, global.)
global economy, 10, 20, 24, 62, 68, 145–46, 148, 167, 168, 210, 219, 242
globalization, 2, 10, 11, 13, 25, 55, 62, 81, 83, 85, 123, 168, 171–72, 236
of education, 5, 77, 81
forces of, 2
and gender, 171–72
and restructuring, 13, 25
Gordillo, Gastón, 8, 13, 177–90, 242, 248, 264
government
and anthropology, 65–66
agencies, 65, 180
of Ecuador, 112, 116, 161
indigenous, 50
of Italy, 138, 141–45, 147
Mexican, 172–73
military. (*See* military, governments.)
need for, 105
officials. (*See* state, officials.)
policies. (*See* state, policies; *see also* Ontario, government, policies.)
retreat of, 195

Gramsci, Antonio, 8, 9, 69, 72n.2, 123, 191, 192–93, 196–97, 199, 200, 209, 210, 215, 253. (*See also* hegemony.)
Great Britain. (*See* Britain.)
Greece, 139, 145
Guayaquil, 111, 112, 115, 153–61 passim
Gupta, Dipankar, 5, 6, 91–106, 123, 124, 162n.1

habitus, 74, 124
hacendado, 158, 176
hacienda, 7, 152, 154, 158, 160. (*See also* Tenguel, hacienda.)
Hall, Stuart, 72n.2, 196, 203
Harvey, David, 11, 21, 62, 73, 146, 147, 196, 211–12, 213, 216, 219–20, 252
health (physical), 182–83
healthcare, 47, 194, 195
hegemonic culture. (*See* culture, hegemonic.)
hegemonic discourse. (*See* dominant, discourse.)
hegemonic processes, 25, 44, 150–51, 176, 187, 192, 196, 210, 223, 229
hegemonic projects, 151, 160, 161. (*See also* state projects.)
hegemony (concept of), 8, 15, 56, 150, 186, 229
  counter-, 5, 193, 204
  gramscian, 9, 14, 99, 160–61, 192, 196, 210, 223–24, 228, 233, 250
  role of, in the construction of memory, 8, 120, 178, 179, 183
  studies of, 56
henequen. (*See* sisal.)
hierarchy, 61, 70, 171, 175, 179
  gendered, 222, 232
hindu, 92
historical materialism, 1, 2, 3, 5, 12–13, 14, 36, 68, 71, 224
historical specificity, 10, 123, 224, 257
history. (*See also* memory.)
  analytical uses of, 13–15, 36, 40–42, 60–62, 70, 123, 151, 176, 212, 233, 243
  alternative, 7, 108, 117, 118, 120
  of events, 109, 110, 118, 127–28, 184–86
  local, 60, 128, 238
  official, 8, 108, 114, 117, 186
  popular, 120
  as constitutive of the present, 119–20, 167, 212
  production of, 107–9, 117–20, 243, 245
  selective, 109, 256, 258
  of struggle, 118, 240–41
  social, 70
  versions of, 7, 55, 108, 118, 120, 187
  working class, 239
Hitler, 100
Hobsbawm, Eric, 108, 109, 136, 192, 254
Holland, 76
Hong Kong, 22
households, 53, 125, 139, 169, 171, 175, 180, 227, 228, 232, 265. (*See also* family.)
Howes, D., 19, 20, 21, 23–4
human rights, 56, 99, 141, 174. (*See also* rights.)

idealism, 14, 22, 28
identity. (*See also* class, basis for identity; ethnicity, working class, identity.)
  changing, 169, 226–31 passim
  claims, 123, 133–34
  collective, 122, 210, 242, 250–66
  community, 122, 206, 210, 219
  cultural, 17, 26, 39, 49, 93–94, 252
  defined, 44–45
  formation of, 21, 44, 55, 70, 210, 224, 237
  gendered, 229
  indigenous, 180, 187
  local, 130, 212, 240, 242, 246, 248
  national, 8, 9, 20, 57, 58, 70, 127, 229
  politics, 5–9, 10, 64, 101, 238
  as a property, 6, 15, 60, 169, 211
  racial, 70
  regional, 8, 9, 36, 38, 45, 56, 225, 237, 242, 250

religious, 92
signs of, 237, 246
social, 10, 250–55, 264–65
ideological consensus, 150, 161
ideological struggle, 108–9, 110, 113, 114, 117, 119
ideology. (*See also* state, ideology.), 10
competing, 152
hegemonic (dominant, prevailing), 25, 109, 203, 213
of sacrifice, 201
shifts in, 79, 200
imperialism, 22, 29, 30, 52
anti-, 65
India, 6, 57, 92–3, 97, 98, 100
Indian, 48, 51, 52. (*See also* indigenous peoples.)
Indigenismo, 47, 48–50, 52, 54. (*See also* indigenous.)
indigenous, 57. (*See also* First Nations.)
culture. (*See* culture, indigenous.)
identity. (*See* identity, indigenous.)
movements, 55–57
peoples, 5, 8, 30, 47–57, 155, 158, 177-90. (*See also* Ecuadorean Indians; Maya; Toba Indians.)
and government, 51, 183
rights, 86, 156, 157. (*See also* rights.)
struggles, 14, 183
uprisings, 50, 161
industrial capitalism, 26, 148, 248
industrial development, 47, 51, 131
industrial relations, 193, 197–99, 204, 213. (*See also* collective bargaining.)
industrial revolution, the, 252, 263
industrial sector, 10, 171, 147
industrial society, 255, 256
post-, 256, 258
industrial work. (*See* work, industrial.)
industrial workers. (*See* workers, industrial.)
industrialization, 51, 130, 172, 246, 262
urban, 130, 213
industries, 141, 147, 168, 214. (*See also* shoe manufacturing.)
coal. (*See* coal.)
fish cannery, 235–36, 242, 244–47 passim

garment, 169–70, 172, 173
steel. (*See* steel.)
industry, 9, 76, 140, 171, 142
history of, 260
primary, 10
rural, 124
inequality, 103, 246, 248
economic, 52, 137
ethnic, 59
experience of, 195, 248
gendered, 173, 174, 212, 248
production of, 38, 195
social, 137
Innis, Harold, 24–25
institutions, 13, 71, 201, 204
democratic, 50, 52
political, 23, 71, 256
social, 10, 256
state, 108, 129
intellectual, 5, 6, 73–74, 136
left, 6, 52–56 passim, 63, 67, 68, 136, 192. (*See also* marxists.)
milieu, 59, 61, 71
organic, 192, 193, 197, 233
production, 4, 5, 61, 63
projects, 60
tradition, 11, 28
workers, 4, 5, 28, 66
Intersubjectivity, 98
Iraq, 85
Italy, 7, 13, 136–49, 192

Japan, 146
Jews, 94, 97, 100, 101
Jorgensen, Joseph, 5, 63, 65
Journalists, 110, 194. (*See also* media.)

Keynes, J.M., 136–37
keywords, 7, 152, 193
knowledge, 5, 120, 181, 182
anthropological, 6, 14, 43, 86
policy implications of, 251, 253, 263
political and economic context of, 6
production/reproduction/transformation of, 3, 4, 6, 75, 78, 85–86, 251
Western, 49

labor, 12–13. (*See also* work.)
  appropriation of, 12, 15
  casualization of, 72, 77–8
  child, 38, 257, 261
  day, 126, 130, 224
  exchange, 40
  flexible. (*See* flexibility.)
  force, 52, 77, 166, 170, 172, 175, 179
  free/unfree, 8, 27, 154, 156, 159
  gendered division of, 125–26, 165–76, 170, 173, 215, 222, 224–26, 227, 246
  migration. (*See* migration.)
  militancy, 8, 9, 206, 210, 211, 225, 238, 240
  non-union, 206, 207, 208
  organizations, 112, 142, 162, 203. (*See also* unions.)
  and popular protest, 191, 192, 193–94, 225
  recruitment, 12, 157, 159
  reserve/surplus, 12, 50, 53, 81, 216
  skilled, 28, 77, 137, 199
  wage, 27, 170, 180, 215. (*See also* wages.)
labor market, 13, 169, 207. (*See also* unemployment.)
  for academics, 5, 27, 77, 81
  and gender, 137, 139, 143, 212
  Italian, 139–47 passim
  local, 137
  Mexican, 169
  national, 137
  reform, 146
  Spanish, 125
labor movement, the, 192, 193, 194, 197
  divisions within, 202, 204
Labor Party of Britain, 75, 78, 81, 85
laborers. (*See* workers.)
Labrecque, Marie France, 9, 10, 12, 13, 165–76, 247, 248, 264
land reform, 47, 49, 53, 55, 107–20 passim
landowners, 129, 130, 154, 160, 167, 219, 224–25, 247, 231. (See also *hacendado.*)

language, 160, 225. (*See also* English; French; Occitan.)
  conflicts, 91–2, 225–26, 243
Languedoc, 9, 221–33
Latin America, 27, 49, 51, 76, 107, 156, 173
Leach, Belinda, 8, 10, 12, 13, 14, 24, 58, 191–205, 211, 223, 265
leadership
  labor, 193, 201–2, 206
  political, 113
  union. (*See* union, leadership.)
Leclau, Ernesto, 250, 251, 254
left, the (political), 52, 63–65, 68, 72, 161, 191. (*See also* anthropology, left in; intellectual, left.)
  in Italy, 13, 137–48
  political project of the, 192, 196
  strategies, 111, 136, 137, 145, 193, 243
legal system, 23, 99
legislation, 23, 94–95, 99, 113, 120, 123, 156–62 passim
  related to agriculture, 157–58
  environmental, 195
  labor, 142, 144, 147, 194, 195, 197, 208, 262
  social, 94–95
Lem, Winnie, 9, 10, 12, 13, 15, 45, 58, 124, 183, 190n., 221–34, 246, 248, 262, 265
Lenin, Vladimir, 95, 192
Levine, S.K., 11, 12, 15n. 4
liberal democracy, 97, 105, 122
liberal discourse, 6, 7, 152, 159, 160
liberalism, 104, 151, 160
livelihood, 13, 213, 219, 251, 261. (*See also* struggles, livelihood.)
  as a field of inquiry, 13
  defense of, 195, 207, 215, 221–34, 235, 242, 256, 263
  strategies, 122, 125, 131, 134, 211
Llobera, Josep, 16n. 5, 37, 46n. 5
local, 61, 56. (*See also* place.)
  analysis, level of, 51, 168, 170, 196
  in relation to the broader social field, 10, 11, 38, 39, 60, 72, 122, 123, 127,

152, 156–60, 168, 214, 219, 226, 264
culture, 44, 99, 103, 215, 222, 248, 257
economic issues, 201, 241
events, 111, 200
loyalties, 210
political action, 194, 203, 231
politics, 22–23, 184, 193, 196, 213, 222
practices, 210, 174
processes, 13, 174
specificity, 68, 130–31, 134
locality. (*See* place.)
Longue durée, 53
Lortie, Lucie, 171–72, 176

Maastricht, 142
machismo, 167, 174
Malinowski, Bronislaw, 51, 58n.3, 79
Malvinas (war in the), 180, 188
Maoists, 136
maquiladoras, 54, 165–76, 264. (*See also* workers, *maquiladora.*)
Marche (region), 137
Marcus, George, 61, 62, 73
marginalization, 54, 94, 137, 146
market, 95, 136
  domestic, 25
  forces, 53, 147, 224
  free, 143
  in fresh fish, 25, 236
  global, international or world, 25, 53, 77, 131, 152, 153, 154, 226
  internal, 152, 155, 157
  national, 53, 57, 131, 158
  protectionism, 51
Marx, Karl, 1, 7, 10, 11–15 passim, 34, 35, 62, 64, 68, 124, 136, 192, 243, 250, 265n.3
Marxist analysis (Marxism), 1–2, 4, 9, 11, 23, 33, 34, 52, 61–62, 64, 70, 219, 223
  anthropology, 4, 11, 34, 36–39, 61
  centrality of class to, 11, 27, 194–95
  and critique of political economy, 1, 11–12, 68
  French, 34, 37, 53, 67–69

neo/post- , 27, 47, 250
  theories, 146
Marxists, 4, 6, 64, 119
material conditions, 2, 8, 10, 12, 74, 129, 224, 228, 232, 256
material processes, 36, 150, 151
materialism. (*See* historical materialism.)
Maya, 167, 168, 169, 170
meaning, 21, 152, 161
  changing, 222
  conflicting, 152, 161, 208–9
  contingent nature of, 21, 186, 187, 206, 222, 224
  multiple, 206
media, the, 108, 110–14, 116, 117, 205, 214, 216, 228. (*See also* journalists.)
memory, 92, 119, 177–90 passim. (*See also* experience, and memory.)
  collective, 178, 236
  historical, 161, 185
  production of, 183, 235
  social, 8, 118, 177–78, 179, 183, 186, 197, 218
  of struggle, 235, 242, 244
men, 166–73 passim, 177, 182, 195, 212, 230, 233. (*See also* domination, male; farming, masculinization of; gender; labor, gendered.)
  activities of, 230, 238
  ideological construction of, 100, 178, 228
  studies concerning, 212
  on welfare, 143
  work of, 125, 126, 227
Menzies, Charles, 9, 10, 12, 13, 14, 178, 235–49
Merida, 167, 168
mesizaje, 48–57
mestizo, 22, 49–51, 55, 57, 167
metaphors ("root"), 6, 91–106 passim, 182
methodology, 3, 14, 36
Mexico, 5, 22, 30–34, 47–58, 165–76. (*See also* labor market, Mexican.)
  history of, 48, 53
  research institutes in, 50, 52, 57

migration (labor), 26, 53, 54, 56, 57, 131, 134, 155, 156, 181, 187–88, 217, 218
military, 112–18 passim, 177–78, 181, 184–89, 216, 218
  governments, 115, 169
missionaries, 178–80, 184, 186, 188
mobility, 10, 93, 125, 251
mode of production, 34, 37, 53, 68, 69
modernity, 55, 57, 98, 154, 159, 167. (*See also* state, projects.)
  acceptance/rejection of, 55–56, 57, 154, 159
  characterized, 98, 257
  as historical context, 167
modernization, 7, 9, 15, 51–52, 54, 102, 130, 131, 152, 155, 157, 158, 166
  of agriculture, 157, 222, 226–27, 232, 155–58
  capitalist, 51–55, 143, 166, 230, 245
  discourse. (*See* discourse, modernization.)
  as state project, 7, 9, 15, 124, 130, 134, 152, 225–32
  theory, 47, 166
Modes of Production theory, 37, 53
Mondragón, 40
Moreno, Isidro, 36, 37, 46n.3
movements. (*See also* social movements.)
  indigenous. (*See* ingenous.)
  labor. (*See* labor movement, the.)
  national, 93, 101
  political movements, 2, 54, 63–65, 67, 120, 191
  working class, 161, 193, 246
multiculturalism, 6, 22–24 passim, 87
multinational corporations, 22, 166, 167, 174
Murcia, 35, 38, 121–24
Muslim, 92

NAFTA, 173
Narotzky, Susana, 4–5, 29, 64, 46n.9, 52, 125
narrative, 60, 62–63, 118, 178, 180, 184, 190, 231

Nash, June, 60, 198, 211
nation, 7, 19, 55–57, 102, 229
  as "imagined community," 17, 19, 91, 124, 188
nation-state, 5, 6, 24, 39, 91–106, 177, 178, 187, 243
  integration of, 39
national
  borders, 4, 57, 189. (*See also* United States-Mexico border.)
  culture. (*See* culture, national.)
  identities. (*See* identity, national.)
  interests, 52, 159
  markets. (*See* markets, national.)
  movements. (*See* movements, national.)
  struggles. (*See* struggles, national.)
  territory, 157
  unity, 24, 50
nationalism, 19, 22, 23, 36, 101
  Quebecois, 22
  Mexican, 47–58 passim
  regional, 9, 34
  trans-, 10
Nationalist
  discourse. (*See* discourse, nationalist.)
  dissent, 33
  ideologies, 93
  issues, 34, 35
  politics, 38
  positions, 86
  project, 22, 36
Native People. (*See* First Nations.)
Nazi, 100, 101
neoconservatism, 205
Neoliberal
  discourse. (*See* discourse, neoliberal.)
  economic policies, 2, 206
  politcal and economic order, 1–6, 79, 175, 206
neoliberalism, 144, 173–74, 250
  effects of, 78, 81
New Democratic Party (NDP), 194–203 passim
Newfoundland, 25, 26, 31
Nicaraguan revolution, 119
North America, 40, 100, 102, 167

Northern Ireland, 80
Nova Scotia, 206–20 passim

Occitan (language), 225–26, 230
Occitania. (*See* Languedoc.)
Ontario, 8, 13, 24, 26, 191–205
  Days of Action, 192, 193, 195
  government of, 193–94, 202
  policies, 191, 192, 195
  labor movement. (*See also* unions.)
Ontario Federation of Labor (OFL), 194
ownership, 25, 114, 181, 243–44, 248. (*See also* landowners.)

Palerm, Angel, 34, 36, 37, 45n.1, 52, 53, 58n.6
Palerm, Juan Vicente, 34, 36, 37, 45n.1, 46n.3, 4
Palmer, B. D., 198, 201–2, 204, 246
Paraguay, 178
particularism, 59, 92, 134, 140, 213
  cultural, 246, 247
  militant, 206, 211, 214–16, 219
patriarchy, 165–67, 172, 173, 174, 175, 176
patriotism, 92, 103
patron-client relations, 53, 126. (*See also* clientelism.)
peasants. (*See also* Ecuadorean Indians, Ecuadorean peasants; workers, rural.)
  agriculture, 246
  as a category, 48, 59, 121, 191, 229
  characterized, 52–54, 162
  economic conditions, 131, 248
  identities, 168–69, 235
  indigenous, 156–58
  landownership by, 131, 247
  in Mexico, 5, 47–57 passim
  organizations of the, 112
  in relation to the state, 5, 53, 127, 130, 134, 156
  revolts (revolutions, uprisings, mobilizations), 54, 113, 117, 118, 236, 246
  studies of, 34, 37, 38, 52, 53, 150
Peru, 39, 150
place, 13, 213, 250–66. (*See also* community, as place, local.)
  belonging to, sense of, 56, 70, 134
  historical construction of, 123
  and identity, 212, 250
  politics of, 214, 220
  significance of, 10, 13, 123–24
  as sites, 116, 124–25
  and work, 250–66
plantations, 168, 181, 188
political
  actors, 193, 232
  action, 3, 8, 13, 14, 56, 119, 192, 193, 212–13, 220, 221–23. (*See also* political protest.) passim
  activism, 35, 67, 120, 188, 202
  aspirations, 119, 160–61, 202
  authority, 156, 158
  change (transformation), 1, 13, 195. (*See also* class politics, and social transformation.)
  coalitions (alliances, alignments), 191, 192, 196, 218, 248
  consensus, 140, 161
  control, 17, 19, 140
  crisis, 162
  dissent, 33–38
  environment, 2–3, 6, 38, 51, 59, 61, 69, 63, 116
  experience. (*See* experience, political.)
  force, 3, 4, 31, 86, 190, 232
  institutions. (*See* institutions, political.)
  mobilization, 10, 13, 52, 67, 183, 193. (*See also* movements, political.)
  parties, 7, 37, 52, 67, 81, 137, 138, 141–45, 162. (*See also* communist party; Falange party; PRI; socialist party.)
  practice, 13, 183, 250
  processes, 23, 151, 160
  strategy, 201
  subordination, 47
police, 208, 241
political economists, 11, 250
political economy, 3, 4, 5, 6, 7, 11–12, 19–27, 86, 123, 132, 136, 137, 145, 150

approaches to anthropology, 33–45, 69–72, 250
and culture, 212
feminist, 170
global, 21, 73, 166, 171
of knowledge, 33, 73–87
of the State, 6
transformations of, 206, 242
political projects, 7, 9, 152, 196, 221, 222, 224, 228–32 passim
political protest, 194, 200, 205, 217–18, 221. (*See also* Ontario Days of Action.)
class basis of, 195, 198, 237–38, 241–44
politicians, 136, 208, 218
politics, 99, 136, 144, 145, 182
academic, 63–67, 73
as a field of study, 2, 6, 233
labor, 199, 206, 211
oppositional, 205, 225
populism, 24, 112, 162, 247
Portugal, 139, 145
positivism, 59, 60
post-Fordism. (*See* Fordism, post-)
post-modern, 2, 15, 21, 47, 57, 73, 250
poverty
as cause of struggle, 243
gendered, 131, 170, 175
generalized, 52, 55, 81, 84, 133, 144, 173, 182, 230
rural, 109, 117, 122–32 passim, 129, 131
urban, 47, 54, 55, 215
power
abuse of, 50, 156
administrative, 201
as an analytic construct, 5, 61, 70, 71
to appropriate culture, 209
coercive, 117, 209
differences, 116, 145, 170, 213
fields of, 73, 151, 223
in institutions, 223
male, 227, 231, 232
management's, over unions, 199
political, 137, 153, 152
relations, 4, 9, 23, 37, 73, 107

gendered, 222, 226, 265
state, 7, 157
structures, 4, 7, 14, 79, 232
of unions, 211, 218
powerholders, 85, 159 160
praxis, 3, 65
PRI (Institutional Revolutionary Party of Mexico), 52, 54, 55, 56
private property. (*See* ownership.)
private sector, 130
privatization, 143, 195, 206
production, 173, 219, 223–24. *(See also* factories; fordism; *maquiladoras.)*
Asiatic Mode of, 52
cooperative, 8. (*See also* cooperatives.)
colonial context of, 240
of culture. (*See* cultural, production.)
of knowledge. (*See* knowledge, production of.)
gendered, 10, 126, 131, 171, 175, 227. (*See also* labor, gendered.)
means of, 151, 227
mode of. (*See* mode of production.)
organization of, 125–26, 221, 237
petty commodity, 26, 27, 38, 180
process of, 2, 10, 121, 125, 134, 169
relations of, 14, 26, 38, 53, 122, 126, 133, 180
industrial, 236, 238, 248
spheres of, 129
theory, 70
proletarianization, 146, 246, 247
proletariat, 156, 191, 219, 262
protests. (*See* political protest.)
Public
debt, 25
health, 81, 181
sphere, 98–99
works, 156–57
public sector
jobs in the, 180, 183
spending, 5, 25, 76–79, 130, 141
Puerto Rico, 173

Quebec, 22, 24, 26, 30
Quito, 111, 112, 153, 160

race, 22, 39, 49, 51, 59, 93, 97. (*See also* discourse, racialized; identity, racial; violence, racially motivated.)
  and gender, 60, 201
  and labor, 20
racism, 21, 22, 23, 39
rationalism, 28, 30
regions, 36, 251. (*See also* Bigoudin; Brittany; Cape Breton; Catalan; Chaco, el; Languedoc; Marche Murcia; Third Italy; Yucatán.)
  as a field of study, 36, 81
  histories of, 25, 263
regional
  culture, 9, 17, 36, 49, 225, 230, 257–58, 263
  economies. (*See* economies, regional.)
  elites. (*See* elites, regional.)
  formations, 53
  identity. (*See* identity, regional.)
  variations, 13, 138, 143, 147
regulation, 6, 79, 81 , 83, 193, 256
  capitalist, 5, 76
religion, 50, 91, 92–93, 95, 180
repression, 35, 51, 52, 112, 113, 115, 120, 187
reproduction
  of capital, 22, 255
  production and, 12–13, 14, 38, 129, 171
  social, 40, 254
republican Spain. (*See* Spain, republican.)
resistance, 71, 150, 218, 229. (*See also* struggles.)
  and accomodation, 8, 207, 212, 213, 219, 220
  to economic conditions, 10, 158, 159, 176
  everyday forms of, 118
  history of, 236
  local, 240
  stories of, 177, 186, 190, 246
restructuring
  of agriculture, 221, 226, 228
  capitalist, 8–9, 11, 232
  economic, 2, 10, 13, 25, 79–85 passim, 120, 193, 195, 200, 203, 232
  policies, 191, 195

public sector, 195
  of universities, 6, 79–85
Reyneri, E., 138, 139, 140
right (political), 13, 24, 192, 203, 243
rights, 157, 159. (*See also* civil rights; human rights; indigenous rights.)
  citizenship, 77, 100, 157, 159, 195, 205, 243
  collective, 159
  individual, 156
  lesbian and gay, 200
  management, 211
  minority, 6, 100, 101, 106
  property, 241
  workers', 194, 198, 204
Roseberry, William, 4, 5, 7, 10, 12, 16n.5, 30, 31n.4, 35, 36, 71, 72n.1, 74, 85, 150–51, 233
Russia, 111, 113, 117

Sabel, C., 257, 261, 266n.4
Said, Edward, 73, 96, 98
service sector, 147, 245
shoe manufacturing, 125, 128, 131, 137
sisal, 8, 167–68, 170
Smith, Adam, 136–37
Smith, Gavin, 10, 13, 14, 40, 42, 46n.9, 58, 123, 150, 178, 186, 190n., 195–96, 197, 199, 220, 233n.4, 234n.8, 237, 248, 250–66
Social. (*See also* differentiation, social; inequality, social; institutions, social; reproduction, social; structure, social.)
  change, 1, 138, 161, 171–72, 192, 195, 196, 199, 202, 214
  conditions, 182
  control, 129, 140
  Darwinism, 57
  democracy, 141, 148, 248
  forces, 29
  justice, 194, 198, 201
  order, 210, 211
  position, 9
  processes, 3, 74, 192, 211
  programs, 125

Social *(continued)*
  spending, 141, 144, 148, 206, 212, 215
  subjects, 8, 187. (*See also* public sector, spending.)
  training, 209–10, 213
social movements, 2, 10, 54, 64–65, 119, 120, 167, 237, 250
  new, 255, 262
socialism, 1, 219
  post-, 138
socialist, 40, 64
  consciousness, 192, 197, 218
  government, 39, 142
  organizations, 63
  parties, 34, 97, 112, 192, 240
  politics, 211, 214, 219
Soviet Union, 136, 253. (*See also* Russia.)
Spain, 4, 8, 33-46, 121–35 passim. (*See also* Franco, Spanish state under.)
  fascist, 4, 125. (*See also* fascism.)
  Post-Franco, 4, 40
  republican, 40, 52, 122, 127–29
  under Franco, 8, 33–40, 127, 131
Spanish Civil War, 34, 35, 38, 39, 40, 122, 125, 127, 134
Spanish conquest, 52, 169, 178
Spanish language, 48
specificity, 68, 122, 134, 174
  cultural, 43 193
  historical, 193
  local, 196, 246
  regional, 68, 167
state, 6–8, 13, 15, 24, 36, 62, 85, 86, 134, 144, 146, 148, 166, 190, 218. (*See also* institutions, state; modernization, as state project; power, state; welfare state.)
  benefits, 140, 141
  discourse, 47, 52, 123, 127, 130, 157, 178, 210
  and ethnic difference, 5
  formation, 6, 23, 24, 104, 124
  hegemony of the, 197, 230
  ideology, 20–21, 48, 85, 123, 127, 134
  intervention, 83, 109, 130, 221, 226, 247–48

  multinational, 56
  officials, 111, 113, 131, 156, 160
  opposition to the, 186, 187, 225, 231, 237
  patriarchal, 167, 172–74. (*See also* patriarchy.)
  political economies of the, 6
  and subjects, 6, 7, 91–106
state policies, 25, 51, 105, 123, 137, 221. (*See also* Ontario, government, policies.)
  anti-discrimination and affirmative action, 192, 200, 201, 202
  economic
    (Canadian), 22
    (Ecuadoran), 154, 157
    (French), 226, 237, 238
    (Italian), 142, 144, 148
    (Mexican), 5, 54
  immigration, 192
  as object of protest, 191, 195, 221, 237
  of the Spanish, 38, 130
state projects, 6, 104, 123–24. (*See also* hegemonic projects.)
  French, 225–30
  Mexican, 5
  resistance to, 14
  Spanish, 125, 127, 129, 130 134
statelessness, 94
steel industry, 206, 213, 217
steel workers, 192, 193, 195, 199–201
  union, 198, 203. (*See also* USWA.)
Stelco steel plant, 193, 197, 200, 203
Steward, Julian, 45n.1, 60, 61
Striffler, Steve, 7, 8, 12, 15, 107–20, 135n.3, 162n.3
strikes, 161, 196, 204
  fish, 237–39, 240, 242
  general, 194, 195, 204–5
  historical meaning of, 259
  industrial, 236
  and union discipline, 216, 218, 229, 231–32
  women's participation in, 200, 221
Structural Adjustment Programs, 175
structural-functionalism, 41, 42

structuralism, 69, 70
structure, 44–45, 167, 168, 170, 171, 175, 195
social, 127, 170
struggles, 8, 9, 119, 150, 152, 158, 160, 162. (*See also* class struggle.)
  autochthonous, 14, 183
  cultural, 208, 213, 230
  gender, 14. (*See also* gender, and political struggle.)
  national, 14
  popular, 109
  political, 64, 110, 120, 210, 212, 214, 219, 224, 235–49, 254, 256
  students, 59–65 passim, 195, 201
subalterns, 30, 85, 178
  changes in, 222
  formation of, 6, 13, 123, 213, 229, 231–32
  gendered, 223
  inter-, 98
  modern, 227
  social, 251, 254
subjects, 6, 8, 13, 61, 124, 166, 187, 200, 229
  individuated, 134, 210, 211, 213
subordination, 47, 56, 57, 118, 119, 172
subsistence, 129, 154, 183
surplus
  appropriation, 11, 12, 15
  extraction, 9
  value, 54, 146
sweatshops, 169
Swedenburg, T., 108, 178, 186
symbolic processes, 150, 151, 182
symbols, 242–47

Tanzania, 167
technology, 21, 6
Tenguel, hacienda, 102–20. (*See also* hacienda.*)
Terradas, Ignaci, 36, 38, 42, 43, 44, 45n.2, 46n.4
Terray, Emmanuel, 34, 68
terrorism, 8, 178, 186–88, 190
textile production, 169, 259

Thailand, 66
Thatcher, Margaret, 5, 75, 80, 137
Third Italy, 256–57, 261
Third World, 52
Thompson, E.P., 36, 69, 72n.2, 75, 151, 259
Toba Indians, 8, 177–90 passim, 264
trade unions. (*See* unions.)
tradition
  as historical practice, 168, 232, 245–46
  malleable quality of, 9, 108, 210
  national, 19, 104, 105
  as source of identity, 226, 230
transnational corporations. (*See* multinationals.)
transnational populations, 25
Trouillot, M.R., 107, 179, 187

underdevelopment. (*See* development.)
unemployment
  benefits, 148
  fear of, 203, 217
  as a field of inquiry, 13, 136–37, 261–62
  in Italy, 136–48
  statistics, 125, 260
    for Italy in contrast to Europe, 137–39
unemployment compensation. (*See* state, benefits.)
unions, 92, 196, 210, 213, 260. (*See also* USWA.)
  anti-, 229
  in coalitions, 52, 193
  and governments, 199
  in Italy, 142–48 passim
  leadership, 193, 197–98, 201–2, 209
  militancy of, 208, 209, 216, 236, 240
  in Ontario, 18, 191–205
  organizing, 12, 64, 72, 110, 239
  public sector, 205
  rank and file membership of, 67, 197–98, 202
United Fruit Company, 107–20
United Kingdom, 22, 27, 28, 29, 31, 31n2, 4. (*See also* Britain.)

United Mineworkers' Union (UMW), 217–18
United States of America, 4, 23, 59–72 passim, 175
  anthropology in the. (*See* anthropology, American.)
  consumer market, 173, 175
  culture and values, 21, 22, 175
  economy, 137, 146–47, 155, 168
  education in the, 76. (*See also* students.)
  history, 93
  imperialism, 22, 27–29, 31
  society, 97, 100
  unions in the, 198
USA-Mexico border, 55, 166, 169, 170, 175
United Steelworkers of America (USWA), 193, 199–201, 201
universities, 5–6, 34, 35, 74–87, 98
  as institutions, 28, 42, 59–72 passim, 75, 77–87 passim
  departments of anthropology in, 27–28, 34, 36, 49
  transformation of, 76
urban
  centers, 50, 212
  growth, 155
  industrialization. (*See also* industrialization, urban.)
  populations, 59
  studies, 250

Vicencio, Claudia, 7, 8, 15, 94, 108, 120, 121–35, 161
Vietnam War, 64, 65
violence, 170, 174–75, 178
  racially motivated, 194
  state, 186–88
viticulture. (*See* wine production.)

Wages, 255, 260–61
  and gender and age differentials, 147, 165, 228
  protection of, 140
  reduction of, 143–44, 146, 147, 165, 211, 225, 228
  reliance on, 259, 260–61
  union-negotiated, 198–99, 209
  women's, 170, 171–72
Warman, A., 47, 53, 54
Weber, Max, 103
welfare policies or programs, 192, 194
welfare recipients, 201
welfare state, 7, 81, 83, 122, 131, 132, 137–40. (*See also* state, benefits.)
Western Europe. (*See* Europe.)
white males, 195, 199, 200, 201, 202. (*See also* men.)
Williams, Raymond, 44, 69, 72n.2, 124, 152, 161, 183, 209, 210, 211–12, 213, 219, 220, 229, 255
wine production, 38, 221–32 passim
Wolf, Eric, 5, 45n.1, 53, 60, 61, 62, 63, 66, 168, 254
women, 30, 222, 230. (*See also* gender; labor, gendered; patriarchy; power, relations, gendered; strikes, women's participation in.)
  anthropology of, 60
  as heads of households, 165
  as "housewife," 227–31
  job opportunities for, 137, 166, 170, 245, 263
  and labor force participation, 9, 10, 38, 125, 126, 131, 137, 138, 143, 146, 147, 166, 169, 171, 200, 261
  and political participation, 221–33
  rural, 9, 166, 169, 171, 221–34, 263
  subordination of, 172, 229, 232, 233
  in the USA, 165
work, 2, 10, 13, 39, 125, 153. (*See also* labor.)
  communal forms of, 39
  domestic, 171–72
  as a field of enquiry, 2, 12–13
  industrial, 10, 38, 122, 197. (*See also* industries.)
  part-time, 147, 200
workers, 12–13, 54, 137, 140, 142–45, 154, 161, 162, 173, 179, 192, 195, 206, 219, 250–66. (*See also* coal, miners; labor; steel workers.)

agricultural, 140, 221–34
Fordist, 193. (*See also* Fordism.)
government, 194
identity, 235–49 passim, 254
indigenous, 154–62 passim
industrial, 122 140, 197, 203–05, 206–20
interests of, 142, 210
maquiladora, 9, 165–76. (See also *maquiladoras*.)
peasant. (*See* peasants.)
rural, 59, 168
unionized. (*See* unions.)
working class, 13, 191–205, 206–20, 255.
(*See also* culture, working class, movements, working class.)

conservative politics of the, 201, 205, 219, 229
formation of the, 55
militancy. (*See* labor, militancy.)
politics, 40, 191–205, 206–20
white, 24
working conditions, 173, 179, 228, 238
World Bank, 173
world systems theory, 37, 53, 69

youth, 137, 138, 142, 143, 146, 147, 168, 171, 173
Yucatán, 9, 165–76

Zapatistas, 173
Ziedenberg, J., 194, 195, 202, 204